THE COMPLETE STAMPS & STAMP COLLECTING

Author's Dedication:
For my granddaughter, Sophie

This edition is published by Lorenz Books,
an imprint of Anness Publishing Ltd,
Blaby Road, Wigston, Leicestershire LE18 4SE

Email: info@anness.com

Web: www.lorenzbooks.com;
www.annesspublishing.com

Publisher: Joanna Lorenz
Editorial Director: Helen Sudell
Project Editor: Catherine Stuart
Text Editor: Beverley Jollands
Designer: Nigel Partridge
Senior Production Controller: Steve Lang
Photography: Martyn Milner and Malcolm Craik

ETHICAL TRADING POLICY

Because of our ongoing ecological investment programme, you, as our customer, can have the pleasure and reassurance of knowing that a tree is being cultivated on your behalf to naturally replace the materials used to make the book you are holding. For further information about this scheme, go to www.annesspublishing.com/trees

A CIP catalogue record for this book is available from the British Library.

NOTE

The stamps reproduced in this book do not appear at their actual size. A small defacing bar has been added to mint issues, where applicable, to indicate that they are a reproduction.

PUBLISHER'S NOTE

Although the advice and information in this book are believed to be accurate and true at the time of going to press, neither the authors nor the publisher can accept any legal responsibility or liability for any errors or omissions that may have been made.

PICTURE ACKNOWLEDGEMENTS

All stamps illustrated in this book and on the jacket were supplied by Dr James Mackay, from his private collection, unless indicated below.

The publisher would like to thank the following organizations and individuals for allowing us to reproduce their pictures in this book:

Key: l=left; r=right; t=top; m=middle; b=bottom

American Philatelic Society: 71tl (all pictures in box), 76 (all pictures), 77br, 78t, 78bl, 80 (all pictures), 82 (all pictures), 85t, 87br

Bath Postal Museum: 7tr, 10bl, 12tr, 14bl, 14br, 16bl, 22bl, 23tl, 23bl, 25bl (in box), 40bl (both pictures in box), 48 (all pictures), 50tr (three pictures), 50br (in box), 52tr, 52bl (in box), 53ml and 53bl, 58tl, 58bl, 59tr (in box), 73tl

Arthur H Groten, MD (from his private collection): 55 (all pictures), 62mr (in box)

Trevor Lee took the photographs appearing on pages 25tr and 85tr

National Philatelic Society 75br, 77bl, 79bl (in box), 81bl (in box)

Philatelic Traders Society Ltd: 79tr

Royal Mail British Stamps © Royal Mail Group plc. All rights reserved. Reproduced with the permission of Royal Mail Group plc

Penny Black and the Penny Black stamp are the registered trade marks of Royal Mail Group plc in the United Kingdom. Anness Publishing Ltd would like to thank Royal Mail Group plc for allowing us to reproduce images of this stamp on the jacket spine and on the following pages: 5tm, 12t, 13b, 14b, 16bl, 76tr (in box), 126tl

Royal Mail Heritage: 42bl, 45bl, 70br, 74bl

© Royal Philatelic Society London: 81tr

The publisher would also like to thank:

The Bath Stamp & Coin Shop, 12–13 Pulteney Bridge, Bath BA2 4AY, United Kingdom, for supplying the equipment featuring on pages 26, 27, 28bl, 29ml, 29tr (in box) and 31tr (in box)

Linns Stamp News, Sidney, OH 45365, USA for allowing us to reproduce extracts from *Philatelic Forgers: Their Lives and Works* by Varro E. Tyler (1991) on page 58

Stanley Gibbons, 5 Parkside, Christchurch Road, Ringwood, Hampshire BH24 3SH, United Kingdom, for allowing us to reproduce images of their equipment on pages 26, 27 and 28

The stamps illustrated in this section appear on the following pages: p1: (clockwise from top-left) 144, 190, 226, 242, 218, 168; p3: 159, p4: (top, from left) 71, 34, 71, (middle) 17, (bottom) 142; p5: (top, from left) 37, 126, 226, (middle, from left) 120, 134, 228, (bottom, from left) 89, 181, 235; p250: 244; p251: 239; p252: 224; p253: 217; p254: (left) 207, (right) 144; p255: (left) 211, (right) 167; p256: (left) 183, (right) 127.

p2: Swedish miniature sheet (1991) reproducing "The Coronation of Gustav II" by Carl Gustav Pilo, designed by Czeslaw Slania.

CONTENTS

THE WORLD DIRECTORY OF STAMPS 86

INTRODUCING STAMPS AND PHILATELY

Philately, to give stamp collecting its proper name, has been called "the king of hobbies and the hobby of kings" – alluding to the fact that George V and Edward VIII of Britain, Carol of Romania, Alfonso XIII of Spain and Farouk of Egypt were all enthusiasts. The most famous non-royal head of state who was a lifelong philatelist was Franklin Delano Roosevelt. In *The Second World War* Winston Churchill has left a description of President Roosevelt engrossed in his hobby. In May 1943 the two statesmen were staying at Shangri-la, Roosevelt's mountain retreat in Maryland:

> The President had been looking forward to a few hours with his stamp collection. General "Pa" Watson, his personal aide, brought him several large albums and a number of envelopes full of specimens he had long desired. I watched him with much interest and in silence for perhaps half an hour as he stuck them, each in its proper place, and so forgot the cares of State.

All too soon, however, Bedell Smith arrived with an urgent message from Eisenhower. "Sadly F.D.R. left his stamp collection and addressed himself to his task…"

When American GIs entered Hitler's mountain lair at Berchtesgaden in May 1945 one of them retrieved the Fuhrer's stamp album, but it was actually a volume prepared for him for geopolitical reasons, with the stamps of the British Empire arranged to show the Nazi leader the rich prizes that would one day fall into his grasp. There is no evidence that Hitler took a personal interest in stamps, although the Third Reich was quick to harness this medium for propaganda.

WHY COLLECT?

Different people take an interest in collecting stamps for different reasons. Schoolteachers used to encourage the hobby because it stimulated an interest in history and geography, but most collectors are initially attracted by those fascinating little pieces of paper, inscribed in exotic languages, with unfamiliar currencies and views of faraway places. Although stamp collecting is an acquisitive hobby, you do not have to spend any money on it at the outset; the stamps from the letters of friends, relatives and work colleagues will get you off to a flying start.

However, by investing a little more time and money in the hobby, you may soon find yourself on a unique and absorbing journey. In this book we take a look at the various methods of starting a collection and the ways in which it can be developed to suit your own interests and requirements. We discuss the mechanics of collecting, including various tools, equipment, albums and accessories that can greatly enhance the systematic development of a collection. You should always remember that stamps are fragile things, originally designed to do no more than perform postal duty once and then be discarded. We look at the best ways to house these delicate treasures so that they are protected from the adverse effects of heat, humidity, sunlight and atmospheric pollution, and how to make sense of their arrangement – chronological or thematic – on the pages of an album.

Above: Definitive sets of mounted stamps are widely available to purchase, and are often favoured by collectors who organize their stamps by country.

FINDING YOUR NICHE

There are many ways of personalizing a stamp collection. Many collectors begin with a modest idea and then find they lean naturally towards a particular aspect of a country, period or theme. You may enjoy playing the detective, delving into the background of each issue to find out the reasons for the

Left: A 1947 stamp from Monaco showing Roosevelt at his stamp collection. It was designed by Pierre Gandon and does not set a good example for stamp collectors, for its subject is about to scuff the stamps with the cuff of his shirt. It must be presumed that Gandon exercised some artistic licence.

Right: A multi-tiered collectable bearing an Egyptian stamp, a contemporary Army Post stamp and a cancellation made by British field post handstamp E 602 in 1940.

Above: This attractive first flight cover of the Italian Airmail Service, issued on 16 May 1917, bears what is generally recognized as the world's first official airmail stamp. Augmented further by its historic cancellation, this cover has all the elements of a highly collectable piece.

introduction of a change of colour or watermark, why one design was introduced or another hastily scrapped, or why one printer lost the contract and another gained it.

The diligent collector need not limit the search to adhesive stamps. Until the early 20th century collectors indiscriminately took everything associated with the postal service, including stickers and labels, postal stationery and anything that remotely resembled a stamp. These sidelines fell out of favour as stamps became more prolific, but in recent years they have once again become legitimate subjects for study and competitive exhibition. Many of the world's finest collections now encompass much of the ancillary material associated with the production and issue of stamps, from postal notices, leaflets, brochures and other ephemera, to artists' drawings, printers' proofs, colour trials and actual stamps overprinted "SPECIMEN" or endorsed in some other manner to prevent postal use. Add to these items the souvenir folders produced by stamp printers, presentation packs sold by postal administrations, first day covers and souvenir postcards, not to mention the analysis of the stamps themselves, and you will find yourself embarked on a vast and interesting project.

FINANCIAL RETURNS

Every collector dreams of one day stumbling across a cache of ancient letters franked with stamps of immense rarity. Many of the fabulous gems of philately were discovered by ordinary people, even children, and the story of these rare finds and their subsequent history as they advanced in value every time they changed hands is the very stuff of romance and adventure.

Today, stamp dealing is a global business; thousands of people make a decent living from trading in stamps and no modern postal administration can afford to ignore the revenue accruing from philatelic sales. Philately is one of the few hobbies to offer its followers the opportunity to make a profit at the end of the day. Advice on buying is essential, as are tips on the best methods of disposal and on gauging the value of your stamps, whether solo or part of a larger collection.

The rise of online dealing has taken stamp buying and selling to a new level. All kinds of collectors – from the amateur just starting out to the professional seeking a rarity to complete a prize-winning exhibit – correspond across the globe and undertake bidding wars on international auction sites. Such is the scale of the new e-shopping culture that many philatelic societies now enable members to participate in club trading circuits via email.

GETTING INVOLVED IN THE HOBBY

Philately is highly organized, with clubs and societies at local, regional, national and worldwide levels. Many offer online membership to draw collectors from far and wide, and are an excellent source of information and contacts.

Exhibiting remains a popular objective for the many collectors who like to show off their treasures. The beginner of today, making his or her first display to the local stamp club, may one day aspire to win an international gold medal. This book gives advice on arranging and annotating your collection, and on the different approaches to displaying material, depending on whether the collection is arranged on traditional lines (by country or period) or topical, or perhaps devoted to telling a story, postal history or sidelines such as air, war or charity issues.

A WORLD OF STAMPS TO CHOOSE FROM

Every country in the modern world has produced stamps at some time. At present there are some 240 countries that issue distinctive stamps, and there are at least three times that number of "dead" countries, which no longer exist as political entities or have changed their name, but which have left their mark in the stamp album.

The world directory of stamps, which forms the larger part of this volume, provides a survey of all the existing countries that currently issue stamps, as well as many obsolete entities – former German, Italian and Indian states, for example – that issued them. Some countries are grouped according to common links in their political and philatelic histories, while others stand alone in the extent of their contribution to philately. In addition to tracing the cultural and economic shifts of the modern world, these intricately designed pieces of paper are a testament to the sheer volume of material available to today's collector.

Below: A historic Madras War Fund charity label produced during World War I to raise funds for a hospital ship.

IRAN
1R.
JUGOSLAVIJA
20
1865
30
DEUTSCHE BUNDESPOST
Deutsche Bundespost
50
DEUTSCHE BUNDESPOST
RSA
5c
RSA
5c
10
DEUTSCHE BUNDESPOST
80
DEUTSCHE BUNDESPOST
STMARKE 20

A GUIDE TO COLLECTING STAMPS

People have been collecting adhesive stamps ever since they first appeared in 1840. While the methods of prepaying postage have diversified considerably since the very first mailing of a letter bearing a Penny Black, most countries continue to appreciate the revenue to be gained from the sale of adhesive stamps and first day covers to collectors. The result is that the number of new issues generated each year now exceeds 10,000. This chapter is divided broadly into three key sections. The first takes a look at how stamps have originated and evolved, and how differences in the use of paper, ink, perforations and watermarks may considerably affect the value of two stamps that look the same. The second section discusses the various methods of collecting – from tools and display techniques to choosing a theme to unite your stamps and stationery – and looks at the choice of what there is to collect, from airmail, sea mail and military posts to the study of the postmarks relating to a country, region or even a single town. Finally, we trace the evolution of philately from its inception in the 1850s, and explain how to reap the rewards of a diverse and exciting hobby in an age of technological innovation – whether making contact with fellow collectors around the globe, bidding online for rarities, or researching the history of an unusual stamp.

Above, from left: Olympic philately is one of the largest branches of thematic collecting. It is little surprise that Greece, which issued these three stamps in 1968, 1972 and 1906, is so prolific on this subject.

WHAT ARE STAMPS?

We usually think of postage stamps as small pieces of printed, gummed paper, but in fact stamps, labels and seals have evolved in response to various postal functions, and a wealth of distinctive formats – and affiliated stationery – now exist.

Left: A United States commemorative celebrates the centenary of its country's stamps in 1947.

THE ORIGINS OF POSTAL SERVICES

Almost as soon as writing evolved, communications of a sort came into being. Postal services were certainly in existence in China as long ago as 4000 BC and in Egypt and Assyria a millennium later. The Chinese and Egyptian services were confined to imperial court circles, but in Assyria the service was open to the mercantile class as well. Not only are these ancient services well documented in contemporary chronicles, but actual examples of letters have survived, in the form of clay tablets bearing messages written in cuneiform (wedge-shaped) script. An immense hoard of such correspondence was discovered at Kultepe in Turkey in 1925 and included clay tablets dating from at least 2000 BC.

Below and right: Cuneiform writing on a Mesopotamian clay tablet, dating from the 21st or 20th century BC; this was celebrated on an Austrian stamp of 1965 issued for the Vienna International Philatelic Exhibition.

EARLY POSTAL SERVICES

A regular postal network was established by Cyrus the Great in Persia in about 529 BC, and detailed descriptions of it were written by the Greek historians Herodotus and Xenophon, both of whom commented on the speed and efficiency of the horse relays that carried letters to the furthest reaches of the Persian Empire.

By this time, the Chinese had a highly sophisticated network of post relays. In the 13th century Marco Polo described the imperial service as having over 25,000 relay stations, but as late as 1879 it was still confined to the court, and the general public were barred from using it on pain of death.

The Chinese were also the first to use paper as a writing material, by the 2nd century BC. The Romans wrote their letters on wax tablets and later on thin sheets of wood, while the Egyptians favoured papyrus. Parchment was the preferred medium in Europe until the 15th century, when paper was introduced from China via Asia Minor and the Byzantine Empire.

Right: A medieval Latin manuscript on another Austrian stamp of the WIPA series of 1965.

By the Middle Ages there were many postal services in Europe, but none was in general use. They operated almost exclusively for trade guilds (such as the Metzger Post of Germany, which served the guild of butchers), the merchants of the Hanseatic League, Venice and

Above: Postmen from the Middle Ages to more modern times are depicted on stamps of Austria, USA, Belgium and France.

the Italian city states, the universities and the great religious houses. When state services were instituted, these gradually died out or were merged with them.

THURN AND TAXIS MONOPOLY

By the 15th century the Holy Roman Empire had an efficient postal service operated by the Counts of Thurn and Taxis, whose range extended from the Baltic to the Adriatic and from Poland to the Straits of Gibraltar. The service survived into the era of adhesive stamps, and issued these in various states of Germany until 1867, when the Thurn and Taxis family (which had backed Austria, the losing side, in the

Seven Weeks' War of the previous year) was forced to give up its postal monopoly to Prussia, receiving 3 million thalers in compensation. The family business had lasted over 420 years, and the last hereditary Grand Master of the Posts died in 1871. (The 500th anniversary of this first great international post was celebrated by a joint issue of stamps in five countries in 1990.)

National postal services evolved from communications established to keep rulers in touch with regional governors. Sometimes a temporary service would be organized to serve the monarch while campaigning against enemy countries. In Britain, Henry VII had such a service in the late 15th century while fighting in Wales and Ireland. Out of the temporary arrangement set up when Henry VIII went to war against the Scots came the rudiments of the service along the Great North Road. Charles I opened the Royal Mail to the general public in 1635 as a way of raising money without recourse to Parliament (which he had dissolved), and the service was completely overhauled after the Restoration of the monarchy in 1660.

A Postal Dynasty

In 1952 Brussels hosted the 13th Postal Union Congress. Belgium marked the occasion with a set of 12 stamps portraying members of the princely family known as the Counts of Thurn and Taxis, who operated an international postal service from 1490 to 1867.

Below: A Roman cursus publicus *mail coach on an Austrian stamp of 1959, a "ball-wagon" designed to thwart robbers who would fall off after leaping aboard (Denmark, 1951) and the Bath–London mail coach on a British stamp of 1984.*

EARLY AMERICAN POSTS

The first postal service in America was established in November 1639, when Richard Fairbanks of Boston became Postmaster to the Massachusetts Bay Colony. Services were organized in Virginia (1657), New York (1672), Connecticut (1674), Philadelphia (1683) and New Hampshire (1683), and were united in 1691 under Thomas Neale as Deputy Postmaster General (under the Postmaster General in London). He was responsible for the handling of all mail arriving from abroad and destined for the various British settlements in North America.

Internal postal services originally radiated from the capital city, but by 1680 cross posts provided a more direct route. The first domestic service was organized by Duncan Campbell of Boston in 1693, operating between there and New York. Other routes, linking Philadelphia to Newport, Virginia (1737) or New York (1742), Boston to Albany, Baltimore to Annapolis and Philadelphia to Pittsburgh, were amalgamated in 1792. The year also saw the first regular exchange of mail between the USA and neighbouring Canada.

CONVEYING MAIL

Mail in the Roman Empire was conveyed by the *cursus publicus* ("public course") using light carts that rattled over paved roads, but the breakdown of the infrastructure in the Dark Ages meant that for many centuries most mail was carried by foot or horse posts. This continued well into the 19th century – the term "postmaster" originally meant a horse-hirer. When the age of steam dawned in the 1830s, however, mail by rail began to supersede horses and coaches, just as sailing packets gave way to the first steamships. Although the modes of transport were becoming speedier, the cost of sending or receiving letters remained prohibitively high until 1840, when national postal services underwent revolutionary change.

Left: A US 2c stamp of 1869 showing a Pony Express rider.

Below: A block of four showing historic mail transport, issued for the 20th Congress of the Universal Postal Union in 1989.

BIRTH OF THE ADHESIVE POSTAGE STAMP

On 22 August 1839 the British Treasury was authorized to implement a plan for an affordable postal service, put forward by the reformer Rowland Hill (1795–1874). Seeking inspiration, the Treasury announced a competition for designs and suggestions as to how prepayment of the new Penny Postage might be shown. Prizes of £200 and £100 were offered for the best design and the runner-up. This was widely publicized and eventually drew some 2,700 entries. Although prizes were awarded, none of the winning entries was actually used. One design showing the head of Queen Victoria was submitted by Sir George Mackenzie of Coul, Ross-shire. Recently discovered in the Royal Collection at Buckingham Palace, it is now regarded as the prototype for the first stamp, the Penny Black of May 1840.

Sir Rowland Hill

Born at Kidderminster in 1795, Hill trained as a schoolmaster but also involved himself in social improvements and colonization projects before turning to postal reform in the 1830s. His plan for uniform penny postage was adopted in January 1840, precipitating the use of adhesive stamps.

THE FORERUNNERS OF THE POSTAGE STAMP

All the elements that made up the first stamps were in fact already in existence. Revenue stamps embossed on blue paper had been around since 1694. They were attached to parchment documents by means of lead staples, secured at the back by small rectangular pieces of white paper – the size of the future Penny Black – bearing the crowned royal cipher, and they even had plate numbers and corner letters, just like the early postage stamps.

Newspapers were subject to a tax as a means of raising revenue, often for defence, although they were allowed free transmission by post. It was the extension of this levy to the American colonies in 1765, via the Stamp Act, that helped to trigger the opposition which culminated in the War of Independence a few years later. From 1802 onwards many taxes were denoted by adhesive labels. Indeed the tax stamps applied to patent medicines were not unlike some of the essays submitted in the Treasury competition.

The adhesive labels denoting prepayment of freight charges are thought to have been used by shipping and freight companies

Above: A tax stamp embossed on blue paper and fixed with a lead staple.

Below: An adhesive label used to secure the back of the lead staple (left) and an impressed newspaper tax stamp of the American colonies, 1765 (right).

Above: The first issues of the Penny Black (top left) and Twopence Blue (bottom), as they appeared in May 1840, with an illustration of the crown watermark (top right).

from about 1811, though none is now extant. So the concept of using adhesive stamps to denote prepaid mail was a natural development.

POSTAL REVOLUTION

The Penny Black and Twopence Blue, introduced in May 1840, were a team effort, conceived by Hill, drawn by Henry Corbould from the effigy sculpted by William Wyon for the Guildhall Medal of 1838, engraved by Charles and Frederick Heath and recess-printed by Perkins, Bacon of London. The rose engine used to engrave the background was patented by the American engineer Jacob Perkins, who had devised a method of engraving steel plates to print banknotes that were proof against forgery.

The new-fangled stamps were slow to catch on. At first they were on sale only at stamp offices operated by the Board of Stamps and Taxes, and postmasters had to obtain a licence to sell them. Until 1852 the public had the option to prepay postage in cash, and such letters bore a red postmark to indicate this. Letters could still be sent unpaid, but attracted a double charge of 2d per half ounce.

WORLD FIRSTS

Brazil is generally credited with being the first country to follow Britain's lead, with its celebrated Bull's Eyes of 1843. In fact the New York City Dispatch Post was using 1c stamps portraying George Washington a year earlier. Henry Thomas Windsor, the proprietor of this private local service, was an Englishman who imported the idea from his native country.

The Swiss cantons of Basle, Geneva and Zurich adopted stamps in 1843–5. In 1845 the US Post Office (USPO) authorized postmasters to issue their own stamps, and two years later the first federal issue consisted of 5c and 10c stamps portraying Benjamin Franklin (first Postmaster General of the USA) and George Washington respectively. Every American definitive series from then until 1981 included a representation of Washington, though Franklin was dropped after 1965.

In 1847 Mauritius was the first British colony to adopt adhesive stamps, although Trinidad had a local stamp that year, for mail carried by the *Lady McLeod*, a steamship run by a private company. Although this showed the ship it was not the first pictorial design to be produced. As early as 1843 the Broadway Penny Post of New York had a stamp showing a steam locomotive.

Bermuda adopted adhesive stamps in 1848, the postmasters of Hamilton (W.B. Perot) and St George's (J.H. Thies) producing them by striking their handstamps on gummed paper.

Right: Obverse of the 1838 Guildhall Medal, sculpted by William Wyon.

Below: A miniature Isle of Man sheet of 1990, showing the evolution of the Penny Black.

Above: The Brazilian 90 reis stamp of 1843, nicknamed the Bull's Eye.

Below: The first stamps issued for use throughout the USA: the 5c Franklin and 10c Washington of 1847.

Above: The 1d Post Office stamp of Mauritius, 1847, and the Bavarian 1 kreuzer, 1849.

Right: The Belgian Epaulettes issue of 1849.

Below: Switzerland's Double Geneva cantonal stamp of 1843, the world's first discount stamp – 5c each or the double for 8c.

In 1849 Bavaria, Belgium and France produced their first stamps and the first decade ended with stamps extending to Austria, Austrian Italy, British Guiana. Hanover, New South Wales, Prussia, Saxony, Schleswig-Holstein, Spain, Switzerland and the Australian state of Victoria. New South Wales had anticipated Britain's adoption of prepaid postage by introducing embossed letter sheets as early as 1838, but adhesive stamps lagged behind by 12 years.

Thereafter, the use of adhesive postage stamps spread rapidly. In 1851 Baden, Canada, Denmark, Hawaii, New Brunswick, Nova Scotia, Sardinia, Trinidad, Tuscany and Württemberg joined the stamp-issuing entities. In 1852 another 11 countries adopted the system, including the Indian district of Scinde (now part of Pakistan), the first country in Asia. With the arrival of the celebrated triangular stamps of the Cape of Good Hope in South Africa in 1853, stamps had spread to every inhabited continent.

THE PARTS OF A STAMP

A postage stamp is the sum of many different parts and processes, and two issues that look the same on the surface may in fact conceal subtle variations. An American 32c issue of 1995–7, known to collectors as the Flag Over Porch issue, illustrates this point. To the untrained eye, these stamps look very similar, but their additional features make them really quite different. Although the same printing process (multicolour photogravure) was used throughout, the stamps were produced by four different printers: Avery-Dennison, J.W. Fergusson & Sons, Stamp Venturers, and the Bureau of Engraving and Printing. There are also differences in the gum: some have gum arabic on the back, which has to be moistened, while others have a self-adhesive backing. Some of the stamps were issued with phosphor tagging to assist electronic sorting and cancellation, while others were not. Fortunately the paper was the same throughout and there were no watermarks to contend with, but different qualities of paper and watermarks in many older issues can dramatically affect the value of seemingly similar stamps.

Above: Superficially these 32c Flag Over Porch stamps of the USA are the same, but they were produced by different printers; they are either conventionally gummed or self-adhesive, and are taken from sheets or coils.

PHOSPHOR TAGGING

The 32c Flag Over Porch stamps are all of much the same value, whether in mint (unused) or used condition, but sometimes a very slight variation can make a vast difference to a stamp's worth. Phosphor is used in Britain to distinguish second and first class mail, the stamps having one or two bands, or an all-over coating detected only with an ultraviolet lamp. The British halfpenny stamp of 1971 may be found with two phosphor bands (in sheets) or a single central band (in coils and booklets) and both types are very common. However, in 1972, a prestige booklet in honour of the Wedgwood pottery legacy included a halfpenny stamp in a mixed pane (the term for a page of stamps) with a single phosphor band at the left side only. Today it is catalogued at 100 times the price of the normal versions.

PERFORATION

Rows of holes are punched out of the sheet between the stamps to make them easy to separate, and variations in perforation are the feature that usually distinguishes stamps. Their size and spacing varies, and a gauge is used to measure the number of holes in a length of 2cm/¾in. Stamps may be comb-perforated, when three sides are punched at a time, or line-perforated, producing a characteristic ragged effect at the corners.

Before true perforation was perfected in the 1850s, stamps were sometimes rouletted: the paper was pierced by blades on a wheel, but not punched out. This method has survived intermittently to the present day but is more usually confined to postal stationery and stickers. Although perforation is redundant in self-adhesive stamps, it is often retained, in the form of die cuts, for aesthetic reasons.

WATERMARKS

The commonest form of security device, watermarks can usually be detected by holding stamps up to the light. Very few countries now use them, but until the 1970s they were widespread. British stamps of the period 1953–67 may be found with three different watermarks or none at all.

When it is necessary to compare different watermarks a detector is required. The traditional method was

During the first decade of their existence, adhesive stamps were cut, or even torn, from a sheet by the local postmaster. Then, during the 1850s, Henry Archer invented a machine to perforate stamps by punching rows of holes along the white spaces between the stamps to ease separation. This perforating machine (left) is one of the few working Victorian examples left in the world. The Penny Red (above right) issued in 1854, shows a triple perforation – an example of the early teething problems experienced with the new-fangled perforators.

Left: This block of Polish stamps of 1919 was perforated by a comb machine: the regular holes intersect perfectly.

Above: A miniature sheet issued by New Caledonia in 1999 shows reproductions of its first stamp, produced using five different printing processes.

to place the stamp face down on a polished black surface and apply a drop or two of benzine, which momentarily renders the stamp transparent. Nowadays there are various electric devices that are more effective.

PRINTING METHODS

Stamps are printed by a number of different processes, so it's important to recognize their salient characteristics.

The earliest stamps, and most US stamps until the 1970s, were recess-printed from steel or copper plates with the design cut into them (a process sometimes described as intaglio). These can be recognized by the slight ridges (as on a banknote) that result from the paper being forced under great pressure into the recesses of the plate. The opposite process is relief-printing or letterpress, often called typography by philatelists, in which the lines of the design on the plate are raised. Ink is rolled across them and pressed into the paper, producing a smooth surface but often with the design showing through on the back of the stamp.

British low-value stamps were printed by letterpress until 1934, when photogravure was adopted. For this the plate is engraved photographically, allowing fine gradations of tone. When magnified the image can be seen to consist of fine lines due to the screening process. It was first used by Bavaria in 1914 and became popular in the 1930s. In recent years it has given way to multicolour offset lithography, perceived as a cheaper and more reliable process, whereby the image is chemically applied to the printing plate and the ink is "offset" on to a secondary medium, such as a rubber mat, before being transferred to the paper. The image is made up of fine dots.

A few stamps from 1847 onwards were embossed, with the portrait or emblem in relief. Recent attempts to create three-dimensional effects have given rise to laminated-prismatic stamps, stamps in metal foil, images raised by thermography, and holograms.

The Many Lives of a Famous Stamp

1 2 3 4

The Austrian 1s stamp holds the world record for being printed using four different processes at different times. Designed by H. Strohofer to mark the 800th anniversary of Mariazell Basilica, it began life on 22 June 1957 [1], engraved by G. Wimmer and recess-printed (intaglio). On 25 October 1957 it was reissued as the first denomination in a new definitive series devoted to buildings. This issue [2] was typographed (letterpress), retaining Wimmer's name in the margin. It is similar to the first: the chief differences are the solid value tablet (the intaglio version has criss-cross lines) and the clouds, which are stippled rather than cross-hatched. The rest of the series, as it gradually appeared, was lithographed, and a version of the 1s in this process appeared in January 1959, easily distinguished by the omission of the engraver's name and the lighter colour [3]. Finally a smaller format was adopted for the version of February 1960 printed in photogravure by the British printer Harrison and Sons of High Wycombe [4]. Apart from the Allied occupation set of 1945 (printed in Washington), this was the only Austrian stamp printed outside the country.

STAMPS FOR EVERYDAY USE

In 1840, when the first stamps were issued, there was only one kind, intended to prepay the postage on ordinary letters. When registered mail was introduced a year later, the British Treasury ruled that the 6d fee had to be prepaid in cash, as registration was not classed as a postal service. It was only in the early 20th century, as postage stamps designed to prepay a range of different services became increasingly available, that the permanent issues came to be known as "definitives".

Britain has retained the small upright format of the Penny Black for the vast majority of definitives, and today every denomination, from 1p to £5, is the same size. However, at various times since 1867, larger sizes have been used for the higher values, while the first ½d stamp, issued in 1870, adopted a small horizontal format, half the size of the 1d stamp. Because most early definitives portrayed a head of state, the upright shape came to be known as the portrait format.

Above: Canada issued its first stamp, the Threepenny Beaver, in 1851.

Below: Africa's first stamp: The Cape of Good Hope Triangular of 1853.

DEFINITIVE SERIES

In establishing a definitive series, most countries followed Britain's lead, although Canada pioneered a horizontal (landscape) format in 1851 for its Threepenny Beaver, and this shape was later adopted by New Brunswick (1860) and the USA (1869).

Above: One year after the birth of the British penny postage, the Penny Red and "improved" Twopence Blue replaced the original 1840 designs, as part of the Post Office's bid to stamp out postal fraud. While effigies of rulers continue to be adapted or created anew by their designers, the basic format of many "portrait" definitives worldwide remains exactly the same.

The British colonies in North America were innovative in the matter of shape: New Brunswick started with a diamond format in 1851, while Newfoundland's first series (1857) adopted square or triangular shapes as well as a larger portrait size, with a corresponding landscape format from 1865. The Cape Triangular (1853) is said to have been adopted to help semi-literate postal workers sort the mail, though this is unlikely as all Cape stamps up to 1864 were of that shape.

SALE OF DEFINITIVES

British stamps were printed in sheets of 240, so that a row of twelve 1d stamps could be sold for 1s and the full sheet for £1. This pattern was followed in those dominions and colonies that used sterling currency, but elsewhere sheets of 100 or 200 were the norm. In recent years, the tendency has been to produce much smaller sheets, notably in Germany, where sheets of ten are now issued with decorative margins, a marketing ploy to encourage philatelists to collect complete sheets rather than single stamps. In the USA sheets of 20 or 18 are now common.

Above: A portion of a self-adhesive US booklet by Stamp Venturers, 1995–6.

AMERICAN PORTRAITS

The subject matter of definitive stamps has also broadened considerably in the past half century. From 1847, US policy was to portray dead presidents and politicians and occasionally other historic figures. The series of 1918 revived the landscape format, briefly used in 1869 for $2 and $5 stamps portraying Benjamin Franklin; this was expanded in 1922–5, when all denominations from 20c to $5 used the horizontal shape to show landmarks, scenery and a buffalo to best effect.

The series of 1938 again portrayed dead presidents. The denominations up to 22c portrayed the president of the

Above: Definitive designs: a UK Machin (left) flanked by a Scottish "country" definitive (right).

corresponding number (for example, the 17th president, Andrew Johnson, was shown on the 17c stamp). Most American definitives since 1954 have broadened the scope to include men and women prominent in many different fields.

Postwar German Definitives

The division of Germany after World War II into the Federal Republic, the Democratic Republic and West Berlin resulted in separate issues of stamps in each area. West Germany's definitive stamp designs ranged from the symbolic (posthorns) to presidential portraiture before settling on the themes of technology and famous buildings. West Berlin featured famous Berliners and architecture, while the Democratic Republic favoured socialist celebrities and communist symbolism.

NATIONAL THEMES

Monarchical countries such as Britain and Spain prefer a uniform series with a single portrait of the ruler. Indeed, the effigy of Elizabeth II, designed by Arnold Machin, has adorned British stamps since 1967 and several hundred different varieties have now been issued. For their low value stamps, the Scandinavian countries and the Netherlands have a penchant for designs based on the numerals of value. Norway's Posthorns have been in longest continuous use, since 1871, but Denmark's Wavy Lines are not far behind. Higher values, however, stick to royal portraits. Republics such as France, Switzerland and Portugal prefer allegorical figures.

Above: Small format definitives issued by St Lucia, 1912 (left) and Sudan, 1921 (right).

Below: Dominica's 1923 series coupled a royal portrait with a colonial emblem.

Above and right: Pictorial definitives from Italy (castles), Austria (religious foundations) and Australia (cartoons).

Below: Historic ships appeared on the Barbados series of 1994–8.

PICTORIAL DESIGNS AND MULTICOLOUR STAMPS

Definitives depicting scenery and the occasional fauna and flora became popular in the late 1890s, beginning with New Zealand, Tonga and Tasmania and spreading to the Latin American countries. By the 1930s the colonies of the British and French empires were indulging in bicoloured pictorials.

The advent of multicolour photogravure, and later offset lithography, broadened the scope in the postwar era, and fully pictorial definitives became the fashion. At first these sets had a mixture of subjects but as the tendency to change sets more frequently has developed, such sets have usually adopted a specific theme, such as birds, flowers, insects or wild animals. Other subjects that have proved very popular include women's costume (Austria), antique furniture (Hungary), coins (Portuguese India) and civic arms (Lithuania).

Definitives are produced in vast quantities – even the Penny Black of 1840–1 ran to some 72 million – but technical alterations during the production, or changes in postal rates, can produce elusive items that soar above their peers in philatelic value.

SHEETS, COILS, BOOKLETS AND STATIONERY

Definitives were always issued in sheets until the 1890s, but other methods of providing stamps have since come into use. In that decade several companies on both sides of the Atlantic devised machines that would dispense stamps. Some were coin-operated but others were intended for use in large company mailrooms, saving staff the time it took to tear up sheets.

COILS AND SHEETS

At first coils of stamps were made up from strips cut from sheets, with parts of the margins used to join one strip to the next; specialists like to collect the coil-join pairs. Later, special printings of stamps from rotary presses produced continuous reels, giving rise to joint line pairs, with a narrow vertical line of colour where the ends of the printing plate met as they were curved round the cylinder. In many countries coils are numbered sequentially on the back of every fifth or tenth stamp in the row.

Apart from the lack of perforations on opposite sides, either vertically or horizontally, coil stamps can be distinguished by their sideways watermark (in Britain) or two or more different stamps side by side to make up the value paid. Similar multivalue coil strips were produced in Britain and later in South Africa in connection with offers made by the *Reader's Digest*.

Left: A US coil of 1912, with private perforations.

Below: A US coil pair of 1983, showing the vertical joint line.

Above: The cover of a British booklet of 1920, advertising Harrods department store.

Right: A Canadian booklet of Flag stamps, 2004.

Sometimes a different theme is used for definitives in coils and sheets. Thus the USA features prominent Americans on sheets and modes of transportation on coils; Germany has portrayed famous women on sheets and landmarks on coils.

Automatic stamps, pioneered by the Frama company of Switzerland in the 1970s, are dispensed by inserting a coin in the slot and using a keypad to tap out the value of the stamp required. The earliest Frama labels were very prosaic, in shades of red ink, but they have become multicoloured and pictorial. Similar systems are operated by Klussendorf (Germany), Creusot (France), Epelsa (Spain) and others.

BOOKLETS AND MINIATURE SHEETS

Booklets of stamps were pioneered by Luxembourg (1895), spread to the USA (1902) and Britain (1908) and are now universal. The stamps are often imperforate on two or more adjoining sides and may be found with inverted watermarks (in Britain) or with different stamps or advertising labels side by side. Originally, booklets were stitched, often with advertising on the covers and interleaves, but in most the panes are now stuck to the cover in a style developed by Sweden. Britain pioneered the prestige booklet in the 1970s, with mixed panes of definitives as well as combinations of regional stamps or special issues.

Luxembourg also pioneered miniature sheets (1921–3), which have spread around the world. One or more stamps, sometimes forming a large composite design, are set in a decorative margin, with the image on the stamp often projecting out to the edges of the sheet.

POSTAL STATIONERY

These collectables include all kinds of envelopes, letter sheets, postcards and wrappers with some kind of stamp printed on them.

Stamped letter sheets denoting prepayment of postage were in use in Sardinia by 1818. Although the "stamp" actually represented a tax, they were allowed to pass through the post without further charge, so they are often regarded, in Italy at least, as the world's first stamps. Other countries, such as New South Wales (1838),

Below: A composite sheetlet of 12 stamps issued by the United Nations in 1998 for International Year of the Ocean.

Above: On this Australian booklet pane of 1967, 4c stamps were uprated to 5c.

The Mulready Envelope

William Mulready was the designer of Britain's first postal envelope, issued in 1840 but withdrawn in 1841. Its rather pompous decoration, portraying Britannia sending forth her winged messengers to all parts of the far-flung British Empire, inspired a satirical poem in *Punch* magazine and numerous lampoons, resulting in its withdrawal but also triggering off a craze for pictorial stationery.

Russia and Finland (1845) and some German states (1845–8), had similar stamped sheets long before resorting to adhesive stamps. Even Rowland Hill pinned his faith on wrappers and letter sheets designed by his friend William Mulready, issuing adhesive stamps only as an afterthought. The "Mulreadys" gave way to envelopes bearing an embossed stamp (the Penny Pink, which continued in use until 1902). Special envelopes with crossed blue lines for registered mail were adopted in 1878 and "Official paid" stationery, pioneered by the USA, spread to most countries by the early 1900s. Stamped postcards were invented in Austria in 1869, offering cut-price postage, and spread abroad a year later despite reservations about the messages being read by postal workers and servants.

Left and below: Impressed stamps from a 2002 Italian commemorative postcard and a US airmail postcard issued in 1981.

OTHER STATIONERY

Newspaper wrappers with printed stamps developed in the 1870s. Lettercards – cards folded and sealed along the outer edges by perforated strips that were torn off by the addressee – were first used in Belgium (1882), while Newfoundland (1912) alone produced reply lettercards, with a smaller card inside. Britain briefly flirted with postnotes, folded sheets with an impressed stamp, in 1982. Telegram forms with impressed or embossed stamps were once common.

Special stationery used by government departments has included jury citations and vaccination certificates. Distinctive stationery for use by armed services or prisoners of war is of particular interest to collectors of military postal history. Austria and prewar Czechoslovakia made enthusiastic use of prestamped postcards for tourist publicity. In Australia, prestamped envelopes and postcards are often employed to commemorate events not deemed to merit adhesive stamp issues.

Since the 1970s there has been a trend towards stationery with a device indicating that postage has been paid, without specifying the amount. Instead the class of postage is expressed, overcoming the need to reprint stationery every time postal rates are increased.

Below: The world's first stamped postcard, issued by Austria in 1869.

COMMEMORATIVE AND SPECIAL ISSUES

The notion that stamps could be used for purposes other than merely to indicate that postage had been paid was slow to catch on. In 1876 the USA produced envelopes with embossed stamps to celebrate the centenary of the Declaration of Independence, but the idea was not adopted for adhesive stamps until the Columbian Exposition in 1893. In the interim, a German local post, the Privat Brief Verkehr of Frankfurt-am-Main, issued a stamp in July 1887 in honour of the Ninth German Federal and Jubilee Shooting Contest. The following year several local posts issued mourning stamps following the deaths of German emperors, William I and his son Frederick III. Many other German local posts had commemorative stamps (including one from Breslau to celebrate the Jewish New Year), but Germany itself did not issue any such stamps until 1919.

FIRST GOVERNMENT ISSUES

In May 1888 New South Wales celebrated the centenary of the colony with a long series captioned "One hundred years". The stamps remained in use for 12 years, undergoing numerous changes in colour, watermark and perforation. Most commemorative issues since that time, however, have been on sale for a short time only, and in some cases from restricted sales outlets. Britain's first adhesive commemorative stamps, for example, publicizing the British Empire Exhibition at Wembley in 1924–5, were sold only at the exhibition's post offices.

Left: The first adhesive commemorative stamp was issued by Frankfurt-am-Main in July 1887, on the occasion of a shooting contest.

Right: New South Wales celebrated its centenary with a commemorative set, issued in May 1888.

Above: The first Mothers' Day stamp, released by the USA in 1934, aptly used Whistler's portrait of his mother.

Below: Marshall Islands stamp, 2004.

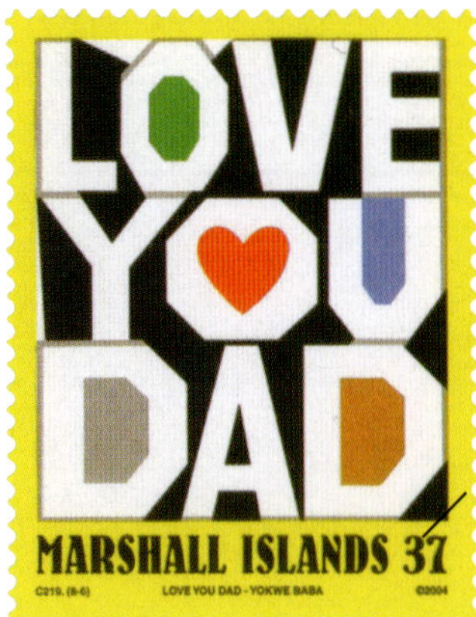

Commemoratives spread throughout the world. Hong Kong overprinted a stamp in 1891 for the colony's 50th anniversary; El Salvador and Nicaragua issued sets in January 1892 to mark the 400th anniversary of Columbus's arrival in America; Montenegro produced Europe's first commemoratives, overprinting the definitive series in 1893 to mark the quatercentenary of printing; and the Transvaal issued Africa's first commemorative in 1895, to mark the adoption of penny postage.

Not only are commemoratives issued with increasing frequency to honour historic events and personalities, as well as to publicize current events of national or international importance, but often the subject of the commemoration is used as an opportunity to issue a set of stamps. Thus the maiden voyage of the *Queen Mary 2* in 2004 was the pretext for a set of six stamps depicting famous British ocean liners.

Propaganda Stamps

Stamps have been used for propaganda purposes since 1892, when Venezuela sought to advance its claim to British Guiana by issuing stamps featuring a map on which the contested territory was highlighted. In 1900 stamps were employed to promote the unity of Germany under the Kaiser, and later, in the Stalinist era, they were widely used for propaganda purposes by both the Third Reich and the USSR. In the 1960s and 1970s Communist countries such as the DDR used stamps to show their solidarity with "unconquerable Vietnam" in its struggle against American aggression.

SPECIAL ISSUES

Many postal administrations now augment their definitives with "special issues", a term that covers anything with a restricted lifespan. These issues are generally thematic in nature, often all of the same denomination and increasingly printed side by side in the same sheet. They include stamps for Christmas, Easter, Mother's Day and many other such occasions, as well as sheetlets or booklets containing greetings stamps, covering everything from the birth of a baby to "Get well soon" or "I love you, Mom".

STAMPS AND PHILANTHROPY

Philately is the only collecting hobby able to support good causes of all kinds, through the medium of stamps that include a sum payable either to charity in general or to a specific organization. Such stamps are known generally as charity stamps (although in the USA they have been described more accurately as semi-postals, as only part of the charge goes to the postal service).

The concept originated in Britain in 1890, when pictorial envelopes were issued to celebrate the golden jubilee of penny postage. They were sold for 1s but were valid for only 1d postage, the other 11d going to the Rowland Hill Benevolent Fund for Post Office Widows and Orphans.

In 1897–1900 some of the Australian colonies – New South Wales, Queensland and Victoria – issued stamps for Queen Victoria's diamond jubilee or Boer War funds, selling them for 1s, 2s or 2s 6d but providing postal validity for only 1d, 2d or 2½d. The example was followed by Russia and Romania in 1905, but without the outrageously high premiums. These stamps, like the Australians, were issued for specific charities, notably the Russo-Japanese War of 1905, but when the idea spread to other parts of Europe, proceeds were devoted to ongoing good causes, especially child welfare. The stamps issued by Switzerland from 1913 for child welfare, inscribed in Latin "Pro juventute", consisted of short sets, usually with a specific subject. Later this concept was extended to other good causes, bearing the inscription "Pro patria" ("For the fatherland").

WELFARE STAMPS

Germany began issuing welfare stamps (*Wohlfahrtsmarken*) in the 1920s and later added stamps with the inscription "*Weihnachtsmarke*" ("Christmas stamp") or "*Jugendmarke*" ("Youth stamp"). The concept continues to this day. The Netherlands produce stamps inscribed "*Voor het kind*" ("For the child") or "*Sommerzegel*" ("Summer stamp"). Since 1929 New Zealand has issued stamps for children's health camps. Some countries, such as Yugoslavia and Portugal, had charity tax stamps whose use was compulsory at certain times, and even issued special postage due labels with which to surcharge mail not bearing the stamps.

Excessive premiums brought charity stamps into disrepute and the actual charity portion is now seldom more than 50 per cent of the postal value. Britain, which started the ball rolling in 1890, did not issue a charity stamp until 1975 (for health and handicap funds), while the USA's first charity stamp (raising money for breast cancer research) appeared in 1988.

Above: Stamps in aid of the Ludwigshafen explosion disaster in 1948 and New Zealand health camps (1949).

Right: A Netherlands Antilles definitive overprinted for the relief of Dutch flood victims in 1953.

Above: A Belgian charity stamp issued in 1996, illustrating the Museum of Walloon Life.

Left: The envelope for the golden jubilee of penny postage contrasted mail communications in 1840 and 1890.

AIRMAILS AND SPECIAL SERVICE STAMPS

Sending messages by air goes back to the 5th century BC, when inscribed arrows were used during the siege of the Corinthian colony of Potidaea. Messages carried by kite date from AD 549 in China, and pigeons have been used since the Siege of Leyden in 1575. The first balloon message was carried by Vincenzo Lunardi in September 1784, and the first official airmail was carried between La Fayette and Crawfordsville, Indiana, by the balloon *Jupiter*, on 17 August 1859.

FIRST AIR MAIL STAMPS

The first regular air service was set up during the sieges of Metz and Paris in the Franco-Prussian War in 1870–1, for which special message forms were inscribed 'Par Ballon Monté' ("By manned balloon"). Within five years of the first faltering flight by the Wright Brothers in 1903, mail was being flown by plane from Paris to St Nazaire. In 1909 the Peruvian aviator Jorge Chavez carried the first airmail between two countries: Switzerland and Italy.

The first air stamp was a private 5c label produced in 1877 by Professor Samuel King for use on mail carried by his balloon *Buffalo* from Nashville, Tennessee, and showed the balloon in flight. In 1898 1s stamps were issued in connection with the Original Great Barrier Pigeongram Service in New Zealand. Semi-official stamps for souvenirs flown by heavier-than-air machines at aviation meetings were first issued in 1909 at Bar-sur-Aube, France.

Above: A French stamp of 1955 showing a balloon flight during the Siege of Paris in 1870.

Right: Private 5c stamp for mail carried by the balloon Buffalo, *1877.*

Left: This 1959 US airmail stamp marked the centenary of the Jupiter *balloon flight.*

Below: Loading mail on to the biplane Horatius *at Croydon, south of London, in the early 1930s.*

MAIL CARRIED BY AIRCRAFT

India organized the world's first mail service by aircraft (Allahabad to Naini, February 1911), closely followed by Britain, Denmark, Italy and the USA. These services had special postmarks but used ordinary stamps. The USA was the first country to issue a stamp depicting an aircraft, in 1912, but it was part of a parcel post series and had no relevance to airmail. Several other countries featured planes on non-airmail stamps in 1914–15.

Italy produced the first airmail stamp, overprinted for the Rome–Turin service in 1917. The first definitive air stamps were issued by the USA in 1918 and featured the Curtiss Jenny biplane. The 24c with inverted centre was the first airmail error. Thousands of airmail stamps have been issued since, though nowadays many that are specific to airmail rates are no longer thus inscribed.

The Inverted Jenny

The USA released a set of three stamps in 1918 depicting a Curtiss JN-4, popularly known as the Jenny. The 24c was printed with a red frame and a blue centre, but one sheet of 100 was discovered with the centre inverted – one of the greatest American rarities.

Above: Airmails have spawned colourful stationery over the years. As shown by this postcard, it was popular to include illustrations of the planes themselves.

Below: Collectable airmail cigarette cards featured the famous pilots of the day and historic airmail planes.

Colombia, Germany, Mexico and Thailand had lightweight airmail stationery from 1923 onwards, but air letter sheets, or "aerogrammes", were pioneered by Iraq in 1933, followed by Britain (1941) and other countries after World War II. The first British aerogrammes were used for mail sent to prisoners of war and were inscribed in English, French and German.

"BACK OF BOOK" STAMPS

Stamps that were neither definitive nor commemorative but intended for special services have traditionally been tacked on the end of the main listing in stamp catalogues. They are therefore known as "back of book" stamps (BOB for short), a phrase that originated with American collectors. The largest group are not strictly postage stamps at all, but labels indicating that money has to be recovered from the addressee, either because an item is unpaid or underpaid, or because some special fee (such as customs duty) has to be collected. These are known as postage due labels, although many of them are inscribed "To pay" in the relevant language.

Because they are used internally, few of these stamps bear a country name, and identifying them by their inscriptions or currency is often a headache for inexperienced collectors. Most are quite functional in design, with numerals of value, but more recent issues tend to be pictorial. They were pioneered by France in 1859 and gradually spread around the world.

Stamps for Parcels, Express Delivery and Other Services

Belgium produced the world's first parcel stamps in 1879, but many railway and freight companies had been using them since the 1840s, if not earlier. Britain's only stamps in this category were definitives overprinted from 1883 onwards for use on government parcels. The USPO introduced a parcel service in 1912 and briefly issued a series of red stamps, mainly depicting aspects of postal communications.

Special and express delivery stamps have appeared mainly in Latin American countries but also in Canada and the USA. The latter also issued stamps denoting special handling in 1925–9. Distinctive stamps for registration, sometimes incorporating a serial number, were issued by Canada, Liberia, Montenegro, the USA, Australian states and several Latin American countries.

Official stamps are those provided for the use of government departments. Stamps for separate departments were issued by the USA, Britain, South Australia and Argentina, but elsewhere all-purpose stamps were produced. Definitives were also overprinted or perforated with initials for this purpose. Stamps inscribed or overprinted to denote a tax on mail during wartime were pioneered by Spain (1874–7) and widely used in World War I.

Stamps have also been produced for many other purposes, such as advice of delivery (Colombia), concessional letters (Italy), journal tax (Austria), late fee (Latin America), lottery or prize draw (Japan and Norway), marine insurance (Netherlands) and newspapers (Austria, New Zealand, USA).

Above: The 1968 US $1 stamp enabled servicemen overseas to send parcels home at a special rate.

Below: Postage due labels from the USA (1879) and Yugoslavia (1948), the latter applied to mail not bearing the compulsory Red Cross charity stamp.

Right: Advice of delivery stamp from Montenegro, 1895.

Below: Parcel postage due label, USA, 1912.

HOW TO COLLECT STAMPS

Armed with a few essential items and some knowledge of stamp care and mounting, the ways you can organize a collection are limitless. Sometimes the choice of what to include seems too great, but, as explained here, there are logical ways to narrow the focus.

Left: An Egyptian "stamp on a stamp", issued in 2004 for the 25th anniversary of the Philatelic Society.

STARTING A COLLECTION

There are many different reasons why people take up stamp collecting. A lucky few may inherit a collection from a parent or relative, so they can get off to a flying start and just carry on where the previous owner left off, but most people have to start from scratch. It may be as simple as seeing a particularly eye-catching stamp on an item in your own mail, perhaps from an interesting place you once visited, or depicting a subject that fascinates you, or that is related in some way to your profession or to a school project. The desire to keep it might just be enough to trigger off the notion of forming a stamp collection with a related theme.

We are by nature acquisitive animals, given to collecting items that may serve no utilitarian purpose but which are nontheless decorative or desirable. As collectable objects, stamps offer variety, rarity, scholarly interest and aesthetic appeal. Ever since the Penny Black first appeared, stamps have been admired and hoarded by collectors for their aesthetic qualities as miniature works of art and masterpieces of engraving, and as exponents of cultural and political ideals.

Below: The theme of the Europa stamps in 2004 was holidays, exemplified by this stamp from Guernsey.

Above: Pictorial stamps from China and Hungary in 2004 illustrate the popular themes of birds and animals.

PHILATELY TODAY

Not so many years ago most pieces of mail that came into the average household bore adhesive stamps, and it was a relatively easy matter to clip stamps off envelopes. Before long you had the nucleus of a collection, mostly stamps of your own country, but augmented with the occasional foreign stamp culled from holiday postcards or, in some cases, from correspondence sent to the workplace. The chances are that your local town had one or more stamp shops with attractive displays of the world's latest issues in the window to tempt passers-by.

Adhesive stamps are now virtually confined to social mail such as personal letters and postcards, as most business and "junk" mail bears meter marks or some other indication that postage has been prepaid by a bulk mailer. Meter marks and PPIs (postage paid impressions) do have their own devotees, but they lack the universal appeal of adhesive stamps. Because stamps are now not very plentiful on mail this particular incentive to start a collection, especially among children, may not be so great as it was. However, this does not mean that philately is becoming less popular. On the contrary, postal

Above: Shops dealing in goods for the stamp collector are fewer than they were, but those remaining are often well stocked and helpful. As they are almost always run by keen philatelists, they are great places to get advice if you are just starting out. Most stamp shops stock starter packs, interesting collections of stamps, and equipment for the specialist.

Below: Presentation packs, often collected as mementoes by the non-philatelist as well as the keen collector, are an important source of revenue for philatelic bureaux.

administrations all over the world now spend a small fortune on advertising on television and in the press, as well as producing lavish brochures and sales literature promoting an ever-increasing number of special issues and first day covers. The response comes mainly from adults, many of whom may have collected stamps as children and given up the hobby, but returned to it later. Yet philatelic bureaux are also keen to issue stamps bearing themes of interest to children and young adults, and the prospect of swapping issues with a fellow collector – at a local stamp club or via internet contact – establishes philately as a great interactive pastime.

Every Stamp Tells a Story

Every stamp tells us something about its country of origin, but occasionally the postmark reveals a bigger story. This Irish cover was salvaged from the fire that burned down the Rotunda, Dublin – itself being used as a temporary GPO after the main office was destroyed during the Easter rising of 1916.

BE AN INDIVIDUAL

Despite the high-pressure sales tactics, not every newcomer to the hobby slavishly collects the offerings of the national philatelic bureaux. Many start out along that road but quickly tire of following the herd and decide to assert their individuality.

What impels them to continue with stamps may be determined by many other factors. They may be attracted to the stamps of another country because of holidays, military service or business connections there, the latter being particularly useful for continuing and developing the collection. In America, while most philatelists collect US stamps, many are drawn to the country from which their ancestors emigrated. The stamps of Israel and the Vatican are immensely popular with Jews or Roman Catholics for religious reasons. And it may simply be the lure of far-off places that explains the popularity of stamps from places such as Pitcairn and Tristan da Cunha.

These are the main reasons for embarking on a straightforward country collection. You begin with the latest issues, sign up to a dealer's new issue service or perhaps get your stamps and first day covers direct from the philatelic bureau of your chosen country, and gradually work back in time, filling in the gaps with purchases from dealers or bidding at auction: all these methods are discussed more fully later.

It is often the case that children begin with a general collection, embracing the stamps of the whole world and including anything that looks remotely like a postage stamp. As they grow older and the difficulty of attempting to form a meaningful collection on such a broad scale becomes apparent, collectors gradually narrow their interests and begin to specialize in a single country or even a particular reign or period.

In the past half century, however, other forms of collecting have developed. Paramount is the collecting of stamps according to the subject or purpose of issue, regardless of the country of origin. Others have developed an interest in postmarks and graduated to postal history, studying and collecting cards, covers and other pieces of mail, not primarily for their adhesive stamps but because of their cancellations and other postal markings.

Left: One of a set of 12 issued by the Vatican in 1946, celebrating the 400th anniversary of the Council of Trent.

Below: A stamp promoting tourism for the Pitcairn Islands, 2004.

TOOLS AND TECHNIQUES

Like any other hobby, stamp collecting requires certain basic essentials, aids and tools. If you buy a starter kit you will find that most, if not all, of these items are included, although as you progress in philately you will probably want to add more advanced versions, as well as other gadgets.

The most obvious necessity is a magnifying glass – the higher the magnification the better. For handling stamps, a pair of tongs or tweezers with flattened "spade" ends is a must. To distinguish the subtle differences between stamps you will need a perforation gauge. These range enormously in sophistication (and price), from the basic transparent plastic model with dots or lines to electronic gauges. Similarly, watermark detectors range from a small black tray to machines with lights and filters. An ultraviolet lamp is used to detect different fluorescence and types of phosphor bands.

KEY
1 Stamp catalogue
2 Colour key
3 & 4 Perforation gauges
5 Large magnifying glass
6 Sliding stamp magnifier
7 Small plastic tongs
8 Larger metal tongs
9 Small scissors
10 Starter pack of stamps
11 Small magnifier
12 Stamps attached to pieces of envelope.

WHERE TO FIND STAMPS

Sooner or later you are going to be confronted with used stamps in their raw state, still attached to pieces of envelopes or postcards, either clipped off your own mail or purchased in bulk from a dealer who gets his supplies from the various charities that save stamps to raise funds. Banks and mail-order firms are other good sources. You will find details of the latter in any monthly stamp magazine.

Above: It is possible to buy world stamps in bulk from a stamp dealer at a relatively low price. Many of these will still be attached to pieces of envelope, or postcards, and will require careful detaching with the aid of a few useful tools before they are mounted.

Postal administrations have also got in on the act. In many countries stamps were not affixed to parcels but were

Perforation Gauge

Invented in the 1860s, a perforation gauge measures the number of holes in a space of 2cm (3/4in). You simply lay the stamp alongside the rows of holes on the gauge until you find the one that fits. This will give you a "perf measurement".

attached to cards that accompanied the parcel to its destination. The cards were then retained by the post office for some time before being scrapped. The stamps, clipped off the cards, eventually found their way into bags sold to dealers and collectors by the kilo – hence the term "kiloware" which is often applied loosely to any mixture of used stamps on paper sold by weight.

DETACHING STAMPS

Once you have sifted through the mixture and selected the stamps you wish to retain, they have to be carefully parted from the envelopes. In the days when most stamps were recess-printed in monochrome, collectors would quite happily drench them in hot water – but not any more, for modern stamps are printed by less stable multicolour processes on glossy paper with a high chalk content, with fugitive inks and phosphor bands that would be damaged by total immersion. The soaking procedure described above holds good for the vast majority of self-adhesive stamps, which now have a water-soluble backing. However, some issues from the 1980s, notably from France, the USA and Australia, are backed with a rubber-based adhesive, which defies soaking. All you can do with these is keep them on their paper, trimmed neatly.

Below: When trimming the attached paper around self-adhesive stamps, take care not to damage the perforations, as this detracts from their value.

Step-by-Step Soaking Sequence

1. Float the stamps face upwards in a basin or large bowl of lukewarm water. Do not soak them.

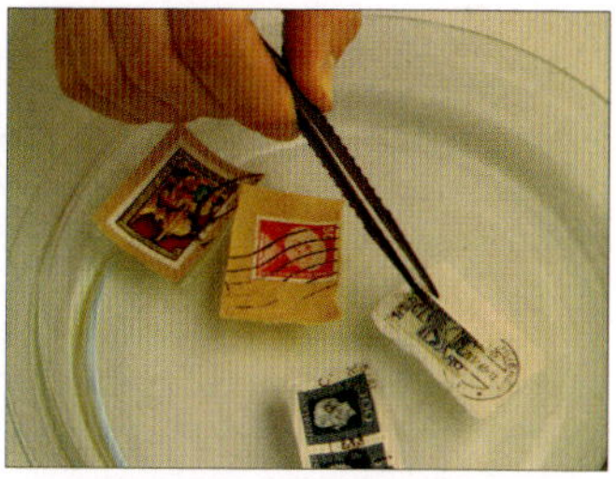

2. The stamps will curl away from the paper almost immediately, but you can test this by gently lifting a corner.

3. Remove the stamps from the water and, with care, use the tweezers to detach from the paper completely.

4. Lay the stamps face down on the top half of a clean sheet of white porous paper to dry.

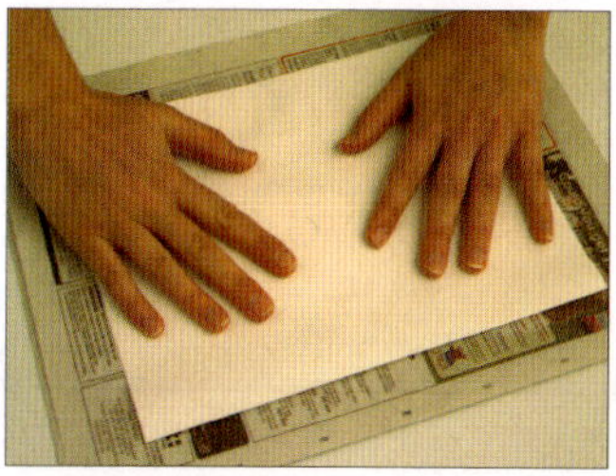

5. Fold the bottom half of the white paper so that it rests over the top of the stamps, then place the folded sheet between layers of newspaper.

6. Place heavy weights on top and leave for 24 hours before removing the dried stamps and sorting into packets. They are now ready to mount in an album.

MOUNTING STAMPS FOR DISPLAY

When stamp albums became popular in the 1860s the best of them – fixed-leaf, of course – had printed outlines of the appropriate shape for every postage stamp of the world then known to exist, with the denomination and colour of the stamp in each space. By the 1870s some albums even attempted to illustrate the stamps as well, although the images were often rather crude. The ultimate de luxe albums of the late 19th and early 20th centuries were those with spaces and illustrations on the right-hand page and catalogue descriptions and technical data on the left-hand page. They were sumptuously bound in full morocco leather and fitted with a heavy brass lock.

Above: A fast-bound printed album, with stamps mounted on facing pages.

ONE-COUNTRY ALBUMS

As the number of stamps increased, such albums became less practicable. As late as the 1940s, Minkus of the USA was still offering the "Master Global" album with a space for every stamp since 1840, but this was a philatelic dinosaur and was eventually killed by its sheer bulk. By that time some publishers, notably Schaubek of Germany, were producing one-country albums along similar lines and this fashion continues to the present day with several companies in America and Europe offering a comprehensive range of such loose-leaf albums, together with annual supplements. The ultimate is the one-country hingeless album with clear mounting strips already in place over each illustration. The collector with plenty of money but perhaps limited time to devote to the hobby can subscribe to the new issues from a philatelic bureau and merely tip them into the appropriate page.

Although simple, this method is unlikely to appeal to collectors for whom the pleasure of the hobby comes not from acquiring new specimens, but from arranging them, mounting them in albums and annotating them to suit their individual taste. To them, a blank album page, adorned with nothing more than the feint squares that provide a guide to keeping the rows of stamps straight, is a challenge to be faced with enthusiasm. Avoiding the rigid constraints of the printed album, these collectors relish the opportunity to express their individuality, not only by the manner in which they lay out the stamps on the page, but also in the methods adopted to annotate them, demonstrating their technical expertise as well as their calligraphic skills.

Below: An album page showing a World War I cover mounted with photo corners and neatly annotated by hand.

Below: A page of Austrian stamps in hingeless mounts, accompanied by manuscript captions.

Mounting Pairs and Blocks
Multiples can be mounted with hinges if they are in used condition, otherwise Hawid strips can be cut to fit. Provided at least two corners of the block are imperforate, photo corners can be used without blunting the perforations.

Above: A page from a beginner's printed album of the 1950s.

Above: A balanced arrangement of Tuva stamps of different shapes.

LAYING OUT STAMPS

It's a good idea to spread out the stamps you intend to mount on the page and move them around until you achieve a balanced effect. Do not attempt to cram too many stamps on to the page – a common mistake of even experienced collectors. Of course, if you wish to display an entire definitive series you may be constrained by the number of stamps in the set, although the average definitive range consists of about 15–20 stamps. Longer sets, such as the Prominent Americans or Transportation coils, would require two or three pages at least, while the prolific Machin series of Great Britain could fill an entire album.

Try to avoid rows containing the same number of stamps, especially if they are all of the same size and format. Most sets are a mixture of horizontal and vertical formats and stamps for the highest denominations are often larger, but where they are all the same size you can impart some variety by laying out the rows to form a pyramid.

Below: A late 19th-century printed album with a space for each stamp.

Commemoratives and special issues may present more of a problem, but also offer greater leeway to indulge your artistic skills. Less rather than more should be the keynote. In some cases you may need a row for each stamp, pair or short set, but sometimes you can get two single issues side by side.

ANNOTATING THE PAGES

The number of stamps you can display on a page is also dependent on the amount of annotation you plan to add. The basic data would be the date of issue and the title of the set or stamp. Then you could add the names of the designer and printer and the printing process used. Further information might include details of perforation and watermark, captions for each stamp and even some notes on the reason for the issue, such as additional denominations or changes of colour necessitated by increased postal rates. It is a good idea to map out the text on a scrap sheet to ensure you get the balance right.

If you are annotating the page by hand you should use a fountain pen or a drafting pen, and preferably black ink. Never use a ballpoint pen because the ink may smudge, and pencilled notes will simply fade.

ADVANCED DISPLAY TECHNIQUES

In a stamp album it is permissible to mount appropriate first day covers and souvenir cards. For a more specialized study ancillary material might include original artwork, essays and rejected designs, die and plate proofs and colour trials, as well as covers, cards and wrappers for registered mail and airmail, illustrating the actual usage of the stamps. As well as a straightforward set you would have separate pages for a range of shades, in chronological order of printing, strips and blocks of stamps to show such marginal markings as plate or cylinder numbers, printers' imprints, alphanumeric controls indicating the year and sequence of printing, or multiples illustrating the exact position of plate flaws and other varieties occurring in the sheet. Information on these topics of interest to the advanced collector will be found towards the end of this section.

The more specialized a collection, the more writing-up is likely to be involved. In extreme cases a single stamp might be mounted on a page with several hundred words of annotation to explain the technical minutiae that make this specimen extraordinary.

Above: A corner of a sheet showing two strips of the Spirit of 76 US stamps, with "Mail early" slogan and Mr Zip.

Below: Plate block of the $5 US definitive of 1975, featuring a railway conductor's lantern.

INCLUDING POSTAL EPHEMERA

The collectable material associated with the lifespan of a postal service or a particular stamp is often described as "ephemera". For example, a cover or entire letter from the "pre-stamp" era might require all kinds of additional material to illustrate details of the route taken from sender to recipient, the computation of the postal charges and other fees (such as registration or express delivery) and any infringements of the regulations that necessitated a fine or some kind of endorsement in manuscript or by handstamp. Other related ephemera might include press cuttings, photographs or engravings.

The inclusion of collateral material, as it is known, is at the discretion of the individual. At one time, too much of this in relation to the actual piece of mail was frowned on, but it is now positively encouraged and is even regarded as a separate class, known as social philately, in competitions. In this area, considerable ingenuity is required to incorporate bulky and even three-dimensional items, as the notion of philately is stretched to the limit.

Right: Picture postcard of the German battle cruiser Derfflinger, *scuttled at Scapa Flow in 1919, with a postcard bearing the ship's postmark.*

Above: Reconstruction of a quarter sheet of New Zealand stamps issued in 1893, displayed to show the advertisements printed on the reverse of the stamps.

Above: Photographic postcards, such as this issue from St Kilda (1919) showing bales of hand-woven tweed, make eye-catching additions to a stamp display.

Below: This thematic treatment of wartime evacuees includes a billeting permit and a meter mark urging people to "Stay Put!"

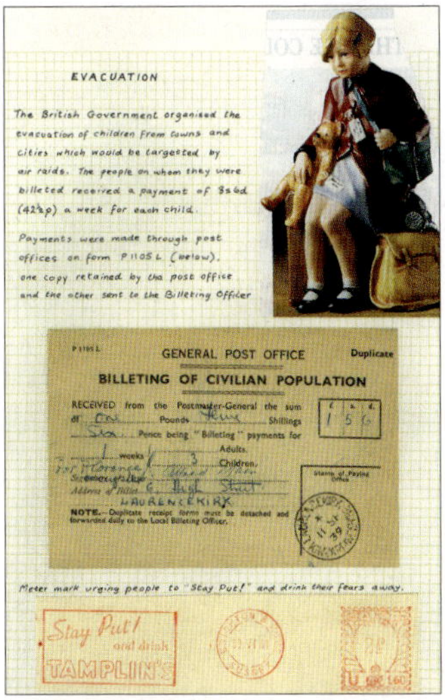

PHILATELY IN THE COMPUTER AGE

At one time the use of a typewriter to produce neat album pages was looked down on, and in competitive exhibitions such entries often lost marks for presentation. In the days of manual typewriters and fixed-sheet albums, the captions and headings had to be typed on sheets of paper, then cut out and pasted to the album pages. The advent of electric typewriters with variable settings and a choice of fonts helped considerably, but now it is a relatively simple matter for the collector to generate album pages on a personal computer and print the results on good quality A4 card, preferably around 160gsm in thickness. Packs of this card cost a fraction of the price of standard album pages and have the advantage that they fit most computer printers; album pages, being generally wider, require a printer with a broader platen.

COMPUTER-AIDED LAYOUTS

The major drawback associated with planning layouts on plain card is that there are no grid lines or "graph paper" squares to guide you in mounting the stamps in neat rows. However, software available for laying out album pages includes a facility enabling you to draw rectangles of varying sizes and shapes.

The requisite captions and other data can then be typed in, using an infinite range of fonts and type sizes, and adding bold or italic variants as required. There is even scope for the use of colour, although you should not get too carried away with this. It is best reserved for bold headings at the tops of pages, but it is also useful for printing the inscriptions on postal markings where the originals are in colours other than black. This makes the text stand out more effectively.

WEB DOWNLOADS AND SOFTWARE

Computers have, of course, many uses apart from generating your own album pages. Collectors are only beginning to wake up to the fact that the search engines on the internet can be used to discover everything you would ever need to know about many of the people and events depicted on stamps.

You can also download all kinds of images germane to your stamp display, such as the actual Old Master painting on which a postage stamp design is based. In some cases there are fees and copyright implications, particularly if you plan to exhibit such material as part of a competitive display, and it does not hurt to enquire about these if you cannot find the relevant information on the site. Many image libraries do not, however, object to the use of

Above: Many word processor documents offer an automatic grid to help you position shapes equidistant from each other: the empty boxes "snap" into place when you drag them into position. While this facility makes for a neat arrangement, it may prevent you from resizing the boxes by delicate amounts to fit the often variable sizes of stamps.

low-resolution digital pictures within a personal collection that will receive limited exposure.

Most importantly, many software packages enable you to create your own catalogue or inventory, complete with regular updates of values, or a database of stamps still required to complete your collection. This field is ever-changing and regular columns in some of the stamp magazines give up-to-date information on such software, as well as a number of websites devoted to helping the collector make the most of the latest information technology.

Collateral Material

Bulkier items, such as this piece of St Kilda tweed, can be mounted in an album or on an exhibition panel by inserting the object in a clear envelope which is itself held in place by photo corners.

COLLECTING BY COUNTRY

Half a century ago there was only one way to collect stamps, and that was according to the country of issue. Within that framework, collectors arranged their stamps by reigns or political periods, in chronological order of issue, and within each issue stamps were laid out in ascending order of face value. Until the 1950s, it was still possible for philatelists to collect stamps on a global basis. In the 1930s the number of stamps issued annually seldom exceeded 1,000, but it began to rise in the 1940s and had doubled by the early 1950s. By 1984 it had risen to over 6,000 stamps a year and today it has risen to almost 15,000. To some extent, this is due to the number of stamp-issuing entities now in existence.

Above: Stamps from Bavaria, the Sudetenland and the French zone of Germany, together with the stamp celebrating German reunification.

Above and right: The 5M stamp of 1900, the only German stamp to portray Kaiser Wilhelm II, and a West Berlin pictorial of 1957 which celebrated the 725th anniversary of Spandau.

THE GERMAN EXAMPLE

Someone taking all the issues of Germany would, technically, be little more than a general collector of a single country. However, it is a colossal field that encompasses the stamps of 17 states before the formation of the German Empire in 1871, the stamps of the Reich up to 1945, German occupation of neighbouring territories during the Franco-Prussian War and both World Wars, and all the issues made by the victorious allies when they invaded and occupied the Third Reich. Then there are the stamps of the Democratic and Federal republics (East and West Germany) and the distinctive stamps of West Berlin. The separate issues of the GDR and Berlin ceased when the Berlin Wall came down and Germany was unified in 1990.

Below: The stamps of Hawaii, as listed in The Stamp Collectors' Handbook *(1874), an early stamp catalogue.*

July, 1859. 1st Provisional.—Numeral in lettered frame (as cut), HAWAIIAN POSTAGE on the left side, UKU LETA (paid letter) to right. Ten types of each, *on pale blue-grey or greenish-blue paper.* Col. imp. rect.

1 cent . pale blue | 2 cents . . black

1862.—Head of Kamehameha IV., on lines, in lettered frame, UKU LETA overarched above, ELUA KENETA (or two cents) at base, leaves at sides, numeral in rect. at top corners. Col. imp. rect.

2 cents, vermilion (copper-plate) | 2 cents . rose (lithograph)

Jan., 1863. 2nd Provisional.—Same as 1st Provisional, *on blue-grey paper.* Col. imp. rect. Ten types.

1 cent . . . . black | 2 cents . . . . . blue

May, 1864.—Head of Kamehameha IV. on lines, in oval, as cut. Col. imp. rect. *perf.*

2 cents . . . . . vermilion

1864. 3rd Provisional.—Same as 1st and 2nd Provisional, *on white paper.* Col. imp. rect. Ten types.

1 cent . . black | 2 cents . black

Note.—On laid paper in 1865, being on plain wove at first.

May, 1865. 4th Provisional.—Numeral in lettered frame, like the other Provisionals; UKU LETA at top, HAWAIIAN POSTAGE each side, on blue paper. Col. imp. rect. Ten types.

5 cents . . . . . blue

As above, but INTERISLAND on left side, *on white paper.* Col. imp. rect.

1 cent . . dark blue | 2 cents . . dark blue

1866.—Head of Kamehameha V. on lines, in oval, as cut. Col. imp. rect. *perf.*

5 cents . . . . blue

1867. 5th Provisional.—Type as 4th Provisional, 1 and 2 cents above; viz., INTERISLAND on left, on blue paper. Col. imp. rect. Ten types.

5 cents . . . . blue

Associated with this group are the stamps of the various districts (from Allenstein to Upper Silesia), which, in the aftermath of World War I, were the subject of plebiscites to decide their future. One of these, the Saar, was also the subject of a plebiscite after World War II. Add the stamps of the ten German colonies (1888–1918) and the German post offices in China, Morocco and the Turkish Empire, and you have a formidable body of material. Throw in the private posts that flourished up to 1900 and the emergency local issues, mainly in the Soviet Zone in 1945–6, and you can see the impossibility of tackling this area on anything but a fairly simplified basis.

REGIONAL ISSUES

British stamps are by no means as prolific or complex, but they are difficult enough. Before 1922 there was only one stamp-issuing authority in the British Isles. Today there are nine. The Irish Free State (now the Republic of Ireland) began in 1922. In 1958 regional stamps appeared in Scotland, Wales and Northern Ireland, as well as Guernsey, Jersey and the Isle of Man. England was the last UK country to get

Below, clockwise from top-left: Regional stamps issued for England, Scotland, Wales and Northern Ireland.

its own definitives, in 2001. Regionalization has also affected other countries. Relative newcomers to the stamp album include the Faroe Islands (Denmark), Åland Islands (Finland), Azores and Madeira (Portugal), the Grenadines, Carriacou and Petite Martinique (Grenada) and Bequia, Mustique, Union Island, Palm Island and the Cays of Tobago (St Vincent).

CHANGING BOUNDARIES

Political upheavals in eastern Europe have seen Czechoslovakia split into the Czech Republic and Slovakia, and Yugoslavia disintegrate into Bosnia and Herzegovina, Croatia, Slovenia, Macedonia, Serbia and Montenegro. There have been separate stamp issues for those parts of Bosnia under the rule of Sarajevo, the Croats and the Serbs respectively. As for the mighty USSR, the solitary issuing authority in 1990 has been superseded by separate stamps for the Russian Federation, Armenia, Azerbaijan, Belarus, Estonia, Georgia, Kazakhstan, Kyrgyzstan, Latvia, Lithuania, Moldova, Tajikistan, Turkmenistan and the Ukraine.

NARROWING THE FIELD

As the number of different stamp-issuing territories has increased, the volume of stamps produced each year has escalated. Consequently, no one could possibly collect the stamps of the world in the fashion prevalent before World War II.

Above: Regimes that broke away from the USSR have enjoyed their own stamps. This issue from Kyrgyzstan appeared in 1992, one year after the country's independence.

A surprising number of philatelists do still maintain a general collection, although their criteria have altered over the years. For example, instead of subscribing to a new issue service taking all the stamps of the British Commonwealth, they may restrict their interests to used stamps off their mail. This is not such a limited exercise as it might appear for it is interesting to see which stamps actually get used.

Other collectors take the issues of related countries. Interestingly, Irish stamps once had very little appeal to British collectors, partly due to political reasons but mainly on account of the strange script (monastic uncials) and language (Gaelic); but in recent years Irish stamps have tended to stick to English inscriptions and have found favour with collectors who now regard the British Isles as a compact group, large enough to keep them occupied.

Right: Portugal issues regional stamps for the Azores and Madeira.

Below: Even Guernsey has regional stamps, for its dependency of Alderney.

The global tendency nowadays is for collectors to focus on the stamps of their own and immediate neighbouring countries. Thus American collectors tend to take the issues of Canada, the United Nations, and the former trust territories of the Marshall Islands, Micronesia and Palau. Philatelists in Italy concentrate on the prolific issues of San Marino and the Vatican, and French collectors go for the stamps of Andorra and Monaco, and perhaps the country's few remaining overseas colonies in the Pacific, Caribbean and Antarctic.

The natural grouping of countries is often facilitated, indeed encouraged, by the marketing policies of philatelic bureaux, which now tend to handle the issues of neighbouring countries as well as their own. In the People's Republic of China you can buy the stamps of Hong Kong, Taiwan and Macao, and this reciprocal arrangement applies in the "special administrative regions" as well. Thus ordering the stamps of the French group is just as easy as obtaining the stamps of France itself and can be done on the same order form or by shopping online.

Ephemeral Nations

Throughout the history of the stamp, governments have used new designs to highlight or stake claims to territory. This *se-tenant* pair of 1993 constitutes the sole issue of Nakhichevan, an autonomous region of Azerbaijan.

Below: This stamp of Taiwan (2004), issued by the People's Republic of China, illustrates its scenic splendours.

INTRODUCING THEMATICS

As stamps broke away from the tradition of royal or presidential portraiture, heraldry and allegory at the end of the 19th century and became increasingly pictorial in character, there gradually developed an alternative to the traditional style of collecting stamps by countries. By the 1920s this approach had become sufficiently established for books on stamp collecting to hint at the possibilities of arranging stamps not by their country but according to the subjects they depicted.

Creating a Thematic Display

This page is taken from a collection formed on the theme of the Vikings, who terrorized, then colonized, much of north-western Europe in the 8th–11th centuries. Intrepid seamen and hardy navigators, they discovered Iceland, Greenland and even North America by the year 1000. The collection is broken down into various subjects, such as Norse mythology, metalwork, arms and armour and stone-carving, but their longships could form a separate collection, with stamps from many parts of the world depicting their striped sails and dragon prows. Even ships can be subdivided into river and coastal craft, trading vessels and warships. This collection is mounted on A4 cards with computer-generated headings.

THE FIRST SCENIC STAMPS

Pictorial stamps were, of course, issued almost as far back as adhesive postage stamps themselves. The locomotive of the Broadway local post appeared in 1842, the Basle dove in 1845 and the *Lady McLeod* steamship of Trinidad in 1847. British North America and the USA added several stamps with the themes of fauna and transportation between 1851 and 1869, and the earliest scenic stamps appeared a decade later. But these were isolated examples and did not encourage collectors to try a new approach.

PICTORIALS AND PUBLICITY

The period between the two World Wars saw pictorialism in full flood, with the British and French colonial empires and the countries of Latin America leading the field. Ships and trains vied with aircraft as many countries tried to show how modern their communications were. Exotic birds and animals jostled with landmarks and scenery as countries began to realize the publicity potential of stamps. Newfoundland had been producing pictorial stamps since 1865 but used the diamond jubilee of Queen Victoria in 1897 and the 400th anniversary of British settlement in 1910 as pretexts for long sets publicizing the scenic delights of the colony. From 1923 onwards it produced several definitive sets that were frankly aimed at promoting the growing tourist industry.

In Europe, France was an outstanding exponent of pictorialism, not only in its increasingly numerous commemoratives from 1917 onwards but also in the definitives. Representations of Marianne (symbolizing the triumph of the French Republic) were favoured for the middle values, but the lowest denominations featured arms of cities and provinces while the higher values since 1929 have depicted monuments and landmarks, beginning with the Arc de Triomphe, Reims Cathedral and Mont-Saint-Michel.

The combination of much more frequent issues of all kinds and multicolour printing processes has widened the scope of stamp design. It is now

Below: Since 1929, many French definitives have depicted scenery and landmarks and could form the basis of collections devoted to specific regions.

Above: A US $4.40 booklet of 1985 containing stamps showing seashells.

virtually impossible to think of a topic that has not been depicted on a stamp somewhere, at some time. Thematic collecting has liberated philately from the constraints of collecting stamps solely by country.

SUBJECT COLLECTING

The basic idea of thematic collecting is to group stamps according to the subject of the design. When the American Topical Association was formed in 1949 its primary aim was to provide members with checklists of stamps showing different subjects. Today, the ATA has over 50,000 members in almost 100 countries, and has published countless booklets detailing a wide range of different subjects. These have been basic lists enabling collectors to locate the stamps of their chosen subject with the aid of a standard stamp catalogue. However, in recent years major catalogue publishers have begun to produce thematic catalogues, fully illustrated and often in colour.

These catalogues follow a well-trodden path and cover such popular subjects as ships, aircraft, trains, cars,

Below: Chinese and Greek stamps for the railway enthusiast – but you have to look hard to spot the locomotives in the background of the designs.

Above: A Marshall Islands sheet of 50 showing US warships named after each state, from Alabama to Wyoming.

flowers, animals, birds, insects, sports, religion and fine art, as well as such international movements as the Red Cross or the Boy Scouts. There are even catalogues that list all the stamps depicting fungi, seashells and insects such as butterflies, and catalogues that deal exhaustively with ball games or the Olympics. However, many of these categories are broad and it is important to define limits within your chosen subject. It would be impossible to collect every stamp that showed a bird, for example; it makes more sense to focus on individual species that appeal to you, such as robins or puffins.

EUROPA STAMPS

Stamps inscribed "Europa" began to be issued in 1956, and have become one of the mainstays of pictorial subject collecting. Originally, the stamps were confined to the six countries of the European Coal and Steel Community (France, Germany, Italy, Belgium, the Netherlands and Luxembourg). During the 1960s their administration was taken over by the European Conference of Posts and Telecommunications (CEPT), now known as PostEurop, and the scheme has expanded to countries from Greenland to Turkey and the Ukraine. At first the stamps had identical designs but in the 1970s this gave way to individual interpretations of a common theme.

You can either collect all the stamps with "Europa" in their inscription, or take those Europa stamps that fit the subject you are collecting. In 2004, for example, the theme of the Europa stamps was holidays. Some countries (such as Ireland) opted for tourist attractions such as scenery and landmarks, while others concentrated on sailing, swimming or just lounging on the beach. Many stamps have more than one element in their design. The primary subject will be very obvious, but often there is a secondary subject, perhaps tucked away in the border or the background, and it is the sharp-eyed philatelist who recognizes it who gains points for observation and originality in competitive exhibitions.

Right and below: Stamps from Slovenia, Latvia, the Czech Republic and Greece expound on the holiday theme of the 2004 Europa stamps.

PURPOSE-OF-ISSUE COLLECTING

This branch of thematics, which is also known as incidental philately, deals with the building of a collection around a particular event. A classic example might be a periodical celebration such as an anniversary, but occasionally a single event in history is chosen as a theme.

Anniversaries were among the first of the "global" themes to adorn stamps and labels. The first time stamps were issued in several countries to mark an event occurred in 1892–3, when the United States and several countries of Latin America celebrated the 400th anniversary of the first voyage of Columbus to the New World. In 1897–8 seven countries of the British Empire issued 56 stamps among them to mark Victoria's diamond jubilee; although Britain did not issue stamps, a number of commemorative labels were produced. Around the same period Portugal and its colonies celebrated the exploits of Vasco da Gama. Issues marking the 450th and 500th anniversaries of Columbus, and numerous others on this theme from Spain, Italy and the Western Hemisphere in between, make this one of the largest subjects in this category.

Above: British royal portraiture in stamps has developed enormously, from the restrained, two-colour intaglio pictorials of George V's silver jubilee in 1935 to the multicolour photogravure and offset lithographic stamps of recent years, celebrating Elizabeth II's golden jubilee in 2002 and paying tribute to the Queen Mother following her death.

OMNIBUS EDITIONS

Identical commemorative sets issued simultaneously in many territories became fashionable in the French and British Empires in the 1930s. Sets from numerous colonies and protectorates celebrated the Colonial Exposition in Paris (1931) and the silver jubilee of George V (1935). With uniform designs differing only in the country name and denomination, these set the pattern for many other omnibus issues until the 1970s. Since then, different motifs within an overall uniform style have been preferred. Royalty remains a popular subject, as seen in birthday and jubilee editions and numerous memorial issues for Diana, Princess of Wales.

Below: A Portuguese stamp of 1894 marked the 400th anniversary of the voyage of Vasco da Gama to India.

THE CONQUEST OF SPACE

Space is a vast, global topic with many different strands to be explored, from the Chinese invention of rockets to the Apollo moon landings and beyond, the probes of Mars and Venus and the development of the Hubble telescope. The space race between the USA and the USSR could be illustrated not only by stamps but also by souvenir covers and postcards. A straightforward subject collection might consist of the different types of spacecraft, while purpose-of-issue collecting could concentrate on the Apollo 11 mission of 1969 and the stamps that celebrated anniversaries of Neil Armstrong's first "step for mankind", or the issues around the world that mourned the victims of the Columbia and Challenger disasters. The exploration of space might be linked to the devel-

Above: A se-tenant *pair – with two designs printed side by side – from the German Democratic Republic, marking the flights of Vostok V and VI in 1963.*

opment of the telescope and the science of astronomy. All these aspects now form a distinct branch of the hobby, under the title of astrophilately.

OLYMPIC PHILATELY

In 1896 Greece hosted the first modern Olympic Games and issued a set of 12 stamps, from 1 lepton to 10 drachmae. Although designed, engraved and printed in France, they were wholly Greek in concept. Apart from the 1d and 10d, which depicted the Acropolis and the Parthenon respectively, the designs were derived from ancient Greek sculptures of athletes, or statues symbolizing the spirit of the Games.

Greece produced a second Olympic set in 1906 but this precedent was not followed by any other host country until 1920, when Belgium issued a set of three, establishing an enduring trend whereby the host nation issues stamps to mark the event. In 1932 the USA became the first country to issue stamps for the Winter Olympics as well. In 1954–5 Australia broke new ground by issuing stamps as advance publicity for the Melbourne Games of 1956. This tradition has now reached the point at which countries begin issuing pre-Games stamps as soon as the winning bid is confirmed.

The Games now include around 30,000 participants, and if you take into account all the stamps marking the anniversaries of national Olympic committees, as well as the stamps and postal stationery provided for the use of the International Olympic Committee in Switzerland, plus souvenir cards and covers, it is not hard to appreciate what a huge subject this has become.

Right: A pre-publicity stamp for the Melbourne Olympic Games of 1956.

Below: A Greek miniature sheet publicizing the Athens Olympic Games, 2004.

SOCCER STAMPS

If the Olympic Games dominates world sport, the World Cup Football Championship (first held in Uruguay in 1930) is not far behind. Like the Olympics, the World Cup takes place every four years and is now almost as prolific in stamp terms. In the interim, however, the European Cup is beginning to rival the global championships in terms of the outpourings of stamps from participants and non-participants eager for revenue from portraying the great soccer stars. In addition, FIFA, the International Federation of Association Football, celebrated its centenary in 2004 and virtually every affiliated country issued stamps to mark the occasion. There have been stamps for women's football (Nigeria and Sweden), children's soccer (Alderney) and even one-legged football (El Salvador).

Above: This sheetlet from Niger in 2000 was one of a series charting each decade of the 20th century.

Left: One of the stamps issued by Sweden to celebrate the FIFA centenary of 2004 portrayed famous women footballers.

OTHER THEMES

Other aspects of purpose-of-issue collecting are more focused, with worldwide issues for United Nations campaigns, the 75th anniversary and centenary of the Universal Postal Union (UPU) in 1949 and 1974, Rotary International (1955 and 1980), the Millennium (2000–1) and memorial issues for leaders of international renown, such as Franklin D. Roosevelt (1945) and Winston Churchill (1964–5). Many nations brought out iconic stamps to mourn the assassination of President John F. Kennedy in 1963, followed by another set to mark the first anniversary.

The First Olympics

Commemorative stamps were still a novelty in 1896, and a long set with a high face value, as issued by the Greek authorities to mark the Athens Olympics of that year, was roundly condemned at the time. Today, however, the series is highly valued and is the key set for any collection with an Olympic theme.

CHOOSING THEMES AND TELLING STORIES

The third distinct branch of topical collecting offers the greatest scope for the collector's individuality, because it involves selecting and arranging material in such a way that it tells a story. Certain topics in this field are extremely popular because of the range and availability of stamps associated with them.

Raw material for a collection illustrating "The American Dream", for example, is to be found in the definitive sets portraying presidents and other prominent figures, numerous commemoratives or special issues and, in recent years, *se-tenant* strips or entire sheets of different stamps featuring outstanding personalities, from country and western singers to choreographers. More manageable US themes might be "How the West was Won" or "The conflict between North and South." There are also many stamps rather more overt in their promotion and definition of the American way of life, bearing iconic images and inspiring messages to the people of the country.

Above: Commemorative and special US issues, usually priced at the domestic letter rate, publicize all aspects of American life. This group highlights youth: the Boy Scouts, Girl Scouts and the National Apprenticeship Program. Even the Automobile Association stamp (1952) stresses the youth angle.

DIDACTIC STAMPS

Almost from their inception, American stamps have had a didactic element, teaching migrants from many lands something of the customs, history and geography of their adopted land. Stamps "saluted" young Americans with carefully contrived issues highlighting the importance of useful, beneficial activity, such as the Boy and Girl Scouts stamps. The American work ethic was hammered home in numerous celebratory portraits of the blue-collar industrial worker, on issues such as those depicting rail and automobile engineers, postal workers, rangers, apprentices and the country's "future farmers".

In contrast to these, more recent issues address health concerns such as obesity and poor levels of fitness by actively promoting physical exercise. A rather idealized version of the American

Suffragette Mail

A suffragette nails the colours to her mast before a demonstration (left). Some members of the suffragette movement in Britain actively targeted public services, such as the postal network, in a bid to draw attention to their campaign. In some cases, public works buildings were set on fire, while other campaigners resorted to more prosaic, local vandalism to make a point. The envelope below was a victim of such an attack: it was heavily damaged when a suffragette poured ink into the letterbox of an unpopular household.

woman as "homemaker" features on several issues, while others champion peace, liberty and diplomacy.

THE TOURIST TRAIL

Another popular approach to creating a narrative collection is to describe a tour around a country, island or even an individual city, illustrating it with appropriate stamps.

Paris and Berlin are excellent subjects for such treatment, because France and Germany (and especially West Berlin when it issued its own stamps) have produced numerous stamps showing everything from panoramic views to individual landmarks. Washington and London might present more of a challenge but it is surprising how many stamps from other countries have portrayed their prominent features. New York City would be much harder. Of course, there are many stamps of the world showing the famous downtown skyline, but only a handful mourned 9/11 with views of the ill-fated Twin Towers. Stamps from many countries marked the New York World's Fairs in 1939 and 1964. The USA issued a stamp in 1953 for the tercentenary of the city, contrasting the Dutch town of New Amsterdam with the modern skyscrapers. New York's Coliseum (1956), University Library (1981), Stock Exchange (1992) and the Brooklyn (1983) and Verrazano Narrows (1964) bridges have all appeared on American stamps, but they are overshadowed by the numerous stamps from the USA and elsewhere featuring the Statue of Liberty, an interesting theme in its own right, particularly for collectors concerned with iconography in stamps.

Below: Stamps from Nauru in the central Pacific showed solidarity with the USA in the wake of 9/11.

POLITICAL MATTERS

Many countries and regimes have used stamps extensively as political propaganda. Fascist Italy started this trend in the early 1920s but it was taken to new levels by Nazi Germany, and by the countries in the communist bloc when the Cold War was at its height. An interesting collection could be made of the propagandist stamps issued by the former German Democratic Republic, and the means by which it sought to denounce the ideals of the West. From 1940 onwards, the United States has issued many stamps that promote democratic ideals, contrasting the four freedoms enshrined in its constitution with the oppression of the nations then under Nazi occupation or – later – behind the Iron Curtain.

Some stamps, such as those issued by the Isle of Man, vividly illustrate the struggle to win votes for women, featuring portraits of the leaders of the suffrage movement, or the campaigns in many parts of the world to achieve racial equality and civil rights for all. In countries such as Britain, exponents of universal suffrage actually targeted the postal services as part of their national campaign, and remnants of the graphic vandalism exist to this day.

The range of topics with a quasi-political slant is enormous, ranging from the rise and fall of the Roman Empire to the collapse of communism in the 1990s. The French Revolution and its worldwide repercussions and the power struggle that led to World War I are themes that lend themselves well to a philatelic treatment.

Above: Many stamps of the GDR commemorated the Nazi death camps, and also portrayed victims of the Holocaust (left).

Below: An American patriotic label from the Cold War era.

COLLATERAL MATERIAL

To illustrate a story in real depth, it's important to look beyond the stamps themselves. Increasingly, related material is being brought into play. First day covers (special envelopes bearing stamps cancelled on the first day of issue) and maximum cards (postcards with an appropriate stamp affixed to the picture side, cancelled by a matching postmark) augment mint stamps, but you can also include non-postal labels (sometimes called poster stamps), perhaps commemorating an event or anniversary, or even advertising diverse products in connnection with the event. Pictorial meter marks and postmarks are other items that can be effective in a thematic display.

COLLECTING POSTAL HISTORY

In its broadest sense, postal history encompasses the study of the development of the posts over the centuries. In practice, as a branch of philately, it embraces the collecting of everything pertaining to the transmission of mail, from the cuneiform tablets of ancient Assyria down to the junk mail that popped through your mailbox today. Although postal services of some kind have been around for thousands of years, no one thought of studying the ephemera and artefacts associated with them until the late 19th century – well after the adoption of adhesive stamps and postal stationery.

Above: An early example of an American machine cancellation, dated 1900, appears adjacent to a 2c George Washington stamp.

Below: "Dumb cancels" (those that do not contain a town or country name) appear in many forms, the impressions often made from shapes cut into cork.

CANCELLATIONS

The earliest philatelists preferred to collect mint stamps; the cancellation was considered merely to be something that detracted from their appearance. By the 1870s, however, a few collectors were beginning to take note of the cancellations as well as other markings on mail, such as datestamps, charge and explanatory marks, and route and transit marks, which appeared mainly on the backs of the envelopes.

In Britain, some dedicated individuals even travelled round the country trying to persuade postmasters and counter staff to give them impressions of their datestamps, a practice that was regarded in official circles with the gravest suspicion. Although such impressions, on otherwise blank pieces of paper, seem rather childish, had they not been preserved many of the marks would be otherwise unrecorded. The advent of the parcel post in 1883 gave an impetus to postmark collecting, although it was not until 1904 that every post office in the UK was equipped with a datestamp.

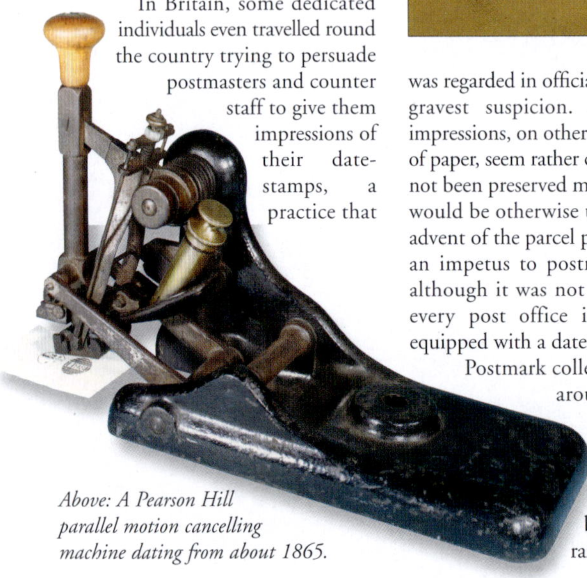

Above: A Pearson Hill parallel motion cancelling machine dating from about 1865.

Postmark collecting developed around the same time in the United States, where collectors were fascinated by the astonishing range of postmarks.

Above and right: A flag cancellation from Boston in 1898 shows the origin of the seven wavy lines found in machine postmarks everywhere. Such postmarks are immensely popular with American collectors as an adjunct to the many stamps featuring the Stars and Stripes.

It was left to the initiative of each postmaster to devise a mark that suited his fancy, and as well as circles and stars there were numerous pictorial cancellations, cut from pieces of rubber or cork. Around the turn of the 20th century, countless US post offices had

Above: Twin datestamps are typical of the French Daguin cancelling machine.

Below: A dated postmark of Versailles, France, from the pre-stamp era.

machines generating a cancellation whose obliterator took the form of the Stars and Stripes. It is from these "flag cancellations" that the wavy lines in most machine cancellations are derived.

PRESERVING POSTMARKS

The craze for picture postcards from the 1890s to World War I provided an abundance of raw material. Sadly, collectors of the period often cut out the postmark, even cutting into the stamps to achieve a neat little square. This vandalism has destroyed the value of many otherwise rare items. Nowadays collectors keep postcards intact. In the case of ordinary envelopes it is generally sufficient to cut out the stamp and postmark, leaving a generous margin all round. Machine cancellations and slogans are usually kept in strips. Registered, express or other covers subject to special handling, as well as underpaid items surcharged prior to delivery, should be kept whole.

Postmark collecting as a sideline to philately became immensely popular in the period after World War II, when increasing use was made of slogan cancellations that were changed at frequent intervals. Firms would sell the wastepaper from their mailrooms by the sackload for a nominal sum, and this was a fertile source of new material.

Many post offices were still cancelling stamps by hand at that period, but from the 1970s mail was increasingly concentrated and mechanized. Letters and cards are nowadays often transported over long distances to a central automatic processing centre or mechanized letter office, and the cancellations have relatively little relevance to the place where the mail originated. This is true not only of the more industrialized countries such as the USA, Britain, France and Germany, but also of many other countries, which, until quite recently, allowed most post offices to cancel their outgoing mail. It is still possible to get a rubber stamp applied to covers and cards at post office counters in Canada and the USA, but in Britain the only way you can now get a mark distinctive to each office is by tendering a letter or card for posting, and asking for a certificate to confirm this. At one time, a charge was applied for this, but the service is now free.

FROM METER MARKS TO ELECTRONIC POSTAGE

Postage meters were pioneered by Norway and New Zealand in the early 1900s and spread throughout the world from 1922 onwards. Meter marks, which were once despised by philatelists, have become popular in recent years, either as a branch of postal history or as an adjunct of topical collecting (mainly for the pictorial element in their design). Even permit mail markings and postage paid impressions (PPIs), which are extensively used on business mail and bulk mailings, have their devotees: one person's junk mail may be another's collectable material. It is now even possible to download postage through a computer and generate electronic stamps.

Pictorial Meter Marks

From the outset, meter marks offered business users the opportunity to incorporate a slogan showing the company emblem or advertising its products. This also applied to the marks used by offices at local and national government level, and they have often been used to convey road safety or public health messages. Much sought after today are the early meter marks from the United Nations, showing the headquarters building in the "stamp" and the logo and slogans alongside it.

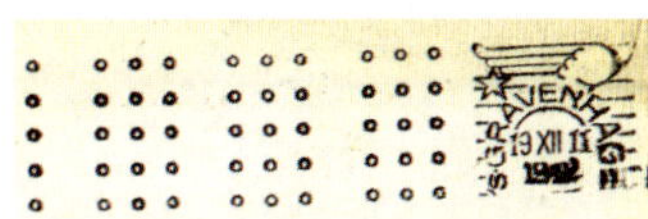

Above: A curious machine cancellation from the Netherlands uses a pattern of dots instead of the usual wavy lines.

Below: Postal history of the future – a postage stamp generated by computer.

COLLECTING SEA MAIL

It is little surprise that sea mail is such a popular subject among postal historians, whose collections often include letters, cards and wrappers indicating how mail was conveyed, or bearing evidence of delay or disruption caused by wars and other international upheavals. Some of the best artefacts hint at fascinating stories of global adventure.

Above: A postcard from Spain to London with the Spanish stamps cancelled by the Southampton ship letter datestamp.

PACKET BOATS

Until the middle of the 19th century the chief medium for the conveyance of mail between countries was the sea. In addition, a great deal of mail from one part of the USA to another, or round the British coast, was carried by ship. From the 17th century onwards there were special regulations concerning the transmission of letters by ship. The British Post Office was the world leader in this respect, organizing a fleet of ships, known as packet boats, which operated from Falmouth in Cornwall and carried mail to all parts of the world. Special postmarks bearing the name of the country of posting, with the letter F at the foot in a fancy fleuron, denoted mail arriving in England from foreign parts via Falmouth.

Below: Ship letter sent from China to Scotland, 1796, via Dover and London.

INTERNATIONAL MAIL

Britain established post offices and postal agencies in many countries, enabling people to correspond across the oceans at a time when those countries had barely organized their internal postal services, let alone created an efficient overseas service. Many hundreds of different postmarks evolved in connection with this operation, from departure and transit marks to accountancy marks, showing the postage due in different currencies and often referring to the article or clause in the postal treaty between Britain and the country of posting. Much international mail was conveyed from one country to another on British ships via British ports, so the stamps and postal markings of three different countries might be involved.

SHIP LETTERS

Mail arriving in the British Isles aboard private ships was treated differently. Ships' captains were entitled to a 1d fee on every letter they handed over to the Post Office on arrival and the recipient paid a ship letter charge of 8d. Special ship letter marks were used by most British seaports – even quite small villages, whose marks are highly desirable.

Many other countries eventually operated similar schemes, but they were consolidated by the Universal Postal Union in 1897 when the French term *paquebot* was adopted. This applied mainly to letters and cards bearing the stamps of one country, posted aboard ships at sea and then landed at a port in another country. Special *paquebot* marks were applied to such mail to explain the use of foreign stamps.

INTERNAL SEABOUND SERVICES

The UK had internal shipping services that regularly conveyed mail and even had shipboard post offices. These operated between Holyhead and Kingstown (now Dun Laoghaire) in Ireland and between Greenock and Ardrishaig in Scotland, and their postmarks are much sought after. Until 1939 cross-Channel steamers had movable mail boxes (*boîtes mobiles*) on deck. They were emptied on the British or French

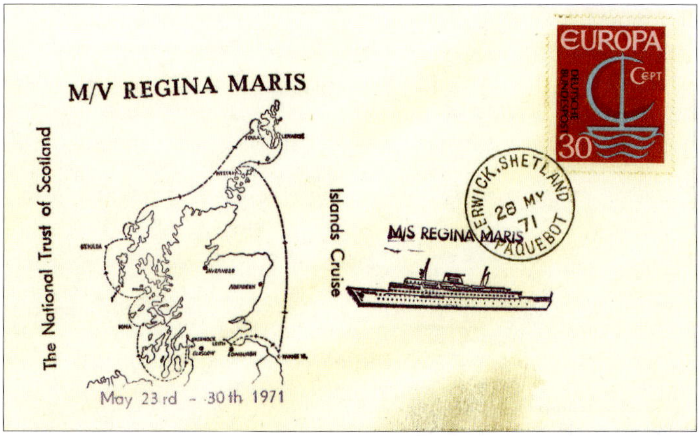

Above: A cover posted aboard the MV Regina Maris *on a National Trust cruise and landed at Lerwick, where the* paquebot *postmark was applied to the German stamp.*

Right: A 25M stamp affixed to a parcel dispatched by commerce submarine from Hamburg to New York in 1916.

Above: A Holyhead paquebot *postmark of 1929 and a backstamp of the Holyhead & Kingstown Packet (1865).*

side, and the contents were postmarked at Southampton, London, Le Havre or Saint-Malo, with the initials "MB" or "BM" above the date.

SHIP MARKINGS

Apart from the internationally used *paquebot*, inscriptions on postmarks in many languages provide a clue to their usage in connection with ship mail. You will find *paketboot* (Dutch or Flemish), or perhaps *vapore* (Italian for "steamship"), *buzón vapor* ("steamer box" in Spanish), *Schiffsbrief* (German) or *skibsbrev* (Danish). Less obviously, Australian and New Zealand stamps are cancelled "Loose letter" to denote individual letters brought in by private ships. "Ship mail room" in Australian postmarks refers to the section of the Melbourne or Sydney sorting offices that processed mail going abroad.

Nowadays many cruise liners have shipboard post offices, complete with pictorial handstamps. The ships that ply along the Norwegian coast between Bergen and Kirkenes each have their own handstamps, indicating the direction, and special postmarks are even applied to mail posted at the North Cape (Nord Kapp).

NAVAL MAIL

Among the most coveted items are those that were conveyed by submarine in wartime. In August 1916, to beat the British blockade, the Germans organized the *Ozeanreederei*, a service to and from the USA using huge submarine freighters, which terminated when America entered the war in 1917; special stamps and cancellations for this purpose were issued by the Deutsche Versicherungsbank. In 1938, during the Spanish Civil War, communications between the Balearic Islands and the Spanish mainland were maintained by submarine and a set of six stamps and a miniature sheet were issued.

Each ship in the German Navy had its own postmark. British naval mail in World War I was marked "Received from H.M. ships", but the inscription "Maritime mail" was substituted in World War II to cover letters from Allied ships as well.

Maiden Voyages

The maiden voyages of mail steamers and latterly cruise liners are often celebrated by special souvenir postcards and covers. These covers from the first eastward voyages of the *Queen Mary*, in 1936, and the *Queen Elizabeth 2*, in 1969, bear US stamps and *paquebot* postmarks.

Below: Paquebot *postmarks of 1956 on these Irish stamps were applied at Dun Laoghaire (formerly Kingstown), the Irish terminus of the Irish Sea ferries.*

COLLECTING RAILWAY MAIL

Railway mail forms one of the largest branches of philatelic collecting. Sub-categories include railwayana (where a variety of collateral material might be collected, from rail tickets to the name plates of locomotives) and railroad ephemera, or "railroadia" (popular in the United States), where collectors will try to get their hands on just about anything connected to the history of a railroad route – even lanterns! Various publications and internet auction sites exist for these enthusiasts, but for those who wish to limit their collection to the role played by the "travelling posts" along these rail routes, there is more than enough material to choose from.

Above: The first purpose-built sorting tender came into use in 1838. The net on the carriage caught the bag of mail suspended at the side of the track.

Below: Postal workers load a travelling post office. The brown overalls guarded against dust and newspaper print.

Mail was first carried in Britain, unofficially, on 11 November 1830 on the Liverpool and Manchester Railway. The first mail conveyed by rail in America was by the *Best Friend* locomotive of the South Carolina Railroad on 15 January 1831, and by the Baltimore & Ohio Railroad in 1832. The first official mail contract was awarded on 1 January 1838 to the latter company by the US Post Office.

British mail was first carried by train on a semi-official basis on 4 July 1837 by the Grand Trunk Railway, between Birmingham and Liverpool. Frederick Karstadt, the son of a British postal official, suggested that mail handling could be accelerated if it could be sorted en route, and he designed the first sorting carriage – a converted horse-box – which began running between Birmingham and Liverpool on 24 January 1838.

TRAVELLING POST OFFICES

The TPO was the brainchild of Briton Nathaniel Wordsell, who experimented with an apparatus that would allow mail to be picked up or dropped off by moving trains. His innovation assisted the development of a national rail post network no end, and by 1855 special all-mail trains were running between London and Bristol, and other services spread rapidly across the British Isles in the ensuing decade. A similar pattern developed in all other countries with rail networks during the second half of the 19th century.

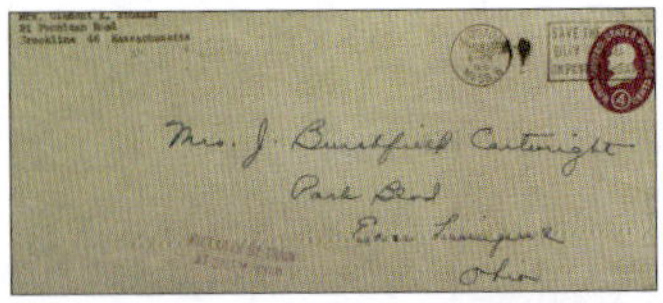

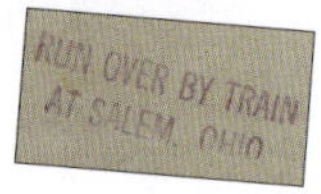

Above and right: The reason for the delay of this miraculously undamaged American letter would be far from apparent, were it not for the unusual postmark: "Run over by train".

Below: A photograph of a Swedish mail train crash at Rorvik, which occurred on 6 September 1954.

THE FIRST POSTMARKS

Distinctive postmarks were evolved for use on mail posted in the special boxes attached to the sides of mail trains or deposited in the late posting boxes at railway stations. In many cases an additional "late fee" was charged, and any items that did not include this were surcharged and fined appropriately. A wide range of explanatory marks also evolved to indicate mail that had been missorted or delayed in transit, while the rarest, and thus most desirable, marks are those applied to mail damaged as a result of a train crash.

IDENTIFYING INSCRIPTIONS

Special postmarks were devised in every country to denote railway mail. The commonest form was an inscription with two or more names, indicating the termini and perhaps an intermediate station en route. Various initials are another clue, and it is important to spot such designations as "ST" (sorting tender), "SC" (sorting carriage), "RPO" (railway post office) or "TPO" (travelling post office). Inscriptions in other languages may include the words *ambulant* (French), *ambulante* (Portuguese), *ambulancia* (Spanish), *Bahnpost* or *Eisenbahn* (German), *banen* (Danish and Norwegian), *jernbanwagen* (Swedish) or abbreviations such as AMB or EISENB. Some marks used by the old German States were inscribed *"Fahrendes postamt"* (literally "Travelling post office").

Subsidiary inscriptions include "Up" or "Down" in British postmarks, indicating the direction of the mail train, while "Day" or "Night" shows the service. German postmarks often include a numeral preceded by "Zug" or "Z", indicating the identification number assigned to the actual train.

Crash Mail

Covers that formed part of railway mails delayed or damaged as a result of train robberies or crashes are very highly prized, despite their poor condition. This charred cover was salvaged from the fire that gutted the bag tender on the London–Edinburgh TPO, when the train crashed at Grantham on 19 September 1906.

Above: French TPO postmarks can be recognized by their scalloped edge and two place names.

Right: German TPO marks are rectangular or oval, with two names and even a train ("Zug") number.

While the railway postmarks used in Britain, Canada and the USA conform to the patterns for datestamps in general, many European countries have favoured distinctive patterns. Austria, Germany and Czechoslovakia used large horizontal oval shapes, whereas French TPOs traditionally have a scalloped edge. In Spain and Portugal the postmarks are octagonal and the Low Countries use a horizontal rectangle.

WHEN RAILWAY MARKS DO NOT MEAN RAILWAY MAIL

Because of the immense popularity of railway mail, and the premiums paid for covers and cards whose postmarks show that they were carried by rail, it is important not to confuse the railway marks with others that appear to have a rail connection, but do not in fact indicate railway mail.

Many postmarks include words that mean "railway station", such as *Bahnhof* or *Hauptbahnhof* (German), *gare* (French), *stazione* or *ferrovia* (Italian) or *stasjon* (Norwegian). These merely indicate a post office that happens to be located at a railway station, rather than mail transported by train.

Above: Spanish TPO marks are octagonal, bearing the abbreviation "Amb" for ambulancia *(moving).*

In fact, collecting covers, cards and parcel labels from such station post offices has become quite a study in its own right, but even here some caution has to be exercised. Many country post offices in Scotland included the word "Station" in their name. Of course, the post office may actually have been in the station at one time but in most cases places such as Annbank Station and Drymen Station were villages in their own right. With the closure of many railway lines, the station names have become redundant and the villages have changed their names: these examples are now known respectively as Mossblown and Croftamie.

Below: Many of the preserved railway lines in the UK issue their own stamps, complete with special cancellations and souvenir cachets.

COLLECTING WARTIME MAIL

It is remarkable that even at the height of the worst conflicts, the mail still manages to get through. The Universal Postal Union was the only international organization that continued to operate reasonably smoothly throughout both World Wars, often relying on elaborate routing of mail through neutral countries. Of course, a vast quantity of mail was trapped as the tide of war ebbed and flowed and it was several years before some could be safely delivered.

FPO AND APO POSTMARKS

Special provisions for the handling of letters to and from soldiers and sailors in wartime date from the Napoleonic Wars, and many distinctive postmarks were employed by both sides. The British and French had efficient facilities for the smooth collection and delivery of forces' mail during the Crimean War (1854–6) and from then on special postmarks were employed in virtually every campaign.

A varied, almost chaotic, range of postmarks appeared during the Boer War (1899–1902) but by the outbreak of World War I a system of field post offices (FPO) was in place and this has continued to the present time, with regular numbers identifying the location of units at home and overseas.

Left and below: An Austrian field postmark of 1915 and a letter to Geneva from French troops in Holland during the Napoleonic War.

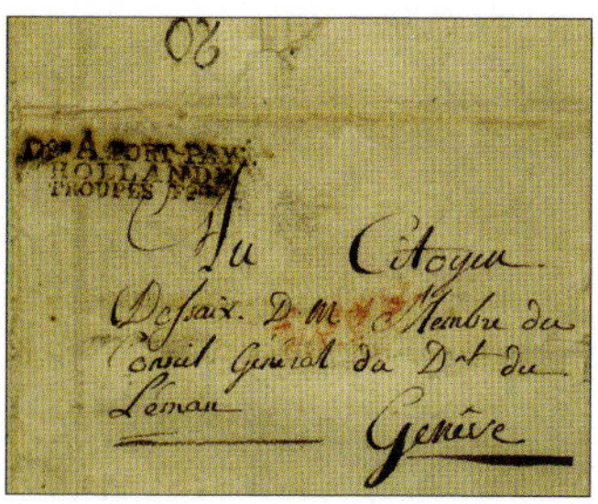

Above: Two APO cancellations dating from 1900 during the Boer War. The scrawl across the top envelope points out that "no stamps [were] obtainable", while the hand stamp below explains that the envelope was "recovered from mails looted by the Boers on June 8".

The transmission of mail to and from soldiers in the American Civil War (1861–5) was often haphazard, but enlivened by a wealth of patriotic covers. A regular service by army post offices (APO) emerged during the Spanish-American War (1898) and was greatly expanded in World War I. The APO system continues today, with numbers identifying offices in Iraq, Afghanistan and other trouble spots.

Below: A stamp postmarked in July 1939 at Camp de Septfonds, a French internment camp for Spanish refugees during the Civil War.

Above: In Britain, the Home Postal Centre in Nottingham was the hub of mail distribution for much of World War II. This clerk is checking a vast index that gave the location of units.

Air raid mail

These two pieces of postal ephemera – a badly damaged newspaper wrapper and a remarkably clean envelope with stamps intact – both survived the carpet-bombing raids targeting southern England in World War II. Note the missile-shaped postmark, applied to wartime mail delayed by enemy action, shown on the bottom envelope.

NAVAL MAIL

Since the mid-19th century a system of special postmarks for military and naval mail has been developed by almost every country around the world. The Franco-German War of 1870–1 and the Pacific War of 1878–83, involving Bolivia, Chile and Peru, yielded a rich crop of military markings, as well as provisional stamps intended for use by the victors in conquered territory.

Naval mail constitutes an enormous area of philately in its own right. While the French and German navies had distinctive datestamps for each warship, the US Navy often resorted to ships' names and other inscriptions set between the obliterating bars of rubber stamps. British vessels, in contrast, retained their anonymity for security reasons. Mail landed from these ships was marked with a handstamp or machine cancellation which read "Received from H.M. Ships". This was altered in World War II to "Post Office Maritime Mail" so as not to exclude deliveries from Allied ships. In World War I each ship was responsible for censoring outgoing mail and a wide variety of marks was employed; these have enabled students to identify many of the individual ships.

Left: Postmark from the German warship Deutschland, *which was interned at Scapa Flow in 1919.*

Below: A World War II cover from England to neutral Switzerland, examined and resealed twice by both British and German censors.

For security reasons, mail landed from warships during World War I was not cancelled by the ordinary postmarks of seaports; instead various dumb cancels were employed on handstamps, in the form of barred circles, concentric circles or crosses. Even cancelling machines had their normal inscriptions replaced by crosses or plus signs. Canada took this concept a step further in World War II, using daters in machine cancellations, devoid of any names or locations.

OCCUPATION, INVASION AND LIBERATION

Occupation stamps were first issued by the German Federal Commissioners in the duchy of Holstein in 1864, following the invasion by Austrian and Prussian forces. It was, incidentally, when the Allies fell out over the administration of the duchies of Schleswig and Holstein that the Seven Weeks' War of 1866 erupted, resulting in many different *Feldpost* markings on both sides. The distinctive stamps for use in occupied territory alone constitute a formidable branch of philately, but the range of covers, postcards and distinctive postmarks is almost infinite.

Special military stationery ranges from the Franco-Prussian and Russo-Turkish wars of the 1870s to the forces' air letter sheets used in Iraq in 2004. Special provision for stamps, stationery and postmarks in connection with the invasion of other countries dates from the 1930s and includes material relating to the Italian invasions of Abyssinia (1936) and Albania (1939), the German invasion of Czechoslovakia (1938–9), Memel, Danzig and Poland (1939), the Hungarian invasion of Slovakia (1938) and Ruthenia (1939). An interesting sideline is the partial erasure of postmarks by the conquerors, cutting out the indigenous version of placenames in bilingual datestamps.

In World War II the Allies made provision for liberation stamps and postal stationery in the aftermath of the landings in Sicily, Italy and Normandy. Stamps were also issued for the Allied

Above: A World War II patriotic cover sent by a soldier in Florida to Canada, transmitted free.

Below: A cover sent from the Cromarty naval base, with the name and date replaced by crosses for security reasons.

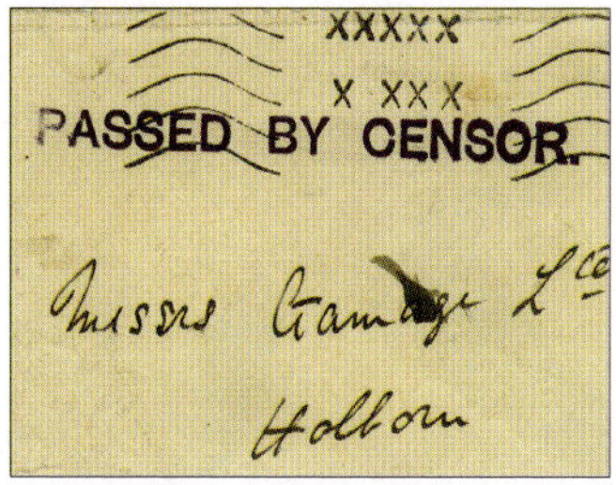

Military Government of Germany in 1945. The stamps of the countries of South-east Asia and the Pacific that were overrun by the Japanese were overprinted following invasion, pending the issuing of distinctive stamps by the occupying power.

SIEGE AND UNDERGROUND POSTS

Distinctive postmarks and cachets are known from various towns under siege, from Paris (1870) to Przemysl (1915); even Mafeking had its own stamps (1900). Underground posts were operated by guerrillas in the Philippines, partisans in Italy and Yugoslavia, and the Boy Scouts during the Warsaw Rising of 1944 (with crude postmarks showing the Scout emblem, carved from half a potato). Internees and prisoners of both World Wars, and even the inmates of the Lodz Ghetto, Theresienstadt and Dachau concentration camp had their own stamps and stationery. Censorship is an enormous subject, with a vast range of re-sealing labels and examiners' marks.

COLLECTING AIRMAIL

The distinctive stamps and stationery devised for mail transported by air has yielded a huge crop of collectable material, and occupies a branch of the hobby known as aerophilately. Yet it is the vast history of the service itself, spanning some two centuries, that often prompts collectors to take a closer interest in this field. Behind the postmarked envelopes and first flight covers are fascinating accounts of some of the most daring, innovative and bizarre methods of carrying mail ever devised.

Left and above: A Swiss stamp celebrating the first round-the-world balloon flight (1999), and the launch of balloons during the Siege of Paris (1870–1).

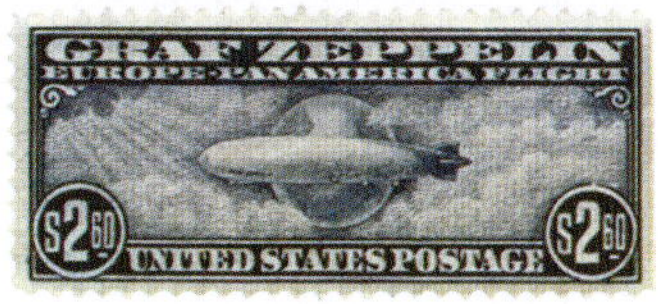

Right and below right: The Graf Zeppelin *moored at Los Angeles on 26 August 1929, following a 79-hour Pacific crossing, and one of three US stamps issued to celebrate its Europe–Pan-American flight in 1930.*

BALLOON POSTS

It was not long after the first hot-air balloon flights by the Montgolfier brothers in France and Vincenzo Lunardi in Britain that attempts were made to carry mail by balloon. In 1807 during the Peninsular War, propaganda leaflets were dropped over the French lines, and thus began a branch of postal history known as "psywar" (psychological warfare) that is of immense interest to airmail buffs as well as military postal historians.

The first commercial balloon posts were organized during the sieges of Metz and Paris in 1870–1. Of the 65 balloons flown out of Paris, six were captured by the enemy, two were blown out to sea and never seen again and the others made safe landings and delivered their precious cargo of letters. These balloons came down all over the place, including one that landed at Lifjeld in Norway, having flown 3,142km/1,952 miles in 14 hours: its record airspeed of 241kph/150mph was not broken until 1915.

Unmanned free balloons were occasionally used to transmit mail during World War I but in the interwar period they were mainly associated with the souvenir mail carried by contestants in the Gordon Bennett balloon races (for which special stamps were also issued). The trouble with free balloons was that they went wherever the wind blew and it was only in 1999 that a balloon capable of reaching the steady airstream in the upper atmosphere could circumnavigate the world, a feat celebrated by a special cover from Switzerland.

Experiments with dirigible balloons by Santos Dumont in Brazil and Count Ferdinand von Zeppelin in Germany led to the airships of World War I and the giant zeppelins of the 1920s and 1930s, which achieved epic transatlantic, polar and global journeys. Zeppelin mail has a large number of devotees, and items include the charred covers from the ill-fated *Hindenburg*, which crashed in New Jersey, in 1937.

The Birth of the US Airmail Service

In 1918, the US Army was persuaded to lend pilots and planes to establish air routes for mail delivery. Within a few years, the service was a thriving commercial enterprise, with airlines dispatching mail at affordable rates.

Above: A souvenir cover from the first night mail flight between Sweden and Croydon, England, in 1928.

HEAVIER-THAN-AIR MACHINES

Within five years of the first flight by the Wright Brothers in 1903, mail was being carried by aircraft in France. Sir Walter Windham, a British pioneer of aviation, organized the first official airmail between Allahabad and Naini, India, in February 1911 and swiftly followed this with the Coronation Aerial Post between London and Windsor in September. Denmark, Italy and the USA all had official airmails launched in the same month.

Mail flown over sea between two countries began with Augustin Parla's flight of July 1913 between Florida and Cuba, and this was followed by the flight of January 1914 between Buenos Aires and Montevideo by Teodoro Fels. Five years later John Alcock and Arthur Whitten-Brown made the first successful non-stop crossing of the Atlantic, flying from St John's, Newfoundland to Clifden, County Galway, Ireland. Ironically, the postal covers that were salvaged from the wrecks of the earlier, unsuccessful competitors in this endeavour now rate much more highly than those from the successful flight.

Above: A cigarette card featuring an "Empire" class flying boat.

Below: US Postmaster James A. Farley helps to stack mail delivered from a flying boat on 22 November 1935.

Above: A first flight cover from the gold-mining town of Herb Lake to The Pas in Manitoba, Canada, 1937.

The heyday of pioneer airmails was the 1920s, when many countries made their first attempts to organize air routes, and the postal subsidies were a major factor in their success. Large countries such as Canada, Australia, Brazil and the USA were in the forefront of this development. In addition to first flight covers with colourful cachets and postmarks, airport dedication souvenirs were produced, notably in the USA where local airports proliferated in this period.

In the 1930s the great transoceanic air routes became commercially feasible, and their development was duly charted by the special covers and postcards associated with the Clipper flying boats. There were also ingenious attempts by France and Germany to accelerate sea mail by using small aircraft catapulted from the decks of ocean liners as they drew near to land. In 1928 France even issued special stamps for this service operated by the liner *Ile de France,* while the catapult mail from the German ships *Bremen* and *Europa* (1929) was marked with distinctive cachets.

HELICOPTER MAIL

Conventional aircraft required a lengthy runway, but the problem of short take-off and landing was solved by the development of the autogiro in the 1930s. Souvenir covers associated with this short-lived aircraft are known from England, Spain, Australia, Canada and the USA between 1934 and 1939. The autogiro was eclipsed by the helicopter, which was developed during World War II and first used to carry mail at Los Angeles in July 1946. At first helicopter flights were confined to emergencies, but in the UK regular commercial mail services were inaugurated in East Anglia in June 1948.

FROM PIGEONGRAMS TO ROCKET MAIL

Carrier pigeons have been used to convey urgent messages since the days of ancient Greece, but the first regular commercial service was organized during the Siege of Paris in 1870–1. More than 300 birds flew messages into the beleaguered city. At first, handwritten flimsies were attached to them but later microfilm *pellicules* were used. The pigeons were taken out of Paris aboard manned balloons. Pigeongrams were widely used in New Zealand from 1896 and in India from 1931 to 1941.

Mail-carrying rockets were devised in Austria and Germany in 1928–31 and were used extensively in India between 1934 and 1944, while Cuba even issued a special stamp for a rocket mail service in 1939.

Below: A cover from the first official helicopter mail flight, from Lowestoft to Peterborough, in 1948.

CINDERELLA PHILATELY

Everyone is familiar with the story of Cinderella, neglected and mistreated by her ugly stepsisters, but transformed by her fairy godmother into the belle of the ball. The parallel between Cinderella and the byways of philately is close, and it is appropriate that the sidelines of the hobby, once despised and ignored, have now developed a strong following and, in fact, form a major branch of philately with its own societies. Many of these have websites where members discuss literature on the subject, specialized auctions and insuring expensive collectables. A list of useful addresses for the aspiring Cinderella philatelist is included at the end of this chapter.

ALBUM WEEDS

Back in the 19th century, when stamp collecting was still in its infancy, collectors did not have at their disposal a wealth of handbooks and monographs, let alone the priced catalogues that are now easily available, or the infinite mass of data on the internet. They therefore operated on the principle of "if it looks like a stamp, stick it in the album". Among these were forgeries and utterly bogus issues, produced solely to defraud collectors. The Reverend R.B. Earee coined the term "album weeds" in the 1870s and such fabrications were the first to go, but many years later philatelists realized that it was important to study forgeries, if only to help collectors distinguish between the genuine and the false.

The brothers Norman and Maurice Williams wrote many books on philately from the 1930s to the 1970s. In one of them, aimed at youthful beginners, they illustrated a range of stamp-like objects – labels, fiscals, telegraph stamps, Christmas seals and the like – declaring sternly, "These have no place in a stamp album." Ironically, the Williams brothers were assiduous collectors of all things Cinderella and for many years were the joint editors of *The Cinderella Philatelist*.

Above: A Frama label (automatic machine stamp) issued by New Zealand.

Right: A self-adhesive service indicator label used at British post office counters in 2004.

Right: The £5 stamp used on British Army telegraphs, and a Victorian label for securing the lead seal on the tax stamps affixed to legal documents.

Below: A page from Collecting Postage Stamps *by L.N. & M. Williams (1950), giving examples of "what not to collect".*

In the course of your search for stamps to put into your collection you are sure to come across some specimens which look like postage stamps but really are not. Examples of some of these miscellaneous stamps and labels are shown on this page, but of course it is impossible to illustrate every type you may find. As a rule, if you have a stamp about which you are doubtful just look at the inscriptions. Many postage stamps bear the words Post, Postage, Postes, Posta, Correio, Correos, or Franco. The 'Puffin' stamp on the cover of this book is a local issue of Lundy.

FISCAL (REVENUE) — AUSTRIAN NEWSPAPER TAX

ENVELOPE CUT-OUT — AIRMAIL LABEL — REGISTRATION LABEL — TELEGRAPH

PROPAGANDA — LABEL CHARITY LABEL — CHRISTMAS SEAL — RAILWAY PARCELS — BOGUS STAMP

20

BEYOND THE CATALOGUE

What is the definition of a philatelic Cinderella? The short answer is anything that is not listed in the standard stamp catalogues. However, this simple answer has to be qualified, for general stamp catalogues often omit items that do find a place in the more specialized catalogues, and quite often what the editor decides to include is arbitrary. For example, some catalogues, especially in Europe, list and price automatic machine stamps, often known as ATM (from the German term *Automatenmarken*), but sometimes referred to loosely as Framas, after the Swiss company that pioneered them. In Britain they are referred to as vending machine labels, and that last word tends to be applied to anything that is not a stamp – despite the fact that the Penny Black and other early British stamps were described in their own sheet margins as labels.

Civil War Cinderellas

These patriotic labels were created around 1861 by the Federal government during the American Civil War. They were produced in sheets (size unknown) of at least 9 images in *se-tenant* blocks. The right-hand image displays one of the labels in place, bound to the envelope by means of a town cancellation – a rare occurrence. The biblical reference shown at the top of this mounted label (Job 39:21) reads: "He paweth in the valley, and rejoiceth in his strength; he goeth on to meet the armed men." Any literate person in those days would have understood its relevance to the war.

Service Indicator Labels – The New Cinderellas?

Postage dues are not postage stamps, as they do not indicate that postage has been prepaid, and for that reason they are strictly termed labels – yet they are invariably included in stamp dealers' catalogues. The distinction between "stamps" (items included in the catalogues) and "labels" (ignored by the catalogues) is becoming more and more blurred. In recent years, for example, the UK has adopted service indicator labels, computer-printed at the point of sale, and these have now virtually ousted the higher denominations of conventional stamps. They prepay postage and perform all the functions of traditional stamps, yet they are completely ignored by the catalogues. Collectors, on the other hand, have had the good sense to realize that these things are just as worthy of study and collecting as the pretty pictures known as commemorative and special issues, most of which never perform any actual postal duty and merely serve to raise revenue for the postal services.

Many other countries operate a similar system. In the USA, in particular, such self-adhesive labels have been available at postal counters for many years. In fact, the difference between conventional stamps (more and more of which are produced to generate philatelic sales) and operational labels (which are gradually usurping the traditional role of stamps in prepaying postage) is becoming difficult to define. Catalogues continue to list, price and illustrate stamps whose status is questionable and which, in many instances, never see the country from which they purport to come, while ignoring the increasing number of "service labels" that now play a vital part in the smooth operation of the mails.

Both Scott (USA) and Gibbons (UK) list the labels involved in an experimental self-service mailing system that was tried in Washington and Kensington, Maryland, in 1989–90. Gibbons describes them simply as machine labels, whereas Scott more accurately refers to them as computer-vended postage. While Gibbons illustrates and describes them, Scott lists and prices them in some detail. These different approaches are also evident in the case of the more permanent issues in use since 1992.

Neither catalogue gives space to the parcel stamps of Belgium and the Netherlands, denominated by weight, or the range of special service labels produced by Germany, all of which cost money and indicate the service provided. The moral here is "ignore the catalogues". If you are specializing in a particular country, everything to do with the postal service deserves an equal place in your collection.

POSTAGE PAID IMPRESSIONS

Businesses, local authorities and mail order companies, which at one time used a postal frank, meter mark or bulk posting prepaid in cash denoted by a special red postmark, now make extensive use of systems such as permit mailing (in the USA) or postage-paid impressions (in most other countries). These impressions, handstruck or printed, are applied either directly to the cover, card or wrapper, or to a self-adhesive label. An increasing number of postal administrations now encourage local businesses to custom their own design, upon which they will be issued with an identification number. Thanks to their propensity for unique thematic appeal and pictorial motif, PPIs have already gained many devotees, and may indeed be Cinderellas of the future.

Above: These two triangular stamps are "phantom" issues – a popular branch of Cinderella philately. They were created by a Viennese stamp dealer, S. Friedl, to commemorate the discovery of a group of glacial islands during an Austro-Hungarian expedition attempting to reach the North Pole in 1872–4. The green item names "Cap Pest", the yellow refers to "Cap Wien". The pair is much sought after by collectors of polar issues.

SOCIAL PHILATELY

This is the newest branch of the hobby of stamp collecting, having originated in Australia in the late 1990s. In 1999 a competitive class for social philately was inaugurated at the Melbourne International Philatelic Exhibition. The concept spread to the Northern Hemisphere shortly afterwards, when it was included in the London Stamp Show of May 2000. It was basically a reaction against the strictures of the traditional and thematic philately classes in national and international competitions, which disqualified exhibitors if they strayed off the straight and narrow path laid down by the rules.

If an exhibitor included items that were not strictly stamps, either mint or affixed to covers or cards, the exhibit was severely marked down. More and more collectors were finding these restrictions increasingly irksome. They felt that – far from detracting from their displays – the judicial inclusion of non-philatelic items, such as ephemera or photographs, that were relevant to the stamps made the exhibit far more interesting, especially to the general public, who would not necessarily appreciate a show devoted to stamps alone. There was a very real danger of philately becoming esoteric and elitist, and the gulf between the "pot hunter" dedicated to winning competitions and the ordinary collector was becoming wider every year. More importantly, however, as competitive philately became more rarefied and confined, the potential for attracting and recruiting newcomers to the hobby decreased sharply. Competitive displays were beginning to appear boring to many collectors, let alone the general public.

Below: A page from a collection devoted to the floating mail of St Kilda.

ST KILDA FLOATING MAIL

Army Mailboat No. 1

Launched on 3 June 1959 by Captain David Boddington, RAMC (shown in pin-striped suit!), watched by Alec Warwick, Alan Aitken and Steve Scola. It was recovered by John Macarthur of 'Sandick', Doune Carloway, Lewis on 15 June, a voyage of 60 miles in 12 days. It also marked the debut of the Army's 'Tin Can Mail' cachet. Postmarked at Stornoway at 1pm on the same day as it was found.

A NEW WAY TO COLLECT

Recognizing this problem, the organizers of philatelic shows tentatively suggested an Open Class where anything was permissible and entries were judged by popular vote. However, this merely represented an extension of the existing system and ran the risk of becoming subject to similar rules and regulations if aspiring winners hoped to progress beyond it.

It was the collector Pat Grimwood-Taylor, exhibiting for the very first time at Melbourne in 1999, who became the apostle of a new style. She scooped a gold medal at the exhibition and subsequently conducted a seminar on the subject in London, for which the British Philatelic Trust (BPT) produced an attractive pamphlet under the title *What is SOCIAL PHILATELY?* Marking further recognition for the new concept, the definition hinged on the aim of presenting a historical story or illustrating the relevance or impact of a postal system – official or otherwise – within a society.

Straight away, the two fundamental differences between social philately and other forms of collecting were made clear. You do not necessarily have to be an expert philatelist (though a knowledge of the basic techniques of the hobby is a help) and, more importantly, you can include many types of non-philatelic material and ephemera (such as maps, prints, coins, medals, cigarette cards and banknotes) in your collection to make it tell the story.

Floating Mail

From 1885 until the island was evacuated in 1930 the people of St Kilda launched "mailboats" during the winter months when they had no other regular communications with the outside world. This photograph of 1896 shows Finlay McQueen dispatching a boat, which was recovered at Vallay near North Uist a few weeks later.

USING POSTAL HISTORY

The BPT leaflet went on to expand its theme, explaining that you can tell the story of the development of a town or country by using stamps, actual letters and documents of all kinds. Local postal historians have probably been doing this for many years, expanding their interests far beyond the strict boundaries of postal markings and covers or postcards.

Leaflets and mini-posters announcing changes in postal rates or the opening or closure of post offices are strictly relevant, but what about press-cuttings containing human interest stories such as postal workers being bitten by dogs or retiring after 60 years in the service? This kind of material had always previously been something of a grey area, considered suitable for a talk to a local philatelic society, but not for inclusion in a competitive display.

In studying the postal history of a town or locality, the philatelist inevitably becomes immersed in the social and economic development of the place, amassing plenty of material that is fascinating but not actually relevant to the story of the posts. Social philately allows the collector to probe the background of a historic event, or chain of events, and include both conventional and non-conventional philatelic material to tell the tale.

A PERSONAL STUDY OF ST KILDA

Relating this to my own experience, and arising out of time I spent with the British Army on the remote island of St Kilda in 1959–61, I formed a collection of that island's postal history that eventually ran to nine volumes. From the outset, however, I was not content merely to acquire covers and postally used postcards bearing the single-circle datestamp, or even explore by-ways such as the island's unique floating mail, airdrops, emergency helicopter flights or mail carried from St Kilda by French lobster-boats and Spanish trawlers that ended up in Camaret-sur-Mer or San Sebastian.

I added maps, ranging from that of Martin Martin, the first visitor to describe the island in detail in 1698, to a contemporary flight plan for one of the earliest airdrops in 1959. Ephemera in the collection ranged from leaflets produced by the National Trust for Scotland (who now own the island) to a spoof certificate purporting to be from King Neptune and retrieved from a bottle washed up on the shore. This was one of several thousands launched off the east coast of the USA in 1959 as a stunt celebrating the bicentenary of the Guinness brewery; most of the bottles came ashore in America but some drifted all the way across the Atlantic on the Gulf Stream. This find also gave me the opportunity to include a Guinness bicentenary beer-bottle label, arguably the first commemorative of its kind, which had been included with Neptune's parchment inside the bottle.

Below: Another page on the floating mail of St Kilda, showing a letter sent in this manner in 1897 and a photograph of an original "mailboat" complete with sheep's bladder float.

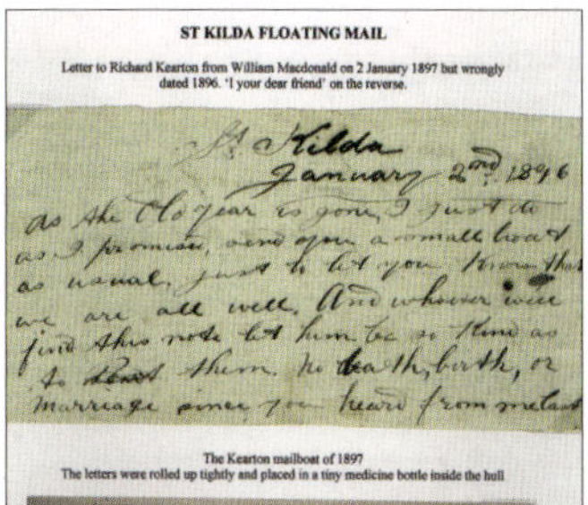
ST KILDA FLOATING MAIL

Letter to Richard Kearton from William Macdonald on 2 January 1897 but wrongly dated 1896. 'I your dear friend' on the reverse.

The Kearton mailboat of 1897
The letters were rolled up tightly and placed in a tiny medicine bottle inside the hull

FLOATING MAILS

The earliest letter I possess from St Kilda dates from 1738. It has no wrapper or postmark and would probably have been disqualified in any conventional postal history display, despite its immense historical interest. It is a letter written by Lady Grange, who was kidnapped in Edinburgh by friends of her ex-husband and eventually imprisoned on St Kilda for fear that she would expose her husband's implication in a Jacobite plot. Her letter, written in ink "from the soot of my lamp and mine awin blood", was discovered three years later in a half-buried whisky bottle on the beach at Baleshare, an island of the Outer Hebrides. It eventually found its way to the addressee, her cousin in Edinburgh, but by the time he took action the poor woman had been moved to the Isle of Skye, where she

ST KILDA FLOATING MAIL

Report in the *Scottish Daily Mail* of 23 July 1959; the allusion to Arch to Arc referred to a joint-Services race from London to Paris.

Rocketmen's mail goes faster by tin can

WHILE the Services battle with each other to shave seconds off the Arch to Arc time the Army is grappling with another communications problem in this supersonic age.

Above: Newspaper cuttings are a useful adjunct to a social philately collection.

Right: Parchment found in a Guinness bottle launched in the 1950s.

died. This letter, and the covering note from the tenant of Baleshare, form the basis of my own social philately display of the floating mails of St Kilda, developed by the islands in the 1870s and continuing until 1930 when the island was evacuated.

Reoccupied by the RAF and the Army in 1957, and regularly visited since by work parties from the National Trust for Scotland, St Kilda has been the scene of many "mailboat" or "tin can mail" launches over the past 45 years. Some have been picked up on the west coast of the Hebrides within 48 hours, while others were recovered more than three years later, as far away as eastern Iceland and north Norway, Orkney and Shetland.

Although the collection includes stamps, postmarks, cachets, charge marks, mixed franking of British and Norwegian stamps and even postage due labels (on covers recovered abroad and treated as unpaid because British stamps are not valid in Norway), the bulk of the display is devoted to photographs of launches and recoveries and a mass of press cuttings and articles about this remarkable phenomenon. It is entirely two-dimensional because I have not yet acquired one of the actual mailboats, consisting of a piece of driftwood hollowed out to form the hull, attached to an inflated sheep's bladder.

FORGERIES, FANTASIES AND POSTAL FRAUD

The subject of stamp forgery attracts collectors, not simply because of the tales of derring-do often attached, but also due to the challenge presented by comparing the likeness between real and fake. Forgery has dogged stamp-issuing authorities since the birth of the Penny Black. In fact, British authorities hired an American inventor, Jacob Perkins, who devised a rose engine capable of producing such an intricate background that the forger would be deterred. In fact, only one attempt to forge the Penny Black was detected, and that was such a poor travesty that it was easily spotted.

VICTIMS OF STAMP FORGERY

Countries where cheaper processes such as letterpress and lithography were in use, or where postal authorities paid less attention to good intaglio engraving, often fell victim to forgery. The earliest attempts at forgery were usually intended to defraud the revenue.

Above: In a bid to beat the forgers, the Twopence Blue was issued with check letters in all four corners in July 1858. The combination of numbers identified each stamp's position in a printed sheet.

Below: These British 6d stamps were produced in doubly fugitive ink with the value surcharged in red letters – another attempt to deter fraudulent use.

Yet even the British postal service was not exempt from this humiliation. The 1s stamp was forged in 1872–3 and vast quantities were passed off as genuine at the Stock Exchange (where this denomination was commonly used on telegrams), but the crime did not come to light until 1898, by which time the trail had gone cold. It was thanks to the vigilance of philatelists that the forgery was detected at all, because the counterfeiters had used combinations of corner letters that did not exist in the genuine stamps. Although the Post Office placed its faith in the check letters as a deterrent to forgery, postal staff apparently never gave them a second glance. Today, the Stock Exchange forgeries fetch higher prices at auction than the genuine stamps, such is the demand for them.

Postal forgeries continue to this day. In recent years British and French definitives have been forged for sale to the public at discount prices, and it was for this reason that elliptical perforations were introduced, the theory being that forgers might produce a passable imitation of a stamp but they would never get the perforations right.

FAMOUS FORGERS

Once philately became an established hobby and definite market values emerged for the scarcer stamps, it was inevitable that the stamp trade should be infiltrated by unscrupulous people who turned to forgery as a means of robbing gullible collectors. The activities of such master forgers as François Fournier, Erasmus Oneglia, Jean de Sperati, S. Allan Taylor and Albert C. Roessler are well documented in literature such as Varro E. Tyler's *Philatelic Forgers: Their Lives and Works* (1976) and, indeed, some important collections of their wares have been formed.

Many forgers achieved notoriety in their day. S. Allan Taylor, an American born in Ayrshire, Scotland, in 1838, was known as "the Prince of Forgers" and produced hundreds of fakes and forgeries during the latter half of the 19th century, some of which were assumed to be authentic for many decades. He put his own portrait on bogus charity and local post stamps, and a self-likeness of the mature Taylor was incorporated into a label produced by a short-lived group of admiring Cinderella philatelists, the S. Allan Taylor Society.

An accomplished forger of more recent times, the Italian Jean de Sperati (1884–1957) was the most technically competent of his peers, producing some 566 forgeries purporting to originate from more than 100 countries.

Bogus Bill

Abkhazia, which seceded from Georgia, briefly had a genuine postal service with distinctive stamps, but long after the secession was suppressed stamps continued to appear in its name, including a notorious miniature sheet showing President Clinton and Monica Lewinsky. Georgia even apologized to the Clinton family and offered them a free holiday at the Black Sea resort of Soukhumi in recompense.

A Dishonest Postmaster

Fraudulent usage of postal material does not always involve the forgery or manipulation of stamps. This rare envelope, shown here front and back, which eventually arrived at Everest Base Camp in 1936, informs the recipient that their letter "Suffered detention in Gangtok post office owing to the Postmaster's failure to affix postage stamps and to forward them in time. The Postmaster has been sent to jail for his offence."

Above: Genuine and forged versions of the French 25c Hermes, the latter produced by British Intelligence.

He even wrote books on the art of philatelic forgery, in which he expressed his contempt for the "experts" who had tried to foil his efforts.

COLLECTING FORGERIES

Many of these colourful characters had a taste for risk and illegality, and no doubt relished the thrill of creating immaculate forgeries that fooled even the most diligent of postal watchdogs. But there are other instances of forgery, where the primary motive – financial gain – appears to lack a well thought out plan. Where stamps are plentiful and cheap in the genuine state, it does not seem to have been worth the forger's expertise to perpetrate such imitations. Nevertheless this is not as unusual a phenomenon as might be thought. Many stamp clubs have a forgery collection, which members may consult in order to check doubtful specimens in their own collections.

Many of the forgeries produced in the 19th century would fool no one nowadays, either because the wrong printing process was used (such as lithography instead of intaglio) or because the draughtsmanship was relatively crude, but it must be remembered that 19th-century collectors did not have the well-illustrated reference works so readily available nowadays. The study of forgeries is germane to any specialized collection, which explains why forgeries often fetch high prices at auction, even when clearly exposed for what they are.

PROPAGANDA FORGERIES

Arguably the most desirable of all forgeries are those that were manufactured by various belligerents in wartime as part of a propaganda campaign. During World War I, Britain forged German and Bavarian stamps, which were affixed to letters or cards dropped in enemy or neutral countries to give the impression of coming from Germany while disseminating subtle propaganda or defeatist literature. This worked well enough to encourage the British to repeat the exercise in World War II, but this time they produced clever parodies of Nazi stamps as well. Stamps of the Vichy French regime portraying Marshal Petain were also forged by the British.

The Germans were adept at creating propaganda forgeries of British stamps, including a large number of George VI definitives overprinted "Liquidation of Empire" and the parody of the 1937 Coronation stamp, with Stalin replacing Queen Elizabeth.

BOGUS STAMPS

The term "bogus" describes stamps that are pure fantasies, often purporting to come from non-existent countries. This was a favourite ploy of conmen in the late 19th century, using such stamps to lure investors in fictional colonial projects. Sadly, these fabrications have their modern counterparts. The break-up of the Soviet Union in the 1990s proved to be a fertile ground for a host of bogus issues, aimed at unsuspecting philatelic buyers.

Below: Bogus stamps attributed to South Moluccas, New Atlantis, Albania, Atlantis and Sedang.

POSTER STAMPS

The term "poster stamps" was devised in the interwar period, when multi-colour lithography was frequently used to create posters in miniature for the promotion of tourism. The description of such items as "stamps" is in fact a misnomer, because although they resemble stamps in appearance these bright, colourful and attractive labels have no connection with the postal services. They were produced by tourist boards, chambers of commerce and even private individuals. They were also extensively employed to advertise the products of many companies, especially after the concept of brand names and trademarks developed in importance in the late 19th century.

Right: A poster stamp produced for the Leipzig Fairs of 1906–7.

Above: Something of a philatelic first, the Shakespeare Penny Memorial label both commemorated the Bard's birth and sought to fund a new theatre.

Below: A label publicizing the Pan-American Exposition in 1901.

COMMEMORATIVE LABELS

Although commemorative postage stamps did not materialize until the late 1880s, labels that celebrated historic personalities or documented important events were in existence many years earlier. The first of these was an embossed medallic label produced for an exhibition in Vienna; although it bore the effigy of the Emperor Ferdinand it was a private production by Apollo Kerzen-Fabrik. In 1851 a label was issued in connection with the Great Exhibition in London; in fact, there is a theory that it was devised to frank the correspondence of Royal Commissioners, but it is of such great rarity that little is known about it.

All of the early labels were produced in connection with international fairs and exhibitions, but in 1860 a label portraying Garibaldi celebrated his expedition to Sicily as part of the campaign for the unification of Italy. Garibaldi was also the subject of a label in 1863 mourning his defeat at Aspromonte. The first label to mark a historic anniversary was produced in England in 1864. Inscribed with the legend "Shakespeare Penny Memorial", it portrayed the Bard himself and celebrated the 300th anniversary of his birth. As the inscription implies, it was also intended as a fundraiser for the projected Memorial Theatre at Shakespeare's birthplace, Stratford-upon-Avon, completed in 1879.

Up to 1873 very few labels were recorded each year, but when Vienna hosted the International Exhibition that year there were embossed scalloped

Rare Label

This poster stamp for Crane's Chocolates is arguably the rarest of its kind, as only four copies are documented in the world. It was designed between 1910 and 1920 by Maxfield Parrish, a major American illustrator. The image is listed in a price guide for its appearance on a full-sized box of chocolates, but this stamp is unlisted. It was intended as a seal on a small box containing a single chocolate and would therefore almost always have been destroyed when the box was opened. The last copy to come on the market was sold for US $1,500 to a Parrish collector, not a poster stamp collector – an example of how rare stamps can cross over into other realms of valued collectables.

Below: A French patriotic label of 1915 recalling the Revolution (left) and a German patriotic label of the same year captioned "God punish England!"

labels for the various commissioners, as well as the label reproducing the gold medals awarded, with the effigy of the Emperor Franz Joseph on the obverse.

A NEW CENTURY

The generation of commemorative labels reached its zenith at the Exposition Universelle in Paris in 1900. This exhibition, to celebrate the achievements of the previous century and progress in the next, was the greatest of the world's fairs at that time, and resulted in the issuing of many hundreds of different labels.

By the end of the 19th century, production of commemorative labels had grown enormously, with publishers producing sets of colourful labels for every conceivable occasion. The labels for the Paris show could be divided into general publicity, the numerous series that featured the landmarks and scenery of Paris, the issues of the many French learned societies, the labels published by companies advertising goods displayed at the fair and the *timbres recompensés*, reproducing the various gold, silver and bronze medals. In addition, A. Baguet alone produced five sets of labels, 40 in all, honouring each of the national pavilions. Some students of poster stamps have devoted a lifetime solely to collecting the different labels from the Exposition Universelle.

The first phase of poster stamps ended with the onset of World War I but over the next four years the publicity labels of the earlier years gave way to long sets showing regimental flags, portraits of military and naval heroes and all the weird and wonderful weaponry conjured up by the conflict. Inevitably France and Germany vied with each other in the production of labels, which moved effortlessly from publicity to propaganda.

TOURIST PUBLICITY

The return to peace saw a dramatic change in the labels. By the 1920s the notion of commemorative postage stamps was well established, and consequently far fewer labels of a commemorative nature were produced. It was now that the publicity element came into its own with the rise of cheap foreign travel. Tourist organizations were quick to perceive the benefits of advertising through this medium. Many of the rather garish posters of the period were automatically reduced to the medium of poster stamps and adorned envelopes containing promotional leaflets and brochures. There was an attempt in continental Europe to produce booklets of different scenic labels, but this fashion was already waning when the outbreak of World War II killed it off.

PHILATELIC EXHIBITIONS

One sphere in which the poster stamp has held its own, despite the vagaries of fashion or the competition from postage stamps, is in philately itself. The first issue in this connection consisted of a series of 1pf stamps of the Circular Post of Frankfurt-am-Main in 1887, available in five different colours. Since this time, every national and international philatelic exhibition has spawned a shoal of labels, and latterly miniature sheets, used either as advance publicity stickers or as mementos of the show. They provide a colourful adornment to the various covers and postcards produced for the occasion, and augment the commemorative stamps with their pictorial cancellations.

Above: Prewar poster stamps from Tournoel in France and Newquay in Cornwall, England.

Right: A Swiss tourist label publicizing autumn holidays.

Below: A sheetlet depicting views of the Smithsonian Institution in Washington, DC.

SOCIETIES

The collecting of poster stamps is closely affiliated to Cinderella philately, and you may get information on significant issues from the societies devoted to that field. There are, however, organizations and exhibitions devoted predominantly to the study and collection of poster stamps. The American Poster Stamp Society offers membership and a regular bulletin. An address for the society can be found at the end of this chapter.

CHARITY SEALS AND LABELS

From the Shakespeare Penny Memorial label of 1864, an increasing number of labels were devised to raise money for good causes. Although many are not official postage stamps, and may not be listed in catalogues, their often colourful and highly visual designs make them of natural interest to collectors.

Left: The Prince of Wales's Hospital Fund label, 1897.

Below: World War I charity fundraising labels from New Zealand and Russia.

Right: Einar Holboell, who devised charity seals, was portrayed on a Belgian anti-TB stamp in 1955.

THE QUEEN'S COMMEMORATION

Queen Victoria's diamond jubilee of 1897 yielded several sets of purely commemorative labels, but there was a particular issue that stood out on account of its intricate design.

Line-engraved by De La Rue (who produced the British postage stamps) the issue consisted of 1s and 2s 6d labels, each depicting the allegorical figure of Charity aiding poor children. At the top was the inscription "1837 The Queen's Commemoration 1897" but at the foot was the facsimile signature of the Prince of Wales (the future Edward VII) and the words "Prince of Wales's Hospital Fund". Although these labels had no postal validity they had the tacit support of the Post Office and were intended to adorn letters and postcards – so long as they were kept well away from the proper postage stamps. Used examples are scarce, suggesting that most were purchased to keep as souvenirs of the jubilee.

The success of the venture induced the promoters to issue 5s and 10s labels as well, but this was going too far and not surprisingly the high values are of the greatest rarity today. The resultant fiasco put a damper on attempts to repeat the exercise and it is significant that no fundraising labels appeared in Britain at the time of the Boer War (1899–1902). There was a belated resurgence during World War I though the idea found greater favour in India and Australia than it did in Britain. Nevertheless, charity labels are among the most enduring of the Cinderellas on a worldwide basis, despite the fierce competition from charity stamps.

Korean Charity Labels
It is easy to detect the American influence on these labels for Boys Town and Girls Town charities in Korea, which by the 1960s were caring for almost 4,000 orphans in the cities of Pusan and Seoul.

CHRISTMAS AND EASTER SEALS

It was in December 1904 that a Danish postal official, Einar Holboell, came up with the notion of producing labels to be affixed to the envelopes of greetings cards, the money thus raised being given to the national anti-tuberculosis fund. His idea was enthusiastically endorsed by the Danish Post Office, which even arranged for the Christmas seals to be sold at post offices. The scheme was taken up by the other Scandinavian countries the following year. At first a single design was produced annually, but in more recent years different motifs have appeared on each label, often forming a composite design covering the sheet. Holboell has himself been portrayed on charity stamps of Denmark and Belgium.

The labels spread to the Faroes, Iceland, Greenland and the Danish West Indies (now the American Virgin Islands), and from there spread to

Above: A booklet containing French anti-TB Christmas seals.

Below: This Swedish envelope bears the 1903 Christmas seal alongside a stamp.

Above: Even charity seals occasionally carried commercial advertising. This French booklet pane promotes various items, such as toothpaste, in its margins.

many other countries, notably Canada, Mexico, the USA, France and South Africa. In the last two countries the seals were produced in booklets, which were sold at post offices. French stamp booklets carried commercial advertising on the top and bottom margins, and this practice was extended to the charity labels, often with incongruous results. A factor unifying most Christmas seals, no matter where they are issued, is the red Cross of Lorraine, the international emblem of the anti-tuberculosis campaign.

In the 1940s the concept was extended to Easter seals, which were sold in aid of funds for the handicapped. Recurring themes of these labels were the Easter lily or a crutch to symbolize the disabled. In New Zealand, however, Easter seals support the St John Ambulance movement and incorporate the Maltese Cross emblem. In recent years many other charities have begun producing their own versions of Christmas and Easter seals to raise funds for cancer research, epilepsy and the prevention of blindness, while organizations like the Red Cross issue charity labels in many lands that can be used all year round.

Below: A bilingual pair of Christmas seals from South Africa (1938).

Above: A Danish Christmas seal (1904) and a Thorvaldsen Foundation seal from Iceland (1953).

Below: An Easter seal produced by the St John Ambulance Brigade, 1970.

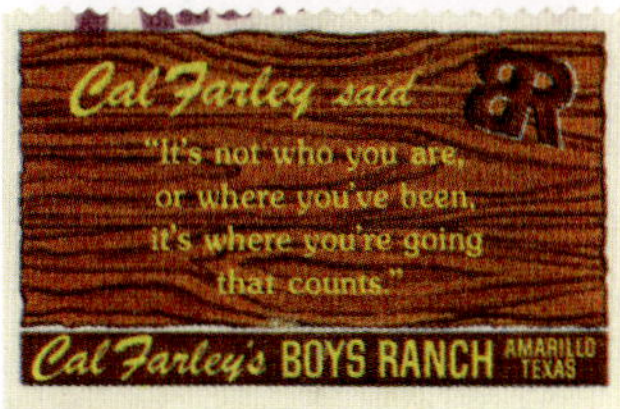

Above: Christmas seals from Boys Town, Nebraska and Cal Farley's Boys Ranch, Texas.

Left: Dürer's "Praying Hands" on a Christmas seal of the Omaha Home for Boys.

CHILDREN'S CHARITIES

A group of charity labels with a strong thematic appeal is that devoted to the care of orphans and homeless children. The vast majority of Easter seals come into this category, notably the American labels showing disabled children overcoming their handicap, accompanied by slogans such as "I'm a fighter" or "Back a fighter".

The best known of the children's charities producing annual labels is Boys Town in Nebraska, founded by Father Edward Flanagan. Many of its labels feature the poignant figure of a boy with a youngster asleep round his neck, saying, "He ain't heavy, Father, He's m' brother." Based on a real incident that has since been immortalized in a statue, this motif is the logo of Boys Town. Separate labels exist for affiliated Boys' and Children's home charities.

Below: Charity labels issued by France and Spain. The French Red Cross label (left) raised funds for military hospitals during World War I; the Spanish "2 pesetas" was one of a number produced in the 1930s and '40s to help provide for the widows of postal workers.

FISCAL STAMPS AND SPECIAL SERVICE LABELS

Adhesive stamps and labels issued to denote dutiable goods, payment of a licence, or simply bearing special instructions to customs or to postal authorities, are among the most diverse of Cinderella collectibles.

FISCAL STAMPS

Adhesive stamps embossed on deep blue "sugar-bag" paper were used for revenue purposes at the Board of Stamps and Taxes in London from 1694 onwards. They were an innovation imported by William of Orange from his native Holland, where they had been in use since the early 17th century. Later fiscal stamps (known as revenue stamps in the United States) were embossed directly on to boxes and bottles containing patent medicines, or the wrappers of dice, while the elaborate device on the ace of spades in a deck of cards was, in fact, a tax stamp.

The excise duty on a wide range of articles, from hair powder to gloves, was indicated by such stamps. Adhesive stamps were produced in perforated sheets for matchboxes, tobacco and cigarettes, wines and spirits, entertainment duty and even phonograph records. The range of fiscal stamps in Britain in the 19th and early 20th centuries was enormous, from additional medicine duty during World War I to travel permits and unemployment insurance. As a result of the Local Stamp Act of 1869 there were even revenue stamps of purely local validity, from Alderney to Winchester, and separate issues for Scotland and Ireland. Savings stamps, introduced in many countries in World War I, continued until the 1970s and have since been replaced by individual issues by banks and public utilities.

A similar pattern operated in many other countries, with a wide range of national duties and numerous taxes imposed at cantonal or communal level. In the USA it was illegal to use a revenue stamp for any purpose other than the specific tax inscribed on it, and up to 1862 there was a proliferation of stamps for many duties. Thereafter a general issue of documentary stamps by the Bureau of Internal Revenue could be used indiscriminately with the exception of the distinctive stamps applied to proprietary articles, such as matches and medicines, introduced in 1871. In 1962 the centenary of the documentary stamps was marked by what is probably the world's first commemorative revenue stamp, and facilities were exceptionally made for it to be used on first day covers. The use of such stamps ceased in 1967.

In 1934 the USA introduced migratory bird hunting permits and stamps denoting payment of the fee. In addition, many individual states have their own annual migratory hunting stamps.

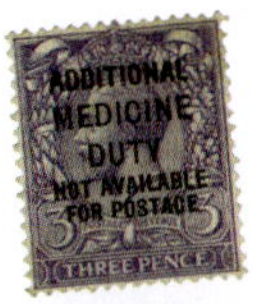

Left: A British 3d postage stamp overprinted for use as an additional medicine duty stamp.

Above: A patent medicine tax stamp, used to seal pill boxes.

Below: Fiscal stamps of the Cape of Good Hope and Malta.

Below: A US cigarette tax stamp portraying De Witt Clinton, a documentary stamp featuring a battleship, and an Ohio vendor's receipt stamp.

Below: The US migratory bird hunting stamp for 1954: the design was changed annually to feature different species.

Bomb Warning

Perhaps the most sombre labels in current use are those of the Israel Postal Authority, inscribed in Hebrew, English, Arabic and Russian, warning the recipient of a parcel that if there is any suspicion that it contains a bomb it should be taken to the police.

TELEGRAPH, TELEPHONE AND TELEVISION STAMPS

At one time there were separate issues of stamps for telegrams in many countries, as well as the issues of the private

Above: Telegraph stamps issued by Britain, Spain and Tangier.

Left: A British telephone stamp of 1884.

telegraph companies. In Britain, the National Telephone Company even had its own stamps (1884–91) portraying its chairman, Colonel Robert Raynsford-Jackson. They were used as an early method to pay for telephone calls at local offices, to avoid the need for an exchange of money. The stamps were finally withdrawn from use in 1891, due to the Post Office's belief that they could be confused with normal postage stamps. Despite this, special stamps were used until relatively recently in some countries to help people save towards the cost of a TV licence.

POSTAL SERVICE LABELS

Labels denoting specific postal services originated in the 1870s when Germany and Sweden introduced stickers bearing names of towns and serial numbers for use on registered packets. The system was later extended to the serial labels affixed to the cards that accompanied parcels. In Britain, distinctive parcel labels were issued to every post office from 1883 to 1916, but registration labels were not adopted until 1907, although the UPU had decreed this in 1881. Distinctive serial labels have also been used for certified mail (USA) or recorded delivery (UK), with equivalents in most other countries. In recent years labels distinctive to each post office have been largely replaced by a national series of barcode labels. Resealing labels for damaged or broken packets and explanatory labels marked "Deceased", "Gone away" and "Return to sender" in different languages are also to be found.

AIRMAIL *ETIQUETTES*

France pioneered special stickers for airmail in 1918, and for that reason they are still generally known to collectors by the French term *etiquettes*. Their use is on the increase as it is now mandatory to affix them to all letters and cards going abroad by air. In many countries nowadays their place has been taken by A-Priority labels, although these retain the general pattern of white inscriptions on a blue background. In such countries there is usually the equivalent of a second-class service denoted by white on green B-Economy labels. The Postal Union Congress at Madrid in 1920 decreed the introduction of green labels for Customs declaration and these, in various modifications, are still in use, generally inscribed in French and a national language. For dutiable goods on which the tax has been paid there are labels inscribed in French "*Franc de droits*" (Free of dues).

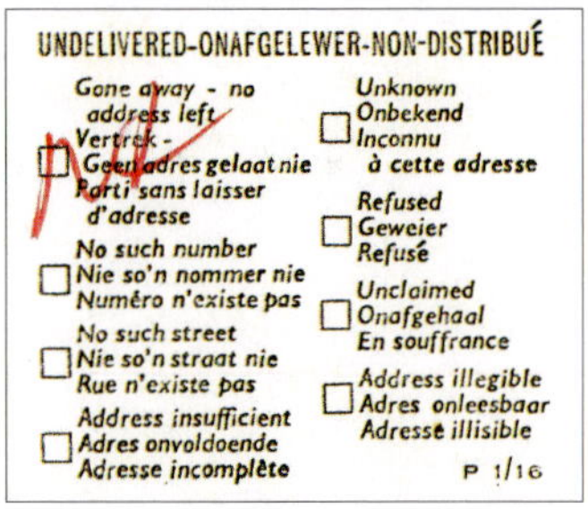

Above: Reasons for non-delivery are explained in English, Afrikaans and French on this South African label.

Below: A pre-stamped postcard from the Åland Islands, bearing an airmail "priority" sticker, issued in 2004.

LABELS FOR SPECIAL TREATMENT

At various times from the late 19th century there have been special labels for express and special delivery services, warning labels affixed to parcels of eggs or containing fragile or perishable substances, and even labels for packages containing live creatures, pathological specimens or radioactive materials. There are also stickers to mark parcels containing Braille reading material for the blind. These labels often conform to an international convention of easily recognizable symbols, such as a wine glass (fragile), a rabbit (live animals), the staff of Aesculapius (pathological specimens) or a blind person carrying a white stick.

Right: A label from the Czech Republic for use on parcels containing live animals.

Right: An early United States Customs label.

Below: An insured parcel card for a dispatch from Vienna to Berne in 1911, bearing an impressed 10 heller stamp.

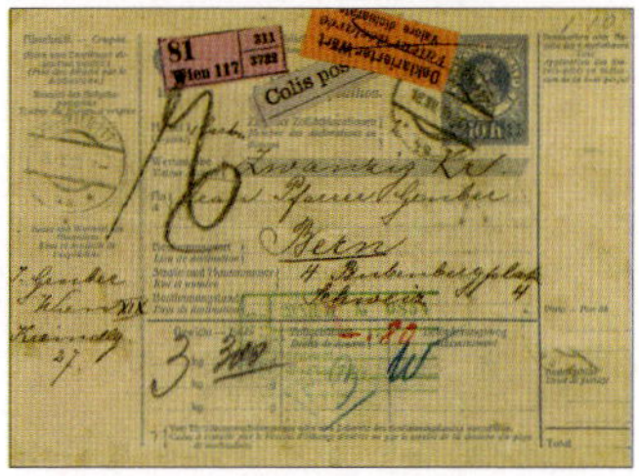

LOCAL STAMPS AND PRIVATE POSTS

The stamp catalogues of the 19th century included postage stamps of all kinds, whether issued by government posts or local services operated by private enterprise. Later, the sheer number of government issues forced all but a few highly specialized one-country catalogues to drop nearly everything else. Thus the stamps of the many local and private posts were consigned to limbo.

CARRIERS STAMPS

US carrier stamps are among the only semi-official issues that continue to be listed. These local stamps originate from the period before 1863, the year the US Post Office finally established a general town delivery. For some 20 to 30 years prior to this, the gap was filled by numerous local dispatch posts known as "carriers", many employees of which later worked for the government as part of the national postal network. In 1842, a 3c carrier stamp became the first ever stamp to be issued under government authority, thanks to the merging of a private firm, City Despatch Post, and the state-run New York City Carrier Department. US carrier stamps are comprehensively listed in the Scott *Specialized Catalogue of U.S. Stamps*, but ignored everywhere else.

Left and below: Two undenominated stamps, depicting Benjamin Franklin and the American eagle, produced in 1861–3 to denote the 1c charged for delivering mail from US post offices to householders. Their use was confined to New York, Philadelphia and New Orleans.

Above: Two stamps used for the Chesterfield Scouts Christmas post.

Left: Shotts Scouts in Lanarkshire, Scotland, produced this 75th anniversary stamp for their 1998 Christmas postal service.

In Germany, from the 1860s to 1900, the Reichspost did not provide a service for commercial mail and printed matter such as circulars, and it was left to private operators to fill the gap. Over 200 services came into existence, many functioning within a single town and others maintaining a nationwide network. In March 1900 they were nationalized and absorbed into the Reichspost. Their heyday was the 1880s and 1890s and they pioneered various issues such as commemoratives, mourning stamps and Christmas or New Year greetings stamps. Similar local services, complete with distinctive adhesives and pre-stamped stationery, operated in Denmark, Norway and Sweden during the same period.

ZEMSTVO POSTS

By far the largest network of local posts was that operating in tsarist Russia. The imperial post served only the cities and larger towns, and in 1864 local authorities were empowered to establish their own postal services in rural districts and to link them to the imperial service. The stamps issued by these local posts are popularly known as "zemstvos" (from the Russian word for a unit of local government). Vetlonga established its service in 1865 but the honour of issuing the first stamps went to Schluesselburg the following year. From 1870 onwards the zemstvo posts were given a completely free hand in matters of design and some of the most colourful stamps of the 19th century resulted.

By the time these services were closed down as a result of the 1917 uprising by the Bolsheviks, many

Right: A Russian zemstvo stamp from Lebedyansk, showing the civic emblem, a swan.

The World's Rarest Stamp

There are quite a few stamps of which only a solitary example has been recorded, but this zemstvo stamp, issued in June 1869 by Kotelnich, in the Viatka province north-east of Moscow, is truly unique, since only half the stamp is now known to exist. It consisted of a right-hand square that was affixed to the letter while the left-hand portion was intended to be retained by the sender as a receipt. Strangely, the complete stamp was illustrated in the catalogue published in the 1880s by the Belgian dealer, Jean-Baptiste Moens.

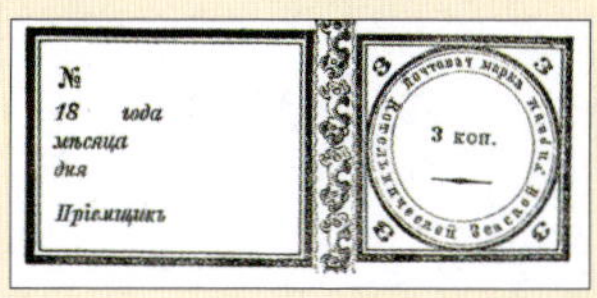

Above: Two local 1/2d stamps dating from 1865–7, issued by Clark & Co of Edinburgh and the Circular Delivery Company in Glasgow.

thousands of different stamps had been released. They include the world's rarest stamp, that from Kotelnich (illustrated in the box opposite).

CIRCULAR DELIVERY STAMPS

In 1865 a number of circular delivery companies, set up to carry mail to designated households and districts, sprang up in Britain, undercutting the postal service with rates of 1/2d or 1/4d for the delivery of printed matter. In a court case of 1867 they were held to infringe the Postmaster General's monopoly and suppressed, but the Post Office was eventually obliged to lower postal rates in 1870 and allow printed matter – including newspapers and companies' advertising postcards – to be sent by post for 1/2d.

OTHER LOCAL POSTS

Although the heyday of the local posts was the late 19th century, there have been some interesting developments in more recent years. In 1929 M.C. Harman, the proprietor of Lundy Island in the Bristol Channel (who also held the mail contract), began issuing his own stamps to defray the costs of transmission of mail to and from Bideford, the nearest mainland post office. To the present day, close to 400 different stamps have been produced and the Lundy issues have a worldwide following. In the 1960s, however, several islands off the Scottish coast also began issuing stamps ostensibly to pay for local carriage, but in fact to a large extent promoted by dealers in popular themes such as Kennedy, Churchill and space travel – subjects that were irrelevant to the islands themselves. To be sure, the issues that have stayed the course have maintained their integrity and cater to real needs.

Since 1981 the Royal Mail's monopoly has been waived by the British Telecommunications Act to allow church and youth groups to organize local posts between 25 November and 1 January. Mail is collected and delivered by volunteers and the modest fee for greetings cards handled by these posts goes to charity. Most of the services produce stamps and these have become very popular with collectors.

Below: One of a series of stamps issued by the Suez Canal Company in 1868 for mail conveyed by its ships.

TRANSPORTATION COMPANIES AND AIRLINES

Postal services have been run by many shipping lines and freight companies, especially in underdeveloped parts of the world where government services were either sporadic or non-existent. Many private railway companies have enjoyed the privilege of transporting mail, and stamps for this purpose – often categorized with fiscal stamps – have been employed in countries as far apart as Denmark and Australia. The conveyance of parcels has often fallen to local carriers who produced distinctive stamps for this purpose. Similarly, commercial airlines in many countries issued stamps to cover the fees charged on letters and parcels carried over their routes. Several remote islands around Britain have a private service conveying their mail to the nearest post office and for this purpose local carriage labels are often employed. Where a regional dialect is spoken, these local stamps may have bilingual inscriptions.

POSTAL DEREGULATION

In the course of the 20th century most of the private or semi-official services were suppressed or taken over by the government posts, but from the 1980s onwards this trend has been gradually reversed. Postal services have now been deregulated in many countries. In Britain, for example, courier companies are now permitted to carry letter mail so long as they charge at least 50p for the service, and a similar proviso exists in Germany. Elsewhere, notably in Holland and Sweden, private local posts have proliferated in recent years. In New Zealand, the service known as Pete's Post and other private companies provide a feeder service for New Zealand Post, and conversely mail bearing their stamps is often delivered by the government posts.

An interesting development in the past decade has been contract remailing, whereby mail from country A is air-freighted to country B and then sorted and forwarded to country C. Apart from the extraordinary permutations this produces, it has also given rise to the issue of private stamps by carriers such as TNT, which are affixed to tourist postcards everywhere from Spain and Italy to Australia, then flown to European hubs for sorting and transmission. The stamps associated with these services are often referred to in inscriptions as "Post paid tickets".

Below: This local stamp produced by the Scottish Isle of Canna is inscribed in both English and Gaelic.

ESSAYS, ARTWORK AND PROOFS

Postage stamps do not materialize out of thin air. In most cases a considerable amount of planning is involved and many months may elapse between the commissioning of an artist to produce a suitable design and the release of the finished product to post offices and other retail outlets.

Each stage in the evolution of a stamp yields a certain amount of material, all of which is of immense interest to the truly dedicated specialist. Much of it is rare, if not unique, and inevitably it usually commands very high prices, so you have to be not only very committed to your hobby but also wealthy enough to afford it. In the end, however, it is this material that makes the difference between a good collection and one that stands a chance of winning a gold medal in competitive philatelic exhibitions.

Above: Die proofs of the engraved portraits used for a pair of Swedish stamps issued in 2004.

ESSAYS AND ORIGINAL ARTWORK

An essay is a design that has been submitted for a forthcoming stamp but is rejected. Strangely, such "unadopted designs", as they are also known, often seem superior to the design that is eventually selected. Either way, essays are of interest as examples of what might have been.

In many cases, even when designs are accepted they are subject to modification and it is therefore possible to find a whole series of stages of a design, progressing from the artist's original concept through minor alterations to the finished model.

Original artwork came to prominence in the 1960s, when stamps were produced by one or other of the processes that involved photographing the artist's drawing or watercolour. In addition to these miniature works of art, with or without the overlays for lettering, value and standard features (such as the monarch's head or a coat of arms), the preliminary pen and ink thumbnail sketches are fascinating as they show how the design gradually evolved in the artist's mind.

DIE AND PLATE PROOFS

In the days when the vast majority of stamps were produced by intaglio (line-engraving or recess-printing) or typography (letterpress or relief-printing), the artist's drawing would be passed to an engraver who sat down at his bench and worked with burins and other tools to produce a master die. In intaglio, the engraver cut the design into a piece of soft steel, which was then chemically hardened. A soft steel cylinder was rolled over it under great pressure, transferring the design to the cylinder. In turn it was hardened then rolled the required number of times over a sheet of soft steel to produce the printing plate.

In relief-printing the engraver might work in soft metal or even a block of wood. A plaster mould would be taken from this and lead "clichés" produced. A thin layer of copper might be deposited by electrolysis and the clichés locked together in a "forme" to make the printing plate.

At each stage the master die, intermediate punches, secondary dies (with different denominations engraved on them), transfer roller and finished plate might be checked by inking them and taking a proof on soft card, India paper or some other material. These die and plate proofs might be endorsed "Before hardening" or "After hardening" and annotated with the date and the initials of the printer or examiner.

Die proofs usually appear as single impressions in pieces of card or paper with wide margins all round, whereas

Left: Black proofs of 1938 Czechoslovak stamp designs, which were rejected.

Right: This photograph of a flat-bed cylinder press is an early example of intaglio printing. The press itself can still be seen at Somerset House in London.

Lewis and Clark Commemorative Issue

On 27 April 1954, the US Post Office announced a new 3c stamp to mark the the anniversary of the Lewis and Clark Expedition to Sioux City, Iowa. Six designs were submitted by Charles R. Chickering of the PO Bureau of Printing and Engraving – the one finally approved appears top left. Chickering's figures were inspired by the Lewis and Clark Monument at Charlottesville, Virginia, and the statue of Sacagawea – the Indian woman who guided the explorers and helped them gain the friendship of the Shoshone Indians – at the State Capitol grounds, North Dakota.

Left: Specimen stamps from Germany, Cyprus and Taiwan.

plate proofs may consist of an entire sheet, a block or a strip. Single items will have very little margin as they are cut from the proof sheet.

Although die and plate proofs are normally pulled in black ink, they are often found in various colours to give postal officials the opportunity to select a shade most suitable for the finished stamp. These variations are regarded as colour trials and though they are usually imperforate they are sometimes perforated to give a better idea of what the finished stamp will look like. Both colour trials and examples of finished stamps without perforations may also be encountered with some form of overprint, either "Cancelled" or "Specimen" or the equivalent in another language. These items were often circulated among postal officials but were overprinted to prevent anyone trying to use them on mail.

ADDING COLOURS

With the advent of multicolour printing it became customary to take proofs of each colour separation, both individually, and in the combinations that culminated in a complete design. These are known as progressive proofs. Proofs in unadopted colours or those finally selected for the finished stamps were sometimes overprinted or punched to provide the printer with samples that could be shown to prospective clients from other postal administrations. Sometimes printers would opt to use imperforate stamps for this purpose, overprinted of course to prevent them being used postally.

Nowadays presentation packs are available from post offices along with mint stamps and FDCs, but in the past special packs were produced either for the media or for presentation to government officials and other dignitaries. All of these things help to build the story of a stamp from its initial concept to the finished article.

Below: Pairs of New Zealand stamps (1926), in rejected and issued colours.

FLAWS AND MARGINAL MARKINGS

After narrowing the focus of a collection to take in the stamps and postal history of a particular country, period or theme, the logical next step for the ambitious philatelist is to create a study of the subtle minutiae of stamps from different printings or produced by different contractors. In order to do this successfully, it is necessary to employ tools and techniques which are far beyond those in general use.

Above: The line-engraved trade card of Waterlow & Sons, printers of stamps and banknotes for much of the 19th and 20th centuries.

Right: US 37c stamp for the Athens Olympic Games, 2004, showing a marginal marking indicating the plate position. Other marginal markings include plate or cylinder numbers, printer's name and first date of sale.

TOOLS OF THE SPECIALIST

Instead of an ordinary perforation gauge, which measures quarter fractions, the advanced philatelist may rely on an electronic device such as the Perfotronic machine, which measures the gauge in tenths. While most collectors might be content to determine whether a stamp has one or two phosphor bands, or a single band on left or right, the specialist will want to distinguish between phosphor wavelengths and colour fluorescence, so a good ultraviolet lamp is essential.

LOOKING BENEATH THE SURFACE

Most collectors may be satisfied with sorting out different printings according to the watermark (as in the British Wilding definitives of 1955–67), but if you are studying the classic issues of the 19th century you will need to distinguish between wove and laid paper, hand- and machine-made paper, and even between different kinds of paper. Apart from the watermark detector you will need a micrometer to check the exact thickness of the paper and a really powerful illuminated magnifier to check the characteristics of the fibres that determine the quality or character of the paper.

In the period between the World Wars New Zealand had its stamps printed on paper supplied by different firms. Specialists therefore distinguish between De La Rue, Samuel Jones, Art, Cowan and Wiggins Teape papers. The wartime issues are known on first fine paper, second fine paper and coarse paper, further sub-divided according to whether the mesh of the paper is horizontal or vertical.

Some specialists end up spending all their time in the study of a single stamp. The Penny Black of 1840 and its eleven plates attract many specialists, but many albums could be filled with a detailed examination of the Penny Lilac (1881–1902), sometimes dubbed the Poor Man's Penny Black. The US George Washington 2c (1894–1900) and New Zealand's Penny Universal (1901–8) are also selected for study.

Wilding 2d Flaws

A constant flaw occurred in sideways coils of the Wilding 2d stamps from roll 5, the left hand numeral being very weak in the original printing. This weakness was rectified by retouching the figure but this, in turn, produced irregularities in its shape. The "retouched 2" remained constant in these coils, throughout changes from dark to light colour as well as changes of watermark.

Above: The British Customs and Revenue Act of 1881 provided for stamps that served both postal and fiscal purposes. The Penny Lilac, inscribed "Postage and Inland Revenue", was widely used on bills and receipts as well as mail until 1902, providing a wealth of material for advanced study, hence its nickname: the Poor Man's Penny Black.

FLAWS AND VARIETIES

Apart from the inks, papers and processes that distinguish the work of one printer from another, the advanced collector must pay attention to the stamps themselves. Each printing method creates its own little quirks, resulting in minor blemishes in the stamps that are known to collectors as "flaws". They may be constant, appearing in the same plate or cylinder position throughout the print-run, such as the "screwdriver" flaws – white gashes caused by damage to the plates. Constant flaws help specialists to reconstruct entire sheets, a process known as "plating". Flaws may also be ephemeral, such as "confetti" flaws – patches of white on some stamps caused by small pieces of paper (often the fragments punched out by the perforators) adhering momentarily to the plate.

Weaknesses in line engraving can be corrected, causing a slight doubling of lines known as a "re-entry". Varieties in photogravure stamps can be corrected manually but the result is still obvious and is known as a "re-touch".

Flaws and varieties are best collected in positional blocks to show their relation to the sheet margins. Controls and cylinder blocks are generally kept in corner blocks of six (three by two) and arrow markings in blocks of four.

MARGINAL MARKINGS

Specialists are also preoccupied with the paper that surrounds sheets of stamps because of the useful information it contains. Back in 1840 the sheets of Penny Blacks included the plate number and instructions regarding the correct attachment of the stamp to the letter as well as the price per row (1s) or sheet (£1). From 1881 until 1947 British stamps bore a control letter alongside numerals indicating the last two digits of the year.

American and Canadian stamps had control numbers referring to the plates released to the printers. De La Rue stamps often had a numeral in a chamfered rectangle, the "current number", which indicated the order in which a plate was printed. Other sheet markings include arrows (to guide the counter clerks in dividing up the sheets in their stock), the printer's imprint or logo, and the exact date of printing.

Thick bars were inserted in the margins in 1887 to prevent wear on the plate. Known as "jubilee lines" (because they first appeared in the jubilee definitives of that year) they are a feature of British stamps to this day. Sheets of stamps in the early 20th century often had strange cuts in the jubilee lines, believed to be made by the printers to identify certain plates. This feature sometimes forms part of the product description on sheets up for auction.

Modern offset litho and photogravure stamps have cylinder numbers in one margin and "traffic lights" (the printer's colour dabs) in the other. The stamps of many countries have the cumulative values of each row printed at the top or bottom to assist accounting. These "reckoning numbers" are not only helpful in plating but are often slightly changed and thus help to identify a particular printing.

Above: A stamp from Israel's Ottoman Clock Tower series (2004) showing an accountancy mark in the right margin and a tab below.

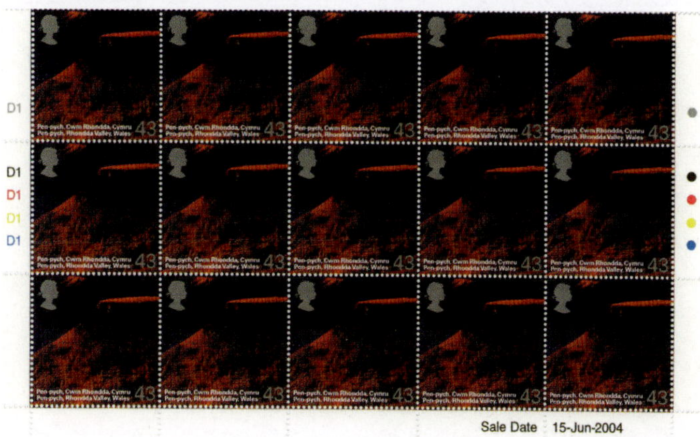

Below: Part of a sheet of Welsh Scenery 43p stamps (2004) showing cylinder numbers, colour dabs and the sale date.

A GLOBAL HOBBY

From its origins in the late 18th century, stamp collecting has emerged as the world's largest and most universal hobby. It is thought that more than 50 million people around the globe now collect, from crowned heads to schoolchildren.

Left: A famous philatelic commemorative produced for an American-hosted exhibition of 1926.

THE ORIGINS OF THE HOBBY

Philately is an extremely interactive pastime, supported by a strong network of societies, magazines, study circles, websites, web-based discussion groups, and exhibitions of interest to both the amateur and the specialist. Some clubs, such as the Invalid and Lone Collectors Society in Britain, exist to establish links between collectors living in remote areas or who, perhaps due to ill health, lack the opportunity to meet others sharing their interest. For the serious collector, there are stamp auctions and dealers' bourses where the outstanding rarities have been known to change hands for seven-figure sums.

EARLY COLLECTORS

Perhaps surprisingly, the earliest stamp collection was put together long before adhesive postage stamps (as we know them today) came into existence. As long ago as 1774, John Bourke, then Receiver-General of the Stamp Duties in Ireland, started a collection of revenue stamps shortly after they were introduced in that country. However, the father of stamp-collecting in the accepted sense was Dr John Edward Gray, Keeper of the Zoological Department of the British Museum. He took a very close interest in postal reform and was one of several people who later challenged Rowland Hill's claim to have invented stamps.

On the day the Penny Black went on sale (1 May 1840) Dr Gray purchased some examples of the stamp, which he kept as mementoes of a historic occasion. He subsequently added the Twopence Blue when it appeared on 8 May, and collected other stamps as soon as they were issued. In 1862 he was the compiler of one of the earliest stamp catalogues, and he also published sets of gummed titles, intended for collectors to cut up and use as headings for the pages of their stamp albums.

Apart from Dr Gray there must have been other men and women who were quick to perceive the innate interest in these tiny scraps of paper and began forming collections of them. By 1850, when stamps from about 20 countries had appeared, and the number of issues in circulation had reached three figures, stamp collecting was well established as a hobby. As early as 1842 references to this strange new craze began to appear in newspaper and magazine articles. More significantly, advertisements of stamps wanted or for sale were being published by 1852. In that year a Belgian schoolmaster is said to have started encouraging his pupils to collect stamps, to improve their knowledge of geography.

THE Stamp Collector's Magazine.

CONTENTS.

POSTAL CHIT-CHAT.

FEB. 1, 1863.] THE STAMP COLLECTOR'S MAGAZINE. 15

Left and above: The first page of the inaugural issue of The Stamp Collector's Magazine, *February 1863, and a page advertising the sale of readers' stamps, labels and covers.*

Below: Female postal workers examine love letters sent on St Valentine's Day. Despite frivolous portraits such as these, many 19th-century women took a serious interest in stamps, and some became avid pioneers of philately.

Stanley Gibbons

Edward Stanley Gibbons was born in the same year as the Penny Black (1840) and began trading in stamps in 1856 from his father's shop in Plymouth, having purchased a collection of South African stamps from two sailors who had just returned to the port. Stamp trading apart, he led a colourful life, marrying five times.

THE FIRST DEALERS AND CATALOGUES

The hobby was certainly well established in Belgium by 1854, by which time Louis Hanciau and Jean-Baptiste Moens (who later became leading dealers) were avid enthusiasts. Edward Stanley Gibbons began dealing in stamps in 1856, a window of his father's pharmacy in Plymouth being devoted to mouth-watering bargains. Nine years later he published his first catalogue, the forerunner of the extensive range of general, specialized and thematic catalogues now on offer.

Oscar Berger-Levreult and Alfred Potiquet both began publishing catalogues in France in 1861 and not long afterwards there were regular magazines devoted to the hobby. One of the earliest was *The Stamp Collector's Magazine*, which first appeared in February 1863, and contained in its opening pages a very vivid account of the open-air selling and swapping of stamps conducted in Birchin Lane, Cheapside, in London, and the similar al fresco meetings of "timbromaniacs" held in the gardens of the Luxembourg and the Tuileries in Paris.

THE BIRTH OF PHILATELY

Timbromania, the original pseudo-scientific name for the hobby (from the French word *timbre*, a stamp), was soon replaced by something more dignified, if less easy to pronounce. Again it was a Frenchman, Georges Herpin, who coined the word "philately", but his logic was as faulty as his grasp of Greek. He tried to convey the idea of something on which no tax or charge was due because it was prepaid (*philos* = love, *a* = not, *telos* = tax), and thus ended up with a word that meant a lover of no taxes. Some have argued that "atelophily" would be more correct. Significantly, the Greeks themselves use the term *philotelia*, which omits the negative element, implying that stamp collectors are lovers of taxes rather than of the stamps that signify their payment.

FIRST STAMP CLUBS

Among the pioneer collectors was the Reverend F.J. Stainforth, who organized the first indoor meetings when the police began to discourage the obstruction caused in Birchin Lane. In the 1860s collectors met on Saturday afternoons in his rectory at All Hallows Staining in the City of London – its Dickensian ring is hardly surprising as it features in Dickens's novel *Dombey and Son*. The gatherings included Charles W. Viner, editor of *The Stamp Collector's Magazine*, Mount Brown, who published an early catalogue, Judge Philbrick and Sir Daniel Cooper, who became president of the Philatelic Society, London, when it was founded in 1869. A society had been formed in Paris in 1864 but it did not last long. The London society, now the Royal Philatelic Society, is still in existence and, if not the biggest, is certainly the most prestigious in the world.

Although stamp collecting is sometimes regarded as a male-dominated hobby, women have always played a prominent role in the field. Among the earliest female enthusiasts were Charlotte Tebay, who helped organize the earliest London exhibition, and Adelaide Lucy Fenton, who was a prolific contributor to the stamp magazines but, like some female novelists of an earlier generation, preferred to write under the masculine pen name of "Herbert Camoens".

The English school of philately was noted for its general approach, whereas the French school had a more scientific bent, paying greater attention to the minute variations in stamps. It was one of their number, Dr Jacques-Amable Legrand, who invented the perforation gauge in 1866 and wrote the earliest treatise on watermarks a year later.

Below: A society for young philatelists was, indeed, the brainchild of a young philatelist. Fred Melville was just 17 when he established the group in 1899, following his disappointment at being rejected as a member of the London Philatelic Society on account of his age. The first meeting is believed to have been held in a shop in Clapham, South London, and the Junior Philatelic Society went on to become the National Philatelic Society, which celebrated its centenary in 1999.

ORGANIZED PHILATELY

Stamp collecting endured a sticky patch in the 1870s (*The Stamp Collector's Magazine* ceased publication in 1874, and its rival *The Philatelist* in 1876, for lack of support), but somehow it managed to keep going and steadily gained ground in the 1880s. By then it was well established throughout Europe and North America, with numerous dealers and stamp auctions.

GROWTH OF STAMP CLUBS

The reason for the loss of interest in the 1870s was probably the paucity of stamp clubs; without the interaction of fellow enthusiasts, many of the original collectors lost heart and gave up. The resurgence of the hobby began in continental Europe, where a national philatelic society was revived in France at the end of 1875.

A stamp club had started in New York in 1867 but soon faded into oblivion and it was not until 1886 that the American Philatelic Society (APS) was formed. Chartered by Congress in 1912, it is now the world's largest stamp club, with its headquarters and magnificent library in State College, Pennsylvania. About the same time the Manchester Philatelic Society was established in England. The Edinburgh & Leith Philatelic Society, founded in 1890, was almost entirely composed of expatriate German businessmen and for the first three years the minutes were recorded in German. By the beginning of the 20th century there were 34 philatelic societies in the UK, a score in the British colonies, a dozen in the USA, 19 in continental Europe and nine in Latin America.

EARLY STAMP EXHIBITIONS

In 1887 the first stamp exhibition took place at Antwerp. Two years later similar shows were organized in New York, Amsterdam and Munich. In 1890 – the golden jubilee of adhesive postage stamps – exhibitions were staged in Vienna, Birmingham, Edinburgh and Leeds as well as London (for which some of the earliest special postmarks were produced). Undoubtedly such exhibitions attracted the general public and drew many new recruits.

World Fair Stamps

New York's fair of technology and science, held from 1939 to 1940, brought hope to an era of international tension. A commemorative stamp was issued by the USPO in the Fair's first year. Some participating countries, such as Iceland, issued postage stamps to fund their attendance at the two-year global exhibition. The Centennial Stamp Exhibition was one of many around the world that marked the centenary of the Penny Black.

Below: The American Philatelic Society, established in 1886 as the American Philatelic Association, has hosted annual conventions for many years.

Philatelic literature, including handbooks and monographs as well as general catalogues, had grown to such an extent that, by 1889, the Munich exhibition included more than 500 volumes. The first exhibition devoted to stamps of particular countries took place in 1893 when the Philatelic Society of London staged a show of British India, Ceylon and the West Indies. The Society's exhibition the following year was dedicated to rare stamps in general.

The first London exhibition in 1890 had been a major landmark. Although the centenary exhibition in 1940 was muted as a result of the outbreak of World War II, it set the precedent for

Above: The label for the Centenary International Philatelic Exhibition, New York, 1947, celebrating the centenary of the first US stamps.

Below: A souvenir sheet for the London International Stamp Exhibition, 1960, portraying Colonel Henry Bishop and the many different "Bishop marks" used by staff to record acceptance of mail from the 1660s to the late 18th century.

the great international shows that have been held in London at ten-year intervals ever since.

NATIONAL CONGRESSES AND REGIONAL FEDERATIONS

The Philatelic Congress of Great Britain was inaugurated at Manchester in 1909 as an opportunity for fellow collectors to meet and discuss the hobby. It has been held annually ever since, with the exception of the war years, in different venues, and has generated sufficient material, in the form of souvenir covers, postcards, labels, miniature sheets and postmarks, to make a sizeable collection.

With the proliferation of stamp clubs after World War II, an intermediate tier of organization was created in Britain, with federations of clubs at county or regional level but including national associations in Scotland, Wales and Northern Ireland, all coming under the aegis of the Association of British Philatelic Societies. Similar federations at state or provincial level exist in the USA and Canada and the great majority of countries in the rest of Europe, Australasia and Latin America.

Major international exhibitions are now held several times a year in different parts of the world. The governing body is the Fédération Internationale de Philatélie (FIP), which sets out the rules for competitions and judging. It also attempts to apply the brake on excessive and unnecessary stamp issues. This is a perennial problem that has so far defeated the continuing efforts of the Universal Postal Union and the International Federation of Stamp Dealers Associations (IFDSA).

Below: The Junior Philatelic Society of the United Kingdom organized a number of national exhibitions during the first half of the 20th century. Due to a falling-out between the London and Manchester branches, the 1909 exhibition held at the latter failed to draw any mention from the society's journal, Stamp Lover.

CLUBS AT LOCAL AND NATIONAL LEVEL

Most towns of any size now boast at least one stamp club, meeting monthly or more frequently, where collectors can exchange unwanted duplicates, buy and sell stamps and attend talks and displays by prominent philatelists.

In recent years, specialist society or study groups have emerged, drawing together collectors of similar interests and specialization at national or even international level. Although these societies hold regular meetings, the main medium for intercourse is the club magazine, in which new research is published, and nowadays most if not all of these specialist organizations have excellent websites. Most clubs, at both local and national level, also maintain a club "packet" – a system that enables all members to add to their collections with the minimum of expense.

Below: In October 1926, first day covers were issued at the International Philatelic Exhibition for the very first time. Although FDCs with 16 October 1926 date stamps are known, this is widely regarded as an error. It is now believed the postal clerk simply forgot to change the date stamp as stamps were officially issued on 18 October.

EXHIBITING STAMPS

Stamp exhibitions have been around for almost 120 years and during that time they have changed from being confined purely to competitive and invited displays by private individuals to becoming the great crossroads of philately, where dealers and philatelic bureaux congregate and collectors flock from all over the world to examine their merchandise.

Purists may decry this trend and feel that the stamp displays have been relegated to a secondary role. The British Philatelic Exhibition (BPE) was, in fact, established as a rival to Stampex (the other major British national show) to try to return to a situation where stamp displays were the main attraction of the event. However, the organizers were forced to admit the dealers' stands at subsequent shows because their absence meant that attendance figures slumped. In the 1970s Stampex was held in February or March and BPE in October or November. Nowadays, both shows are organized under the aegis of the Philatelic Traders' Society (PTS) and are known as the Spring and Autumn Stampex. In turn, they now have a rival in the form of Philatex, which is held more or less simultaneously, with a bias towards postal history.

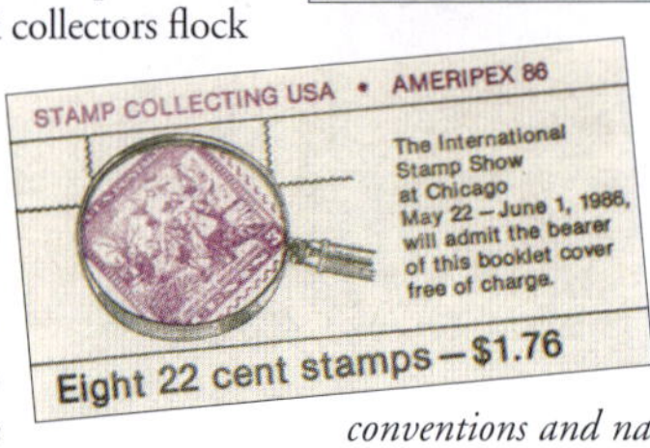

Above and left: The USA has perhaps the largest number of exhibitions, dealers' and collectors' conventions and national bourses, many of which attract collectors from all over the world.

Below: The US-hosted International Philatelic Exhibitions provided good opportunities to promote the sale of souvenir sheets or new commemoratives.

EXHIBITIONS AT ALL LEVELS

There are numerous regional exhibitions and conventions in Britain, usually organized by the federations of philatelic societies. These shows tend to lay more emphasis on competitive displays, though dealers' stands are also a major attraction. A similar pattern is to be found in other countries.

The USA leads the way in organizing philatelic exhibitions, but they are also staged each year at club, regional and national level all over Europe, Australasia and an ever-increasing number of countries in the Third World. The most phenomenal growth in recent years has taken place in Singapore, Hong Kong and the People's Republic of China. The annual stamp shows in Beijing and Shanghai, for example, attract crowds in excess of 300,000 – an astronomical attendance. Six-figure attendance has also been recorded at exhibitions in Prague, Budapest, Warsaw and other capital cities that, not so long ago, were suffering from numerous restrictions under communist rule.

Above: Philatelic exhibitions occur throughout the world each year. This event was hosted in Helsinki, Finland.

Many countries have a national stamp day, stamp week or even stamp month, when their postal administrations collaborate with the trade bodies to promote the hobby by means of exhibitions. Sales of special stamps for these events go a long way in subsidizing the shows.

ENTERING COMPETITIVE SHOWS

Those who aspire to take part in the competitive sections of the international exhibitions must first earn a silver medal or a higher award at national level: this ensures that the standards of the entries in the main annual exhibitions are kept high. To attain this level may take many years of competing at a local club show, gradually improving the layout and writing-up of the display, and acquiring those philatelic gems that make all the difference between the mediocre and the first-rate, till the collection is ready for the big national shows. The coveted silver medal, however, is no more than the key to the door of the most prestigious events, and such an entry at international exhibitions may receive only a certificate of participation at the first attempt.

Such is the competitive instinct in many stamp collectors that initial disappointment will merely spur them on to greater efforts, and over the years they will climb the ladder of international awards from bronze and bronze-silver medals, through silver, silver-gilt or vermeil awards to small and large gold medals. At the pinnacle of the awards system are the national and international Grand Prix and the special trophies in each class. Thereafter the Grand Prix winners may be invited to exhibit *hors concours* (out of contest) in the Court of Honour, alongside exhibits from the world's most prestigious stamp collections, such as those belonging to Queen Elizabeth II or Prince Rainier of Monaco.

It is when you see these dazzling arrays of the great rarities that you appreciate the old adage about stamp collecting being "the king of hobbies and the hobby of kings", although today's biggest collectors are more likely to be property tycoons, industrial millionaires, film stars and pop idols, while the greatest rarities are probably owned by investment syndicates and union pension funds.

However, stamp collecting is still primarily the hobby of countless millions of ordinary men, women and children all over the world, and it is with them that its enduring strength lies. These are the collectors who are the mainstay of the exhibitions, preparing their competition entries of 16 or 32 sheets (the minimum basic requirement at regional level) or multiple frames of 16 sheets at national and international level.

Competitive Philately

Records held by the National Philatelic Society of the United Kingdom help to characterize competitive philately during the 1920s. The Society's first International Stamp Exhibition was held in London in 1923, and planning began at least two years before. There was a design competition for "Air Post Stamps", with premiums of twenty and ten guineas (£21 and £10.50) for the two best entrants. The American millionaire collector Arthur Hind exhibited his rare Mauritius 1d and 2d values and there was even an early nod to thematic and Cinderella collecting in competitive categories such as "War and Post-War Stamps" and "Etceteras", the latter including displays of proofs, essays, specimens, errors, forgeries, embossed stamps, Mulready envelopes and Chinese treaty port material.

Above: Large stamp exhibitions have often attracted people of note, including royalty and politicians. At this British exhibition during the 1950s the future prime minister, Harold Wilson, examines Cape Triangular stamps.

FIP MARKING SYSTEM

Under the rules of the Fédération Internationale de Philatélie, entries are given marks for presentation, philatelic material, philatelic treatment and philatelic knowledge. Presentation covers overall appearance, including marks for the title page, which should act as an index to the display itself. Material deals with the stamps and other items, their quality and rarity, while treatment pertains to the ways in which they are set out. Philatelic knowledge accounts for a third of the marks, and this is where exhibitors can really shine by demonstrating their original research. But you must study the rules carefully to make sure that you do not include anything that will detract from the display and lose you marks that might mean all the difference between a gold and silver medal.

Below: Promotional stamps and stationery are often produced in conjunction with exhibitions and national stamp centenaries or commemorative dates introduced to plug the hobby.

BUYING AND SELLING STAMPS

Although it is possible to collect stamps with little or no outlay, concentrating on the stamps off your mail, sooner or later you are going to have to buy material if you are to make any real headway in the hobby. There are four main methods of acquiring stamps by purchase: from other collectors, from a dealer, from an auction and direct from a post office counter or philatelic bureau. The first three outlets are also useful for disposing of stamps.

GRADE AND CONDITION

Before you start trading it is worth understanding the principles behind grade and condition if you want to be able to calculate the approximate value of a stamp.

The "grade" of a stamp is determined by the actual position of the printed design on the paper, in relation to the perforated edges. The relative imprecision of perforating methods in the past means that the "margins" (the area of unprinted paper surrounding the printed design) of many older stamps vary considerably in width. Stamps with larger margins tend to attract collectors more than examples where the design is tight against the edges. Grading in catalogues such as Gibbons or Scott uses terms such as "fair", "good", "fine", "very fine", and so on. It is generally assumed that if the stamp has a balanced appearance and the design is well clear of the edges, it counts for a "fine" or "very fine" grade. Imperforate stamps should present three normal-size margins.

"Condition" is based on a greater number of factors: the effects of production, whether the stamp is hinged, the nature of the cancellation on a used stamp, or any evidence of damage (such as missing perforated "teeth", tears or faded colour due to prolonged exposure to sunlight). Of course, the grade of the stamp can also affect its condition. All of the above may detract from a stamp's commercial value, although some of the more quirky or historically weighty cancellations may render some used issues highly sought after by collectors.

Below: Collectors browse through booklets of stamps available for sale at the bourse of a large stamp show.

TRADING WITH OTHER COLLECTORS

You can buy, sell or swap stamps with other collectors at a stamp club, either face to face or through the medium of the club exchange packet or "circuit". This usually consists of a box containing a quantity of small booklets with stamps, cards and covers mounted on their pages, with the prices clearly marked. Trading circuits organized by societies such as the APS have designated sales books, and even specific mounts for displaying material, but the principle remains the same. In most cases it is customary also to add the catalogue number with the catalogue price (for mint or used).

When trading among themselves, collectors generally work on a quarter to a fifth of the catalogue price, a basis that allows you to add to your collection with the minimum of expense. This may not seem like a good deal from the vendor's viewpoint, but it probably amounts to a more generous percentage than is obtained by selling to a dealer. The only snags about selling through the club packet are that it is time-consuming to mount and price stamps individually (although many collectors actually enjoy this) and, of course, many months may elapse before the packet has been around everyone on the circuit and you get back the (hopefully) empty booklets with a tidy sum of cash, less the modest commission due to the club funds.

Swapping Stamps

Trading with fellow enthusiasts is an enjoyable, informal way to develop a collection and learn more about your stamps. Here, a society meets to browse and trade stamps at a shopping mall.

DEALERS

Even stamp dealers usually offer material at a discount off the catalogue price, although if the stamps are particularly elusive you should be prepared to pay over the odds sometimes. Catalogue prices are usually a fair indication of relative value, but occasionally even these are at odds with reality. While in some (though not all) cases the catalogue represents the selling price of a major dealer, that dealer may be deliberately keeping prices low (when, for example, the company wishes to buy material for stock). Other dealers recognize this and will often ignore the standard catalogue and fix their own price, based on what they had to pay at auction.

If you decide to sell to a dealer you may be in for quite a shock. What he offers you may be only a fifth of what you paid – sometimes less – especially if you are trading in your entire collection rather than selected items. The reason for this large differential between buying and selling price is mainly economic. When appraising a collection, dealers ignore all the common stamps (of which they will already have a large stock that is slow to turn over) and will base their valuation on the scarcer or more expensive individual items. Selling stamps this way, however, means that you get cash on the spot – useful if you need money in a hurry.

FINDING THE RIGHT DEALER

For every dealer with a retail shop there are probably 100 whose business is postal or by appointment only. Some of the world's largest dealers operate in quite a modest manner, acting on behalf of a few very wealthy clients who will regularly spend large sums with them. They are truly international, traversing the world in search of major rarities, relying on their laptops, bidding at auctions online and emailing clients to set up new deals.

At the other end of the scale are the vast majority of dealers, who are content to make a modest living, meeting potential customers on the fair circuits, which have now largely superseded the retail shops. Others have found niches specializing in certain countries or types of material, sending out price lists to regular clients and laboriously making up approval booklets in which stamps and covers are mounted and priced.

Apart from the excellent directories of dealers published by such bodies as the American Stamp Dealers' Association (ASDA) and the Philatelic Traders' Society (PTS) in Britain, the easiest way to contact a dealer specializing in your field is to scour the classified advertisements in the philatelic magazines. If yours is a popular subject the choice of dealers will be bewildering, but whatever your interests – no matter how esoteric – somewhere there will be at least one dealer specializing in them. As a rule, the dealers with a retail shop tend to hold general stocks as they have to cater to all tastes, whereas the postal dealers are more likely to concentrate on specific subjects. Many of them are leading authorities in their chosen speciality and you can usually rely on their judgment and integrity.

AUCTIONS

The stamp auction is where the best stamps and postal history material come up for sale, and this is where you are most likely to find entire collections and specialized studies that can form the basis for further expansion, as well as the more choice single items that fill that long-felt want.

If you attend a sale, make sure you know before it begins what your spending limit is, and stick to it. Too often, a couple of bidders get carried away in their reckless attempt to secure a coveted item and one ends up paying well over the odds. You also need to remember that most auctions nowadays charge a buyer's premium (usually 15 per cent) and that a general consumer tax may be payable on that, so the net sum you have to fork out on a purchase could turn out to be substantially more than your final bid.

It is also possible to place your bid by post. In this case you need to state the maximum you are prepared to pay on each lot and the auctioneer will let you have it at the next step above the highest room bid or the next highest postal bid to yours.

If you have good material to dispose of, selling at auction offers the best method of ensuring the maximum return, but bear in mind that the auctioneer takes a percentage of the sum realized, and many months may elapse between sending stamps to the auction and the sale itself, as material has to be appraised, lotted and described, catalogues printed and dispatched to prospective bidders, and then all the paperwork after the sale completed before you receive a remittance.

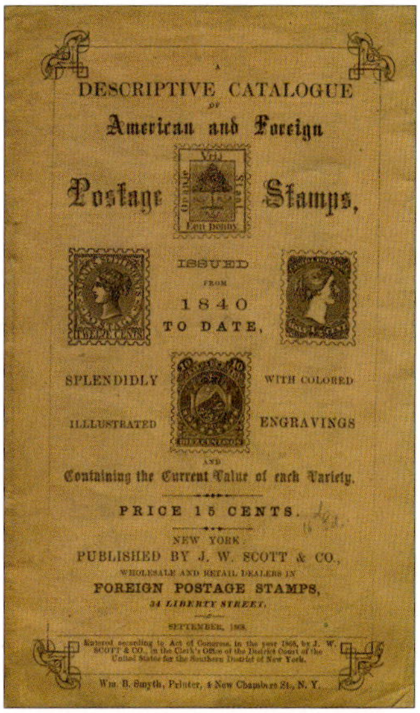

Above: An early auction catalogue. The first auction devoted entirely to stamps was held in Paris in 1865. Five years later, the American philatelist J. Walter Scott (founder of the Scott philatelic empire) organized his first sale in New York, and by the 1880s stamp auctions were a regular occurrence, with firms established solely to generate philatelic sales. Although London was dominant for many years, today there are many excellent stamp auctions in Geneva, Sydney, Singapore and Hong Kong.

PHILATELIC BUREAUX

Virtually every national postal administration now operates a philatelic bureau, selling stamps, postal stationery, FDCs and other products direct to collectors, and all transactions can be made by credit card. You pay only face value for your purchases, plus a small handing charge in many cases, but this ensures you get everything relevant to your chosen country, and sometimes a bonus such as a proof or special print unavailable across the post office counter. Bureaux produce annual catalogues of back stock as well as their own magazines, usually quarterly, announcing forthcoming issues, often with excellent background stories.

PHILATELY ONLINE

Above: Some of the larger philatelic societies offer a rigorously organized form of online "club packet", which enables members to swap stamps and even submit queries about a purchase.

We are living in the heart of an IT revolution that impacts on every aspect of our lives, from split-second global communications to online shopping and banking, and information retrieval. Stamp collecting is also currently being transformed by the advent of the internet, with countless societies, clubs, magazines, dealers, auctioneers and centres of research offering online facilities to assist in the expansion and refinement of collections.

In addition to the ever-growing number of internet research outlets, there are also numerous software packages that assist the collector with everything from forming an inventory to calculating the value of stamps or downloading pre-designed album pages. Magazines, journals and societies often publish reviews of the latest philatelic software, and their merits (or pitfalls) are regularly debated in online discussion forums – which are themselves one of the fastest-growing resources available to the online philatelic fraternity. Another hotly debated topic is the advantages or disadvantages of purchasing stamps online, which is becoming an increasingly popular alternative to local, face-to-face dealing.

RESEARCH AT THE CLICK OF A MOUSE

One of the biggest problems facing the thematic or topical collector is finding out about the subjects of stamps. The basic details such as the reason for the issue are given in stamp catalogues, but for a topical collection you often need to get the whole story – the why and the wherefore as well as the hidden meaning. It is ferreting out such information that gains good marks in competitive displays.

This is where search engines such as Google and Yahoo come into their own. There is, seemingly, absolutely nothing under the sun that cannot be found in this way, providing you type in a clear and concise phrase rather than a single keyword, which might yield far more than you require, much of it irrelevant. The search engines are also invaluable for researching postal history, and can help you to locate masses of information on the places whose postmarks you are interested in, as well as simply drawing your attention to organizations that can help further. Long-established thematic societies, such as the American Topical Association, also have their own websites, with useful tips and links for the keen researcher.

DATABASES, INVENTORIES AND WANTS LISTS

Stamp catalogues remain key to the process of identifying and valuing individual issues or long-running series. Yet there exists an increasing demand among collectors to be able to tailor these set-format reference tools to meet their individual needs. Some of the biggest catalogue publishers, such as Scott, are now working in conjunction with philatelic software producers to combine the entire catalogue of a country with the benefits of a personal inventory, so that a collector can itemize their prized possessions and identify gaps in their collection.

The idea is that the collector will not only be able to sort and display stamps by numerous categories, such as catalogue number and issue date, but also use the software to generate a personal record of their own collection.

Viewing Stamps Online

Stamps for sale on the internet are often accompanied by digital images of such quality that it is possible to discern individual fibres in the paper and verify the distance between the perforations. This Bavarian stamp displays a number of missing, or "pulled", perfs, which can affect value.

Current software offers the opportunity to revise information on value, add further details on format, grade and condition, and even upload digital scans. The best packages offer considerable space for editing data on each stamp – sometimes up to one page per issue. The collector can also inventory reports, calculate the value of a bulk of stamps, and generate wants lists to mail to dealers and other collectors.

Some of this software can be downloaded direct from the supplier's website, although before purchasing it is worth checking that the dealer is reputable and that a full mailing address, with customer service contact, is given. There may be free trial downloads, so that you can check that you are happy with the format of the software before purchasing it.

BUYING AND SELLING ONLINE

The ability to trade online is probably the most significant part of the internet revolution in stamp collecting. Stamp dealers who scraped a bare living catering to customers living in their neighbourhood have now found that by creating their own website their stock is available to the world at large. Collectors have found thousands of dealers and auctioneers, large and small, general and specialized, whose wares are to be found simply by clicking on to their websites. Most philatelic bureaux have also embraced this technology and it has become a very simple matter to select what you want and pay for it by credit card.

Apart from the various auctioneers, who also have websites nowadays and enable you to bid online, there are larger, less esoteric organizations such as Ebay, where online sales are in continuous operation. Nor does buying online always require putting in a bid. In America, *Linn's Stamp News* runs a site at www.zillionsofstamps.com – open to all – that gives the collector the opportunity to input data on a wanted stamp and then search by dealer. The American Philatelic Society runs its own stamps store for members at www.stampstore.org, where the collector can browse stamps, selecting them by keyword, catalogue number, country or even type, such as "air mails". APS members can also submit information on stamps they wish to sell to other collectors.

For all forms of buying and selling, the computer scores heavily because it is now possible to download high-resolution images of stamps, which make even the most sumptuous of printed catalogues look crude by comparison. Fakes (stamps that have been tampered with to improve their appearance or altered by cleaning off the cancellation to convert a cheap used stamp into a valuable mint one) are no longer such a headache for potential buyers, because high-resolution images of stamps will immediately show up any imperfection, repair or other signs of alteration.

DISCUSSION FORUMS

One of the latest developments in this interactive hobby is for collectors to meet and chat with fellow enthusiasts from anywhere in the world via online messaging services. This can be done by posting notices to message boards, or by participating in a "live" discussion. Many philatelic forums have countless discussions running at any one time – on every subject from catalogue prices to the latest commemoratives, how to get started in collecting or experiences of online auction bidding. A code of conduct is usually encouraged during these discussions – namely that the participants stick to the subject at hand. Two of the busiest stamp collector forums, with spirited discussions, are the Virtual Stamp Club (www.virtualstampclub.com) and Frajola's Board for Philatelists (www.rfrajola.com). These sites also offer other standard facilities such as a bookstore and archive search facility.

Below: Global auction sites such as Ebay have embraced online philatelic trading. The number of bids is often displayed in a "counter" at the bottom of the screen. If you are not too familiar with the stamps you are bidding for, check that the seller has included their catalogue value with the lot, otherwise you may end up paying over the odds. Before getting involved in a bidding war, determine the maximum amount you wish to pay per stamp.

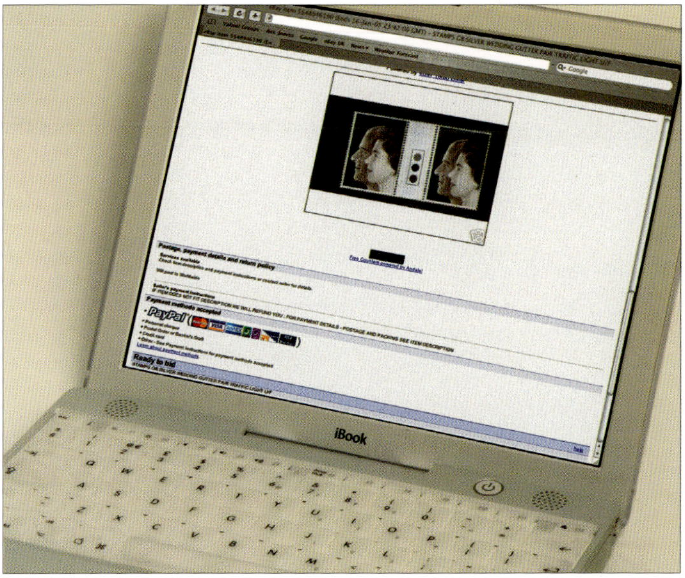

USEFUL SERVICES AND ADDRESSES

For the vast majority of collectors the standard stamp catalogues, published by long-established firms such as Gibbons (UK), Scott (USA), Michel (Germany) or Yvert et Tellier (France), are their bibles. The more advanced collectors are not content with one or other of the great general catalogues but require the specialized catalogues of their chosen countries – which may entail learning a foreign language as the best of the detailed catalogues, monographs and other reference works tend to be confined to the language of the country under study.

RESEARCHING THE MACHINS

The following example may help to illustrate the difference between the different levels of catalogues. The Machin decimal definitives of the UK, launched in 1971 and still going strong, occupy a column in the Gibbons *Stamps of the World* (2004 edition), which lists 120 stamps by denomination and colour only. The same stamps, classified by printer, printing process, perforation and phosphor, occupy nine columns in the Gibbons *British Commonwealth* volume 1, while volume 4 of the *Specialised Stamp Catalogue*, devoted entirely to the decimal definitives, now runs to almost 950 pages. This catalogue explains the differences in the stamps produced by Harrison, Enschedé, Questa and De La Rue (photogravure), Questa, Waddington and Walsall (lithography) and Bradbury Wilkinson, Enschedé or De La Rue (intaglio). It details the variations in the queen's effigy (high or low), whether chemically etched or computer engraved, and distinguishes the numerous types of paper, gum, perforation (normal or elliptical in different gauges), cylinder varieties, marginal markings, booklets and coils.

Left: Three British second class Machin definitives, printed by Walsall, Harrison and Questa, can be identified by the sheet markings.

Many advanced collectors prefer the *Complete Deegam Machin Handbook* compiled by Douglas Myall, who is also the author of the *Deegam Catalogue of Machin Se-tenant Pairs* and even a catalogue of *Elizabethan Coil Leaders*. Beyond that, an absolute must is membership of the Great Britain Philatelic Society, which has a separate Machin chapter, or the Decimal Book Study Circle, which publishes *The Bookmark* detailing the latest research by members. In fact, it is the pooling of information by individual collectors, who devote a considerable amount of time and money to researching the latest printings, that helps to maintain the extraordinary momentum of interest in this series.

CHECKING PREVIOUS RESEARCH

There is a vast literature on all aspects of philately and postal history, from monumental treatises running to several volumes, to articles in general and specialist magazines. A great deal of research by countless students into the most subtle minutiae of stamps and more esoteric aspects of postal history is to be found. Much of it has probably never been distilled and published in even the advanced catalogues. One task for the collector researching his material in detail is to find out what has already been published on the subject; sourcing all this secondary material takes quite a lot of research in itself.

MUSEUMS AND ARCHIVES

Many countries have at least one museum devoted to philately. In the USA the Smithsonian Institution in Washington has one of the world's largest philatelic collections, or rather a whole host of different collections pertaining to stamps, from a general whole-world reference collection to specialized studies and a wealth of postal history material. There are excellent facilities for studying these collections. The American Philatelic Society's extensive premises in State

Which Catalogue?

The following is an alphabetical list of the geographical areas covered by the key stamp catalogue producers. Although some of the larger publishers, such as Gibbons and Scott, also produce "world guides", they are listed here according to the country of which they have the most extensive coverage.

Australian Commonwealth Specialized Australia
AAMS US and Canadian Air Mail Covers
Bale Israel/Palestine
Barefoot European Revenues and British Revenues
Brookman United States
Campbell-Paterson New Zealand
Higgins & Gage Global Postal Stationery (10 yr)
Michel Germany
Minkus/Krause United States, Canada and United Nations
Nederlandsche (NVPH) Netherlands
Sanabria Airmail Catalogue Global Air Mail stamps (10 yr)
Sassone Italy
Scott United States
Springer Handbooks Non-Scott-listed US Revenues
Stanley Gibbons Great Britain
Steven's Mexican Revenues (10 yr)
Unitrade Canada and Provinces
World Perfin Catalogue Worldwide (printed in sections)
Yvert-Tellier France
Zumstein Switzerland

College, Pennsylvania also has some amazing reference collections, often donated or bequeathed by members, but its strong point is its library – one of the finest in the world.

At the other end of the spectrum is the National Postal Museum in London. This was located in the old General Post Office in the very heart of the City, but since the Post Office sold the building for redevelopment the museum has been in storage, under the management of the Post Office Heritage Collections. In the country that invented stamps and did so much to develop postal services this is a scandal of international proportions. The British Library is home to the Tapling Collection, containing many of the world's greatest rarities, as well as many other collections, available for research.

Elsewhere in the world, from Paris to Pretoria, there are postal museums and archives crammed with source material. The following associations may be able to offer advice on how to broaden the scope of your study.

Philatelic Societies

American Philatelic Society
100 Match Factory Place, Bellefonte, PA 16875, USA, www.stamps.org (*The American Philatelist, Philatelic Literature Review*)

American Poster Stamp Society
3654 Applegate Road, Jacksonville, OR 97530, USA

American Topical Association
PO Box 50820, Albuquerque, NM 87181-0820, USA (*Topical Time*)

Australian Philatelic Federation Ltd, PO Box 829, South Melbourne BC VIC 3205, Australia

British Philatelic Centre
107 Charterhouse Street, London EC1M 6PT, UK, www.ukphilately.org.uk
Association of British Philatelic Societies
British Philatelic Trust
National Philatelic Society (*Stamp Lover*)

The Philatelic Traders' Society Limited, PO Box 371, Fleet, Hampshire GU52 6ZX

Right: The American Philatelic Research Library, based at the APS premises in Bellefonte, Pennsylvania, is the largest public philatelic library in the United States. It houses classic periodicals and catalogues, and is open to the general public.

The Cinderella Stamp Club
www.cinderellastampclub.org.uk
(*The Cinderella Philatelist*)

Collectors Club of New York
22 East 35 Street, New York, NY 100016-3806, USA, www.collectorsclub.org
(*The Collectors Club Philatelist*)

The Ephemera Society of America, Inc.
PO Box 95, Cazenovia, NY 13035-0095, www.ephemerasociety.org (*Ephemera Journal*)

Invalid and Lone Collectors Club
12 Appian Close, Kings Heath, Birmingham, B14 6DS, UK

Philatelic Foundation
21 East 40th Street, New York, NY 100016, USA

Royal Philatelic Society
41 Devonshire Place, London W1N 1PE, UK, www.rpsl.org.uk (*The London Philatelist*)

Philatelic Magazines

Canadian Stamp News
Trajan Publications, 103 Lakeshore Road, Suite 202, St Catharines, Ontario L2N 2T6, Canada, www.trajan.ca

Gibbons Stamp Monthly
5 Parkside, Christchurch Road, Ringwood, Hampshire
BH24 3SH, UK
www.gibbonsstampmonthly.com

Global Stamp News
PO Box 97, Sidney, OH 45365-0097, USA

Linn's Stamp News
PO Box 29, 911 Vandemark Road, Sidney, OH 45365-0065, USA, www.linns.com

The Philatelic Exporter
PO Box 137, Hatfield, Hertfordshire, AL10 9DB, UK, www.philatelicexporter.com

Scott Stamp Monthly
PO Box 828, Sidney, OH 45365, USA, www.scottonline.com

Stamp and Coin Mart
Trinity Publications Ltd, Edward House, 92-3 Edward Street, Birmingham, B1 2RA, UK, www.stampmart.co.uk

Stamp Collector
700 East State Street, Iola, WI 54990-0001, USA, www.krause.com

Stamp Magazine
IPC Media, Leon House, 233 High Street, Croydon CR9 1HZ, UK, www.stampmagazine.co.uk

Stamp News
PO Box 1410, Dubbo, NSW 3830, Australia

Right: The Bath Postal Museum, England, is situated in the building from which one of the first letters bearing a Penny Black was sent on 2 May 1840 – four days ahead of the official date.

BELGIË
BELGIQUE
20 DIENSTMARKE 20
15 CENTS
STERNA
SINGAPORE
CHRISTMAS
DEUTSCHE DEMOKRATISCHE REPUBLIK
DEUTSCHE DEMOKRATISCHE REPUBLIK
Deutsche Bundespost
50 BUNDESPOST
100 BUNDESPOST
30 BUNDESPOST
60
Bundespost
Johannes Faust

THE WORLD DIRECTORY OF STAMPS

Stamps function rather like miniature posters: they reflect what a country thinks of itself, or how it wishes to be seen by the world. In the following pages you will find a survey of the stamps of the whole world from 1840 to the present day. Each section covers the stamps of a particular continent, and, within these parameters, the stamps of individual countries, or a group of nations, that are related politically or geographically. The stamps often chart interesting developments. The United States, for example, has remained remarkably stable since the inception of its stamps, yet even in this instance the Civil War gave rise to the separate issues of the Confederate States. At the other extreme are countries that have frequently changed their political status (such as Albania, which has been a principality, a republic, an independent kingdom, an Italian colony, a people's republic and now a democracy), or have changed their name (such as Southern Rhodesia, which became Rhodesia and is now Zimbabwe). There are stamps that reflect the economic upheavals of the past century and a half and those that mark civil wars, or were issued by occupying forces in wartime or as part of plebiscites to decide a country's future. Each continental section includes a thematic feature illustrating stamps that reflect the culture, art or history of a particular region.

Above, from left: After Germany became a federation of 32 states in 1849, many towns and duchies issued their own stamps, including Brunswick (in 1852), Bergedorf (1861) and Mecklenburg-Schwerin (1856).

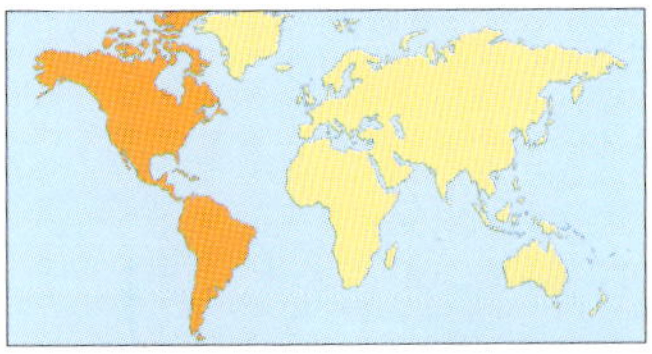

1

2

3

4

5

6

7

8

9

AMERICA

The American continent was quick to follow Britain in introducing adhesive stamps during the 1840s, and America took the lead in adopting pictorial stamps from the 1850s onwards. The continent's vast size and scattered population encouraged the early development of airmail.

CANADA

One of the world's largest countries, Canada was colonized by the French after 1534. Britain acquired Hudson's Bay, Newfoundland and Nova Scotia in 1713 and gained control of New France in 1763 after a decisive victory at Quebec in 1759. Thereafter, exploration and settlement extended British influence from coast to coast. Upper and Lower Canada (Ontario and Quebec) acquired self-government in 1837. They joined with New Brunswick and Nova Scotia in 1867 to form the Confederation of Canada; British Columbia (1871) and Prince Edward Island (1873) joined later, but Newfoundland was not admitted until 1949. Until recently all Canadian stamps were printed by the intaglio process.

Left: This stamp of 1927, celebrating the 60th anniversary of the Confederation of Canada, shows how much its territory had grown over the period since the union was formed.

BRITISH NORTH AMERICA

Before confederation, the individual British colonies issued their own stamps. Canada led the way in 1851 by separating its postal services from the General Post Office in London. In the 1860s stamps were produced for use on both Vancouver's Island and British Columbia [1], but these were followed by separate issues due to differences in the value of their currency [2]. New Brunswick's diamond-shaped stamps (1851) were followed in 1860 by a pictorial series that was quasi-commemorative, the 1c stamp celebrating the opening of the railway [3].

Newfoundland's first stamps were issued in 1857 [4], with square, upright rectangular and triangular stamps featuring the heraldic flowers of the United Kingdom. Pictorial stamps, with a penchant for royal portraiture [5], followed in 1865, and from 1898 onwards there were long scenic sets. Newfoundland's last issues (1947) before joining Canada celebrated the 21st birthday of Princess Elizabeth and the 400th anniversary of Cabot's sighting of "the new found land" [6].

Nova Scotia issued the world's first diamond-shaped stamps in 1851, beating New Brunswick by four days. The advent of the dollar in 1860 resulted in a series issued by the American Bank Note Company of New York with a full-face portrait of Queen Victoria [7]. By contrast, most of Prince Edward Island's stamps were rather crudely typographed in London [8].

A LITTLE BIT OF FRANCE IN NORTH AMERICA

When France ceded all its territory on the mainland to the British it retained the two tiny islands of St Pierre and Miquelon, off the coast of Newfoundland, as a base for fishing on the Grand Banks. French colonial general issues were followed by distinctive stamps in 1885, most of them with motifs alluding to the fishing industry [9]. In more recent times a wider range of subjects, such as scenery [10] and bird life, have been covered, reflecting the growing importance of tourism.

CONFEDERATION

The stamps of Canada introduced in 1851 were extended to the rest of the confederation from 1867 onwards. The dominion favoured portraits of Queen Victoria in a wide range that showed her at different stages throughout her long life. Her diamond jubilee in 1897 was the occasion for a set of 16, from 1/2c to $5, showing the Chalon portrait of 1837 and Von Angeli's bust of the 1890s [11]. The advent of imperial penny postage in 1898 gave rise to the world's first Christmas stamp [12] showing a world map with the territories of the British Empire coloured red. The history of Canada was charted by commemoratives, including a single stamp of 1917 for the golden jubilee of confederation [13]: this motif was reprised ten years later, along with others, for the 60th anniversary.

As with the issues of Newfoundland, a strong thread running through Canadian stamps is royal portraiture, notably for coronations, jubilees and royal visits [14]; to Canada belongs the only stamp ever to refer to Elizabeth II as Duchess of Edinburgh [15].

Stamps of 1951 and 1991 reproduced Canada's first stamp, the Threepenny Beaver. A long-running series consisted of pairs portraying former prime ministers [16]. Canada and the USA issued identical stamps for the opening of the St Lawrence Seaway in 1959, one of the earliest joint issues,

Below: Canada's first stamp inscribed solely in French marked the occasion of the Montreal Jazz Festival in 2004.

Works of Art

Since 1988 Canada has issued a large stamp each year reproducing an outstanding painting by a Canadian artist. These stamps are greatly enhanced by the use of gold or silver foil frames. The stamps have been produced in small sheets with descriptive text in the sheet margins, encouraging philatelists to collect them entire.

while the US bicentennial yielded a stamp portraying Benjamin Franklin, a reminder that he had been Deputy Postmaster General for the whole of North America [18].

Like the USA, Canada includes at least one stamp in the definitive range showing the national flag in various settings [17] but also has an alternative stamp at the basic domestic rate portraying Elizabeth II. Modern stamps are imperforate and produced in self-adhesive booklets. Canadian stamps were originally inscribed only in English, but from 1927 onwards they were regularly inscribed in French as well. Now stamps are captioned solely in French where relevant.

While it was once a conservative country with regard to stamp production, Canada broke new ground in 1994 with the world's first customized stamps, which offered the customer a choice of different circular labels to add to the basic stamp.

10

11

12

13

14

15

16

17

18

1

2

3

4

5

6

7

8

9

10

11

12

UNITED STATES DEFINITIVES

Although a New York private post had a stamp by 1842, and postmasters were authorized to issue their own stamps in 1845, it was not until 1847 that the US Post Office adopted stamps nationwide. At this time 5c and 10c stamps sufficed, and the USA chose portraits of Benjamin Franklin, the first Postmaster General of the United States, and George Washington, the "Father of His Country". Every definitive series from then until the 1970s portrayed George Washington, and he has seldom been far from the scene since. Benjamin Franklin was included in every series up to the set of 1970–4.

Left: George Washington on America's "Penny Black", the 10c stamp of 1847, based on a portrait by Gilbert Stuart.

DEAD PRESIDENTS

Thomas Jefferson, the third president, was also the third man to appear on US stamps, on the 5c stamp of 1856, but in the series of 1860–1 he had to vie with Franklin on two values and Washington on the other five. The necessity for a 2c stamp in 1863, for local letters, led to the admission of Andrew Jackson on one of the oddest American stamps of all time, with a full-face portrait that seems to overflow the confines of the design [2]. A 15c in grey-black was added in 1866 and portrayed Abraham Lincoln within months of his assassination [1].

BROADENING THE SCOPE

Franklin [3], Washington and Lincoln graced the 1869 series, which introduced the concept of pictorial motifs [4], including creditable attempts to reproduce historical paintings of the landing of Columbus (15c) and the Declaration of Independence (24c). This novelty was short-lived, and the following year reverted to the portrait gallery approach, with images of politicians Edwin Stanton and Henry Clay, Daniel Webster, General Winfield Scott, the lexicographer Alexander Hamilton and Commodore Perry.

ADVENT OF PHOTOGRAPHY

All the 1870 stamps bore profiles sculpted like classical busts, but in 1875 a 5c stamp was added to the series that bore a facing portrait of General Zachary Taylor taken from a daguerroetype. James Garfield, assassinated the previous year, was the subject of a 5c stamp in 1882, also derived from a photograph. Thereafter the classical profile gradually died out. In the series of 1890 only the three lowest values (1–3c) showing Franklin, Washington [5] and Jackson [6] and the two top values featuring Jefferson (30c) and Perry (90c) retained that style, while the six middle values (4–15c) were based on photographs. The only newcomers to this line-up were Ulysses Grant [7] and General Sherman on the 5c and 8c stamps. In 1894–5 the designs were modified and the opportunity was taken to add the fourth president, James Madison ($2) and the jurist John Marshall ($5), whose portraits were based on oil paintings.

For the new century definitive design took a backward step, setting the portraits [8] in very fussy frames, though the designs repay a second glance as Franklin on the 1c was flanked by allegorical figures holding electric light bulbs aloft. Newcomers included Admiral Farragut, hero of the recent Spanish–American War, and Martha Washington, the original First Lady, and first woman to appear [9].

There seems to have been a reaction against this surfeit of the great and good, for the definitives of 1912–22 were confined to profiles of Franklin

Non-portrait Definitives

Apart from portraiture, the series of 1975–81 (combining landmarks and symbols of the American Revolution with an assortment of musical instruments) and the coil series of 1985–93 (transportation from the Conestoga wagon to the school bus) have a strong thematic appeal.

and Washington. But by 1922 the public were ready for some variety and the series, which eventually ran to 23 stamps, ranged from the 1/2c [10] showing Nathan Hale (executed by the British as a spy in the War of Independence) to middle values portraying Teddy Roosevelt, William McKinley, James Monroe, Rutherford B. Hayes and Grover Cleveland [11], all of whom had died by that time.

The concept of portraying dead presidents reached its climax with the series of 1938–54, which portrayed every deceased holder of the highest office [12]. Furthermore, up to the 22c value, each president was portrayed on a stamp whose denomination accorded with his number. Above that, the presidents were shown in chronological order with their dates in office, ending with Calvin Coolidge on the $5 stamp. No doubt these stamps helped people to remember which president was which. Fractional values portrayed Franklin, Martha Washington and the White House.

PROMINENT AMERICANS

Dead presidents continued to dominate the 1954–65 series [13–14] but newcomers included General Pershing [15], Paul Revere [16] and Robert E. Lee, and from then on the presidential preference waned. To be sure, later series included Kennedy (1967) and Eisenhower (1970), but from that time the themes would be Prominent Americans (1965–81) [17–19], Great Americans (1980–94) [20–22] and the current series of celebrities that began in 2000 [23–24].

Since May 1978 the US Post Office has issued undenominated stamps at times when the domestic first-class rate is being increased, to cover an anticipated shortage of stamps showing the new rate. The earliest featured a stylized eagle and were lettered A–D (up to 1985) but later stamps had distinctive motifs whose initial letter followed the same code. Thus the increase to 25c in 1988 was covered by a stamp showing the Earth. When the rate rose to 29c in 1991 a Flower stamp was accompanied by a "make-up" stamp inscribed: "This US stamp along with 25c of additional US postage is equivalent to the F stamp rate."

Above: Old images of Washington and Jackson were re-used in a diamond format on the $5 stamp in the 1990s.

13

14

15

16

17

18

19

20

21

22

23

24

1

2

3

4

5

6

7

8

9

10

11

UNITED STATES COMMEMORATIVE AND SPECIAL ISSUES

The first set of adhesive stamps intended for temporary sale, as opposed to the permanent or definitive series, was issued in January 1893, partly to commemorate the quatercentenary of Columbus's arrival in the New World and partly to publicize the Columbian Exposition in Chicago. The set consisted of 16 values from 1c to $5 and cost over $16 in total, a colossal sum for that period.

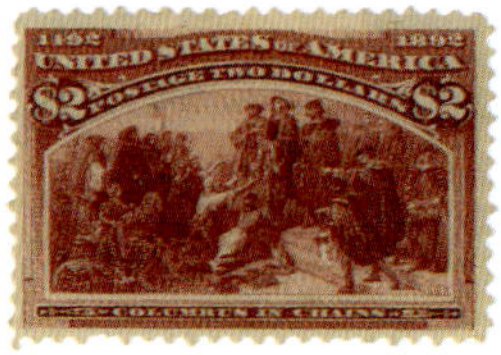

Left: The Columbian series traced the volatile career of Christopher Columbus.

EXPOSITION PUBLICITY

The Trans-Mississippi Exposition at Omaha in 1898 had a more modest nine stamps up to the $2 value [1], while the Pan-American Exposition at Buffalo in 1901 [2] had a mere six stamps, the highest value being 10c. The St Louis International Exposition, doubling up with the centenary of the Louisiana Purchase in 1904, rated five stamps (1c–10c); by the time of the Panama–Pacific Exposition in 1913 four low-value stamps sufficed [3].

The Jamestown Exposition (1907) rated only three stamps while the Alaska–Yukon–Pacific Exposition of 1909 had to be content with a single 2c stamp. Thereafter, most commemorative and special issues were singles [4], and the occasion had to be very special to merit more. In the 1930s there was a rash of small-format stamps celebrating the major anniversaries of the oldest colonies [5]. A return to expensive issues, last seen in the 1890s, came with the release in 1930 of three high-value stamps commemorating the Europe–Pan-American flight of the *Graf Zeppelin*, while the most prolific issue since the Columbian Exposition was a set of 12 for the bicentenary of the birth of Washington in 1932.

FARLEY'S FOLLIES

Most special issues before World War II took note of historic anniversaries or major current events, but in 1934 a set of ten featured scenery in some of the national parks [6]. The issue was quasi-commemorative as it coincided with National Parks Year, although this was not actually mentioned on the stamps.

This was also the era of the Farley Follies, when Postmaster General James Farley, currying favour with Franklin D. Roosevelt (an ardent philatelist), presented him with imperforate blocks of commemoratives. When word got out, collectors clamoured that what was good enough for the president was good enough for them also, and Farley was forced to release special printings. The 1935 American Philatelic Society Convention in Atlantic City was favoured with sheets of six of the stamp showing Mirror Lake and Mount Rainier. In 1936 the third International Philatelic Exhibition in New York saw a miniature sheet of four recent commemoratives in an imperforate block.

COMMEMORATIVE THEMES

A more frankly thematic approach was evident in the four stamps of 1937 showing scenery and landmarks in US territories [8] and reached its climax in the sets of five honouring heroes of the Army and Navy [9]. Sets of five in 1940 honoured famous Americans: authors, poets, educationalists, scientists, composers and artists – a series of 35 in all [7]. This concept was put to good use in the 1943–4 set of 13 showing flags of the oppressed nations [12].

Above: Imperforate stamps of 1934–7, released on the authority of Postmaster General James Farley, were nicknamed Farley's Follies by collectors, whose protests forced the US Post Office to make them generally available.

SOCIAL FOCUS

In the immediate postwar era single stamps were the norm [11], but their frequency accelerated and reached a peak in 1948 [13]. Stamps were issued not only to mark historic anniversaries and contemporary events [10] but, increasingly, to focus attention on social issues and groups – from gold-star mothers [15] to newspaper boys. Different aspects of the American way of life were the pretext for numerous stamps through the 1950s and beyond [14], and this notion of using stamps to raise awareness of important social issues continues to this day, from the "Register and Vote" campaign to concern for victims of AIDS and breast cancer in recent years.

As everywhere else in the world, a topical slant has entered the new issue policy [16–17]. The 1956 trio showing wild animals may have had the laudable objective of making the public conservation conscious but its thematic appeal was overwhelming. Similarly the set of six in 1960–1 showing quotations and autographs attracted topical collectors, although at the height of the Cold War its political message was its main objective. Sometimes the approach was more subtle: the stamp marking the Red Cross centenary in 1963 showed the Red Cross flag over the SS *Morning Light* – the ship that repatriated participants in the Bay of Pigs invasion of Cuba [18]. Most special issues are now self-adhesive [19].

Black Heritage

Protests that Black Americans had been neglected in US stamps led to the introduction of an annual stamp devoted to Black Heritage. Beginning in 1978 with Harriet Tubman, organizer of the "underground railway" for runaway slaves, the series has ranged from the civil rights activist Ida B. Wells to Jan Ernst Matzeliger, the inventor of the shoe-lasting machine, and W.E.B. Du Bois, founder of the Niagara Movement, precursor of the National Association for the Advancement of Colored People.

12

13

14

15

16

17

18

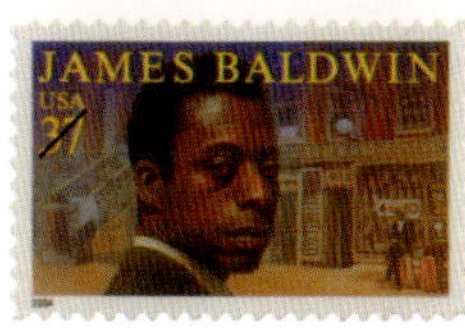

19

1

2

3

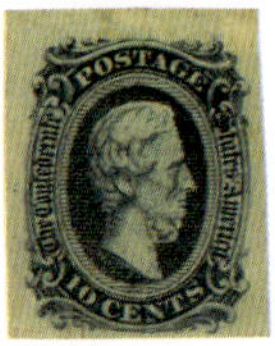

4

5

6

7

8

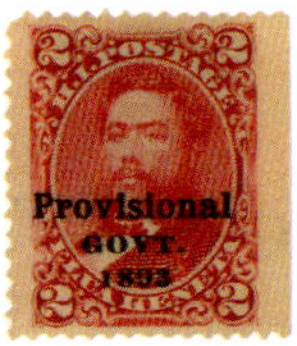

9

10

11

12

13

UNITED STATES POSSESSIONS AND TERRITORIES

A number of administrations, from mainland states and institutions to off-shore territories, formerly had their own stamps but are now part of the United States of America and employ the latter's issues. This includes even the extra-territorial post office of the United Nations, located in the head-quarters building at the eastern side of mid-town Manhattan, New York City. It should be noted that many similar stamps, inscribed in French or German, are used at the other UN post offices in Geneva and Vienna.

Left: To celebrate the 55th anniversary of the founding of the United Nations, stamps were issued in 2000 showing the headquarters building, both while under construction and at the present day. This stamp presents an unusual view looking southwards, with the East River on the left and Brooklyn in the distance.

CONFEDERATE STATES OF AMERICA

Eleven states seceded from the Union in 1861 over the vexed question of states' rights, with particular regard to slavery, and formed a federal republic under the title of the Confederate States of America. At first it was left to individual postmasters to furnish stamps to their own design. Many, such as the 2c stamp produced in Memphis, Tennessee, bore the name of the post-master rather than the town [1]. Other stamps, many unique or extremely rare, were crudely handstamped.

The first issues for general use were 5c and 10c stamps, printed by Hoyer & Ludwig of Richmond, Virginia; they portrayed Jefferson Davis [2] and Thomas Jefferson respectively. A supply of stamps was procured from De La Rue of London [3] – the only stamps of continental USA produced outside the country. Later stamps portrayed Jefferson Davis [4] and George Washington [5], a reminder that the Father of His Country had been a slave-owning Southern gentleman.

HAWAII

The Polynesian kingdom of Hawaii in the north central Pacific introduced stamps in 1851. Crudely typeset, they are popularly known as Missionaries as most of them were used by Christian missionaries to send mail back to New England: some stamps bore the inscription "H.I. & U.S. Postage". Stamps portraying Kamehameha III appeared in 1853, followed by a veritable portrait gallery of Hawaiian royalty, including Kamehameha IV [6], Kamehameha V [7] and Princess Victoria Kamamalu [8].

In 1887 King David Kalakaua [9] was forced to accept a Western-style constitution that curbed native power. When his successor, Queen Liliuokalani, attempted a coup to restore the old laws, American business interests overthrew the monarchy and proclaimed a provisional government. On 4 July 1894, the Republic of Hawaii was proclaimed [11]. The islands were annexed by the USA on 12 August 1898. During this interim period (1899–1900) Hawaii's very last stamp portrayed the statue of Kamehameha I [10]. Ordinary US stamps have been used in Hawaii since 14 June 1900.

SPANISH–AMERICAN WAR

During the war between Spain and the United States in 1898 the US occupied the Spanish territories of Cuba and the Philippines. American stamps were

From General Assembly to Stampex

Two stamps of 1958 depict Central Hall, Westminster, London, where the UN General Assembly met in 1946. For many years in the 1950s and 1960s the hall was the venue of Stampex, the British national stamp show.

overprinted for use during the period of military administration, after which the islands were handed over to the indigenous authorities.

The USA also captured the islands of Guam in the Pacific and Puerto Rico in the Caribbean, both of which were ceded to it by Spain. Apart from occupation by the Japanese in 1941–4, Guam was under the control of the US Navy until 1950. American stamps were overprinted from 1899 to 1901 [12] and ordinary US stamps have been in use since then.

Puerto Rico used Spanish colonial keytypes in the latter part of the 19th century [13–14]. Having been ceded to the US on 10 December 1898, it was under military administration until 1900. Contemporary US stamps were at first overprinted "Porto Rico" [15], followed by the correct spelling in 1900 [16]. Ordinary US stamps have been used since April 1900.

UNITED NATIONS

Distinctive stamps for the use of the United Nations Secretariat in New York City were introduced on October 24 – United Nations Day – 1951. Since then the UN has produced a prodigious number of stamps, mainly publicizing the work of its specialized agencies and promoting causes of international concern. The UN building itself appeared in the first series [17] and has been the subject of many stamps since then, either in splendid isolation [18] or in relation to the neighbouring skyscrapers of Manhattan [19]. Several stamps feature the interior [20] or the gardens, statuary and stained glass windows. Stamps of 1952 [21] and 1995 [22] commemorated the signing of the UN Charter in San Francisco, and featured the Veterans' War Memorial Building in that city.

In the early years a valiant attempt was made to inscribe every stamp in the five major languages of the world – English, French, Spanish, Russian and Chinese – but by the mid-1960s this had been quietly dropped and English predominated in the stamps issued by the office in New York.

By 1967 a more thematic approach was evident, and a long-running series was devoted to works of art donated by member countries. In 1980 the UN embarked on a series depicting the flags of the member countries. These were released in sheetlets of 16, each containing four different flags. This marathon series came to an end in 1989, the final flag being that of the UN itself, but the accession of new countries in the 1990s as a result of the fall of communism led to the issue of a further 24 flag stamps between 1997 and 1999. The latest series is devoted to endangered species of the world.

Below: In recent years the UN has featured sites on its stamps, and the set of 2004 focused on Greece to coincide with the Athens Olympics.

14

15

16

17

18

19

20

21

22

1

2

3

4

5

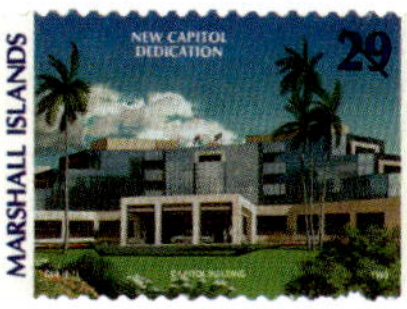

6

7

8

9

10

UNITED STATES TRUST TERRITORIES IN THE PACIFIC

Germany acquired a number of Pacific island groups towards the end of the 19th century. The first were the Marshall Islands, which it colonized in 1855, and in 1899, at the end of the Spanish–American War, Spain sold the Caroline Islands to Germany. At the same time, the Mariana Islands, which had been administered by the Philippines, were transferred by the United States to Germany in November 1899. All three groups remained under German control until 1914, when the Caroline and Mariana Islands were occupied by the Japanese. The Marshall Islands were captured by New Zealand forces but transferred to Japan at the end of World War I. The Marianas were captured by US forces in 1944 and the other two island groups fell into American hands at the end of World War II. All three were declared the United States Trust Territory of the Pacific Islands by the United Nations on 18 July 1947.

Self-government was introduced in 1979 in the Marshall and Caroline Islands. The former group retained its original name but the latter was renamed the Federated States of Micronesia. The following year the Palau group in the western Carolines separated from Micronesia and became a republic in January 1981. In 1986 all three territories entered into the Compact of Free Association with the United States, which remained responsible for defence and external relations.

Left: A joint issue of stamps by the Marshall Islands and Micronesia in October 1996 celebrated the tenth anniversary of the Compact of Free Association; both designs featured a sailing boat alongside their respective flags.

In the Caroline and Mariana islands, which were under German rule from 1899 until 1914, stamps were issued in the contemporary colonial keytypes [1–2]. The Marshall Islands used ordinary German stamps until 1897, when overprinted stamps were adopted. These were followed by the Yacht stamps in 1901 [3]. Ordinary Japanese stamps were later used, followed by American stamps from 1945 onwards, and examples of these with identifiable postmarks of the islands are now much sought-after.

MARSHALL ISLANDS

Postal independence was inaugurated in May 1984 with a celebratory block of four stamps, followed shortly afterwards by a definitive series featuring maps of the various atolls. Subsequent issues have been strongly thematic, with fish, birds and ships [5] featured. In the early years of the Marshall Islands' independence commemorative stamps were issued relatively infrequently and, in fact, stamps relating purely to the islands are few in number [4; 6]. This was more than balanced by the stamps that increasingly looked to the outside world.

In 1989 an ambitious programme was launched chronicling all the major campaigns and battles of World War II. The series eventually ran to 157 stamps, including portraits of the leading figures on both sides of the war [7]. More recent issues include a sheet of 50 showing American warships, from the USS *Alabama* to the USS *Wyoming* – one for each state – and stamps showing solidarity with the United States in the aftermath of 9/11 [8]. Historic ships are a recurring theme [9] for stamps, while figures such as Winston Churchill and Tsar Nicholas II have also been portrayed.

MICRONESIA

The inaugural issue consisted of a block of four showing maps of Yap, Truk, Pohnpei and Kosrae, the groups making up the Federated States of Micronesia, all formerly part of the Caroline Islands. At the same time a definitive series portrayed explorers and island scenes, notably the famous stone money of Yap [11]. A moderate policy of new issues was pursued at first, with most of the stamps devoted to subjects of island interest [10] or commemorating salient events in the islands' recent history [13].

In the early period the stamps were designed and marketed by the Crown Agents in England, and this was reflected in the use of British designers and European printers. In 1991, however, the contract passed to the Unicover Corporation of Cheyenne, Wyoming, which was already printing the stamps of the Marshall Islands. Unicover had its own printing facilities and employed mainly American designers, notably the father-and-son team of Paul and Chris Calle. This inaugurated an era in which popular themes such as fish, butterflies and flowers were the subjects of long sets, often released in sheets of up to 25 different stamps side by side. In 1993 Micronesia introduced a series devoted to pioneers of aviation portrayed alongside their aircraft [14], from the Wright Brothers to heroes of World War II. These stamps were issued in *se-tenant* blocks of eight and continued to appear at regular intervals until 1996.

In the following year the contract passed to the Inter-Governmental Philatelic Corporation of New York, and since then a much more prolific policy has been pursued. There is now a greater focus on events and personalities of worldwide significance, from Elvis Presley to Princess Diana.

Caught in the Act

To mark the Ameripex stamp show in Chicago (1986) Micronesia issued five stamps illustrating the life and crimes of Bully Hayes. In addition to murder and mayhem, he forged rare stamps of Hawaii, as shown on the 33c stamp. Incidentally, the forgery, like the genuine stamp, did not have perforations (as shown below right).

PALAU

This republic had a head start on the others, adopting its own stamps in March 1983. It has maintained a more prolific policy ever since. Successive definitive sets have featured marine life [12], flowers [15], birds [16] and insects. As a popular destination for Japanese tourists visiting the war graves, Palau has made a number of issues relating to its links with Japan [17], and its connection with the USA has yielded stamps featuring Ronald Reagan [18] and Operation Desert Storm [19]. Many sheets vividly illustrated every phase of World War II in the Pacific, notably the fighting over Peleliu in 1944. A self-adhesive die-cut stamp in the form of a Bai gable marked the republic's tenth anniversary.

Palau has been a client of the Inter-Governmental Philatelic Corporation since its inception, and although the flow of new issues was relatively modest in the early years it has greatly increased recently. Sheets of 25–40 different stamps have been prevalent from 1986 onwards, with increasing emphasis on stamps with immense appeal to collectors worldwide, from Disney characters to footballers.

11

12

13

14

15

16

17

18

19

NORTH AMERICAN INDIANS IN STAMPS

When Europeans penetrated North America at the beginning of the 16th century there were probably about a million Native Americans spread across what is now Canada, the USA and Mexico. By the end of the 19th century that figure had been halved, but after 1910 the Native American population began to recover. Driven off their ancestral lands by the encroachment of Europeans, many tribes ended up living on large reservations in areas of little interest or apparent use to the incomers, such as the Dakotas and the arid regions of the South-west.

The first Native American to appear on a US stamp was Minnehaha, the heroine of Longfellow's epic poem *Hiawatha* – and as that was the $60 newspaper stamp of 1875 it is unlikely to figure in most pictorial collections devoted to this theme.

The earliest stamp to show indigenous people in their own right was the 4c value of the set of 1898 publicizing the Trans-Mississippi Exposition. The first Indians to be identified by name on stamps were Powhatan and his daughter Pocahontas, whose microscopic effigies were worked into the framework of the 1c stamp of 1907 portraying Captain John Smith, marking the tercentenary of Jamestown. Pocahontas herself was portrayed on the 5c stamp, all dressed up in the height of Jacobean fashion as Smith paraded her in London.

While the low values of the 1922–32 US definitive series focused on famous Americans, and especially presidents, the 14c showed an unnamed American Indian in feather war bonnet. It later transpired that the image was derived from a photograph of Hollow Horn Bear, chief of the Brule Sioux. After

Above: Chief Hollow Horn Bear of the Brule Sioux (left) and an Indian Head cent on the definitive 13c stamp of 1978 (right).

Right: Pocahontas appears in Jacobean dress on a stamp of 1907.

Below: Blocks of four showing Pueblo decorated pots, 1977 (left) and shamanistic masks, 1979 (right).

Above: Traditional dances and beadwork patterns were featured in a booklet of five 32c stamps in 1996.

Above: Crazy Horse, Sequoyah, Sitting Bull and Red Cloud in the Great Americans definitive series, 1980–94.

that, Native Americans had a very low profile and appeared as minuscule subsidiary figures, such as the Indian woman standing respectfully behind the intrepid explorers on the Lewis and Clark Expedition stamp of 1954.

The turning point came in 1961 with the advent of multicolour intaglio. The first stamp to make use of the new Giori presses marked the centenary of Frederic Remington's birth by reproducing his famous painting *The Smoke Signal*. The first example of Native American art was a totem pole carved by the Tlingit of southern Alaska, chosen as the motif for the 1967 stamp marking the centenary of the purchase of Alaska from Russia.

In 1970 one of the four stamps in the set celebrating the centenary of the American Natural History Museum showed a Haida ceremonial canoe. The Haida, like the Tlingit, settled on the north-western Pacific seaboard, a reminder of the fact that the continent's indigenous races had originally come from eastern Asia across the land bridge up to 30,000 years ago. A 50c stamp of 1991 showed some of the earliest emigrants from Siberia arriving in Alaska.

In 1977 the first set devoted to American folk art concentrated on the applied arts of the Pueblo Indians, featuring decorated pots produced by the Zia, San Ildefonso, Hopi and Acoma peoples. In 1979 the series returned to Native American art with shamanistic masks of the Heiltsuk branch of the Bella Bella, Chilkat Tlingit, mainstream Tlingit and Bella Coola tribes of the north-west Pacific coast.

Two stamps of 1989 showed pre-Columbian carvings, a Mimbres ritual figure and the "Key Marco Cat" carved by Calusa Indians. In 1990 a booklet of five stamps featured war bonnets of the Cheyenne, Flathead, Comanche, Shoshone and Assiniboine tribes.

Left: Indian paddling Father Jacques Marquette's canoe, 1968.

The first Great Americans definitive series of 1980–8 included Crazy Horse, the Sioux leader, and the Cherokee chief Sequoyah, who appeared on the 13c and 19c stamps. The second series (1985–94) portrayed Red Cloud of the Oglala Sioux (10c) and Sitting Bull of the Hunkpapa Sioux (28c). The first Indian woman since Pocahontas to appear on an American stamp was Sacagawea, on a 29c stamp in the sheet of 20 showing Legends of the West, released in 1994. Chief Joseph of the Nez Perce and the Apache leader Geronimo were also featured in this issue as well as a stamp showing a montage representing Native American culture.

In 1996 a set of five in a *se-tenant* strip focused on Native American dances without assigning them to any particular tribes. In August 2004 a 2c definitive showed a silver and turquoise Navajo necklace, and in the same month a sheet of ten stamps was devoted to Native American art from the 11th century to about 1969.

Below: Indian carved figure, 1989 (left) and Remington's The Smoke Signal *(right).*

1

2

3

4

5

6

7

8

BAHAMAS, BERMUDA AND WEST INDIES

It is a popular fallacy that the Bahamas and Bermuda are in the West Indies: they actually lie well to the north of the Caribbean but philatelists put them in the same category as those islands. It appears that the first land sighted by Columbus in the New World was in the Bahamas, as celebrated by sets of stamps in 1942 and 1992. Of the islands grouped here, most are or were under British administration, but some – Curaçao, Aruba and the Netherlands Antilles – came under Dutch rule, while Guadeloupe and Martinique are now French overseas departments. The Danes sold their possessions in the West Indies to the United States in 1917 and they are now known as the American Virgin Islands.

Left: Although the Netherlands were overrun by the Germans in World War II, Curaçao remained in Dutch hands and issued stamps showing Queen Wilhelmina, Princess Juliana and Prince Bernhard with their daughters.

BAHAMAS

The Bahamas were a crown colony before attaining self-government in 1964 and becoming an independent member of the Commonwealth in 1973. Unlike most other colonies, the islands had distinctive stamps from their inception in 1859, including some pictorial designs from 1901. A favoured venue for political summit conferences between Britain and the USA [1], the islands have also become very popular tourist destinations and this is reflected in many issues of recent years highlighting everything from birdwatching to beaches [2–3]. The Bahamas contributed a squadron of Spitfires in World War II, recorded on several issues since 1990 [4].

BARBADOS

This crown colony, settled in the early 17th century, enjoyed autonomy from early times. Its first stamps, reproduced on centennial commemoratives in 1952, showed Britannia seated on sugar bags, a motif also used by Mauritius and Trinidad [7]. The old-world charm of Barbados comes across in designs using ancient landmarks [5], but its relaxed atmosphere is neatly conveyed by the Christmas stamps of 2003 [6].

BERMUDA

This island lies about 1060km/660 miles east of North Carolina. Like the Bahamas and Barbados it has long been a very popular resort for Americans. Stamps were introduced as early as 1848 and were struck by hand by the postmasters of Hamilton and St George's. More conventional stamps, printed in London, were adopted in 1865, but they did not conform to the usual colonial keytypes, except for the high values of 1918–52, portraying George V or George VI. This design, with the profile of Queen Elizabeth substituted, was revived for a $22 stamp in 1996 [8]. Modern issues are very much tourist-orientated, such as the series showing island souvenirs [9] or the idyllic scenery [10]. Many stamps issued since the 1950s have alluded to the settlement of the island by shipwrecked sailors.

TRINIDAD AND TOBAGO

Both islands had their own stamps until 1913. British stamps were used in Tobago until 1879, when a series portraying Queen Victoria was introduced [11], but Trinidad's *Lady McLeod* steamship stamp of 1847 was the first from any British colony in the Western

Bottle-shaped Stamps

Trinidad and Tobago issue very few stamps, but none was so spectacular as the set released in January 2000 to celebrate the 175th anniversary of angostura bitters, distilled from an aromatic bark and a popular ingredient of cocktails. The stamps, produced by Southern Colour Print of New Zealand, were self-adhesive and shaped like the bitters bottles.

Hemisphere, followed by the Britannia design in 1851 [7]. Bicoloured intaglio in the 1930s and 1940s [13] has now given way to multicolour lithography for stamps that illustrate island occupations and, of course, the local passion for cricket [14].

EUROPEAN COLONIES

The Danish West Indies consisted of the islands of St Croix and St Thomas and had stamps mainly in the prevailing Danish designs [12]. They remained valid for a few months after the islands were sold to the USA, and covers with mixed franking of DWI and US stamps are much sought-after.

The Netherlands Antilles comprised the islands of Curaçao and Bonaire, near to coastal Venezuela, together with the Leeward islands of St Estatius, Saba and part of St Maarten, the rest of which formed part of the French colony of Guadeloupe. Stamps inscribed "Curaçao" [15] were used throughout the Dutch islands until 1948, when the term "Netherlands Antilles" was adopted. A stamp of 1959 showed the sea-water distillation plant installed by Weir's of Cathcart, Scotland [16]. Until 1986 Aruba was part of the Netherlands Antilles but since then has enjoyed autonomy and its own stamps, which convey an unhurried lifestyle [17] as well as its popularity with cruise ships [18].

In the 17th and 18th centuries France and Britain fought for control of the Caribbean, and islands frequently changed hands until the end of the Napoleonic Wars. All that then remained in French hands were Guadeloupe and Martinique, two groups of islands in the Lesser Antilles. Guadeloupe comprised two large islands, Basse-Terre and Grande-Terre, together with some smaller islands and the northern part of St Martin (the rest of the island being in the Netherlands Antilles). Martinique was administered as a separate colony.

Originally both territories used the general stamps of the French colonies, but the first distinctive stamps appeared in the 1880s and consisted of provisional surcharges identified by the initials GPE or MQE respectively. In 1946 both colonies became overseas departments of France and their stamps were phased out two years later. They have used French stamps ever since.

Above: Island women and coastal scenery dominated the last definitive series of Guadeloupe (1947).

Below: Government House at Fort-de-France appeared on stamps of Martinique from 1933 to 1945.

9

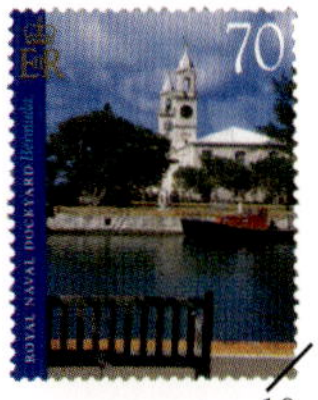

10

11

12

13

14

15

16

17

18

1

2

3

4

5

6

7

8

9

CUBA, HISPANIOLA AND JAMAICA

The three largest islands of the Caribbean comprise the republics of Cuba and Jamaica, with Hispaniola shared by Haiti and the Dominican Republic. Associated with Jamaica are its former dependencies, the Cayman Islands and the Turks and Caicos Islands. All these islands were originally under Spanish rule, but the French later colonized the western part of Hispaniola, while the British captured Jamaica in 1655. Dominican rebels tried to join Bolivar's Greater Colombia in 1821 but were thwarted by the Haitians, who invaded the eastern part of the island and occupied it until 1843. Cuba remained in Spanish hands until the war with the United States in 1898. After a period under American military administration (1899–1902) Cuba became an independent republic, though the USA retained Guantanamo Bay as a military base. Cuba became a socialist state on 1 January 1959, and a centre for Marxist subversion throughout Latin America.

Left: Major Ernesto "Che" Guevara, born in Argentina, trained as a doctor but joined Castro's revolutionary movement in Cuba, becoming finance minister. He left to organize revolutions all over Latin America, but was captured and shot in Bolivia in 1967. This stamp, celebrating Day of the Guerrilla, shows a map of Latin America, highlighting Bolivia.

CUBA

From 1855 to 1898 Cuban stamps conformed to Spanish colonial keytypes [1]. US stamps were briefly overprinted before a definitive series appeared in 1899 [2]. Many republican stamps honoured José Martí, father of Cuban independence [3]. After the rebels, led by Fidel Castro, seized power, stamps became heavily politicized, often making common cause with Vietnam or promoting Marxist ideology, an exception being the set of 1963 honouring Ernest Hemingway [4]. Stamps celebrated anniversaries of the abortive invasion of Playa de Giron, known in the US as the Bay of Pigs [5]. In recent years, however, the Marxist hard line has been played down and stamps have been much more thematic in character.

DOMINICAN REPUBLIC

Occupying the eastern and much larger part of Hispaniola, this republic almost went to war with neighbouring Haiti when the latter protested at the way the map had been redrawn on the definitive stamps of 1900 [6]. The boundary dispute was not settled until 1935, when Dominica's dictator General Rafael Trujillo brokered a deal [7].

The republic was an early exponent of bicoloured stamps, including a set of 1939 for the New York World's Fair, one of which showed the Trylon and Perisphere together with a projected lighthouse to mark the 450th anniversary, in 1942, of Columbus's arrival in the New World [8]. Like other Latin American countries, Dominica regularly issued compulsory tax stamps to raise funds for public works [9]. Since Trujillo's fall in 1961, stamps have become increasingly thematic.

HAITI

The world's first black republic was founded just after the French Revolution but was suppressed by Napoleon. With British help the Haitians threw out the French, and Jean-Jacques Dessalines proclaimed

Presidential Gallery

To mark the bicentenary of the US constitution in 1987 the Turks and Caicos Islands produced a series of sheetlets portraying every American president with a scene representing his time in office. Whereas presidents such as George Washington, Abraham Lincoln and John F. Kennedy have tended to hog the philatelic limelight, these little islands at last gave prominence to Millard Fillmore, Rutherford B. Hayes and others who had been largely forgotten.

himself emperor. Following his murder in 1806 the country split into a kingdom under Henri Christophe and a republic under Alexander Petion.

Stamps were introduced in 1881; the first, showing the head of Liberty, was followed by the national arms [10]. The centenary of independence was celebrated by two sets of 1904 portraying Toussaint l'Ouverture [11] and other patriots, and many later stamps depicted the impressive citadel of Christophe [12]. In recent years restrained intaglio has given way to gaudy lithography [13].

JAMAICA

The largest colony in the British West Indies, Jamaica had a postal service from 1671, using British stamps until 1860, when distinctive issues appeared. They followed the British colonial pattern, although a pictorial 1d stamp appeared as early as 1900. The definitives of 1919–21 took the colourful history of the island as their subject. Self-government was granted in 1945 and independence in 1962 [14], with Elizabeth II remaining head of state. Since then stamps have become much more colourful – not only the small-format definitives but also the special issues marking events of specifically Jamaican importance [16–17]. Even Christmas stamps are used to get across vital public messages [18]. The Jamaican dollar, adopted in 1969, remained fairly stable until the 1990s when it depreciated heavily. As a result, stamps since 1996 have been denominated in as many dollars as they were formerly in cents.

The Cayman Islands used Jamaican stamps until 1900, when distinctive issues were produced. Though best known today as a financial centre, the islands also rely heavily on tourism, reflected in the stamps. Stamps were issued by the Turks Islands from 1867 until 1900 [15] when they joined with the Caicos group (formerly under the Bahamas). Although stamps in joint names are still current, the Caicos Islands have occasionally had distinctive stamps since 1981.

Below: A high proportion of stamps from the Cayman Islands highlight the fauna and flora of the Caribbean, but the leisurely way of life also features.

10

11

12

13

14

15

16

17

18

1

2

3

4

5

6

7

8

9

BRITISH WEST INDIES

The islands generally grouped under this heading are scattered around the Caribbean and fall geographically into two main archipelagos known as the Leeward and Windward Islands. The Leeward Islands at one time formed a political union, consisting of Antigua and Barbuda, the British Virgin Islands, Dominica, Montserrat and St Christopher Nevis Anguilla. It was formed in 1871, putting into constitutional effect an informal federation dating from the 1670s. The Windward Islands, however, were always separate colonies. The West Indies, a major source of sugar for Britain, also assumed an important strategic role after the loss of its American colonies.

Left: Admiral Lord Nelson was commander of the West Indies station in the late 18th century and is commemorated to this day by the naval dockyard. It was from here that he set sail for his final decisive battle at Trafalgar in 1805.

LEEWARD ISLANDS

While each colony of the Leewards originally had distinctive stamps, a general issue was released in 1890 in the prevailing keyplate design. Stamps of this type, differing solely in the profile of the reigning monarch [1], continued until the federal union was dissolved on 1 July 1956. In 1903 the various islands, objecting to the loss of philatelic revenue, had resumed the issue of their own stamps, which were used in conjunction with the general series.

Antigua had its own stamps from 1862. Until 1982 they were thus inscribed [3], but since then they have also borne the name of its dependency Barbuda [4]. Stamps of the Leeward Islands overprinted "Barbuda" were briefly introduced in 1922 but Barbuda did not resume stamps of its own until 1968. A long series (1968–71) portrayed every British monarch since William the Conqueror [2], while stamps inscribed "Antigua & Barbuda" are now overprinted "Barbuda Mail" for specific use there. From 1979 to 1991 the uninhabited island of Redonda, forming part of this group, had prolific issues in its name that pandered to the most popular themes [5].

Dominica introduced stamps in 1874 and these continued in the usual colonial style until 1968, when the island was granted associated statehood and became more prolific and innovative in its issues, notably with the D-framed definitives of 1969 [6]. It became independent in November 1978, assuming the name of the Commonwealth of Dominica [7].

Montserrat's stamps date from 1876. At one time its sole claim to fame was the lime juice supplied to the Royal Navy to prevent scurvy (hence the American term "limey", originally applied to British seamen), but since 1971 it has acquired a reputation for prolific stamp issues, although these have been considerably moderated in recent years. Most issues are generally thematic [8] with a strong element of royal pomp and circumstance [9].

St Christopher [10] and Nevis [11] issued their own stamps from 1870 and 1868 respectively until 1890, then used the stamps of the Leeward Islands. When distinctive stamps were resumed in 1903 they chose the title "St Kitts-Nevis" for a joint series. After the island of Anguilla celebrated its tercentenary in 1950 its name was added to the title, which is now "St Christopher Nevis Anguilla" [12].

Following the grant of associated statehood in 1967, Anguilla agitated for independence and seceded that September, overprinting its stamps accordingly. Its secession was contested at first, but the dispute was resolved by placing Anguilla under a British Commissioner, hence the curious inscription [13]. Since June 1980 the other islands have had separate postal administrations, with stamps inscribed "Nevis" [14] and "St Kitts" [15].

WINDWARD ISLANDS

The Virgin Islands adopted distinctive stamps in 1866 and these continued to be thus inscribed until 1968 [16], when the epithet "British" was added to avoid confusion with the American Virgin Islands. Ironically, the US dollar (discreetly indicated on stamps by the abbreviation "U.S.Cy") has been the currency of the British Virgin Islands since 1962. Unusually for the West Indies, the islands' stamps continue to focus on local customs, marine life and flora, with a strong emphasis on the British royal family. A set of 1969 commemorated Robert Louis Stevenson, whose adventure story *Treasure Island* was set in the islands.

Grenada had a conventional philatelic history from 1861 to 1967, when it was granted associate statehood, but since then it has become one of the world's most prolific issuing countries, producing about 5,000 stamps by 2004. Many sets are produced in sheetlets of from 6 to 20 *se-tenant*, devoted to many subjects that have little relevance to the country, ranging from dinosaurs to American entertainers. The Grenadines of Grenada are almost as prolific, with separate issues

Below: The Virgin Islands paid tribute to the Princess of Wales (left), while Grenada honoured President Reagan's visit with an overprint (right).

Stamps for All Occasions

The smaller the Caribbean island, the more prolific the stamp issues. The Grenadines of Grenada and St Vincent rival each other in their bid to produce stamps for every conceivable occasion and celebrity. The islands that first put Michael Jackson and Madonna on stamps have even produced images of every team that reached the finals of the World Cup football championships in recent years.

for Carriacou and Petite Martinique that often cover the same topics as Grenada itself.

St Lucia began issuing stamps in 1860 and followed the prevailing colonial policy until it was granted associate statehood in 1967, followed by complete independence in 1979. Since 1983 it has liberalized its stamp policy, although there has been some attempt to maintain the integrity of stamps by a relative adherence to subjects of indigenous interest [17].

It pales into insignificance alongside St Vincent. Here, stamps in the colonial style were issued from 1861 to 1963, when the island was granted ministerial government and the stamp contract passed out of the hands of the Crown Agents to an American company. Complete independence was gained in 1979. Since then new issues have risen to several hundred each year. Equally prolific were the issues of the Grenadines of St Vincent (1973–94) [18], followed by the numerous stamps from individual islands Bequia, Canouan, Mustique, Union Island, Palm Island and the Cayes of Tobago.

10

11

12

13

14

15

16

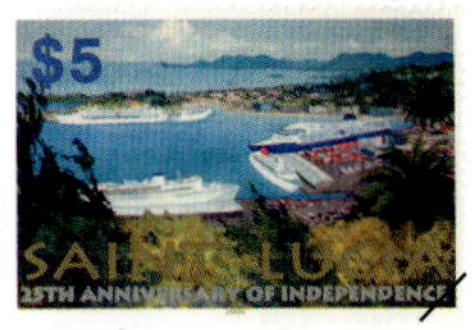

17

18

1

2

3

4

5

6

7

8

9

10

CENTRAL AMERICA

With a long and unenviable reputation for revolution, the countries of Central America were the original banana republics, with one-product economies largely in the hands of foreign (mainly US) investors. They share a common profile, characterized by a mainly impoverished population ruled by a handful of landowners with US business interests paramount, most notably over the development and operation of the Panama Canal. Not surprisingly, the character and subjects of their stamps often reflect their status as client states of the USA.

Left: President Jimmy Carter and President Torrijos of Panama signing the treaty that ceded the Canal Zone back to Panama in 1977.

COSTA RICA

The "rich coast" facing the Pacific began issuing stamps in 1863, and early issues tended to portray dead politicians [1]. Stamps overprinted for the remote province of Guanacaste were in use in the 1880s due to local currency differences [2]. Pictorial themes appeared in the 1930s, sport being a very early topic. Institutions such as Rotary [3] reflected the Americanization of the country. From 1947, when Roosevelt was honoured, the great and good of the USA were often portrayed, ranging from Father Flanagan, founder of Boys Town, on a children's charity set of 1959, to John Kennedy and John Kennedy Junior [4].

EL SALVADOR

The volcano of San Miguel appeared in 1867 on the first stamps of the country named in tribute to the Saviour [5]. The early stamps were often overprinted or surcharged for re-issue but more pictorial designs appeared in the 1930s. Some very attractive sets engraved by American and British firms appeared in the 1940s, notably the Roosevelt memorial issue of 1948, which comprised 12 stamps and two miniature sheets [6]. Stamps of more recent times have been lithographed in full colour and cover a wide range of topics, from sport to wildlife and scenery [7].

GUATEMALA

Another smoking volcano graced the arms stamps of Guatemala [8], adopted in 1871, but its most enduring image is the long-tailed quetzal. First appearing on stamps of 1881 [9], as a national icon it has been reprised on many issues down to the present time, usually in repose but sometimes in flight [10]. Philatelically one of the more conservative countries, Guatemala tends to stick closely to subjects of domestic interest. Such issues include several propaganda stamps laying claim to British Honduras (later Belize).

HONDURAS

The triangular seal of Honduras, with its sun rising over a volcano, formed the motif of the first stamps, issued in 1866 [11], but by 1878 the country had become infected with the craze for dead presidents [12], which continued until the 1930s. From 1946 onwards Honduras discovered a lucrative market in long sets honouring American heroes, starting with Roosevelt. The series of 1959 for the 150th birthday of Abraham Lincoln ran to 24 stamps and included his log cabin birthplace [13] and the Gettysburg address.

NICARAGUA

In the stamps of Nicaragua, from their inception in 1862, the smoking volcanoes really came into their own [14].

Presidential Visit

One of the few stamps to portray Bill Clinton during his term in office was this issue by El Salvador in 1999, marking his presidential visit to the republic. Both presidents, with their seals and flags, are depicted on this *se-tenant* pair.

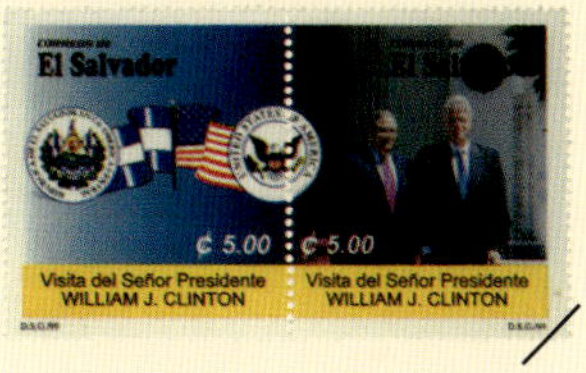

Unfortunately, the series of 1901 showing Momotombo issuing smoke [15] deterred the US Congress from its original plan to drive the canal across Nicaragua, and thereafter the Panama lobby triumphed. Among the non-political US celebrities honoured was the humorist Will Rogers, with a piece of subliminal advertising for Pan-American Airways for good measure [16]. Because of currency fluctuations, stamps were overprinted "B" (Bluefields) in the province of Zelayo [17] and in Cabo Gracias a Dios.

PANAMA

The most southerly of the republics was originally a province of Colombia and from 1887 it issued stamps thus inscribed but showing the isthmus of Panama. In 1903, when Colombia refused to lease territory to the USA for the construction of the canal, Panama declared its independence. The US Navy prevented Colombia from taking action and stamps were overprinted to blot out the Colombian inscriptions. Panamanian stamps grew lavish in their coverage of US subjects. This has been less noticeable since the fall of the Noriega regime and emphasis is now on modernization and social reform.

The canal was not opened until 1915 but from 1904 onwards stamps were overprinted or inscribed with the words "Canal Zone" [18]. Many of them portrayed the engineers who built the canal [19] or depicted its landmarks [20]. The US lease expired in 1999 and ordinary Panamanian stamps have been used since then.

BELIZE

The only British colony in Central America, British Honduras had its own stamps from 1865. Bicoloured pictorials showing local products and Mayan ruins appeared from 1938 until 1962, when a series featuring local birds was printed by multicolour photogravure. In 1964 the colony was granted self-government and was renamed Belize in 1973, the series then current being overprinted accordingly. Continual friction with neighbouring Guatemala (which laid claim to the colony) delayed the grant of full independence until September 1981.

Belize continues to pursue a conservative policy regarding new issues and the vast majority of them concentrate on subjects of indigenous interest. Its stamps are firmly rooted in the colonial past, with numerous issues featuring the British royal family. Among other themes, primary products such as logwood rank highly, but Belize is also proud of its status as the originator of chewing gum [21]. The Cayes of Belize, a chain of islands off the coast, had a typewritten local stamp in the 1890s and this seems to have inspired the "regional" stamps that appeared briefly in 1984–5.

Below: Oliver Stanley was one of the few British politicians to achieve philatelic recognition. The airport of British Honduras was named after him when he was Colonial Secretary.

11

12

13

14

15

16

17

18

19

20

21

COLOMBIA, ECUADOR AND VENEZUELA

Occupying the north-west corner of South America, these countries cover the area from the Atlantic coast to the equatorial region of the Pacific. Once part of the Spanish Empire under the name of New Granada, the region declared independence in 1813 and was united by Simon Bolivar to form the Republic of Greater Colombia, named in honour of the man who discovered it. However, it disintegrated in 1829–30 and the component states have been separate ever since.

Left: This Colombian stamp marked the 150th anniversary of the Spanish rout at Caribobo, which freed New Granada and led to the Republic of Greater Colombia.

1

2

3

4

5

6

7

8

9

10

11

12

COLOMBIA

Following the break-up of the short-lived republic, Colombia reverted to its old Spanish colonial name and by 1859, when its first stamps appeared [1], the country was a loose union of states known as the Granadine Confederation. Two years later it changed its name to the United States of New Granada and in 1862 adopted the name of the United States of Colombia [2]. It changed its name for the fourth and last time in 1886 to become the Republic of Colombia [3].

Relatively crude stamps were lithographed locally but from time to time Colombia went to the great American or British printers. The earliest attempt at a multicolour treatment was in 1947, when Waterlow of London printed a series featuring local orchids, combining intaglio with lithography [4]. Colombia was noted for stamps produced for specific services, such as the "Extra Rapido" service [5]. The vast majority of stamps pertain strictly to Colombia, with only the occasional nod at an international figure [6].

States Issues

The constitution of 1832 divided the country into 18 autonomous provinces, reduced in 1858 to nine. The federal government encouraged the provinces to establish their own postal services and all produced their own stamps at various times from 1865, but after 1886 this was gradually curbed and the last stamps were abolished in 1906.

Antioquia began issuing stamps in 1868 and although not the first to do so it was by far the most prolific, producing almost as many stamps as the other eight states combined. In the first decade the stamps concentrated on the state arms, followed by the head of Liberty in the 1870s and 1880s and finally a portrait of local hero, General Cordoba [7]. Bolivar was the first to adopt distinctive stamps, beginning in 1863 with a stamp showing the national seal that is arguably the smallest stamp ever issued. Later stamps bore a profile of Simon Bolivar, after whom the province was named [8].

Boyaca issued stamps only between 1899 and 1904 but in that short time produced the most varied of all the states issues: a medley of portraiture [9], heraldry and the monument to the Battle of Boyaca during the War of Independence. Cauca issued only two typeset stamps in 1902 [10] while Cundinamarca's stamps, issued from 1870 to 1904, concentrated on the national arms [11]. Heraldry was the principal feature of the stamps produced by Santander between 1884 and

1903 [12] and by Tolima from 1870 to 1904. Stamps were also issued by Panama from 1878 until it seceded from Colombia in 1903.

ECUADOR

At one time the Inca kingdom of Quito and later part of New Granada, Ecuador was liberated in 1822 but left Greater Colombia in May 1830 and was established as a republic, taking its name from the Equator, which runs through it. Stamps were introduced in 1865 [13], national arms being followed by presidential portraits [14].

The 1920s and 1930s were a period dominated by frequent overprints and surcharges. Design improved in the late 1930s and culminated in a set of 14 celebrating the 150th anniversary of the American constitution, recess-printed in New York in four colours – a tour de force for the time [15]. The American connection was reinforced a year later with a long set for the New York World's Fair and since then stamps have included the only one to show Vice President Nixon and one of the few to show little John Kennedy Junior saluting his father's coffin [16]. Nowadays, tourism is the most important industry, reflected in numerous stamps publicizing the Galapagos Islands and other attractions [17–18].

VENEZUELA

Columbus reached the north coast of South America in 1498 during his third voyage and named the region

Below: A stamp of Venezuela was issued in 1969 to mark the 150th anniversary of the Battle of Boyaca.

> **Cartographic Conflict**
>
> At various times since 1894 Venezuela has issued stamps laying claim to extensive tracts of neighbouring Guyana. A series of 1965–6 backed this claim by reproducing various maps published from 1775 onwards showing the disputed territory.

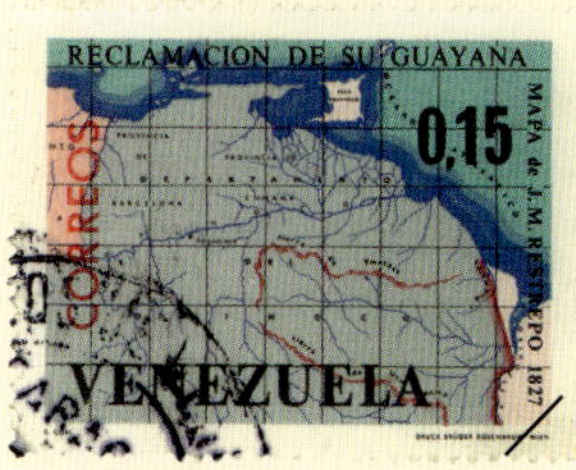

Venezuela (Little Venice) because of the numerous lagoons in the delta of the Orinoco. The first stamps were introduced in 1859 and showed the arms of the Venezuelan Federation.

The country changed its name to the United States of Venezuela in 1866 and stamps thus inscribed were released [19]. From 1871 to 1903 all but a handful of stamps portrayed Simon Bolivar [20]. Apart from a series of stamps issued in 1951–3, which featured the arms of the 24 provinces and ran to several hundreds, Venezuela has pursued a fairly modest policy, with a penchant for patriotic themes. It is interesting to contrast the restrained monochrome engraving of the stamps celebrating the centenary of independence in 1921 [21] with the multicolour lithography of recent years.

In November 1863 a Scottish entrepreneur, Captain Robert Todd, was awarded the contract to convey mail from Venezuela to St Thomas in the Danish West Indies (now the American Virgin Islands). Stamps depicting the SS *Robert Todd* and inscribed with all the names of the ports served were issued between 1864 and 1873. During the Civil War of 1899–1903 many local provisional stamps appeared.

13

14

15

16

17

18

19

20

21

1

2

3

4

5

6

7

8

9

10

BRAZIL AND GUYANA

Brazil occupies approximately half the continent of South America and is the only country in the Western Hemisphere to derive its language and culture from Portugal. It was discovered in 1500 by Pedro Cabral and settled in 1532. During the Napoleonic Wars, when João VI was driven from Portugal, he established his court in Brazil in 1808. In 1822, after his return to Portugal, his son Pedro I declared Brazil to be an independent empire, which continued until 1889 when Pedro II abdicated and a republic was proclaimed.

Left: One of several stamps issued in 1932 to celebrate the quatercentenary of the colonization of Brazil shows a map of South America with the Brazilian territory shaded.

BRAZIL: EMPIRE

Dom Pedro II succeeded his father as emperor in 1831, at the tender age of six, and reigned until 1889. When he was barely 17, Brazil became the first country in the world to follow Britain's example by introducing adhesive postage stamps, popularly known to collectors as Bull's Eyes on account of their circular shape. In 1943 stamps identical but for the inscription marked their centenary [1]. Dom Pedro appeared on stamps printed in New York [2], his beard becoming whiter as he advanced in years. Ousted by a military coup, he was exiled to Europe and died in Paris in 1891.

REVOLUTION AND REVOLT

Although its subsequent history was not as turbulent as that of many of its neighbours, Brazil had its share of rebellions in remote provinces, as well as occasional revolutions. A series of 14 stamps issued in April 1931 celebrated the revolution of 3 October 1930, with portraits of politicians and quotations from their speeches. Obscure at the time, they are well-nigh baffling today. Few now recall why Vargas said: "Rio Grande stands by Brazil", to which Pessoa responded, "I say No!" [3].

A revolt broke out in São Paulo in July 1932 and a provisional government was established. It was suppressed by federal troops on 2 October, but not before revolutionary stamps [4] had been issued. The United States of Brazil became a Federative Republic in 1946, but following a military coup in 1964 the country was a dictatorship until March 1985, when democratic government was restored. None of the later upheavals had any impact on stamps.

REPUBLIC

The vast majority of Brazilian special issues have been single stamps covering a wide range of topics and personalities. A strong feature is the issue of stamps marking visits by other heads of state, a tradition dating from 1920 when Albert, King of the Belgians, paid a visit. In addition to small-format definitives, Brazil has issued very tiny stamps for compulsory use to raise money for child welfare [5].

Most stamps are produced at the Brazilian Mint and the quality of production has improved considerably since the 1950s [6]. Symbolic motifs are frequently used and often demand a second glance [7–8], although the ban on drinking and driving could not be clearer [9]. At the same time there is considerable nostalgia for the past, as exemplified by the bilingual stamp recalling the age of steam [10] and the many stamps harking back to imperial glory [11].

GUYANA

The vast tract of territory on the north-west coast of Brazil, bordering with Venezuela, was colonized by the British, French and Dutch. The first stamps of British Guiana were the extremely rare Cottonreels of 1850. In 1898 the colony belatedly celebrated Queen Victoria's diamond jubilee with a set featuring local scenery [12]. A pictorial definitive series of 1934 included a portrait of Sir Walter Raleigh and his son [13]. British Guiana gained independence in May 1966 and adopted the ancient indigenous name, Guyana. Between 1981 and 1994 Guyana overprinted earlier stamps, yielding almost 3,000 different varieties. Since 1994 sanity has returned, although it still ranks among the most prolific stamp-issuing countries, with a predilection for popular themes [14–15].

The only French colony in South America, French Guiana lies between Brazil and Surinam. It formerly included the notorious penal settlement of Devil's Island, but nowadays the territory is better known as a base for European experiments with the Ariane space rockets. French Guiana began issuing distinctive stamps in 1886, when several of the French colonial general series were surcharged with new values and overprinted "Guy. Franc". By 1892 the general colonial stamps were being diagonally overprinted "Guyane", and these were shortly followed by the colonial keytypes inscribed with the name at the foot.

Below: Surinam was the first country to celebrate Commander Alan Shepard's sub-orbital flight of 5 May 1961.

Most Valuable Perhaps, but Not the Rarest

British Guiana is remembered philatelically for the unique 1c black and magenta stamp of 1856, which was reproduced on stamps of 1967. Though no rarer than any other stamp of which only one example is known, it was at one time the most valuable, having achieved a world auction record price of $935,000 in 1980.

A pictorial series, introduced in 1904, featured a giant anteater, a gold-miner and palm trees in the capital Cayenne; the series was followed by rather garish bicoloured stamps in 1929 and more attractive intaglio pictorials in the 1940s. A definitive series featuring the tricolour was printed in London for the Free French [16], followed by a series showing scenes of native life [17]. French Guiana became an overseas department of France in 1946 and ordinary French stamps have been in use there since 1948. The inland territory of Inini was separately administered and had its own stamps from 1930 to 1946 [18], when it was re-incorporated with French Guiana.

The Dutch colonized Surinam, which issued colonial keytypes from 1873 and later distinctive designs, especially after 1954 when it became an autonomous state. Since then stamps have honoured America's first astronaut, Alan Shepard, and the 30th anniversary of Amelia Earhart's flight to South America [19]. Surinam became an independent country in 1975 but the stamps have continued in the same style.

11

12

13

14

15

16

17

18

19

1

2

3

4

5

6

7

8

9

10

11

BOLIVIA, CHILE AND PERU

Much of the area occupied by these three republics once formed the mighty Inca empire, overthrown by the conquistadors led by Francisco Pizarro in 1531–3. Because of its immense mineral wealth the region became the most prosperous of all Spain's possessions in South America, and it was here that the struggle for independence was fiercest and most prolonged. War at sea eventually gained the countries' independence but it was another naval campaign, the Pacific War of 1879–85, that lost Peru her southern nitrate districts and Bolivia her access to the ocean.

Left: Victories on land by Simon Bolivar and José de San Martín were clinched by the defeat of the Spanish navy by the British naval commander Thomas Cochrane, 10th Earl of Dundonald. Unjustly convicted of fraud, imprisoned, disgraced and dismissed from the Royal Navy, he went to South America and used his considerable talents to secure the liberation of Chile, Peru, Brazil and later Greece. His exploits won him a pardon and reinstatement. Dying an admiral, he was buried in Westminster Abbey.

BOLIVIA

Released in 1867, Bolivia's first stamps featured a condor, symbolic of the Andes [1]. They were soon followed by allegorical and armorial designs recess-printed in New York [2]. In 1901 Bolivia switched to portraits of historical figures [3] but adopted pictorialism in 1916, with scenes of Mount Ilimani and Lake Titicaca [5]. Having lost its Pacific seaboard to Chile, it waged a stamp war with neighbouring Paraguay over the Gran Chaco [4]. Its claims to the Chaco Boliviano eventually led to the war of 1932–5, which left both countries on the verge of bankruptcy.

Many later stamps featured designs depicting the scenery, wildlife and culture of the Quechua Indians of the Altiplano [6]. Commemorative issues harked back to the battles of the War of Independence [7] but the Pacific War was best forgotten in Bolivia.

Like the other countries of UPAEP (the postal union of the Americas) Bolivia now issues stamps each year in the prevailing topic [8]. In 1986 the boliviano collapsed, resulting in hyperinflation. Since the currency reform of 1987 and the introduction of the new boliviano, the country's economy has been relatively stable.

CHILE

The longest of the Latin American countries, extending from the tropics to the sub-Antarctic, Chile is hemmed in between the Andes and the Pacific. Virtually all of its stamps portrayed Columbus from 1853 [9] until 1910. In that year the centenary of independence was celebrated by a long set [11] of which the highest denomination portrayed Admiral Cochrane. The admiral also appeared in ensuing definitive sets [10].

The Pacific War had been fought by Chile to gain access to the nitrate deposits jointly owned by Peru and Bolivia, and this valuable asset was the subject of many stamps in the 1930s and 1940s [12]. Commemoratives tended to concentrate on the struggle for independence, often tastefully recess-printed at the Chilean Mint [14]. More strident offset lithography tends to be favoured increasingly [15]. In the postwar period, Chile became embroiled with Argentina over rival claims to a slice of Antarctica, and this was a frequent subject for stamps.

Chile produced a set of four stamps in 1910 for use in the offshore islands of Juan Fernandez [13] and in more recent years has issued "regional"

Antarctic Rivalry and Co-operation

Both Chile and Peru followed Argentina's example and developed an interest in Antarctica in the years after World War II. While the stamps of Chile and Argentina became increasingly strident, with maps claiming the same territory, Peru's involvement was much more low key. Eventually the Antarctic Treaty of 1988, to which they all subscribed, took the heat out of the situation. They have since tended to co-operate in scientific research.

stamps for Easter Island, which is now a major tourist attraction.

The overthrow of the democratically elected Marxist President Salvador Allende in 1973 ushered in an era of military dictatorship under General Augusto Pinochet, but stamps of this period studiously avoided political controversy. After Pinochet was ousted in 1989, a more liberal policy ensued and a number of stamps portrayed the writer Pablo Neruda (who had been exiled) as well as Allende himself.

Although Chile pursues a relatively moderate policy with regard to new issues, in 1996 it released a set of 60 stamps each warning against a specific accident – in the home, on the roads, at school and in the workplace, as well as warnings on alcohol and drug abuse and hints on safety in leisure activities.

PERU

Pending the introduction of its own stamps [18] in 1858, Peru made use of freight labels supplied by the Pacific Steam Navigation Company. From 1866 most Peruvian stamps were recess-printed by rival New York firms. After the Chilean occupation in 1881 stamps were overprinted with the Chilean arms [16]. When President Morales Bermudez died suddenly in 1894, shortly before his term of office expired, stamps were overprinted with his portrait as a mark of respect [17]. These are arguably the first mourning stamps to be produced by a government postal administration (as opposed to the German private posts in 1888).

Peru was one of the first countries to adopt photogravure, in 1924, and throughout the 1930s many fine examples from England were released, notably the long series celebrating the quatercentenary of Lima in 1935 [20]. Since World War II, however, most stamps have been lithographed locally. Co-operation with other Latin American countries is a recurring theme [21], along with frequent references to the region's pre-Columbian civilizations. Boundary disputes with Chile and Bolivia [19] still fester and have several times brought Peru to the brink of war with her neighbours.

Below: This se-tenant *pair of stamps was issued in 1992 mainly for tourists' postcards from Easter Island, but is also valid on mail from mainland Chile.*

12

13

14

15

16

17

18

19

20

21

1

2

3

4

5

6

7

8

9

10

ARGENTINA, PARAGUAY AND URUGUAY

These three countries, lying south of Brazil, were first visited by Spaniards in 1512–20 but were not colonized until the late 16th century and were still relatively undeveloped when they threw off the Spanish yoke in 1810–11. Argentina and Uruguay lie on opposite sides of the River Plate, while Paraguay is one of South America's two landlocked countries, lying north-west of its neighbours.

Left: The Battle of Maipu in 1818 marked the turning point in the struggle for independence from Spain. Having liberated Argentina, José de San Martín crossed the Andes to free Chile and Peru.

ARGENTINA

Three of the Argentine states had their own stamps in the 1850s, those of Buenos Aires featuring a steamship. Cordoba [1] had an armorial design but Corrientes blatantly plagiarized the Ceres stamps of France. General issues for the Argentine Confederation [2] were issued in 1858–60, followed by stamps of the Republic [3]. Argentina stuck to dead heroes and presidents until the 1930s, San Martín predominating, but had the distinction of producing the first commemorative stamps in the Western Hemisphere in October 1892 to celebrate the quatercentenary of the first voyage made by Columbus [5]. Between 1913 and 1938, stamps were overprinted for the use of eight separate government departments [4].

A set of 25 marked the revolution of 1930 [6], the first of many issues that reflected the turbulent politics of Argentina in later years. Other stamps looked back to the heroic struggle for independence [7] or pursued the government's long-running battle with Britain over the Falkland Islands and territory in Antarctica [8].

PARAGUAY

This landlocked country had the misfortune to be ruled by a series of tyrannical dictators, the last of whom declared war on Argentina, Uruguay and Brazil (1864), almost destroying Paraguay as a result. The first stamps appeared in 1870, the year this disastrous war ended [9]. History repeated itself when Paraguay became involved in a dispute with Bolivia over the Gran Chaco. A war fought in the stamp album with rival map stamps [10] escalated into bloodshed in 1932–5; this time Paraguay won a Pyrrhic victory.

In the 1930s and 1940s many stamps were printed in England [11] but after World War II American printers predominated [12]. Relations with Argentina improved in the 1950s and stamps portraying the two dictators, Stroessner of Paraguay and Peron of Argentina, set the seal on this [13].

Since 1962 Paraguay has issued a prodigal number of stamps, from space research [14] to nude paintings [15], of little relevance to the country itself.

Below: Stamps issued by Buenos Aires in the 1850s bore a steamship, hence their nickname of Barquitos ("little ships").

URUGUAY

In the 17th century this region on the east bank of the River Plate was fought over by Spain and Portugal, and when Spanish supremacy was smashed in 1810 local hero José Artigas tried to create a separate state, known as the Banda Oriental. To maintain independence Artigas had to fight Spain, Buenos Aires and the Portuguese. In 1825 Brazil and Argentina went to war over the disputed territory, and the matter was resolved only when Britain intervened to force the belligerents to recognize Uruguay's independence in 1830. Uruguay, which won Olympic soccer gold medals in 1924 and 1928, hosted the first World Cup in 1930 and celebrated the centenary of independence by winning the trophy.

Uruguay's first stamps, introduced in 1856, are popularly known as the Montevideo Suns. They were followed in 1866 by a series in which the numerals were the dominant feature [16]. The full title República Oriental del Uruguay means "republic on the east bank of the River Uruguay", and it appeared on many later stamps. Unlike most Latin American countries, which followed the US fashion for presidential portraiture, Uruguay preferred allegorical subjects [17] and historical vignettes, either lithographed locally or recess-printed in England. In recent years a more symbolic approach has been adopted, with designs rendered in a semi-abstract poster style. Visits from heads of state of many countries, from France and Italy to Israel [18], have been a fertile source of stamp designs, bolstering Uruguay's sense of its global importance.

Occasionally Uruguay has issued stamps and miniature sheets whose validity has been cast into doubt because they were not on general release in post offices. These include the sets marking the Montreal Olympics, the 30th anniversary of the United Nations and the Apollo-Soyuz joint space mission (1975), and the Nobel laureates, World Cup football championship, Lindbergh, Rubens and Zeppelin sets (1977). Apart from these lapses a fairly modest policy has been pursued, confined mostly to single stamps.

Below: One of a series showing historic engravings of Montevideo (top) contrasts with the poster style of the 1990 stamp honouring the Engineer Corps (bottom).

Land of Fire and Gold Dust

The island of Tierra del Fuego at the southern tip of Latin America was discovered by Magellan in 1520 as he rounded Cape Horn, and named "Land of Fire" by him from the bonfires of the natives. Argentina and Chile partitioned the island in 1881 and six years later Julius Popper established goldmines in both parts. Mail taken to Punta Arenas in Chile bore a 10c stamp – representing neither Chilean nor Argentinian currency but centigrams of gold dust.

11

12

13

14

15

16

17

18

1

2

3

4

5

6

7

SOUTH ATLANTIC ISLANDS

Dotted around the South Atlantic are several remote island groups, the last remnants of the British Empire, consisting of the Falkland Islands and St Helena, with the dependencies of South Georgia and the South Sandwich Islands (to which is appended British Antarctic Territory) on the one hand, and Ascension and Tristan da Cunha on the other. The Falklands, which have been in British hands since 1833, have relied on sheep-farming, and St Helena has been a coaling-station. Only Ascension, with its communications and NASA installations of recent years, has real importance today. The Falklands and South Georgia were invaded and occupied by Argentina in 1981, precipitating war with Britain.

Left: Following the liberation of the Falklands and South Georgia, £1 stamps featuring maps of the islands were sold at a premium of 100 per cent in aid of the reconstruction of the islands. Such a high premium was contrary to UPU guidelines.

FALKLAND ISLANDS

The stamps of the Falkland Islands departed from the usual British colonial pattern in having distinctive designs, even though they stuck rigidly to the tradition of royal portraits. In 1929 a definitive series was introduced with a profile of George V over a tiny vignette of a fin whale and gentoo penguins, but it was not until 1933, with a long series celebrating the centenary of the British colony, that bicoloured intaglio pictorials were adopted. This remained the norm until 1968, when multicolour photogravure became fashionable. The stamps of recent years have sometimes referred to the war with Argentina [1], but birds and seals continue to be the dominant subjects [2], with occasional scenes of island life [3] and visiting ships.

FALKLAND DEPENDENCIES

Although a small undated stamp inscribed "South Georgia" (intended to be marked on letters below the postage stamp) was occasionally used to cancel mail to these territories, it was not an overprint in the true sense. The first stamps of South Georgia, with similar sets for the South Orkneys [4], South Shetland and Graham Land, were issued in 1944, followed by a general series in 1946. In 1954 a pictorial definitive series featured scientific ships that had been associated with the area.

Stamps of the Falkland Islands Dependencies were replaced in 1963 by separate issues for British Antarctic Territory and South Georgia [5]. Stamps inscribed for the former remain in use, but from 1980 to 1985 South Georgia reverted to stamps of the Falkland Islands Dependencies. In 1985 it and the South Sandwich Islands ceased to be dependencies of the Falkland Islands and began issuing stamps bearing their joint names [6].

British Antarctic Territory has issued stamps continuously since 1963. The Silver Jubilee stamps of 1977 alluded to the time spent in the region by the Duke of Edinburgh, unusually portraying him bearded [7]. Other stamps allude to the area's wildlife [8] and the work of the scientific research stations.

ST HELENA

Blue stamps denominated 6d were introduced in St Helena in 1856, but between 1864 and 1880 they were printed in different colours and surcharged accordingly for use as various values from 1d to 5s. In later years the colonial keytypes were used, although some pictorial designs appeared from

1903 onwards. As in the Falklands, the centenary of the crown colony in 1934 was celebrated by a long set of bicoloured intaglio pictorial stamps, establishing a precedent for later issues. Multicolour photogravure was adopted in 1961 [9]. Apart from some stamps alluding to Napoleon's exile, most recent issues have been preoccupied with island scenery and flowers [10]. Stamps in support of the Hong Kong stamp show of 1994 featured islanders' pets, and a wide range of other topics includes sea slugs and medical scientists. The stamps celebrating Elizabeth II's silver jubilee in 1977 showed the royal family visiting the island [11].

ASCENSION

This remote island was an outpost of the Royal Navy and used ordinary British stamps until 1922, when overprinted St Helena stamps were adopted, followed by a pictorial series in 1934. It has since followed the same pattern, issuing more colourful stamps since the 1960s. Many issues refer to its importance as a communications centre, the 1986 Christmas stamps appropriately including an image of George V making the first royal Christmas broadcast for the BBC [12]. Scenery, bird life and landmarks [13] provide the staple fare for its stamps.

Above: The garden on Green Mountain featured on a 1975 stamp marking the 160th anniversary of British settlement.

Below: Base B and the postmark of Deception Island appear on a British Antarctic stamp.

Ducal Connections

The "capital" of Tristan da Cunha is called Edinburgh, named in honour of Prince Alfred, the first Duke, who visited the island aboard HMS *Galatea* in 1867.

TRISTAN DA CUNHA

Named after the Portuguese navigator who discovered it in 1502, Tristan da Cunha remained a desert isle until Napoleon was exiled to St Helena. Its garrison was evacuated in 1816 leaving behind Corporal Glass, who became the patriarch of the little community.

Stamps of St Helena with an overprint were introduced in 1952, followed by pictorial issues that reflect the scenery and wildlife [14] or mark the few historic events, such as the evacuation in 1961 following the eruption of the volcano, or the visits of scientific expeditions [15]. While its first stamps were overprints on those of St Helena, the position was briefly reversed on 12 October 1961, when a quantity of Tristan stamps held in St Helena was overprinted "St. Helena Tristan Relief" and surcharged in sterling (although the stamps were denominated in South African cents). Only 434 complete sets were sold (mostly to passengers of a visiting liner) before the issue was suppressed.

8

9

10

11

12

13

14

15

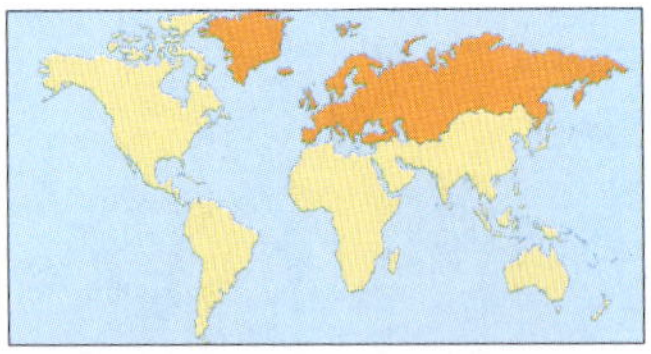

EUROPE

The European contribution to philately is immense: it includes the first adhesive (1840), bicoloured (1843) and pictorial stamps (1845), as well as many technological advances, from intaglio in the 1840s and photogravure in 1914 to holographic stamps (1988) and heat-sensitive inks (2001).

WESTERN SCANDINAVIA

As a collective name for the countries of north-western Europe, Scandinavia is often used to include not only Denmark, Norway and Sweden but also Finland and the North Atlantic islands colonized by the Vikings in the Middle Ages: the Faroes, Iceland and Greenland. The Vikings were hardy seafarers who penetrated even North America around AD 1000; in the early 11th century Cnut (Canute), king of Denmark and Norway, also ruled England. In 1397 Queen Margrethe I united Norway, Sweden, Iceland, Greenland and Finland under the Danish crown, a union that lasted until 1523, when Gustavus Vasa drove the Danes out of Sweden. In the 17th century Sweden was the greatest power in the Baltic, but its expansion into Russia was checked in 1709 and a century later it was forced to cede Finland to the tsar. Norway remained part of Denmark until 1814, when it was transferred to Sweden, but in 1905 the Norwegian parliament voted for independence, electing a Danish prince as Haakon VII. Iceland became a republic in 1944.

Left: The eruption of Hekla in Iceland in 1948 was marked by a set of seven stamps showing different views of the volcano.

1

2

3

4

5

6

7

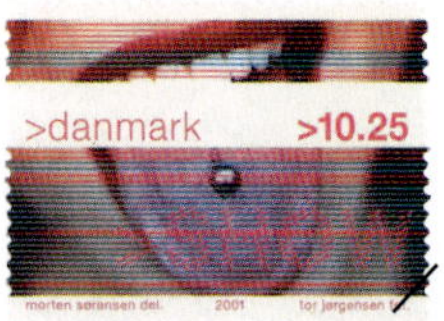

8

9

10

DENMARK

The first of the Scandinavian countries to adopt stamps, Denmark's first issue consisted of the 2rbs and 4rbs (rigsbank skilling) stamps – small, square with a security underprint [1]. A feature common to the main Scandinavian countries is the use of a numeral motif for the low-value stamps that is retained in use for many years. The Danish waves design [2] has been in use, with modifications, since 1905. The first commemoratives appeared in 1920 to celebrate the recovery of Northern Slesvig from Germany [3]. The Nordic countries preferred a small format for special issues, such as the set marking the 400th anniversary of the Reformation in 1936 [4].

From 1953 to 1956 Denmark celebrated its millennium as a kingdom with ten stamps, one for each century. The top value [5] showed the memorial to the war of 1864, in which Denmark was defeated and lost Slesvig to Prussia. Stamps honouring the Red Cross in 1966 bore the titles of international Red Cross organizations in 32 languages, plus a Latin motto – the largest number of different languages on a single stamp up to that time [7]. The postal printing works has continued to use intaglio to this day, but in recent years multicolour lithography has also been employed effectively, as in the stamps celebrating the silver jubilee of Margrethe II [6] and the Youth series, which included a close-up of a tongue with a stud in it [8].

NORWAY

Both Norway and Sweden introduced stamps in 1855 but while Norway portrayed King Oscar of Sweden [9]

Sweden preferred armorial designs. Both countries would later follow the same pattern as Denmark, using a numeral motif for the lowest values and heraldic design for the middle denominations and a portrait of the monarch on the high values. This meant that the only stamps that needed to be changed at the outset of each new reign were the relatively little-used high values.

For the most part Norway preferred the cheap letterpress process, reserving intaglio for the occasional high-value commemorative, but in 1928 the contract passed to Emil Mostue, who used lithography for a short period before introducing photogravure. This was used most effectively in the tourist propaganda series of 1938 [11] and the Queen Maud charity set of 1939 [12].

Both Denmark and Norway were overrun by Nazi Germany in 1940. While Christian X remained in Copenhagen to raise the morale of his people, Haakon VII went to Scotland to regroup his forces there. In Norway the Germans installed Vidkun Quisling [13], whose name has become a byword for treachery; the date on the stamp was that on which he was asked to form a government. The definitives were overprinted with a large letter V for Victory [14], but this boomeranged when the Resistance painted the slogan "Vi Vil Vinne" (We will win) on roads, a scene depicted on one of the stamps issued by the Norwegian government in exile [15].

Increasing use of multicolour lithography has brightened the appearance of Norwegian stamps in recent years [16]. The inauguration of the National Junior Stamp Club in 1997 was marked by two stamps crammed with different thematic subjects [10].

DANISH POSSESSIONS

Iceland had been a Danish colony since Viking times and its earliest stamps [17] were closely modelled on those of the mother country. In December 1918 it was declared an independent kingdom under Christian X but it became a republic in 1944. Since 1938 many of its stamps have featured geysers and glaciers [19], the volcanic destruction of Heimaey and the birth of the island of Surtsey.

Greenland had free postage until 1938, though parcels had to bear special stamps [18]. During World War II, when stamps were unavailable from Denmark, a series was recess-printed by the American Bank Note Company. Since 1950 Greenland's stamps have followed the Danish style but reflect the culture and traditions of the Inuit population. Bilingual inscriptions have been in use since 1963.

The Faroes had the unusual distinction of their own provisional stamps during World War II but did not get a permanent series until 1975 [20]. Since then the stamps have continued to depict the extraordinary scenery of these islands.

Record Longevity

The posthorn design of Norway's low values was introduced in 1871 – and is still in use. Over the years it has changed currency (1877), lettering (1893) and printer several times, and switched from letterpress to photogravure (1934), then intaglio (1962) and multicolour lithography (1997). Norway even celebrated its centenary with a pair showing the 3sk of 1871.

11

12

13

14

15

16

17

18

19

20

1

2

3

4

5

6

7

8

9

10

EASTERN SCANDINAVIA

Sweden was the dominant Baltic power from the Middle Ages to the end of the 17th century. Sverker I (*c.* 1134–56) united the Swedes and the Goths, and his crusade to Christianize the pagan Finns marked the beginning of the Swedish conquest of Finland. The Union of Kalmar (1397) united Denmark, Norway and Sweden under one ruler, but in 1520 the Swedish noble Gustavus Vasa raised a revolt against the Danish king that restored Swedish independence. Under his successors Sweden extended its rule over the whole of Finland and south of the Baltic. Sweden's power was checked when Poland, Denmark and Russia combined against Charles XII in a long war (1700–20), as a result of which it lost Estonia, Livonia and Ingermanland. Finland and the Aland Islands were ceded to Russia in 1809.

Left: Since 1956 the Nordic countries have issued stamps in uniform designs to symbolize their close postal co-operation. In 1967 the subject of these stamps was the Nordic House in Reykjavik, Iceland.

FINLAND

Until 1917 Finland was a Russian grand duchy and its early stamps were inscribed in both Cyrillic and Roman alphabets [1]; later issues were trilingual, with the name of the country in Russian, Finnish and Swedish [2]. When russification was at its height at the turn of the 20th century the stamps were identical to the Russian series [3], apart from the currency (the markka, divided into 100 penniä). Finland's first independent stamps were designed by its leading architect, Eliel Saarinen [4].

Most stamps were recess-printed in single colours [5] until 1966, when multicolour lithography was adopted [6]. Annual issues for the Red Cross and anti-TB campaign followed the same trend, with themes reflecting Finnish scenery and wildlife [7].

Most definitive issues since 1917 are in a small upright format and depict the lion rampant, a device seen on the tombs of the Vasa kings of Sweden. These have varied from time to time and designs featuring scenery and landmarks have been favoured for the high values [8]. Stamps portraying Marshal Gustav Mannerheim were overprinted for Eastern Karelia, occupied by the Finns from 1941 to 1944 [9].

ALAND ISLANDS

The Aland Islands in the Baltic were ceded to Russia in 1809. Of immense strategic importance, their great fortress at Bomarsund was destroyed by an Anglo-French fleet in 1854 and the islands were demilitarized and declared neutral. The mainly Swedish inhabitants were granted autonomy in 1922.

Regional stamps were introduced in 1984 [10] but since January 1993 the Aland postal service has been completely independent. Its stamps concentrate on the islands' scenery and distinctive culture, with a popular annual issue featuring island churches [11]. Their endearingly homespun character is reflected in genre scenes of island life. A beauty contest for cats in 2003 to elect "Missy Aland" resulted in the winners, Tovis [12] and Randi, being portrayed on a couple of stamps.

SWEDEN

Adhesive stamps were introduced in July 1855 and showed arms or numerals [13], a tradition continued in the low-value definitives to this day. No portrait of the king appeared until 1885, when Oscar II was shown on the higher denominations [14]. In 1920 stamp production passed from private firms to the Stamp Printing Office and Swedish stamps were subsequently recess-printed [15] in booklets or coils, distinguished by the lack of perforation on one or more adjoining sides, or two opposite sides [16] respectively.

Sweden was the home of Alfred Nobel, the armaments millionaire who created the prizes named in his memory. He himself appeared on stamps of 1946 to mark the 50th anniversary of his death, and in 1961 Sweden began issuing a set each year portraying the Nobel laureates since 1901 [17].

A joint issue with Finland in 1967 publicized Finnish settlers in Sweden and Swedish settlers in Finland. Each country issued two stamps symbolizing solidarity, designed by Pentti Rahikainen and lithographed at the State Bank Note Printing Works in Helsinki [18]. Since this major turning point Swedish stamps have been much more colourful, increasingly employing offset lithography. At the same time their scope has widened considerably, from rock 'n' roll [19] to the endearing charm of Carl Larsson's paintings [20].

The Greatest Master of Line Engraving

In 1960 a young Polish engraver named Czeslaw Slania began work at the Swedish Stamp Printing Office. Over the ensuing 45 years he engraved more than 1,000 stamps for his adopted land and many other countries (including the UK and USA). Universally recognized as the maestro of portrait engraving, in 1991 he was accorded the singular honour of a souvenir sheet as a 70th birthday tribute – which he engraved himself. Although at the time that was his greatest masterpiece, he surpassed it in March 2000 with this magnificent work, his 1,000th stamp engraving. Appropriately, he reproduced the painting *Great Deeds of Swedish Kings* by the 17th-century artist David Klöcker Ehrenstrahl.

11

12

13

14

15

16

17

18

19

20

VIKINGS IN STAMPS

The word "Viking" came to be synonymous with "warrior", but it originally meant "bay people" and alluded to those who came from the inlets and fiords of western Norway and terrorized all of Europe between 780 and 1050. The image purveyed by the monastic chronicles – of bloodthirsty murderers and ruthless pillagers of Christendom – dies hard, but Viking history has now been substantially revised. Their influence in Britain is evident in place names from Ipswich and Harwich in the south to Lerwick and Haroldswick in Shetland.

Today, the Vikings are depicted in a more positive light, with a highly developed civilization and a strict code of honour. They were not all looters and rapists but accomplished craftsmen in wood, stone and metal, and skilled builders of ocean-going vessels far ahead of their time.

The Vikings had a distinctive religion based on a rich mythology with its own pantheon of gods and lesser deities. Above all, it was their daring seamanship that has proved their lasting legacy. Not so long ago Christopher Columbus got all the credit for finding the New World; now the prior claim of the Vikings has been proven by archaeological discoveries.

Below: The Scandinavian countries issued miniature sheets in 2004 showing characters from Norse mythology, such as Thor and Ran on this sheet from the Faroes.

While Scandinavian philately has been much enriched by Viking subjects, their impact elsewhere has provided material for stamps from many countries. Significantly the longship is the most important symbol of that era, for it was this craft that made possible the extraordinary expansion of the Vikings between 900 and 1100.

Norsemen raided Brittany and Gaul, laid siege to Paris and were bought off by grants of land in what came to be known as Normandy. Although they acquired a veneer of civilization from the Franks, it was the same tough fighting men who invaded and conquered England in 1066. Half a century earlier King Cnut had also conquered England and briefly created a vast Norse empire that stretched from Arctic Norway and Sweden to western Scotland and much of Ireland as well as the Faroes, Iceland, Greenland and the north-eastern seaboard of America.

Above: Viking ship on an early stamp of Estonia (top) and an Arctic Viking stamp from Greenland, showing an Indian arrowhead from a Viking grave and a Viking coin found in Maine.

Below: Floki and his raven on an Iceland miniature sheet, 2003.

Right: Miniature sheet from the Faroes showing the Vikings' Atlantic voyages.

Below: Tynwald, named from the Norse for "assembly field", celebrated its 1,000th anniversary in 1979.

Above: The name Viking remains a byword for exploration: the space mission to Mars, honoured by this American stamp, recalls the intrepid Atlantic voyages of 1,000 years ago.

Right: In 2000 Iceland issued two stamps featuring Viking architecture, including this reconstruction.

Above: Dragon figurehead of a Viking ship on a Danish stamp (left); Leif Erikson's statue in Reykjavik, Iceland, featured on an American stamp in 1968 celebrating his arrival in and exploration of Vinland, believed to be Maine (centre); Viking warriors and longships arriving on the Isle of Man on a stamp of 1973 (right).

While Hrolf the Ganger (later Duke Rollo of Normandy) was carving a large fief in the lower Seine basin, others penetrated the Mediterranean, colonized Sicily and Malta and got as far as Constantinople, which they knew as Miklagard (big garden). The followers of Rurik sailed north into the Black Sea and penetrated the valleys of the rivers Don, Dnieper and Volga, laying the foundations of Russia and the Ukraine. The indigenous peoples invited the strangers, whom they called Rus (red-haired) to bring law and order. Rurik answered the call and founded Novgorod (new town), the first of many cities that included Kiev and Smolensk. Viking ships can be found on the first stamps of Estonia as well as on more recent issues from Poland, Ukraine and Lithuania.

Of all the lands the Vikings settled, Iceland has remained most faithful to Norse culture. They first arrived in 874, driving out or enslaving the Irish hermits they found there. Icelandic stamps recall their arrival at Reykjavik and the establishment in 930 of the Althing, the world's oldest democratic assembly.

Banished from Iceland in 980, Erik the Red and his followers sailed to the far west, where he discovered southern Greenland. Three sets and matching miniature sheets from Greenland in 1999–2000 tell the story of the rise and fall of the Arctic Vikings. Though Greenland was treeless, the abundant driftwood in its bays encouraged Erik's son Leif the Lucky to look for land farther west. Around 1000 he discovered three territories, Helluland (Baffin Land), Markland (Newfoundland) and Vinland (wine country, believed to be Maine). Stamps from many countries, including Canada and the USA, acknowledge Leif Erikson's discoveries.

Many stamps of the Isle of Man, under Norse rule until 1266, allude to its Viking heritage. Stamps of Ireland also reflect Viking history, from the founding of Dublin to the Battle of Clontarf in 1014. Numerous stamps with a Viking theme have been issued by Denmark, Norway and Sweden, illustrating Viking craftsmanship from the carved stones of Gotland to the Jellinge style of curvilinear ornament.

1

2

3

4

5

6

7

8

9

10

11

BRITISH ISLES

Eighty years ago there was a single stamp-issuing authority for the whole of the British Isles. Today, there are five, and of these Royal Mail (which is responsible for the stamps of the United Kingdom) also produces country or regional stamps for England, Scotland, Wales and Northern Ireland. The first division came in 1922, when the 26 counties of southern Ireland became the Irish Free State. Wartime provisional issues in the Channel Islands were followed by the regional issues of 1958, and postal autonomy in 1969 for Guernsey and Jersey was followed by that for the Isle of Man in 1973. At first, regional stamps, apart from those of the offshore islands, were confined to Scotland, Wales and Northern Ireland, but England has also had its own stamps since 2001. In 1840, when Rowland Hill introduced adhesive postage stamps, no country name was necessary, and in deference to Britain's premier position, the Universal Postal Union decreed in 1874 that Britain alone would be exempt from the rule requiring the country name to appear on stamps. Ever since then, the head of the reigning monarch has been sufficient identification.

Left: In 1995 Royal Mail issued two stamps to celebrate the bicentenary of the birth of Sir Rowland Hill, portraying him as a young man and in old age. The latter also incorporated the Penny Black.

CONSERVATIVE POLICY

The design of the Penny Black (1840) was regarded as so perfect that it remained in use for 40 years, changing colour in 1841, adopting perforations in 1848 and acquiring check letters in all four corners in 1858 [1]. When the rate for postcards and printed matter was halved in 1870 the solution was to issue a stamp half the size of the Penny [2]. Separate stamps for revenue purposes were introduced in 1853, but postage and revenue duties were combined from 1881 onwards. As a result, the Penny Lilac [3] is arguably the world's greatest stamp, at least in terms of its being produced in quite astronomical quantities up to 1902.

Attempts to improve the appearance of the Victorian stamps led to the mainly bicoloured Jubilee series of 1887. Most of the designs were retained in the reign of Edward VII, with his profile substituted [4]. The stamps from 1880 onwards were mainly printed by letterpress; the George V series [5] was adapted to photogravure in 1934 [6]. George V, a keen philatelist, requested that the intaglio process, which had been used from 1840 to 1879, should be revived for the high values, popularly known as the Seahorses [7].

FIRST COMMEMORATIVES

Although commemorative postal stationery had been produced in 1890 for the jubilee of penny postage, no adhesive commemorative stamps were issued until 1924, when new stamps were produced for the British Empire Exhibition [8], though sales were confined to the showgrounds. Britain produced very few commemoratives until the 1950s; those that were issued were confined to events of national, international or royal significance [9].

PHOTOGRAVURE

The definitives for the brief reign of Edward VIII broke new ground, using a design that was ideally suited to the photogravure process [10]. The clock turned back again a year later, when the definitives of Edward's brother George VI added the heraldic flowers of the United Kingdom [11]. For the Coronation stamp of 1937 the king and queen were portrayed side by side [12] whereas the Silver Wedding stamps of 1948 featured conjoined busts [13]. Special issues in the immediate postwar years were heavily symbolic in character [14].

EARLY ELIZABETHAN STAMPS

The first definitives of the reign of Elizabeth II, introduced in 1952, were based on a facing portrait of the queen by the photographer Dorothy Wilding [15]. One of the four designs for the Coronation stamps, issued in 1953, showed a full-face portrait with the coronation regalia [17]. The first definitives were superseded in 1967 by a series that returned to the style set in 1936 by the Edward VIII series, using an effigy of the queen sculpted in plaster by Arnold Machin [16].

The tempo of special issues increased in the 1960s; at the same time the first bicoloured stamps since 1910 appeared [18]. Symbolism gave way to pictorialism [19] and the first stamps to commemorate a historic personality appeared in 1964, although the Post Office argued that these marked the Shakespeare Quatercentenary Festival (a major national event) rather than honouring William Shakespeare himself. Nevertheless, protests in Scotland that the bicentenary of the birth of Robert Burns in 1959 had been ignored led to the issue of two commemorative stamps in 1966. That year, in which Post Office policy on special issues broke free, also witnessed stamps in honour of the football World Cup, including a last-minute "special" to celebrate England's victory [20], and the first British Christmas stamps, featuring two designs by young children – another novelty [21].

Below: Four stamps issued in 1964 depicted characters from Shakespeare's plays to mark his quatercentenary, and in 1966 Robert Burns was belatedly commemorated (bottom).

The World's Most Prolific Series

No one could have foreseen that the British definitives first issued in 1967, known as the Machins after the sculptor who modelled the queen's head, would become not only one of the world's longest-running series but also the most prolific of all time. Even on a simplified reckoning there have been well over 200 different denominations and colours since 1967.

The design was retained when Britain introduced decimal currency in 1971. It has been produced by several printers, using photogravure, lithography, intaglio and even letterpress and embossing, in gummed sheets and self-adhesive booklets. But taking into account all the variations in paper, perforation and phosphor bands, the number of collectable varieties runs into thousands.

12

13

14

15

16

17

18

19

20

21

BRITISH REGIONAL ISSUES

Historically the British Isles consisted of three kingdoms (England, Scotland and Ireland), a principality (Wales) and three crown dependencies (Guernsey, Jersey and the Isle of Man). For more than 80 years after the first issue in 1940 the stamps produced by the British Post Office were used in all of these areas. Today, however, separate issues appear for use throughout the United Kingdom, in England, Scotland, Wales and Northern Ireland, and Guernsey, Alderney, Jersey, the Isle of Man and the Irish Republic, reflecting the different history, culture and outlook of each territory, yet often revealing subjects common to all. Many events and personalities that might not be considered to merit the issue of British stamps are celebrated by the offshore islands.

Left: The first of an Irish series issued in 1969 devoted to Irish Art reproduced The Last Supper and Crucifixion, *a stained glass window in the chapel of Eton College in England, designed by the Dublin-born artist Evie Hone.*

1

2

3

4

5

6

7

8

9

10

11

12

RECENT DEVELOPMENTS IN BRITISH STAMPS

In recent years the use of intaglio combined with photogravure has resulted in stamps with much sharper outlines. Many modern British stamps have designs that bleed off into the perforations, although the motifs are often obscure, such as the series of 2002 for the centenary of J.M. Barrie's *Peter Pan* [1]. Just how far British design moved in the latter part of the 20th century can be gauged by comparing the stamps of 1981 and 1986 celebrating the marriages of Prince Charles [2] and Prince Andrew [3]: the latter showed a much more informal approach to its subject. A series issued in 2003 entitled Extreme Endeavours broke new ground by portraying a living person other than royalty on a stamp – it showed Sir Edmund Hillary approaching the summit of Everest in 1953 [4].

REGIONALISM

Although the Channel Islands and the Isle of Man had been agitating for their own stamps since the 1930s, nothing was done to implement this until 1958, when distinctive stamps appeared not only in each of the offshore islands but also in Scotland, Wales and Northern Ireland. Like the "unified" series they bore no name, and all had to bear the Wilding portrait of the queen as their dominant feature. But the stamps, designed by local artists, gained their individuality from the inclusion of heraldic devices and local symbolism: the ducal crown and lily of Guernsey [5], the arms and mace of Jersey [6], the triskeles (three-legged symbol) and ring-chain of Man [7], the crown, thistle and saltire cross of Scotland [8], the dragon and leek of Wales [9] and the red hand of Ulster and flax blossom of Northern Ireland [10].

Following the advent of decimal currency in 1971 the remaining regions received standardized designs based on the Machin portrait with their national emblems in the upper left-hand corner [11–14]. The Manx series was discontinued in 1973 following the island's postal autonomy, but the others continued until 1999–2000, when different motifs were produced for each of four stamps covering the basic postal rates [15]. England joined in 2001.

IRISH FREE STATE

Following the Easter Rising (1916) and War of Independence (1919–21), the 26 counties in the south and west of

Ireland attained dominion status as the Irish Free State, which introduced its own stamps in 1922. At first British stamps were overprinted in Gaelic, using monastic uncials to signify the Provisional Government of Ireland. This was followed by an overprinted series inscribed "Saorstat Eireann" (Irish Free State) [16].

The first of the distinctive stamps appeared on December 6, 1922, the very day the Free State came into being. The designs, rich in Celtic symbolism, included one showing a map of an undivided Ireland [17]. They continued in use until 1968, when they were replaced by a series illustrating ancient Irish art treasures.

REPUBLIC OF IRELAND

The first step to complete independence came in 1936 when Eamon de Valera used the abdication of Edward VIII to draft a new constitution formally abandoning the Free State title in favour of Eire. In 1939 two stamps celebrated the 150th anniversary of the US constitution and the installation of the first US president – they were the first of many stamps that emphasized the close ties between Ireland and the USA [19]. The Republic of Ireland was formally inaugurated in April 1949 with the only stamp ever to use this title for the country [18]. Since then the name Eire has been retained, although the penchant for inscriptions in the Irish language (spoken by only 20 per cent of the population) has greatly diminished. Interestingly, it has been used on recent stamps that reflect Ireland's enthusiasm for the European Union [20–21].

Special issues take pride in Irish inventions such as the air pump, the tractor, the steam turbine and the submarine [22]. Major naval figures include Commodore Barry, co-founder of the US Navy, and William Brown who founded the Argentinian Navy, while the exploits of the polar explorer Sir Ernest Shackleton were the subject of an issue in 2004. The pantheon of heroes and martyrs in the long struggle for independence range from the leaders of the ill-fated Easter Rising to Wolfe Tone, Michael Collins and Eamon de Valera. Literary figures are legion on stamps and range from medieval chroniclers to modern poets and playwrights. Sporting attractions range from Gaelic football and hurling to sailing [23], while scenery and wildlife are well covered. Ireland's devotion to Catholicism is featured prominently but other faiths have also been honoured. Since 1985 Ireland has issued stamps for Valentine's Day, more recent issues linking this to the Chinese Lunar New Year.

Below: Irish stamps issued in 2004 celebrated the jubilee of Pope John Paul II (left) and combined the theme of Valentine's Day with the Chinese Year of the Monkey (right).

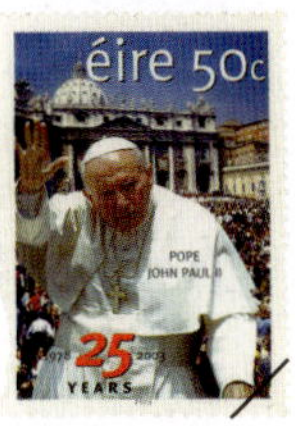

Bogus Fenians

In 1967 Ireland issued two stamps to mark the centenary of the Fenian rebellion in Canada and reproduced the stamps allegedly issued at that time. It was only after the issue that it transpired that the "stamps" were the bogus production of a Boston stamp dealer, "Honest Allan" Taylor.

13

14

15

16

17

18

19

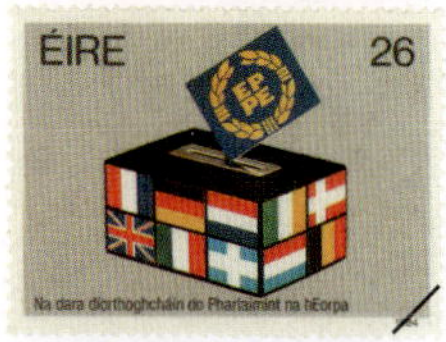

20

21

22

23

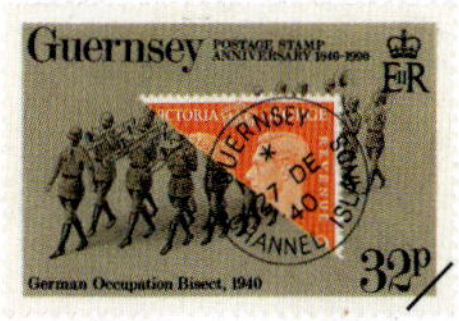

1

2

3

4

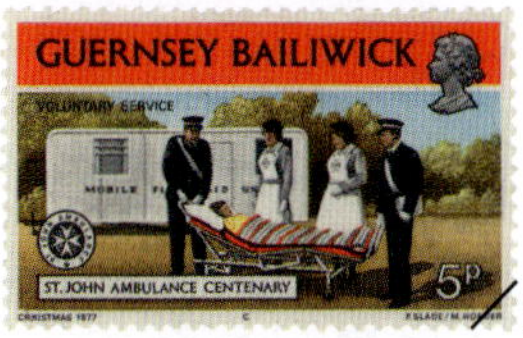

5

6

7

8

BRITISH OFFSHORE ISLANDS

The Isle of Man and the Channel Islands are not, strictly speaking, part of the United Kingdom but are dependencies of the Crown with their own parliamentary systems. The Isle of Man, situated between Ireland, Scotland and England, was under Norse rule until 1266, then briefly ruled by Scotland. The Earls of Derby and later the Dukes of Atholl were the Lords of Mann (*sic*) until 1765 when the island passed to the Crown. The Channel Islands comprise the bailiwicks of Guernsey (with its dependencies Alderney and Sark) and Jersey – the last remnants of the Duchy of Normandy. The Channel Islands were under German occupation during World War II.

Left: In 2004 Jersey issued a set of stamps in se-tenant *pairs to celebrate royal connections dating from the Norman Conquest. Each pair featured an island landmark alongside a portrait of the monarch in whose reign it was constructed.*

GUERNSEY

Both Guernsey and Jersey were occupied by German forces in May 1940 and were not freed until May 1945, during which time they ran out of British stamps. In Guernsey 2d stamps were bisected – as shown on a stamp of 1990 marking the 150th anniversary of adhesive stamps [1] – pending locally printed stamps [2], which ceased to be valid after the liberation. British stamps were used from then until 1969, when both bailiwicks took over their own postal services and introduced distinctive stamps. Guernsey's first definitives showed portraits of medieval rulers based on silver pennies [4].

The stamps of the offshore islands often focused on subjects overlooked by the British Post Office. Guernsey's stamps marked the St John Ambulance centenary [5] and John Wesley's ministry to the island [6] among many other events. Connections with nearby France have resulted in many stamps, such as the series of 1992 showing the cartoon character Asterix the Gaul [7]. In 2004 a set marking the 60th anniversary of D-Day (which bypassed the islands) paid tribute to the Red Cross ship *Vega*, which brought provisions after the island was cut off by the Allied advance in Normandy [8].

Guernsey's dependency Alderney has had "regional" stamps since 1983. Though distinctive to that island, they are also postally valid in Guernsey [9]. Circular stamps marking the centenary of FIFA in 2004 showed "playground school footie" [10].

JERSEY

As well as the armorial stamps issued in 1941–3 Jersey had a set of six pictorial definitives in 1943–4, designed by the well-known local artist Edmund Blampied but printed in Paris. The artist even managed to incorporate the royal monogram GR (flanking the value) under the noses of the Nazis [3].

Scenery and royal portraiture were featured in the definitives of 1969, which were re-issued in 1970–1 with decimal currency, followed by those of the parishes (1976–80) and the arms of the island's prominent families in 1981–8. Flowers, scenery and bird life have been covered in more recent sets.

One of Jersey's first special issues marked the 25th anniversary of the liberation, a subject that has been alluded to in several subsequent sets. Loyalty to the Crown is manifest in the many stamps portraying members of the British royal family: Elizabeth II's golden jubilee was celebrated in 2002 by stamps depicting the Crown Jewels [11]. Short sets are also produced frequently, covering numerous topics from tourist attractions to the island's remarkably diverse wildlife [12]. Since 1996 a £1 miniature sheet has been released annually to mark the Chinese New Year. Designed by Victor Ambrus, these stamps feature the relevant animal of the Chinese zodiac wearing a multicoloured scarf.

ISLE OF MAN

Although it had the option of postal autonomy in 1969, at the same time as Guernsey and Jersey, the Isle of Man did not follow suit until 1973. Following the style of the regional stamps of 1958–71, the first definitives that were issued incorporated the triskeles, the three-legged emblem of the island, and a Hiberno-Norse ring-chain motif. A second series, introduced in 1978, retained the triskeles but dispensed with the curvilinear ornament in order to place greater emphasis on landmarks of the island [13]. Later sets featured island birds (1983–5), Manx railways and trams (1988–92) and ships (1993–7), including the *Waverley*, the world's last sea-going paddle-steamer, which plies the route between Glasgow and the Isle of Man [14].

Special issues have explored the island's Norse heritage but also proudly show the Manx contribution to the world at large. The Lifeboat Institution was founded by Sir William Hillary, a native of the island [15] while Manx connections with the USA have yielded several sets [16]. The Isle of Man granted votes to women in 1881, before anyone else [17]. Members of the British royal family, in their official roles, have been a popular subject, and include the late Princess Margaret and Queen Alexandra, depicted as Princess of Wales for the centenary of the servicemen's charity SSAFA (Soldiers, Sailors and Air Force Association).

The island is world-famous for its Tourist Trophy (TT) motorcycle races and these have appeared on a number of sets since 1973. The most recent combines them with the comedian George Formby, who made his screen debut in *No Limit* (1936), filmed during the 1935 TT races.

Below: Isle of Man stamps have featured Princess Margaret in Guide uniform (1985) and Queen Alexandra as Princess of Wales in 1885.

Puzzle Pieces

Two stamps that often puzzle collectors bear the portrait of George VI. Without a country name, they must be British, but they are not to be found under Great Britain in the catalogues. They were issued by Britain, in 1948, but celebrated the third anniversary of the liberation of the Channel Islands and are thus regarded as the forerunners of the modern stamps. Both depict islanders gathering seaweed for manure, based on paintings by the Jersey artist Edmund Blampied.

9

10

11

12

13

14

15

16

17

1

2

3

4

5

6

7

8 

9

BRITISH EUROPEAN TERRITORIES

British stamps have been issued in a number of territories in continental Europe that it acquired as a result of various military campaigns. The first of these was Gibraltar, which had belonged to Spain since the expulsion of the Moors in 1492. Lying on the northern side of the straits at the western end of the Mediterranean, called the Pillars of Hercules by the ancients, it derived its name from Gibel Tarik (Tarik's rock) after the Moorish chieftain who seized it in the 8th century. It was captured by an Anglo-Dutch expedition in 1704 and remains British despite frequent attempts by Spain to regain it.

Left: The 1960 definitive series of Gibraltar featured a map of the straits, graphically illustrating the strategic importance of the Rock. The badge of the colony is, in fact, a bunch of keys, and it would be true to say that Gibraltar itself was the key to British mastery of the Mediterranean in both world wars, particularly during anti-submarine campaigns.

GIBRALTAR

The postal service was controlled from London until 1886 and used ordinary British stamps, identified only by an obliterator with the letter G in the centre. When control was transferred to Gibraltar itself the earliest distinctive stamps were merely those of Bermuda, overprinted [8]. Pictorial definitives were introduced gradually from 1931, using two-colour recess printing from 1928 to 1953 [1]. A more stylized approach was adopted in 1960 for a series showing the fauna and flora of the Rock, including the famous Barbary ape, the only higher primate found in Europe [2]. Ships [3], insects [4] and views of Gibraltar old and new were depicted on later issues.

Of the special issues, many alluded to the Great Siege of 1779–83 and the importance of the Rock as a British garrison and coaling station, but by the 1960s issues such as the Sea Angling Championships [5] were publicizing Gibraltar as a tourist destination. The first Christmas stamp reproduced a stained glass window from a Glasgow church [6].

Although only an associate member of the EU (through the UK), Gibraltar has produced a number of stamps that relate to it [7], including a sheetlet featuring the euro coinage, despite the fact that Gibraltar uses sterling currency.

MALTA

From the 16th century until 1798 Malta was the base of the Knights of St John, who had been ousted from Rhodes by the Turks. The French under Napoleon seized the island in 1798 but were driven out by a local rebellion assisted by the British, who then took over. Like Gibraltar, the postal service was run from London, and British stamps with the obliterator M were used until 1885, but from 1860 the island had a distinctive ½d stamp for local mail.

Pictorial stamps appeared from 1899 and included a view of the Grand Harbour at Valletta on the ¼d stamps [9]. The strategic importance of the island fortress was shown during World War II, when Malta was besieged by Axis forces. George VI conferred the George Cross on the island in 1942, and thereafter it appeared on many of the stamps alongside the name [12]. Malta also received a commendation scroll from President Roosevelt [10].

Malta became an independent state in 1964, and its first definitive series featured landmarks illustrating its history since the Stone Age [11]. Many later stamps highlighted the glorious architecture and art from the time of the Knights [13]. On December 13, 1974, Malta became a republic within the Commonwealth [14]. In 1989 it hosted a summit conference between Presidents Bush and Gorbachev [16]. Its importance as a holiday destination goes back to the early 19th century, when Sir Walter Scott spent some time there [15]. More recent stamps have noted major international sporting events [17].

CYPRUS

During the Napoleonic Wars Britain gained control of the Ionian Islands in the Adriatic off the Greek coast. Ordinary British stamps were used in

Below: John F. Kennedy on a Cypriot stamp of 1965 (top). Stamps of Northern Cyprus cover international anniversaries (middle) as well as the annual Europa issues (bottom).

Refugee Tax

Compulsory stamps showing a child surrounded by barbed wire have been issued with various dates since 1977, in aid of refugees from Northern Cyprus.

Cephalonia, Corfu and Zante until 1859, when a set was produced of three undenominated stamps portraying Queen Victoria, with their values determined by their colour [18]. These stamps were withdrawn in 1864 when Britain handed the three islands over to Greece.

The Treaty of Berlin (1878) assigned the administration of Cyprus to Britain, and overprinted British stamps [19] were used until 1881. The island was nominally Turkish until 1925, when it was made a British crown colony. Pictorial definitives, dwelling heavily on the Greek classical period, appeared from 1934.

Cyprus became a republic within the Commonwealth in 1960. Although stamps since then have mostly alluded to the glories of its Greek heritage, issues mourning the death of John F. Kennedy quoted his speech on self-determination for Cyprus. Sadly, Cyprus was torn apart by ethnic violence, leading to the Turkish invasion and partition of the island in 1974. A breakaway regime known as the Turkish Republic of Northern Cyprus has had its own stamps since the island was partitioned. Mail to and from Northern Cyprus is routed through Mersin in mainland Turkey.

10

11

12

13

14

15

16

17

18

19

1

2

3

4

5

6

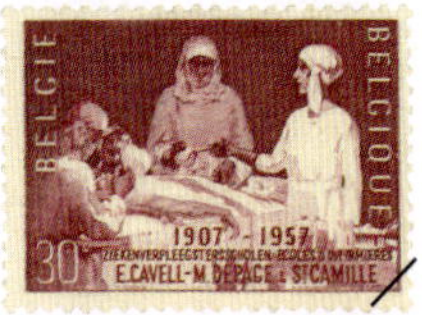

7

8

9

10

11

THE BENELUX COUNTRIES

Belgium, the Netherlands and Luxembourg, historically known collectively as the Low Countries, were at one time ruled by the same monarch, reigning as King of the Netherlands and Grand Duke of Luxembourg, but in 1831 the Belgians seceded and elected Prince Leopold of Saxe-Coburg-Gotha as their king. When William III of the Netherlands died in 1890 the union with Luxembourg was dissolved because Salic Law forbade the succession of a female. The grand duchy passed to Duke Adolf of Nassau, the nearest male heir. When Grand Duke William IV died in 1912 the law was changed to allow his daughter Adelaide to succeed to the throne. All three countries were overrun by the Germans in 1940; when they were liberated in 1944 they decided to form a commercial union known as Benelux.

Left: Since 1964 the Benelux countries have issued stamps in a common design to celebrate important anniversaries of the union, which served as a model for the EEC and EU.

BELGIUM

Adhesive postage stamps were adopted in Belgium in 1849, followed by Luxembourg and the Netherlands in 1852. All three countries have many similarities and parallels in their stamps, reflecting their common historical, political and cultural heritage. Each country has been responsible for innovations. While Luxembourg was the first country to issue stamp booklets (1895) and miniature sheets (1921), Belgium pioneered railway parcel stamps (1879) and continues to produce them to this day [1]. Between 1893 and 1914 stamps were issued with labels attached to signify that mail was not to be delivered on Sundays [2].

In August 1914 the Germans invaded Belgium in violation of the Treaty of London (1839), which had guaranteed its neutrality. The definitive series of 1919–20 shows Albert I wearing a steel helmet, alluding to his command of the Belgian Army during World War I [3].

All three Benelux countries have frequently issued stamps with a charity premium, a recurring theme being the younger members of the royal family. Baudouin of Belgium made his philatelic debut on the Anti-tuberculosis Fund stamps of 1936 [5]. His mother, Queen Astrid, was killed in a car crash in 1935; a black mourning stamp [6] was followed by a set in different colours but with the same portrait edged in black. A stamp of 1957 for the 50th anniversary of the Edith Cavell Nursing School recalls the British nurse, shot by the Germans as a spy in World War I [7].

The Low Countries were overrun by the Germans in 1940. Belgium celebrated its liberation in 1944 with definitives showing the lion rampant and "V" for victory [4]. Since 1893 Belgian stamps have been inscribed in both French and Flemish, but two different versions of the liberation stamps were produced, with the titles rendered as "Belgie-Belgique" and "Belgique-Belgie" to satisfy Flemish and Walloon national pride. Despite deep-seated differences between the two communities, Belgium has been a model for European unity.

Brussels is the seat of the European Parliament, and the first elections were celebrated on stamps of 1979 [10]. Belgium's main artistic contribution to contemporary philately has been the extensive use of images from strip cartoons and comics [8].

NETHERLANDS

Holland remained neutral in World War I but during World War II it was under German occupation from May 14, 1940, until May 6, 1945. Dutch Nazis formed a government that collaborated closely with the invaders, reflected in the wartime definitives showing ancient Germanic symbols [12]. Charity stamps were issued in 1942 – a device to raise money for the Netherlands Legion, a unit of the Waffen SS [9]. The Dutch royal family escaped to England and thence to Canada, and stamps printed in England were used by the exiled administration. Following the liberation in 1945 they were put on sale in the Netherlands.

Since 1866 the vast majority of Dutch stamps have been printed by Johan Enschedé of Haarlem, using a wide range of processes and techniques. In the postwar period Dutch stamp design has been particularly innovative, at times verging on the avant-garde. The silver jubilee of Queen Juliana was appropriately marked by a stamp of 1973 with a silver surface. In 1970, the Netherlands broke new ground with the world's first stamps to be designed by computer [11]. Recent Dutch stamps have ranged from the minimalist [13] to the strident [14], though the design of the stamp honouring Anne Frank was restrained and dignified [15]. Since 1934 special stamps have been issued by the International Court of Justice [16].

LUXEMBOURG

The stamps of the grand duchy were introduced in 1852 (at the same time as those of the Netherlands) and the first issues portrayed William III as grand duke. Later issues paralleled those of Belgium and the Netherlands and showed the same penchant for charity stamps [17], with causes ranging from child welfare to the protection of nature and other worthy causes. In March 1945 liberation from German occupation was marked by stamps thanking the United States [18].

Birth, Marriage and Death

The Netherlands pioneered special stamps for business mail in 1997 and followed this up with a stamp for the announcement of a baby's birth. In January 1998 a stamp symbolizing light across darkness was launched for bereavement notices and condolence, while March the same year saw a distinctive self-adhesive stamp for the announcement of weddings or congratulations to the happy couple. Such stamps have since been emulated elsewhere.

Luxembourg still makes extensive use of intaglio engraving [19] in both portrait and scenic stamps. Most of its stamps are inscribed in French, but occasionally Letzeburgisch (a German dialect) is used [20]. Undenominated stamps lettered A or B indicate first or second class postage [21].

As a founder member of the European Coal and Steel Community – the forerunner of the European Community – the importance of Luxembourg as an administrative centre is reflected in many of the stamps it has issued in more recent years, while historic sets are reminders of the role of the grand duchy in the Burgundian dominions of the Middle Ages.

12

13

14

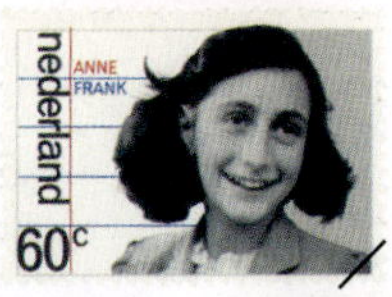

15

16

17

18

19

20

21

1

2

3

4

5

6

7

8

9

10

11

12

SWITZERLAND

The Swiss Confederation was formed in 1291, when Nidwalden, Schwyz and Uri joined forces to resist Austria. Its independence was confirmed in 1648 and today it consists of 24 cantons, each with its own laws and customs. Constitutions of 1848 and 1874 created a union modelled on that of the USA. This gives the cantons considerable autonomy except in defence, external relations and the postal service.

Left: Zurich and Geneva, had their own stamps as early as 1843, while Basle adopted a stamp in 1845. A federal postal system was not created until 1850, with stamps for the entire country.

A PROBLEM SOLVED

The problem of providing stamps for a country with four official languages (French, German, Italian and Romansch) was solved by inscribing them in Latin: the name Helvetia was derived from the Celtic tribe that inhabited the Alpine regions at the dawn of the Christian era. For the same reason, it was important to avoid heraldry or symbolism associated with any particular canton, so the Swiss cross and allegorical figures were adopted [1].

A few stamps, mainly for the Red Cross and the National Fête, were inscribed "Confoederatio Helvetica" [3] but the majority stuck to "Helvetia" [4]. Out of the National Fête issues developed the annual charity stamps inscribed "Pro patria" (For the fatherland) from 1952, usually adopting attractive themes [2]. Since 1913 Switzerland has also produced stamps each year inscribed "Pro juventute" (For youth) and often featuring subjects of interest to young people [5]. In recent years some quirky stamps have appeared, such as the 2000–1 definitives showing typical Swiss scenes in the form of snowstorm paperweights [6].

Until 1932 stamps were printed at the Federal Mint in Berne but thereafter responsibility passed to the postal service, which had its own printing works. Many stamps from that time until 2002 were also produced by the private firm of Courvoisier, which built up a global reputation for fine colour photogravure.

AN INTERNATIONAL HEADQUARTERS

Despite the fact that Switzerland had been the seat of the United Nations and its predecessor, the League of Nations, since 1922, this traditionally neutral country did not become a member of the UN until 2002 [7]. The League of Nations had its headquarters on the outskirts of Geneva and until it was dissolved in 1945 it used Swiss stamps overprinted for the purpose [8]. From 1923 until 1950 Swiss stamps were also overprinted for other international bodies located in Geneva, such as the International Labour Office [9], but distinctive stamps [10] have been provided since then. Subsequently stamps were also provided for the use of the International Education Office [13], the World Health Organization [11], the World Meteorological Organization [12], the International Refugees Organization, the Universal Postal Union in Berne [15], the International Telecommunications Union [14], the World Intellectual Property Organization and the Geneva headquarters of the United Nations itself, occupying the Palais des Nations [16], which originally housed the League. (For stamps issued by the UN

Philatelic Revenue

Before high finance, the mainstay of the economy of Liechtenstein was philately, and many attractive and latterly very colourful stamps were produced from the 1930s onwards with an eye to foreign revenue. To mark the LIBA stamp exhibition in 2002, Liechtenstein issued a pair of stamps that, between them, reproduced no fewer than 23 different stamps dating from 1912 to 2002 to mark the 90th anniversary of the first adhesive postage stamps.

from its headquarters in New York, *refer to* the stamps of the United States Possessions and Territories.)

Switzerland has been in the forefront of philatelic technology in recent years, pioneering a number of gimmicks that have hit the headlines. A sheet marking the centenary of the Swiss chocolate industry resembled a bar of chocolate, with simulated wrapping in the silver foil sheet margins. The stamps gave off the aroma of chocolate when gently rubbed. A set of five stamps in 2002 celebrating the centenary of the teddy bear was produced in different shapes for each stamp. In 2000, it broke new ground with the world's first textile stamp, a self-adhesive Fr5 stamp embroidered by a firm in St Gallen. This has since been copied by other countries. In 2004 Switzerland even produced a Fr5 stamp made from a square section of real wood, the design being the actual grain of the timber.

LIECHTENSTEIN

Associated with Switzerland is the tiny principality of Liechtenstein, founded in 1719. It achieved autonomy in 1806 and became fully independent in 1866. It originally used Austrian stamps but began issuing its own in 1912, although Austria continued to be responsible for the external postal service and its stamps could also be used in Liechtenstein until 1921.

The earliest stamps of the principality included a reference to the Austrian Post at the foot [17]. The Austrian connection ended in 1920 and thereafter stamps made no reference to Austria. Instead, Liechtenstein became aligned with Switzerland and in 1921 it adopted Swiss currency. At first its stamps continued to be printed in Vienna, but after 1924 they were usually printed in Switzerland, either by the postal printing works in Berne using the intaglio process [19], or in photogravure by Courvoisier.

Many of the stamps feature paintings and sculpture in the art collections of the Prince of Liechtenstein, regarded as some of the finest in the world [18; 20]. This tiny country, with a population of only 30,000, may be one of Europe's leading financial centres, but it also has a largely rural economy depending on traditional occupations such as cheese-making [21]. The Ruritania-like quality of Liechtenstein is also reflected in the many stamps featuring knightly escutcheons, with antique lettering to match.

Below: The garnished escutcheon of Georg Marxer, 1745, appeared in the first set devoted to the arms of the Bailiffs of Liechtenstein (1980).

13

14

15

16

17

18

19

20

21

1

2

3

4

5

6

7

8

9

10

11

12

13

14

GERMAN STATES

Germany was a large part of the Holy Roman Empire, a loose federation of about 1,800 kingdoms, principalities, duchies and free cities that endured until 1806. After 1812 Germany was reduced to a federation of 32 states, of which Prussia was the strongest. From 1849 onwards many states issued their own stamps. Under Bismarck, Prussia absorbed several states in the wars of 1864 and 1866 and after it defeated France in the war of 1870–1 the German Empire (Deutsches Reich) was proclaimed at Versailles, completing the process of unification. The Prussian postmaster General Heinrich von Stephan, used his experience of unifying the postal services of the German states to create the Universal Postal Union in 1874.

Left: The highest denomination of Germany's definitive sets of 1900 and 1902 portrayed Kaiser Wilhelm II making a speech at the celebrations marking the 25th anniversary of the German Empire in 1896.

Only half the states in existence before the unification of Germany issued their own stamps; others relied on the services provided by the Counts of Thurn and Taxis from their headquarters in Frankfurt. Separate issues were needed for each currency – which was groschen in the northern states and kreuzer in the southern states – and the designs for these areas had a rectangular or circular format respectively [1–2]. In 1867 the Thurn and Taxis network was purchased by the North German Confederation.

INDIVIDUAL STATES

The individuality of the various states was reflected in their stamps, particularly in the early period. Numeral designs were originally favoured but heraldic motifs soon came into fashion, those of the grand duchy of Baden (1862–71) being typical [3].

Bavaria's first stamps concentrated on numerals but after the accession of the mad King Ludwig II it adopted the fashion for stamps with the coat of arms embossed in colourless relief [5]. Bavaria continued to have its own postal service until 29 April 1920, the last series appearing earlier that year, a curious blend of avant-garde art and traditional Catholic values [4].

At the other extreme was the Hanseatic town of Bergedorf, which introduced stamps in 1861. Each was printed in black on different colours and in different sizes in ascending order of value [6]. From 1420 to 1867 the town belonged jointly to Lübeck and Hamburg, alluded to in the initials in the corners of the stamps.

World Firsts

The Prince Regent Luitpold finally appeared on stamps in 1911, marking his 90th birthday. These stamps have the distinction of being the first in the world to be produced by photo-lithography (left). Luitpold was succeeded as regent by his son, who ascended the throne as Ludwig III in 1913. Ludwig's stamps also broke new ground, being the world's first to be produced by the photogravure process (right).

The imperial free city of Bremen issued stamps from 1855 to 1867, showing the civic arms [7]. The duchy of Brunswick had stamps showing the white horse emblem from 1852 [9], switching to embossed stamps in 1861. Hamburg, a free city from 1510, adopted stamps in 1859, all showing its triple-towered badge [8]. Lübeck, a free city since 1226, joined Hamburg in 1241 to form the Hanseatic League. Armorial stamps were used from 1859 [11] and embossed from 1863 to 1867.

The kingdom of Hanover had armorial stamps from 1851 to 1855, then switched to a numeral design for pfennig values [12] and a profile of George V for the higher denominations. Hanover was on the losing side in the Austro-Prussian War of 1866 and its stamps were suppressed following annexation by Prussia. From 1856 the grand duchy of Mecklenburg-Schwerin issued stamps that could be divided into quarters [10]. The adjoining state of Mecklenburg-Strelitz introduced stamps only in 1864, using the embossed style then in fashion [13] and a similar pattern was followed by the grand duchy of Oldenburg [14].

Prussia adopted stamps in 1850, originally portraying Friedrich Wilhelm IV [15], but his successor Wilhelm I preferred embossed armorial stamps from 1861, setting the trend for other states whose stamps were printed at the Prussian State Printing Works in Berlin. Saxony began with numerals, progressed to royal portraiture and from 1863 used embossed stamps in the Prussian manner [16]. Schleswig and Holstein were German duchies ruled by the Danish monarch but they rebelled in 1848 and issued a stamp in 1850 [17]. In 1864 Austria and Prussia invaded and stamps were issued in each duchy [18]. Disagreement between the allies led to the war of 1866.

The kingdom of Württemberg began issuing stamps in 1851, using numerals followed by embossed arms [19] and numerals again from 1869. Although it joined the German Empire in 1871 it had its own postal service, with distinctive stamps, until 1902. When its posts were absorbed into the Reich service Württemberg continued to issue special stamps for government correspondence until 1920 and municipal service stamps until 1924 – the only states' issue to feel the effects of hyperinflation in 1923 [20]. There were even commemorative issues in each category for the jubilee of William II in 1916, featuring the royal arms and the king's portrait respectively [22]. The only states' pictorials were the official mail series of March 1920, showing views of Stuttgart, Ulm, Eilwangen or Tubingen [21].

British Outpost

The strategic island of Heligoland was seized by Britain during the Napoleonic wars, but its postal service was operated by Hamburg. and stamps portraying Queen Victoria were printed in Berlin, with dual sterling and German values. The island was ceded to Germany on 9 August 1890.

THE MOVE TOWARDS UNIFICATION

The North German Confederation, led by Prussia, was established on 1 January 1868, and the stamps of the member states were replaced by numeral designs [23] in groschen or kreuzer currencies. A special stamp was provided for Hamburg which used its own schillings [24]. Stamps issued in French currency were produced for use in Alsace and Lorraine in 1870, absorbed into the Reich in 1871 [25]. Collectors also regard the semi-official air stamps as states' issues [26].

15

16

17

18

19

20

21

22

23

24

25

26

1

2

3

4

5

6

7

8

9

10

11

12

13

GERMAN REICH

The period from the unification of Germany in 1871 to the fall of Hitler in 1945 was one of immense material progress accompanied by political instability. Pulling together a ramshackle conglomeration of states with their own distinct history and culture was a superhuman feat, although it led to autocracy under Kaiser Wilhelm II. Germany's demand for "a place in the sun" and its commercial rivalry with Britain and France led inevitably to World War I. Resentment at the harsh terms of the 1919 Treaty of Versailles and mass unemployment in turn led to the rise of fascism. The collapse of the monarchies in 1918 had no impact on stamps, which were still inscribed "Deutsches Reich".

Left: Adolf Hitler, an Austrian who served in the Bavarian Army, founded the National Socialist German Workers' Party. Briefly imprisoned for an attempted coup in 1923, he gained power constitutionally in 1933, but rapidly destroyed German democratic institutions. Stamps were issued for his birthday each April, usually with exorbitant premiums for the Hitler Culture Fund. Nazi Germany often used philately for propaganda.

THE EMPIRE

The earliest stamps of the empire featured the German eagle [1], but in 1899 a series portrayed the actress Anna Führing in the role of Germania [2], epitomizing the aggressive style of the kaiser. Remarkably these stamps survived the empire by three years. Under the Weimar Republic the imperial inscription remained but definitives emphasized the working classes [3].

Germany began to suffer the effects of inflation during World War I and it escalated in the early 1920s, reaching its peak in November 1923. The 1 milliard (thousand million) mark stamp [4], released only in Bavaria, is known as the Hitler Provisional because it was issued a few hours before he staged his *putsch* in Munich on 9 November. There were few special issues in the Weimar period but significantly many had premiums in aid of the welfare fund to alleviate poverty [5].

THE THIRD REICH

By the beginning of 1933 the Nazis were the largest party in the Reichstag and President Hindenburg had no alternative but to appoint Hitler as chancellor. Once in power, the Nazis dissolved parliament, banned all political parties except themselves and imprisoned communists, socialists, trades unionists and anyone who dissented from their political philosophy. Hitler was hell-bent on reversing the terms of the Treaty of Versailles. Stamps of the 1930s became increasingly propagandistic, publicizing the annual party rallies [6] and showing the führer in belligerent mood. The stamps for the party rally of 1937 [7] formed a miniature sheet whose slogan translated as "He who will save a nation must think heroically." Other stamps charted the expansion of the Reich, from the restoration of the Saar in 1935 [8] to the union with Austria in 1938 [9].

Later in 1938 Hitler demanded the Sudetenland, the German part of Czechslovakia; Czech stamps were overprinted "Wir sind frei!" (We are free!) with the swastika [10]. Danzig was subsequently absorbed into the Reich on 1 September 1939, its stamps being suitably overprinted [11], and the invasion of Poland the same day was the first act of World War II.

The definitives continued to portray Hindenburg until 1941, when Hitler put his own portrait on the regular

A Breakaway State

In 1923, when Germany was wracked by inflation, the French seized the opportunity to detach the Rhineland (then occupied by its troops) and create an independent buffer state known as the Rhineland Republic. German stamps were overprinted "R.R." for this purpose, but protests from Britain, the USA and Germany itself led to the plan being aborted.

series [12]. Wartime stamps continued the strident Nazi messages [13–14]. As the tide of war turned, Hitler renamed his empire Grossdeutsches Reich (Great German State) and this was expressed on the last issues of the Nazi regime [16]. Ironically the very last stamps, issued as the Russians were advancing through the ruins of Berlin, honoured stormtroopers of the SA and SS [15].

PLEBISCITES

After World War I many districts of the empire from Schleswig to Silesia held plebiscites to decide their future. Under Allied supervision plebiscites took place in Allenstein (East Prussia) and Marienwerder (West Prussia), both of which voted to remain German. Memel was placed under French administration but was seized by Lithuania in 1923. Schleswig was divided into two zones, the north voting to return to Denmark and the south voting to remain in Germany. Upper Silesia was partitioned between Germany and Poland. Distinctive stamps were issued in each district. The Saar, a special case, fell to the French, who wished to secure the rich iron and coal industries. German and Bavarian stamps were overprinted [18] pending pictorials printed in Paris [17]. When a plebiscite was finally held in 1935 the district reverted to Germany.

FREE CITY OF DANZIG

The Baltic port of Danzig had been part of Poland for centuries though it enjoyed considerable autonomy and its population was predominantly German, the descendants of traders who had arrived in search of amber. In 1795 it came under Prussian rule, following the third partition of Poland.

By the early 20th century Danzig was the capital of West Prussia and its inhabitants 95 per cent German, but the newly reconstituted Poland demanded the return of Danzig, a vital outlet for Polish trade and commerce. Under the Treaty of Versailles, the problem of satisfying Polish demands was met by creating the Free City of Danzig, in which Poland enjoyed considerable rights. This source of friction between Germany and Poland was violently resolved when Hitler invaded Poland and Danzig once more became the capital of West Prussia. The politics of the Free City mirrored those of Germany itself, with the local Nazis in power from 1934 onwards.

German stamps were overprinted [19] pending the supply of distinctive stamps showing the crowned double cross or a Hanseatic cogge [20]. The special issues reflected the essentially German character of Danzig, including a set for the 150th birth anniversary of the philosopher Schopenhauer [21].

OCCUPATION

By 1942 Hitler had overrun most of Europe, from the Pyrenees to the Arctic, from the Atlantic to the Black Sea. German definitives were overprinted for use in many areas, from Alsace [23] and Lorraine [22], which were soon reabsorbed into the Reich, to large parts of Russia, redesignated Ostland [24]. After the capitulation of Italy, the Germans occupied territories formerly under Italian control [25].

14

15

16

17

18

19

20

21

22

23

24

25

1

2

3

4

5

6

7

8

9

10

11

12

13

POSTWAR GERMANY

In May 1945 a defeated Germany was partitioned by the Americans, British, French and Russians, and the capital Berlin was divided into four sectors. What began as a scheme to prevent a united Germany from ever again threatening the free world soon turned into the battleground on which the Cold War was mainly fought. Germany split into East and West in 1948 and the breach widened with the Soviet blockade of Berlin and later the erection of the Berlin Wall, which never deterred the truly determined from escaping to the West.

Left: In 1965 the Federal Republic commemorated 20 years of refugees fleeing westward with this 20pf stamp. Mail addressed to the Democratic Republic bearing this stamp was either returned to sender or had the offending stamp painted over.

FOUR-POWER CONTROL

For the Anglo-American zones stamps inscribed "AM" (Allied Military) with a large "M" (Military) in the centre and "Deutschland" at the foot [1] were brought over from the USA, later reprinted in Britain and ultimately in Germany itself. The French had a general series [2] followed by separate stamps for Baden, Württemberg and the Rhineland-Palatinate [3]. The six regions of the Soviet zone each released their own stamps in 1945–6 [4], and many towns also produced their own issues. From February 1946 until 1948 the Soviet zone used the stamps of the Anglo-American zones [5].

Growing disparity in the value of the mark in the East and West led to currency reform in 1948, but it also precipitated the split between East and West. Stamps were overprinted to distinguish their respective use [6–7]. The three western zones became the Federal German Republic in September 1949 and a month later the Soviets created the German Democratic Republic. The western sectors of Berlin became a Land (province) of the Federal Republic on 1 September 1950, and this issued its own stamps until 1990.

FEDERAL REPUBLIC

Stamps with the inscription "Deutsche Bundespost" (German Federal Post) were used in the West from 1950 [8]. From time to time trouble flared between the two republics when the Bundespost issued stamps showing places in the East, such as the Treptow Gate in Neubrandenburg as part of the definitive series of 1964–9, whose theme was 12 centuries of German architecture [9]. One of the first multicoloured stamps marked the centenary of the arrival of the political refugee Carl Schurz in America [10].

After the highly propagandistic stamps of the Third Reich, West German stamps concentrated on historical events and personages. Definitives bore famous buildings or presidential portraits, accident prevention (1971–4) and industry and technology (1975–82). From 1986–7 onwards two series ran side by side, featuring famous women (sheet stamps) and tourist attractions (coil stamps).

WEST BERLIN

Stamps used in West Berlin were often identical to those in West Germany, but with the inscription "Deutsche Bundespost Berlin". However, Berlin often produced distinctive stamps, especially with a theme that was particular to the city. One of the earliest issues featured the Freedom Bell, based on the Liberty Bell and the gift of the American people [12]. Other stamps charted the rebuilding of the city and such landmarks as the Kaiser Wilhelm

Memorial Church, preserved in ruins as a reminder of the war [14]. The Brandenburg Gate, shown on many stamps of the GDR as well as West Berlin [13], served as a symbol of the divided city.

Both the Federal Republic and Berlin issued stamps mourning John F. Kennedy [15], whose impassioned speech at the Berlin Wall struck a chord with his audience. The later stamps of Berlin highlighted the cultural heritage of the former German capital [16] but also paid frequent tribute to the Allies, whose airlift of supplies broke the Soviet blockade of 1949 [17].

DEMOCRATIC REPUBLIC

The stamps of East Germany reflected the doctrinaire politics of the regime almost to the end, with stamps commemorating Communist figureheads [18] and symbolism strongly redolent of the USSR in the Stalinist era [19]. In many ways, the GDR was the conscience of Germany, tackling issues – such as Kristallnacht, when the Nazis destroyed Jewish shops and synagogues [20] – that were ignored or glossed over in the West, such as the atrocities committed in the concentration camps. At the same time, however, many reflected the totalitarian and militaristic nature of the GDR itself [21–22].

In 1973–5 a definitive series featured famous buildings. The last definitive series, introduced in 1980, consisted of the same designs but in a reduced size [23]. A long-running series consisted of stamps issued each spring and autumn to mark the world-famous Leipzig Fair. Normally a pair of stamps was released in each case but an exception was the set of four with matching miniature sheet issued in 1965 to mark the 800th anniversary of Leipzig and an international stamp exhibition held at the same time.

The Ostmark was replaced by the Deutschmark on 1 July 1990, necessitating new stamps simply inscribed "Deutsche Post" [24]. Stamps bearing the letters "DDR" remained valid for postage until 31 December 1991 [25].

History Repeats Itself

After World War II, the Saar was administered by France from May 1945 and had distinctive stamps from January 1947, French currency being introduced in November 1947. The Saar reverted to Germany in 1957 and stamps were then issued with the German inscription "Saarland", often in the same designs as those of West Germany, until July 1959, when German currency was introduced.

UNITED GERMANY

On 3 October 1990, the Democratic Republic was absorbed into the Federal Republic and thereafter only one type of stamp was used throughout Germany. One of the first sets to appear was a pair issued on 6 November that year celebrating the opening of the Berlin Wall [11]. Since 1995 stamps have been simply inscribed "Deutschland".

A casualty of reunification was the separate postal service of West Berlin, whose stamps were discontinued in September 1990. The following January, a stamp of united Germany celebrated the bicentenary of the Brandenburg Gate. Thereafter Berlin, as the restored capital of the whole country, featured prominently. Many stamps since 1991 have portrayed historic figures. In 2003 a stamp portrayed Georg Elser, the man who tried to kill Hitler at a Munich rally in 1939, and previously a stamp showing the date "20 Juli 1944" behind bars alluded to the bomb plot of that year – both rare examples of Germany coming to terms with its past. Stamps of recent years have been more overtly thematic.

14

15

16

17

18

19

20

21

22

23

24

25

1

2

3

4

5

6

7

8

9

10

11

AUSTRIA AND HUNGARY

At the height of its power, the Habsburg Empire occupied most of the basin of the Danube, from Bohemia to Transylvania, from Galicia to the Adriatic. It was a conglomeration of many races, tongues and creeds, held together on the principle of "divide and rule". Hungary had been an independent kingdom since the 10th century but in the 17th century accepted Habsburg protection against the Turks. In 1848, the year of revolutions, the Hungarians rose in a revolt that was suppressed by Austria aided by Russia. Thereafter Hungary was absorbed by Austria, a situation that was inherently unstable. So completely assimilated were these countries that they used the same stamps when they were adopted in 1850 [1]. After the *Ausgleich* (compromise) of 1867 both countries had their own stamps.

Left: The embodiment of the empire was Franz Joseph I, who succeeded in the aftermath of the 1848 revolution, at the age of 18, and ruled his ramshackle dominions for almost 70 years. His private life was marred by tragedy: the execution of his brother Maximilian, the assassination of his wife and the suicide of his son Rudolf.

AUSTRIAN REPUBLIC

The empire survived the aged kaiser by only two years, collapsing at the end of World War I. Not only did Hungary break away, but Transylvania passed to Romania and the Alpine and Adriatic provinces went to Italy, while entirely new countries such as Czechoslovakia and Yugoslavia were created and Poland was reconstituted. Austria, once the heart of a mighty empire, was reduced to the size of Scotland, with a similar population. There was a strong movement in favour of union with Germany, and in 1918–21 stamps were actually inscribed "Deutschösterreich" (German Austria). In 1920 they were overprinted "Hochwasser" to raise money for flood relief [3]. The definitive issues of 1934–8 featured provincial costumes [2].

In the 1930s Hitler, the Austrian-born dictator of Germany, had ambitions to add his native land to the Third Reich, and in 1934 the Nazis murdered the Austrian chancellor, Engelbert Dollfuss [4]. The last stamps of the republic were the first Christmas stamps, issued in 1937. People imagined they could see the baleful image of Hitler in the rose [5], an ill omen. In April 1938, on the eve of a plebiscite, the Nazis marched into Austria without a shot being fired.

Austria was liberated by the Allies in May 1945. The Russians issued stamps showing the hammer and sickle [6] while the French, British and Americans had an innocuous posthorn design, produced in Washington [7]. The second republic was proclaimed soon afterwards. Costumes were the subject of a long-running series [8], rendered this time in photogravure. Various subjects, from scenery and architecture to myths and legends, have been used since then, the current issue being aimed at the tourist industry [9].

Austria is a land of music, and numerous stamps from 1922 onwards have honoured the great composers such as Haydn, Mozart, Beethoven and Strauss, while very recent stamps have portrayed Oscar Peterson [10], Riccardo Muti and Seiji Ozawa as well as the Rolling Stones. Nostalgia for the Habsburgs has seen the release of several stamps portraying Franz Joseph and his wife Elisabeth, assassinated in 1898. Appropriately, "Sissi", as she was affectionately known, is the subject of a new musical [11].

HUNGARY

For a few years after the creation of the dual monarchy in 1867, Hungary and Austria had identical stamps that merely portrayed the man known in one country as Kaiser Franz Joseph and in the other as Kiraly Ferenc Joszef. The only inscription was the abbreviation "kr", denoting *kreuzer* in Austria and *krajczar* in Hungary. The first specifically Hungarian stamps were intended for the imperial tax on newspapers that enabled transmission free of postage. A series portraying the monarch with the Hungarian arms below but no inscriptions appeared in 1871 and it was not until 1874 that stamps bore the country name. A new currency, based on the *korona* (crown) of 100 *filler* was adopted in 1900; stamps thus denominated showed the aged king wearing the Hungarian crown or the Turul, the mythical bird of the Magyar people.

A series depicting harvesters was introduced in 1915 and bore the inscription "Magyar Kir. Posta" (Hungarian Royal Post). The design endured until 1926 but underwent changes of inscription and various overprints reflecting the turmoil of 1919–24. At the end of World War I, Hungary went rapidly from a people's republic [12] to a soviet republic under Bela Kun [13]. A right-wing coup led by Admiral Horthy established a separate government at Szeged [14] and when the communists were driven out their overprints were blotted out by a wheatsheaf [15]. Hungary remained "a kingdom without a king, ruled by an admiral without a navy", as the continued abbreviation for *kiralyi* (royal) in the later stamps indicated [16].

History repeated itself after World War II (in which Hungary had been allied to Nazi Germany) when a provisional government [18] was followed by a republic (1946) and a people's republic (1949). In the communist era Hungary gained notoriety for its large number of stamps, including strictly limited editions of imperforate varieties. From 1949 until 1990, when communism collapsed, stamps were merely inscribed "Magyar Posta" [19–20] but since then "Magyarorszag" (Hungarian State) has been used. The output has been much more restrained but includes themes previously banned. Recent issues include stamps honouring Raoul Wallenberg, the Swedish diplomat who saved the lives of many Jews but died in a Soviet camp [17] and the countdown to Hungarian entry into the European Union in 2004 [21].

MISCELLANEOUS ISSUES

Stamps inscribed "K.u.K. Militärpost" were used in Bosnia and Herzegovina (*see* Yugoslavia) but stamps inscribed "K.u.K. Feldpost" were employed in World War I [22]. As well as a general issue there were separate sets for the occupation of Italy, Montenegro, Romania and Serbia, while stamps issued by the French, Romanians and Serbs marked their occupation of Hungarian territory. The Danube Steam Navigation Company had its own stamps for mail carried on its steamers along the river and in the Black Sea ports, originally denominated in kreuzer but later in the international currency of gold centimes [23].

Soccer Triumph

In 1953 the Hungarian football team defeated England 6–3 at Wembley and re-issued a diamond-shaped sports stamp with the date, venue and winning score. In 2003 Hungary even issued a stamp to celebrate the 50th anniversary of beating England on its own pitch.

12

13

14

15

16

17

18

19

20

21

22

23

CZECHOSLOVAKIA

Czechoslovakia, in the heart of Europe, was a creation of the Treaty of Versailles, uniting the Czechs of Bohemia and Moravia (formerly under Austria) with the Slovaks and Ruthenes (formerly under Hungary). The inclusion of three million Germans and 700,000 Hungarians created problems in the late 1930s. The Czechs and Slovaks spoke very similar languages, but culturally, historically and economically they were very different. They won their independence in 1918 as a reward for helping the Allies against the Central Powers.

Left: The architect of the new country was a Moravian, Thomas Masaryk, who campaigned before and during the war to secure self-determination for Czechoslovakia.

1

2

3

4

5

6

7

8

9

10

11

PREWAR REPUBLIC

Before the creation of the republic, the Czech legions were present at the Western Front, in Italy and in eastern Europe, fighting on the Allied side. During the Russian Civil War the Czechoslovak army in Russia controlled the Trans-Siberian Railway and issued its own stamps [1]. After independence in October 1918 the first postal service was operated by the Boy Scouts [2]. Later, stamps of Austria and Hungary were overprinted [3]. Almost from the outset the republic was beset with problems, at first concerning the Slovaks, who felt they were the junior partner, and later with the large German community in the Sudetenland. In the 1930s both factions were manipulated by Hitler for his own ends.

DISMEMBERMENT

In 1938 Czechoslovakia was forced to surrender the Sudetenland to Germany. At the same time the demands of the Slovaks led to a compromise: to give the Slovaks equal billing, stamps were briefly issued with the country name rendered as "Cesko-Slovensko". That vital hyphen, however, failed to stem the tide. In January 1939 the Slovak parliament was inaugurated [5]. In March stamps of Czechoslovakia were overprinted "Slovensky Stat", soon followed by definitive stamps portraying the Slovak leader, Father Hlinka [4].

On 15 March 1939, the Carpatho-Ukrainian parliament was inaugurated with a stamp inscribed in Cyrillic [6]. By noon the same day the Hungarians had invaded and annexed Ruthenia. It was liberated by the Red Army in 1944 and briefly functioned as an independent republic with its own stamps [7], before it was absorbed by the USSR.

In March 1939 Germany invaded the rump of Czechoslovakia, establishing a protectorate under the name of Bohemia and Moravia. Czechoslovak stamps were overprinted, pending the supply of distinctive stamps inscribed in German and Czech [8]. Following the assassination of Reinhard Heydrich by members of the Czech resistance, a stamp showing his death mask was released [9]. Special stamps were provided for Theresienstadt concentration camp [11]. Many people fled to France and Britain, where an exile government issued its own stamps, including one portraying Josef Gabcik, who assassinated Heydrich [10]. The War Heroes set was subsequently released in Czechoslovakia itself in August 1945.

POSTWAR REPUBLIC

Czechoslovakia was reconstituted in 1945 following liberation by the Red Army [12], but by 1948 the country had been totally absorbed into the communist bloc. Stamps of 1945 marked the first anniversary of the

Slovak Rising [13]. Doctrinaire communism was not reflected in stamps to the same extent as in the other Iron Curtain countries, and at least portraiture of Lenin [14] was rendered with the usual impeccable taste.

Having been an enthusiastic exponent of line-engraving and fine intaglio printing since the mid-1920s, Czechoslovakia developed a very distinctive style. Its delicate motifs are exemplified by the Shakespeare stamp in the Cultural Anniversaries set of 1964, showing Bottom from *A Midsummer Night's Dream* [16]. Several stamps remembered the destruction of the villages of Lidice and Lesaky as a reprisal for the killing of Heydrich, while others recalled the horrors of the concentration camps [15]. Latterly Czechoslovakia produced numerous sets of wide thematic appeal.

CZECH REPUBLIC

Communism collapsed in 1990 when democratic elections brought to power the poet and dissident Vaclav Havel. In April the country officially became the Czech and Slovak Federative Republic (although this was not reflected in the name printed on stamps). This reflected a sincere attempt to hold the country together on an equal basis, but the federation was amicably dissolved at the end of 1992. There was some debate about reviving the name of Bohemia and Moravia but it had too many bitter memories. Instead the term Czech Republic was adopted. A large stamp showing the lion of Bohemia [17] was followed by definitives portraying President Havel [18]. Later definitives have featured landmarks, ornamental doorways [19] and the signs of the zodiac. Special issues are beautifully engraved but a refreshing element of levity creeps in occasionally [20].

Below: One of three stamps of 1997 marking the 110th anniversary of Hašek Jaroslav's satirical novel The Good Soldier Schweik.

Ill Omen

The first Czechoslovakian definitives were designed by Alfons Mucha, the outstanding exponent of Art Nouveau, and showed the Hradcany in Prague. In the original the sun, symbolizing the dawn of the republic, appeared to the right of the castle, until it was pointed out that that was where the setting sun appeared – an ill omen. The stamps were withdrawn and re-engraved without the sun.

SLOVAKIA

If the stamps of Slovakia appear similar, it is because they are engraved and printed in Prague. Like the Czech Republic, Slovakia began with stamps showing the national emblem [21]. Both countries issue large art stamps, a recent one celebrating the work of Andy Warhol, of Slovak origin [22].

Slovakia pursues a moderate new issue policy. The definitives of 1993–2002 are in the old Czechoslovak style, with landmarks and scenery as their subject. Recent issues have become more colourful by printing in a combination of intaglio engraving and offset lithography. The vast majority of special issues are released as single stamps, apart from a trio each January highlighting major anniversaries of the coming year. Regular issues include Europa (May), Christmas (November) and Stamp Day (December).

12

13

14

15

16

17

18

19

20

21

22

1

2

3

4

5

6

7

8

9

10

11

12

13

POLAND

This country in eastern Europe rose rapidly from a small duchy in the late Middle Ages to become an empire that stretched from the Baltic to the Black Sea, encompassing modern Lithuania, Belarus and the Ukraine. It had a very turbulent history, suffering invasion by Mongols, Turks, Hungarians, Swedes and latterly Russia, Prussia and Austria, which took large slices of territory in 1772 and 1793 and then dismembered what was left in 1795. Napoleon briefly restored much of the country but after his defeat the neighbouring powers again partitioned the country, much of which nominally became a kingdom under the personal rule of the tsar. For 120 years Poland in the historic sense ceased to exist.

Left: Poland's finest hour came in 1410 when its army soundly defeated the Teutonic Knights at Grunwald. The battle's 550th anniversary was celebrated by one of the largest stamps up to that date. Jan Matejko's vast painting was engraved by Czeslaw Slania.

Prussian, German or Austrian stamps were used in the areas controlled by these powers. The Russians allowed the Poles a stamp in 1860, which was identical to the contemporary Russian issue apart from the inscription using the Roman alphabet [1]. Following the revolt of 1863–5, however, the stamp was suppressed. During World War I German troops avenged the Teutonic Knights' defeat at Grunwald at nearby Tannenberg, defeating the Russians and occupying much of Russian Poland for the rest of the war.

POLISH REPUBLIC

A republic was proclaimed on 3 November 1918, bringing together the territories previously under German, Austrian and Russian rule. At first German [2], Austrian [3] and Austro-Hungarian military post [4] stamps were overprinted for use in their respective areas. At the same time various local "town" posts had their own stamps [5]. Even when the postal authorities of the new republic issued their own stamps, separate issues had to be made in the north and south, denominated in the currencies of Germany and Austria respectively [7]. Issues for the whole country did not appear until February 1920. The first prime minister was Ignacy Paderewski, the celebrated pianist [8]. Most stamps in the two decades of the first republic were printed in letterpress or lithography, but intaglio was used for a set of 13 in 1938 celebrating the 20th anniversary of independence with a look back at the great events in Polish history since the Middle Ages [6].

NAZI OCCUPATION

On 1 September 1939, Germany invaded Poland, and 17 days later the country was again partitioned, Stalin seizing the land east of the River Bug. While eastern Poland disappeared into the USSR, parts of the west were absorbed into the Reich, while Warsaw and the central region constituted the General Government, a German protectorate. At first, Polish stamps were overprinted, the swastika blotting out the original designs [9], but soon distinctive stamps were released, including a definitive series portraying Hitler [10]. The large Jewish population was herded into ghettoes in Warsaw and Lodz, renamed Litzmanstadt, which had its own posts [11]. From there,

Prisoners' Posts

Large numbers of Polish soldiers were held in the German camps at Grossborn, Murnau and Woldenberg, where they organized their own postal services, complete with stamps engraved and struck by hand. The issues boosted morale and celebrated many events – including, in 1942, the 450th anniversary of the discovery of America with a view of the Capitol in Washington!

Jews were despatched to the extermination camps. Many Poles escaped to other countries, notably Britain, where their forces were reconstituted and fought with great distinction in the Battle of Britain and subsequent campaigns of World War II. A government in exile set up in London issued its own stamps, including a charity stamp of 1944 commemorating the Warsaw Uprising [12], while Polish forces in Russia and Italy had similarly distinctive stamps.

REPUBLIC REGAINED

The Polish republic was proclaimed again in September 1944 at Lublin, which had been liberated by the Red Army. The first stamps portrayed Romuald Traugutt [13] and other heroes of the struggles for freedom in the 19th century. In February 1945 stamps were overprinted as each major city was liberated [14]. Later, stamps were printed in Cracow and included one remembering the horrors of the Majdanek extermination camp [15]. Although Poland was firmly in the communist bloc, its strong Catholic traditions softened the banality of Stalinism. Stamps might pay tribute to Russian space achievements [16] but they also acknowledged the humanitarianism of Eleanor Roosevelt [17]. A tricolour stamp of 1971 celebrated Polish participation in the Paris Commune [19]. The profound influence of Catholicism on this deeply religious society was only enhanced by the election of the first Polish pope. After Cardinal Karol Wojtyla became Pope John Paul II in 1978 his portrait appeared with increasing frequency on the stamps of his native land, culminating in the celebration of the 20th anniversary of his papacy [18].

The collapse of the USSR in 1991 freed Poland from the grip of communism, but under the Solidarity movement, which began in 1980 in the shipyards of Gdansk [21], the country had already begun to move in a democratic direction. As early as 1961 stamps alluding to the rulers of the former Polish kingdom were being released, while Poland's contribution to European culture was emphasized by the frequent appearances of the composer Chopin and the poet Mickeiwicz. Although prewar Poland had a bad record for anti-semitism, the postwar republic compensated with stamps honouring the heroes of the Warsaw Ghetto and individual martyrs of the Holocaust such as the children's writer Janusz Korczak. The one glaring omission was any reference to the Polish home army or the troops who fought on the Allied side in World War II, a deficiency that was not remedied until the 1980s.

In the prewar period Poland had external post offices in Odessa and Danzig (Gdansk) issuing distinctive stamps [20]. Danzig became part of Poland in 1945. The Russians took a large part of eastern Poland (now in Lithuania, Belarus and the Ukraine) but compensated Poland with most of East Prussia and Silesia.

14

15

16

17

18

19

20

21

1

2

3

4

5

6

7

8

9

10

11

BALTIC STATES

The republics of Estonia, Latvia and Lithuania are collectively known as the Baltic States. Though ethnically and linguistically distinct, they have a shared history and many cultural and political links that have been emphasized since the restoration of independence in the 1990s. All three were part of the Russian Empire until the Revolution of 1917, but by that time they had been occupied by the Germans (with whom the Baltic landowning class had close blood ties). They became independent in 1918 but were forced by Stalin to accept Soviet garrisons in 1939. Absorbed into the USSR a year later, they were "liberated" by the Germans in 1941 and re-occupied by the USSR in 1944–5. In 1990 they mounted a protest by forming the Via Baltica, a human chain from Tallinn in the north to Kaunas in the south, as a prelude to demands for independence.

Left: Since independence, the Baltic States have made a number of joint issues, such as this sheetlet of 1995 featuring a map of the three countries linked by the Via Baltica. The stamps depict scenes in the respective capitals.

ESTONIA

The first stamps released in Estonia, in November 1918, were lithographed locally [1] and actually preceded the use of tsarist stamps diagonally overprinted "Eesti Post" [2]. Stamps often had symbolic motifs or showed workers [5]. The last issue of prewar Estonia was a set of four to celebrate the centenary of adhesive stamps [3] only days before the country was swallowed up by the USSR. On 20 August 1991, it declared its independence again and began issuing stamps on 1 October. All stamps since then have been lithographed locally by Vaba Maa of Tallinn, showing scenery and landmarks [4] and including a long-running series showing lighthouses [7].

The definitives issued since 1991 have featured the three lions emblem, reviving the symbol of the prewar republic [6]. The rapid depreciation of the Soviet rouble led in 1992 to the reintroduction of the kroon (crown) tariffed at 16 old roubles and divided into 100 senti. The vast majority of Estonian stamps are issued as singles, with occasional sets of six devoted to the Finno-Ugric peoples, the captive breeding programme at Tallinn Zoo and other somewhat esoteric subjects.

LATVIA

When it declared independence on 18 November 1918, Latvia was still under German occupation, and its first stamps were printed on the back of German military maps. The liberation of Riga was marked by stamps in 1919 showing the city skyline [10]. Stamps for the Red Cross fund (1919–20) were printed on the back of Bolshevik banknotes [8]. The 20th anniversary of independence was celebrated in 1938 and showed General Balodis and scenes from the anti-Bolshevik campaign [9].

In October 1939 the USSR acquired the right to garrison Latvia and a year later Latvia "begged" to be admitted to the Soviet Union, the last stamps showing the arms of the new soviet socialist republic [11]. Along with Estonia and Lithuania, Latvia was liberated by the Germans in 1941 and Russian stamps were overprinted accordingly [12]. The independence of Latvia was recognized by the USSR on 9 September 1991. Soviet stamps were overprinted and surcharged [13], augmenting an arms series issued shortly before [14]. Since then Latvian stamps have covered a wide range of modern themes [15].

LITHUANIA

Having proclaimed its independence in February 1918, Lithuania cast around for a German prince suitable to become king, but monarchy was on the wane and in November 1918 a republic was declared. Following some typeset stamps, Lithuania obtained stamps from Berlin [16] followed in 1921 by a series designed and printed in Kaunas [17].

A major setback was the invasion of Central Lithuania by a Polish volunteer corps under General Zeligowski. Stamps inscribed in Polish were issued in 1920–2 [18] before the area around Vilnius was annexed by Poland. When Poland was invaded and dismembered in 1939, Lithuania's share was the return to it of Vilnius, celebrated by an overprint on the stamps marking the 20th anniversary of independence [19]. In exchange, however, Lithuania had to accept a Soviet garrison and in August 1940 it was absorbed by the Soviet Union.

Independence was declared on 11 March 1990, but was not recognized by the Russians until 6 September 1991. The majority of stamps issued since then have been lithographed in Leipzig or Berlin, often emphasizing the country's long history. Annual issues have portrayed the men who signed the original declaration of independence in 1918 [20].

The overall character of the stamps since the restoration of sovereignty has been to catch up on the historic events and major figures denied philatelic recognition during the Soviet period [21]. The distinctive character of the country is also reflected in the long-running series devoted to provincial costumes, while illustrations from the Red Book of Lithuania cover the country's endangered fauna and flora.

NORTH INGERMANLAND

This territory north of Estonia briefly won its freedom from Russia in 1919–20 and issued its own stamps. The first series was closely modelled on contemporary Finnish stamps but was soon followed by a bicoloured pictorial set that alluded to outrages committed by the Bolsheviks. By the Treaty of Dorpat (Estonia), North Ingermanland reverted to Russia in October 1920.

Still in Business

Many of Lithuania's prewar stamps were printed in Kaunas (the temporary capital) by the firm of Spindulys. Despite expropriation and nationalization under communist rule the company managed to survive and had the honour of printing the first stamps of the restored republic, but as it lacked a perforator the stamps had to be cut apart. In a subsequent printing, grey dots were added to simulate the perforations.

Below: One of a series of stamps issued by North Ingermanland in 1920 shows a church burned down by Bolsheviks.

12

13

14

15

16

17

18

19

20

21

1

2

3

4

5

6

7

8

9

10

11

12

RUSSIA

The world's largest country, Russia attained its greatest size, estimated at 22.5 million sq km/8.6 million sq miles, before the revolution of 1917. The loss of Finland, the Baltic States and eastern Poland in 1918–19 reduced it by 780,000 sq km/300,000 sq miles, but Stalin all but made that good by 1945. Even today, the Russian Federation, shorn of 14 of the republics that formerly made up the Soviet Union, still stretches from the Baltic to the Pacific, occupying the northern part of Europe and Asia. This vast, sprawling country of many different nationalities, languages and cultures, developed over two centuries. Its disastrous involvement in World War I brought down the monarchy, and a moderate socialist republic was soon overthrown by the Bolsheviks led by Lenin, founder of the communist regime that endured for 70 years.

Left: Vladimir Ilyich Ulyanov, known as Lenin, was the Marxist revolutionary who led the Bolsheviks to power in 1917. Numerous stamps were issued from his death in 1924 onwards. This stamp of 1953, marking the 29th anniversary of his death, shows him during the October Revolution.

FALL OF THE TSARIST EMPIRE

Russia adopted adhesive stamps in 1858, having relied on pre-stamped envelopes since 1845. The format of the Russian stamps [1] was much smaller than that adopted by Britain and other countries and, indeed, has survived to this day. Variations on the theme of imperial arms continued up to the October Revolution of 1917, but in 1913 the Romanov dynasty celebrated its tercentenary with a portrait gallery of tsars from Michael I to the ill-starred Nicholas II [2], who abdicated in March 1917.

The Bolsheviks seized power in November 1917 and created the Russian Socialist Federal Soviet Republic (RSFSR). Tsarist stamps were overprinted with a hammer and sickle within a star and surcharged to cope with inflation [3]. Distinctive stamps symbolized revolution and liberty [4] and commemorated the fifth anniversary of the revolution [5]. Images of soldiers, workers and peasants [7] replaced tsarist symbols.

Civil war broke out in 1918 and dragged on until 1922. It was remembered philatelically by the ephemeral issues of breakaway governments from the Crimea to the Far East and the armies of Denikin, Wrangel, Avalov-Bermondt and others [8].

UNION OF SOVIET SOCIALIST REPUBLICS

Before his death in 1924 Lenin had clawed back a considerable part of the former empire, which had broken away at the revolution. In July 1923 he formed the Union of Socialist Soviet Republics, joining the RSFSR to the Ukraine, Belorussia and Transcaucasia. The Uzbek and Turkmen republics were added in 1924, the Tajik in 1929 and the Kazakh and Kirghiz republic in 1936. In 1940 Stalin added the Baltic States.

Following Lenin's death in January 1924 a set of four mourning stamps [9] appeared, and was reissued annually on the anniversary of his death until 1929. Lenin also appeared in many of the subsequent definitive sets, as well as countless special issues thereafter that formed part of the massive personality cult that grew up around him. By contrast, Stalin, his successor, appeared only twice – alongside Lenin on stamps marking the 10th and 20th anniversaries of the latter's death. For much of the Soviet period stamps were extremely propagandistic and introspective, either continually exhorting the workers to do better or trumpeting Soviet achievements, such as the mass flight over the North Pole in 1937–8 [10].

After the outbreak of the Great Patriotic War (set in motion by the German invasion of the USSR in 1941), the majority of stamps extolled the feats of Soviet heroes. However, a rare example of Soviet recognition of the Anglo-American contribution to the war effort came with two stamps of 1943 marking the 26th anniversary of the revolution and the Tehran Conference [6].

The issue of small-format definitives continued unabated from 1929 [11] to the 1960s [12] and beyond. In the post-Stalinist era stamps broadened in scope, noting cultural celebrities of other lands. The USSR was the first country to honour Scotland's national poet, Robert Burns, with a stamp in 1956 on the 160th anniversary of his death [13]. By the 1960s multicolour offset lithography went hand in hand with a more thematic approach and the Soviet Union's participation in international sporting events of the era [15], combined with occasional reminders of the Cold War [16].

RUSSIAN FEDERATION

One of the last issues of the USSR appeared in October 1991 and honoured heroes who helped defeat the attempted coup by communist hardliners [14]. By that time the Baltic States had declared independence and the USSR itself was formally dissolved on 29 December. Since January 1992 stamps have been inscribed "Rossija" and its Cyrillic equivalent. A small-format horizontal definitive series featured landmarks from the tsarist era [17] while special issues ranged from the splendours of old Russian decorative art [18] to wildlife [19] and children's cartoons [20]. Space achievements continued to rank high [21] and included a stamp celebrating a joint Russian–German space flight [22]. The

Stamps As Money

During World War I there was an acute shortage of small silver coins so the government reprinted the Romanov commemoratives of 1913 on cardboard with inscriptions on the reverse signifying their validity as coins.

500th anniversary of the discovery of America by Columbus was marked by a stamp showing the Stars and Stripes and the new Russian flag – actually the old tsarist flag revived.

Under the Soviet regime more than 6,000 stamps were issued, but in the years since the collapse of communism a more moderate policy has been pursued, omitting the political propaganda of the former era. Instead, like other former communist states, Russia has been engaging on a catching-up exercise, honouring personalities and anniversaries that would have been forbidden previously. Numerous sets in the past decade have extolled the glories and achievements of the tsarist period, culminating in the 3r stamp of 1998 commemorating the 80th anniversary of the death of Tsar Nicholas II. This stamp was issued with a *se-tenant* label portraying the entire royal family, murdered by the Bolsheviks at Ekaterinburg in 1918. Other issues have portrayed Peter the Great, notably the series of 2003 for the tercentenary of St Petersburg.

13

14

15

16

17

18

19

20

21

22

1

2

3

4

5

6

7

8

9

COMMONWEALTH OF INDEPENDENT STATES

The Commonwealth of Independent States was the name applied by Mikhail Gorbachev to the countries that emerged from the break-up of the USSR in 1991. In fact, the notion that the republics of the former Soviet Union would present any kind of image of solidarity was soon dispelled as the Ukraine came to the brink of war with Russia over the Crimea and numerous ethnic groups, from Abkhazia to Chechnya and Nagorno-Karabakh, attempted to secede and form independent states. Apart from the Baltic States only the Ukraine and the Caucasian republics had a previous existence as independent countries issuing their own stamps.

Left: The Ukrainian Soviet Republic was proclaimed in March 1919 and allied itself with the RSFSR in 1920. In July 1923 it became one of the constituents of the Soviet Union. Its only stamps were a set of June 1923 with premiums in aid of famine relief.

CAUCASIAN REPUBLICS

A national republic was proclaimed in May 1918 and used tsarist stamps overprinted with a national emblem. In March 1922 Armenia joined the Transcaucasian Federation and in this period issued stamps showing Mount Ararat [1] and other scenery. Since September 1991, when it declared independence, most of its stamps have been printed in England [2].

Briefly a national republic (May 1918 to April 1920) Azerbaijan became a Soviet republic when Red Army troops invaded. In this period it released a set for famine relief [3] before joining the Transcaucasian Federation in March 1922. Independence was declared on August 18, 1991, unissued stamps showing the Caspian Sea being overprinted [4]. Since then Azerbaijan has embarked on many "bandwagon" issues for John Lennon, Princess Diana and other international celebrities.

Nakhichevan, an Azerbaijani enclave entirely surrounded by Armenia, had its own government from 1924. It briefly had its own stamps in 1993 showing a map and portrait of President Aliev, who later became president of Azerbaijan itself [5].

Georgia was a national republic from May 1918 until February 1921 and in that time issued stamps showing St George [6]. It then became a Soviet republic and joined the Transcaucasian Federation, issuing stamps overprinted for famine relief in 1922 [7]. It regained its independence on April 9, 1991, and issued stamps originally inscribed "Gruzija" [8] but titled "Georgia" since 1993 [9].

When the Transcaucasian Federation was formed in 1922 each state continued to issue its own stamps until September 1923, when a general issue appeared [10]. These stamps were superseded by those of the USSR in 1924 and 70 years elapsed before separate issues were resumed.

WESTERN REPUBLICS

The political history of the Ukraine was broadly parallel to that of the Caucasus, with a national republic from January 1918 to March 1919. Most of the stamps issued in this period were tsarist stamps overprinted with the Ukrainian trident, and many variations of this appeared in different towns [11]. History repeated itself when the Ukraine declared its independence in

August 1991, with various trident overprints on the Soviet definitives [12]. Many of the stamps issued since then have been printed in Canada [13].

Neither Belarus nor Moldova had a previous philatelic existence, although they were constituent republics of the USSR, previously known as Belorussia (White Russia) and Moldavia (whose name was changed to avoid confusion with the Romanian province of that name). They became fully independent in August and December 1991 respectively, although Moldova had previously asserted its sovereignty within the Soviet Union in 1990 and its first stamps celebrated the first anniversary [14]. Subsequently Soviet stamps were overprinted [15] pending the issue of stamps printed in Bulgaria, Hungary or Spain. The stamps of Belarus were printed in Moscow [16] but are now produced locally in Minsk.

ASIAN REPUBLICS

The remaining republics, which entered the stamp album only in the 1990s, were all within the territory formerly known as Soviet Central Asia.

Below: These stamps issued in 1992 were among the first independent issues by the former Soviet Central Asian states Turkmenistan and Uzbekistan.

A Feeling of Déjà Vu

The only distinctive stamps of the national republic of the Ukraine were those in a set of July 1918 showing the head of Ceres and various national emblems. After the Ukraine regained independence in 1991, the Ceres design was revived in a reduced size for the definitive series of 1992.

Kazakhstan declared independence in December 1991 and has had its stamps produced in Vienna [17], Paris, Berlin, Budapest, Oslo and Leipzig. Kyrgyzstan became independent in September 1991. Most of its stamps have been printed in Moscow [18].

Tajikistan asserted its sovereignty on 25 August 1990, and its independence on 9 September 1991, producing its own stamps from May 1992 [19]. Turkmenistan became independent on 27 October 1991, and issued a stamp portraying President Niyazov and the national flag to mark its first anniversary. Uzbekistan declared its sovereignty on 20 June 1990, and became independent in August 1991. In matters of stamp production it has remained faithful to Moscow.

PROVISIONAL ISSUES

In 1992–4 there was a tremendous flood of local provisional issues in the territories of the former Soviet Union, allegedly produced by the regional postal authorities during a period of political and economic turmoil, when postal rates rose sharply and there was an acute shortage of stamps. Apart from the definitives overprinted at St Petersburg, most of these have been ignored by the standard catalogues.

10

11

12

13

14

15

16

17

18

19

1

2

3

4

5

6

7

8

9

10

11

ALBANIA

The Balkans were the most unstable part of Europe in the late 19th and 20th centuries. The political upheavals of the dying years of the Turkish Empire, and the struggles between the various ethnic groups that continue today, are reflected in the bewildering array of stamps marking liberation from Turkish rule and the intervention of various European powers, as well as the rivalries of the different nationalities. Nowhere was this truer than in Albania, one of the most remote and backward outposts of the Ottoman Empire, where most of the inhabitants were Muslim and divided into two main tribes, the Ghegs and Tosks, but with large minorities of Greeks in the south and Slavs in the north and east.

Left: A pair of stamps marked the first anniversary of the death of Mikel Koliqi, the first Albanian cardinal, in 1998.

INDEPENDENCE, INVASION AND ISOLATION

During the First Balkan War, Albania declared its independence of Turkey. Its first stamps, issued in June 1913, were contemporary Turkish stamps overprinted "Shqipenia" (Albania) with the double-headed eagle. When these ran out, the Albanians resorted to makeshifts produced by typewriting and various rubber handstamps [1].

In February 1914 the provisional government invited a German prince, William of Wied, to be king. Stamps bearing his portrait were printed in Austria but never issued as such [2], and William returned to Germany when war broke out in August. Albania was a battleground between opposing forces in World War I, but for a time (1914–16) Essad Pasha ruled Central Albania until he was driven out by the Austrians [3]. In December 1916 French troops invaded from Salonika and established the autonomous province of Koritsa, which lasted until the French withdrew in 1920 [4].

A provisional government under Turhan Bey was established at Shkoder (Scutari) in December 1918, backed by an inter-allied commission to protect Albania from the Serbs. Austrian revenue stamps were overprinted and used until 1920 [5]. A regency was created at Shkoder in February 1920, continuing until January 1925. Ironically its first stamps were those of Prince William with the portrait obscured [6].

In December 1924 the national assembly voted for a republic and Ahmed Zogu Bey was elected president. The overprint signifies the return of the government to Tirana [7]. In 1928 the assembly voted for a return to a hereditary monarchy and elected the president, who took the title of King Zog I, the last republican series being appropriately overprinted [8].

On 7 April 1939, Italian troops invaded Albania and ousted Zog. Soon afterwards Victor Emmanuel III of Italy was proclaimed king of Albania [9]. The surrender of Italy in 1943 created a vacuum in the Balkans that was soon filled by the Germans. Stamps overprinted "14 Shtator 1943" (14 September) marked the German occupation [10]. Albanian partisans led by Enver Hoxha drove out the Germans and declared the Democratic State of Albania on 22 October 1944 [11]. The constituent assembly declared Albania a people's republic on 11 January 1946, effecting the country's 12th change of status in 35 years [12].

The doctrinaire communism of the Hoxha era was reflected in stamps portraying Marx, Lenin and Stalin [13] or showing wartime partisans and the triumph of socialism. Stereotyped motifs were not enhanced by the poor quality of the printing. From 1961, however, a more thematic approach was adopted in a bid to earn hard currency, and numerous sets featured birds, flowers, wild animals, cattle, dogs and other popular subjects. At the same time, Albania's gradual emergence from self-imposed isolation as the last bastion of Stalinism in Europe was reflected in stamps marking participation in the Olympic Games and other sporting contests. As the quality of printing improved, numerous sets reproduced paintings, mosaics and sculpture.

On 29 April 1991, Albania cast off communism and became a democratic republic. This change has been reflected in stamps honouring personalities and events banned in the communist era. Another sign of the times is the production of stamps in recent years by Alex Matsoukis, the leading Greek stamp printer.

ITALIAN POST OFFICES

In the closing years of Turkish rule Italy operated post offices in Albania, using Italian stamps overprinted "Albania" [14] or the names of the principal towns of Durazzo [15], Janina [16], Scutari [17] and Valona [18], but surcharged in Turkish currency. The last of them, in Scutari and Valona, were closed in 1918 but the Italians maintained a toehold in Albania, having occupied the island of Sazan (Saseno)

Below: A number of stamps were printed locally during the Greek occupation of southern Albania during World War II. This issue from the town of Erseka was based on the Greek flag.

Handstruck Stamps

The oddest of the Epirus provisionals was the set of four produced by Greek insurgents at Chimara in February 1914, with the skull and crossbones and the countermark of the area commander.

in the Gulf of Valona in October 1914 and remained there until 1943. Stamps were issued in 1923 [19].

GREEK OCCUPATIONS

In 1913 the European powers decided that Epirus should form part of Albania, but the mainly Greek population thought otherwise and rose in revolt. A provisional government was established in 1914 and stamps showing a rifleman were printed in Corfu [20] followed by stamps showing the double-headed eagle and Greek cross flag, overprinted at Koritsa [21]. Other issues were produced at Moschopolis [22] and other towns, including a set showing the Greek flag. In December 1914 the powers agreed that Greece should occupy the territory that had declared its independence, which was now renamed Northern Epirus. Greek stamps thus overprinted were in use from then until June 1916, when the region was occupied by Italian troops and returned to Albania in 1919.

In 1939 Italy seized Albania and from here the invasion of Greece was mounted in October 1940. However, the Greeks counterattacked and not only drove the invaders out but pursued them into southern Albania. Greek stamps overprinted to signify "Greek Occupation" were in use in Epirus until April 1941 [23].

12

13

14

15

16

17

18

19

20

21

22

23

BULGARIA AND ROMANIA

The countries bordering the Black Sea's west coast were important powers in the Middle Ages, but succumbed to Turkish rule until the 19th century. Moldavia and Wallachia united to form the kingdom of Romania in 1881. The principality of Bulgaria, created by the Congress of Berlin in 1878, remained under Turkish suzerainty until independence in 1908.

1

2

3

4

5

6

7

8

9

10

11

Left: After 1878 Bulgaria south of the Balkan Mountains remained under the Turks, who produced stamps for use in Eastern Roumelia, as this area was called. In 1885 the people rebelled and declared the state of South Bulgaria, overprinting stamps before uniting with the north.

KINGDOM AND PRINCIPALITY

The Danubian principalities of Moldavia and Wallachia [1] gained autonomy in 1858, later uniting to form Romania under local hero Prince Alexander Cuza. In 1866 he was forced to abdicate in favour of a German aristocrat, Prince Karl of Hohenzollern-Sigmaringen [2], who proclaimed himself King Carol I in 1881. In 1906 Romania celebrated Carol's 40 years on the throne by issuing no fewer than 43 stamps, including one of the earliest charity (semi-postal) sets showing Queen Elisabeth – better known as the poet Carmen Sylva – spinning, weaving and tending a wounded soldier [3].

The principality of Bulgaria, though nominally under Turkish suzerainty, was politically and economically dependent on Russia and France, as reflected in the centime currency of the first stamps [4]. Prince Ferdinand of Saxe-Coburg was chosen by the European powers to rule the principality, shown on the stamps of 1901. He assumed the title of tsar in 1909, reviving Bulgaria's ambitions to dominate the Balkans [5].

BALKAN WARS AND WORLD WAR I

Bulgaria achieved its greatest extent as a result of the First Balkan War of 1912–13, adding Western Thrace, which gave it access to the Aegean. Stamps overprinted at the time [7] referred to it as a war of liberation, but it triggered off a second war in which Bulgaria faced its erstwhile allies Greece and Serbia and was shorn of Thrace, which went to Greece. Resentment at this led to Bulgaria's alignment with Germany and its old enemy Turkey in World War I. A set of stamps was projected in 1915, when Bulgaria again briefly occupied Macedonia and the Dobrudja, but was not actually issued until 1921 [6].

Romania entered World War I on the Allied side in 1916 but suffered heavy losses in 1917–18. Its reward, however, was the cession by Hungary of Transylvania, for which Romania overprinted Hungarian stamps at Cluj and Oradea in 1919 [8]. During the war Romania was largely overrun by troops of the Central Powers, and stamps were issued or overprinted by Austria, Bulgaria and Germany for those areas under their control [9–11].

THE SHADOW OF FASCISM

Both Bulgaria and Romania embraced fascism in the 1930s and were allied to Germany in World War II. In 1930 Boris III married Princess Giovanna of Italy, a political marriage that drew Bulgaria into Mussolini's orbit [12].

In Romania six-year-old King Michael succeeded his grandfather Ferdinand in July 1927. He was shown on the definitive series of 1928 [13], but abdicated in favour of his father Carol II, who had been passed over on account of his turbulent private life. He gained the throne in 1930 as a result of a coup but was forced to abdicate in 1940 [14]. Michael became king a second time and played a major role in the overthrow of the fascist dictatorship of Antonescu in 1944. Although Romania was occupied by the Red Army Michael held on to his throne until the end of 1947, when Romania became a people's republic [15].

Bulgaria changed sides when it was occupied by the Red Army in 1944 but remained a kingdom under the boy king Simeon [19] until September 15, 1946.

RISE OF COMMUNISM

For a brief period Bulgarian stamps were simply inscribed "Republic" [16] but soon it was officially styled a people's republic, denoted by the inscription "Narodna Republika", later shortened to "N.R." The communist propaganda of the early issues soon gave way to a revival of national pride in Bulgaria's long history [17]. Communism never supplanted the Orthodox faith, which was reflected in numerous stamps featuring monasteries and religious art [18].

As everywhere else in the communist bloc, early issues in both countries were dominated by propaganda, but by the 1960s a more liberal policy was in force. Romania played a prominent part in publicizing international cultural figures such as Shakespeare [20]. This policy has continued to the present day, especially since the overthrow of the Ceausescus in 1989 and the restoration of democracy. Stamps of 1999 portrayed Charlie Chaplin as well as Laurel and Hardy [21].

In the wake of the collapse of communism in eastern Europe, Bulgaria became a democratic republic on 15 November 1990. There was no change in the stamps, which had long since shed the "N.R." inscription and adopted bilingual captions.

The Times Correspondent

In 1921 the first Englishman to appear on a foreign stamp was James D. Bourchier, the Balkans correspondent of *The Times*, whose despatches in 1877 helped to influence public opinion in favour of the Bulgars.

Below: For The Europa Tales and Legends theme (1997), Romania depicted Dracula and Vlad the Impaler.

12

13 14

15

16 17

18

19 20

21

1

2

3

4

5

6

7

8

9

10

FORMER YUGOSLAVIA

The kingdom of Yugoslavia was an artificial creation of the Allied Powers at the end of World War I. At its core was the kingdom of Serbia, a Turkish province from 1458 until 1804, then an autonomous principality under Turkish suzerainty until its independence was proclaimed by the Treaty of Berlin in 1878. It was closely allied to the tiny principality of Montenegro, which, alone of the Christian areas in the Balkans, retained its independence after the collapse of the Byzantine Empire in 1453.

Left: The first special issue of the new kingdom in 1921 was a set of three charity stamps for the disabled soldiers' fund. This stamp reproduced Uros Predic's painting of the Kosovo Maiden *tending a wounded man on the battlefield in 1389.*

SERBIA

While Montenegro had been ruled by a prince-bishop, Serbia was headed by one or other of two rival clans. In 1866, when stamps were introduced, the nation was ruled by Prince Michael Obrenovich [1], whose father Milosh had ousted Kara Georg (Black George). Michael was murdered in 1868 and succeeded by his nephew Milan, who proclaimed himself king in 1882 and abdicated in 1889. His son, Alexander I, succeeded him and reigned until 1903, when he and his consort were brutally murdered by a group of officers. This atrocity brought to the throne Peter, grandson of Kara Georg, whose first stamps were those portraying his luckless predecessor with the portrait blotted out by the royal arms [2]. Peter commanded the Serbian army in the Balkan Wars and the opening campaign of World War I [3].

Although Serbia was overrun by the Central Powers, the Serbian army managed to escape to Corfu, where it used French stamps overprinted [4] – the first instance of a postal service in exile. The Serbs shared this misfortune with their Montenegrin allies.

MONTENEGRO

In contrast with the bloody history of Serbia, Montenegro was ruled for 60 years by Prince Nikita and fought in the Russo-Turkish War (1877–8) and the Balkan Wars. Stamps were introduced in 1874 but to Montenegro goes the credit for issuing the first commemorative stamps by a European government, celebrating the 400th anniversary of printing, in January 1893 [5]. These overprints on the definitive series were followed in 1896 by a long set marking the bicentenary of the Petrovich dynasty [7]. Nikita proclaimed himself king in 1910 [8] but in 1919 he fled to the French Riviera where he died in 1921.

KINGDOM OF THE SERBS, CROATS AND SLOVENES

Nikita's kingdom merged with the new state that was known originally as the Kingdom of the Serbs, Croats and Slovenes. These peoples had been ruled by Hungary and Austria respectively. The kingdom also included part of Macedonia, a melting-pot that had been fought over by Serbia, Greece and Bulgaria in the second Balkan War (and which remains a bone of contention with Greece to this day).

They were joined by Bosnia and Herzegovina, Turkish provinces that had been occupied by Austria-Hungary in 1878. Their early stamps did not even bear a name, the Habsburg arms being sufficient identification [6]. The names (in German) briefly appeared in a pictorial series of 1906 [10] but during World War I an inscription

The Death Mask Stamps

A few months after the murder of Alexander I in 1903, Peter I celebrated his coronation and the centenary of the Karageorgevich dynasty with a set of stamps engraved and printed in France. They showed the conjoined profiles of Kara Georg and Peter but when they were turned upside down people imagined they could see the death mask of the murdered king. The stamps were hastily withdrawn from use as a result.

signifying the Royal and Imperial Military Post was substituted. To this period belongs the set of three stamps issued in 1917 in memory of Archduke Franz Ferdinand and his wife Sophie Chotek, whose assassination by Serb terrorists in June 1914 triggered off World War I [11].

At the end of that war the stamps of Bosnia and Herzegovina were overprinted "Država S.H.S." in Roman or Cyrillic lettering [12] to denote the union of Serbs, Croats and Slovenes. Hungarian stamps overprinted "Hrvatska S.H.S." were used in Croatia [9], pending the introduction of an Art Nouveau series [13]. Slovenia had a series of stamps popularly known as the Chainbreakers [14], as well as long vertical stamps with allegorical themes [15] or a portrait of King Peter [16]. A general issue for the whole kingdom, recess-printed by the American Banknote Company, appeared in 1921, portraying Peter or his son Alexander, who succeeded him that August [17]. A definitive series of 1926–7 portraying King Alexander [18] was printed in Belgrade from plates made in Austria.

YUGOSLAVIA

The name of the kingdom was changed to Yugoslavia ("land of the southern Slavs") in October 1929, in a desperate bid to hold together this ramshackle conglomeration of different religious, linguistic and ethnic groups. King Alexander realized that attempts at democratic institutions had failed and that the only solution was to impose a dictatorship based on fascist models. At the same time, strenuous attempts were made to give the different nationalities parity at all levels and this is reflected in the stamps.

The first issue of the new regime, in fact, celebrated the millennium of the ancient kingdom of Croatia; on two of the stamps King Tomislav, the first ruler of the kingdom in the 10th century, was portrayed alongside Alexander (who named his younger son after the medieval Croat hero). The stamps were released on 1 November 1929, and had obviously been designed and engraved before the political change; it was not until April 1931 that stamps inscribed "Kraljevina Yugoslavija" appeared. Commemoratives of the early 1930s highlighted events or anniversaries in Serbia and Croatia in equal measure. A new definitive series appeared in 1931 showing a facing portrait of Alexander in military uniform.

Alexander's policies, however, failed to appease growing demands from Croat separatists. Just after the fifth anniversary of the united kingdom Alexander was assassinated during a state visit to Marseilles. The entire definitive series was re-issued a few days later with a heavy black border [19] in mourning for the murdered king.

Alexander was succeeded by his 11-year-old elder son Peter. Peter had made his philatelic debut the previous year in the uniform of Sokol, a physical training and sports organization, to mark its meeting in Ljubljana [21]. A definitive series portraying the boy king appeared in 1935 [20], while a grown-up portrait of him appeared on the last definitives of prewar Yugoslavia, in 1939–40 [22].

11

12

13

14

15

16

17

18

19

20

21

22

1

2

3

4

5

6

7

8

9

10

YUGOSLAVIA: DIVISION, RECONSTRUCTION AND CIVIL WAR

As a country of peoples of widely differing linguistic, cultural, historic, religious and ethnic backgrounds, Yugoslavia was ruthlessly held together by strong men – King Alexander before World War II and Marshal Tito after it. Without such figures, it was bound to fall apart, first due to external threat and latterly due to implosion. As ancient rivalries between Serbia and Croatia surfaced, religious or racial tensions involving the Slovenes, Macedonians and Kosovar Albanians erupted into violent warfare, bringing a new expression – "ethnic cleansing", a euphemism for genocide – into common parlance.

Left: After being occupied by the Germans, the Yugoslavs freed themselves thanks to the partisans led by Josip Broz Tito, who formed the communist government that ruled the country until the 1990s.

WARTIME OCCUPATION

On 6 April 1941, Yugoslavia was invaded by German, Italian, Hungarian and Bulgarian forces. The Yugoslavs surrendered 11 days later and their country was dismembered by the invading powers. Germany annexed Lower Styria and Italy grabbed the rest of Slovenia, while also adding to the territory it had previously gained from the invasion of Albania. Hungary acquired territory north of the Sava and Bulgaria acquired those parts of Macedonia that Serbia had seized in 1914. Yugoslav stamps were overprinted by the Italians for use in Lubiana [1], but when Italy changed sides the Germans seized this area and overprinted Italian stamps with the German name of Laibach [2].

The rest of Yugoslavia was partitioned into three states. Croatia was nominally a kingdom but was ruled by the *poglavnik* (dictator) Ante Pavelich. Yugoslav stamps were overprinted with the Croat arms [3] followed by definitives portraying Pavelich [4]. The Croat Legion fought on the Eastern Front [5]. Montenegro used Yugoslav stamps overprinted by the Italians and later the Germans, while Serbia became a puppet state [6].

As in World War I, a government in exile was formed abroad, and distinctive stamps keeping alive the name of Yugoslavia were produced in England for the use of the Yugoslav Merchant Navy working with the Allies [7].

YUGOSLAVIA RECONSTITUTED

Resistance to the enemy was split between two movements: the royalist Chetniks under Draza Mihailovic and the communist Partisans led by Josip Broz, known as Tito. The latter triumphed in 1943; the Chetniks (often accused of collaborating with the Nazis) were discredited, and the communists seized power. Stamps of wartime Serbia and Montenegro were overprinted in December 1944 to signify the Democratic Federation of Yugoslavia [8], composed of the six republics of Serbia, Croatia, Slovenia, Montenegro, Bosnia–Herzegovina and Macedonia, with the federal territory of Kosovo, whose inhabitants were predominantly Albanian.

As everywhere else in the communist bloc, the early stamps were heavily politicized, a notable exception being those of 1948 marking the 80th anniversary of the death of Laurenz

Kosir, the "ideological creator" of the postage stamp. He had proposed the use of adhesive stamps some years before Rowland Hill but his recommendation was merely filed away. By the 1960s, however, a more thematic approach, with stamps featuring wildlife, flowers and Adriatic resorts, reflected an appreciation of the global stamp market and tourism as major sources of hard currency [9].

Obligatory tax stamps (with corresponding postage due labels for mail not bearing these stamps) were a recurring feature of the post-war years. Popular annual issues included stamps for Children's Week, while Yugoslavia was the first communist country to introduce Christmas stamps, in 1966.

A set of stamps marking Tito's 75th birthday in 1967 was retained and expanded as a definitive series, followed in 1971–3 by a long series featuring landmarks and scenery.

COLLAPSE OF COMMUNISM

The collapse of communism in 1991 led to the fragmentation of the Federation, and Croatia and Slovenia seceded in May and June respectively. Both were invaded by Serbia and for a time separate issues of stamps appeared in Kraina [10] and the Baranjska Oblast. Most of the early stamps of Croatia were obligatory tax stamps to raise money for national defence, but by 1993 stamps reflected global events and personalities [11]. This pattern was also followed by Slovenia, beginning with definitives featuring the national emblem [14] but soon paying tribute to UNICEF [13] and the United Nations for its support, or providing colourful images of international appeal.

Bosnia and Herzegovina declared independence in April 1992 and armorial stamps were issued by the Sarajevo government [12]. The country was soon embroiled in war, being fought over by Croats and Serbs, each issuing their own stamps. Recent issues from the Sarajevo government include a stamp for the AIDS appeal.

Diana Remembered

Following the tragic death of Diana, Princess of Wales, in 1997, Bosnia and Herzegovina issued a stamp in her memory. It was a reminder of her work for the eradication of landmines and of the visit she made to the war-torn country shortly before her death. The design featured an informal photograph of the princess in Sarajevo, with red roses and a map of Bosnia in the background.

Following a referendum, Macedonia declared its independence in September 1991. A high proportion of its stamps were for compulsory use, to raise funds for the Red Cross, or emphasizing the cultural identity of this ancient country [15] – a matter that has caused a major rift with neighbouring Greece.

SERBIA AND MONTENEGRO

Stamps inscribed "Yugoslavia" continued to be issued in Serbia and Montenegro, generally carrying on the colourful but bland policy of catering to the international market, but occasionally making a political point, such as the Destroyed Bridges series and Bombed Buildings pair of 1999, lashing out at NATO [16–17]. During this period, however, obligatory stamps were regularly produced for Serbia alone and thus inscribed [18].

The fiction of Yugoslavia ended in 2003 when stamps inscribed "Serbia and Montenegro" were introduced. Designs for these combine the image of a country striving to fit in with the international community [20] with a constant harking back to the glories of medieval times [19].

11

12

13

14

15

16

17

18

19

20

1

2

3

4

5

6

7

8

9

10

11

12

GREECE

The Greeks had been part of the Ottoman Empire since the fall of the Byzantine Empire in 1453, but in 1821 they rebelled and began a ten-year War of Independence in which Britain, France and Russia allied to defeat the Turks. In 1833 the European Powers selected Prince Otto of Bavaria to be King of the Hellenes, but he was deposed in 1862 and Prince William of Schleswig-Holstein-Sonderburg-Glucksburg replaced him, taking the title of George I.

Left: In 2004 the modern Olympic Games returned to Athens, where they had first been held in 1896. Numerous sets of Greek stamps publicized the Games ahead of the event and several others were issued during and after the Olympics.

CLASSICAL TRADITIONS

Stamps were introduced in Greece in 1861 [1]. Until 1911 all definitives portrayed Hermes, messenger of the gods, in various forms, and even thereafter a high proportion of stamps have drawn on the rich store of classical mythology and art. From 1927 onwards different motifs were used for the various definitive issues, and the vast majority were devoted to the glories of Ancient Greece. The 1935–9 airmails focused on mythological characters, while the airmails of 1942–3 drew on the spirits of the various winds. This tradition continues, as can be seen in the sets illustrating the labours of Hercules [3] or the 1988 definitives portraying the Olympian gods [4]. Even modern events and institutions are commemorated by designs that seek a parallel from the classical period.

BALKAN WARS

In the first hundred years of independence Greece doubled its territory. Britain ceded the Ionian Islands in 1864 and Crete (after a period of autonomy within the Turkish Empire but under Anglo-Russian administration) gradually passed into Greek hands after 1906 [2]. The largest accretion came in the Balkan Wars of 1912–13, which not only confirmed possession of Crete but also gave Greece western Thrace [5] and many Aegean islands, such as Lemnos [6] and Samos [7]. In the second Balkan War Greece took Dedeagatz from Bulgaria [8].

Several compulsory tax stamps were issued in this period to raise money for war wounded and widows and orphans [9]. After World War I Greece seized eastern Thrace [10] but had to cede it to Turkey in 1922. This crushing defeat toppled the monarchy, marked by the overprint "Epanastasis" (Revolution), applied ironically to the remaining Victory stamps of 1913 [11]. Attempts to take over the Dodecanese Islands from Turkey in 1912 were foiled by the Italians, who held them until 1944.

MONARCHY RESTORED

The monarchy was restored in November 1935, signalled by the date and crown overprinted on all stamps then current [12]. During the period of the first republic Greece celebrated its centenary of independence with a long set portraying the heroes of that struggle [13]. Previously, two stamps of 1924 had marked the centenary of the death of Lord Byron at Missolonghi [14], and a 1927 set honoured the centenary of the naval battle at Navarino when the combined fleets of Britain, France and Russia defeated the Turks.

Preparing to invade Greece in October 1940, Mussolini issued an ultimatum, to which the Greeks replied with a resounding "Oxi!"(No!); this was

Eating His Words

In 1907 Winston Churchill, then Under-Secretary of State for the Colonies, visited Cyprus and said: "I think it is only natural that the Cypriot people who are of Greek descent should regard their incorporation with what may be called their mother country as an ideal to be earnestly, devoutly and fervently cherished..." When Britain refused the Greek Cypriot demands for *enosis* (unification with Greece) in 1954 his speech was quoted by Mrs Lena Jeger in a House of Commons debate on July 28. The relevant page from *Hansard* (the report of parliamentary proceedings) was reproduced on a set of Greek stamps, with a symbolic black blot across the middle.

the subject of two stamps on its fifth anniversary [15]. When the Italians invaded, the Greeks chased them all the way back to the Adriatic.

Coming to the aid of their allies, the Germans invaded Greece in April 1941. The royal family fled to Cairo, and Greece endured four years of occupation and privation that shattered the economy and reduced the population to starvation level. The currency collapsed and Greece suffered inflation, which was reflected in stamps that ran up to 5 million drachmae in 1944 [17]. A regency headed by Archbishop Damaskinos continued to September 1946, when a plebiscite voted to restore the monarchy.

POSTWAR PERIOD

Greece was one of the few countries to mourn the death of Franklin D. Roosevelt with an issue of stamps [16]. Although the royalist government was pro-western, a powerful communist movement arose out of the wartime partisans, which led to a long-running civil war that was reflected in several issues. A stamp of 1949 showing a column of women and children alluded to the abduction of Greek children to the neighbouring communist countries of Albania and Bulgaria [18].

From 1968 onwards Greek stamps were inscribed "Hellas", the Roman version of the country name, to conform to Universal Postal Union regulations insisting that countries should be identified in the universally recognized alphabet. In 1967 a military junta seized power, but apart from a set of 1972 marking the fifth anniversary of the revolution, the regime made little impact on stamps. In 1973 King Constantine II attempted a counter-coup and when this failed he fled to Italy. The monarchy was abolished in his absence on June 1, 1973.

These political upheavals had remarkably little effect on the stamps, which continued to lean heavily on classical subjects. If anything, references to the glories of Ancient Greece have tended to increase in recent years, as suitable motifs derived from Hellenistic civilization are found for many subjects, from the Greek presidency of the EU (the allegorical figure of Hellas driving her chariot) to the second Pan-European Transport Conference (Hermes leading Selene's chariot). In addition to a wider use of the most popular themes [19] many very recent stamps have given prominence to the Macedon of Philip II and Alexander the Great [20] as a counter to the independent republic of Macedonia. Icons are a popular subject for Christmas stamps in general but especially for the Millennium series of 2000 [21], showing the birth of Christ. Greece issues Europa stamps each year in the prevailing theme [22].

13

14

15

16

17

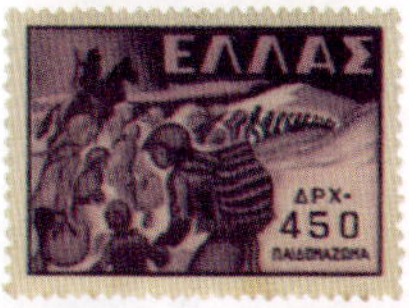

18

19

20

21

22

1

2

3

4

5

6

7

8

9

10

TURKEY

Although most of Turkey is geographically in western Asia, it was formerly a great European power and in 1683 the Turks even laid siege to Vienna. At the height of their power, the Sultans ruled an empire that stretched along the north coast of Africa and included the whole of the Balkans. By the 1850s, however, Turkey was "the sick man of Europe", and it lost most of its European territory in a series of wars from the 1820s to 1914. Siding with Germany and Austria in World War I, it suffered humiliating defeats and lost its Asiatic dominions: Palestine, Syria, Iraq and the Lebanon. When the Greeks attempted to seize the coast of Asia Minor in 1922, the Young Turks rose in revolt. Led by Kemal Pasha, they abolished the sultanate and declared a republic. Kemal Pasha transferred the capital from Istanbul (Constantinople) to Ankara and embarked on a process of rapid westernization, abolishing Turkish dress and compelling everyone to adopt western-style surnames. He himself took the name of Ataturk, "Father of the Turks".

Left: One of Kemal's most important reforms was the replacement of Arabic by a modified form of the Roman alphabet. Stamps of 1938 show him teaching the new alphabet.

TURKISH ISSUES

Turkey introduced postage stamps in 1863 [1], the chief motif being the *toughra* (a combination of seal and signature) of Sultan Abdul-Aziz. Stamps showing the ruler's mark or the Moslem crescent continued for some years [2]. Stamps of 1908 were overprinted "*Behie*" (discount) to compete with the foreign post offices operating in Turkey. In 1914 a new series, recess-printed by Bradbury Wilkinson in England, featured scenery and landmarks [3]. Several World War I issues showed life at the battlefront [4].

Kemal raised the standard of revolt at Ankara in April 1920. Stamps showing the first parliament house of the republic [5] were issued in 1922. By November 1923 Kemal had driven out the Greeks and extended his nationalist regime to the whole country. Since then, Kemal has appeared on more Turkish stamps than Washington has on American issues. The two men appeared on the same stamp following the 150th anniversary of the American constitution in 1939, celebrated with a large Turkish commemorative. [6]

Until 1951 stamps were inscribed "Türkiye Postalari" (Turkish Posts) and then "Türkiye Cumhuriyeti Postalari" (Turkish Republic Posts). From 1956 "Türkiye" alone was used but since 1966 "Türkiye Cumhuriyeti" has been preferred [7]. Modern stamps are lithographed in Ankara or Istanbul. While many special issues highlight the technological progress of the modern state [8], others cover historical events [9] and even foster the colourful regional costumes [10] that Kemal tried to stamp out. Tradition mixes easily with modernization [11]. Above all, Kemal himself is a constant thread running through Turkish philately; he is portrayed here on one of the stamps of 2003 celebrating the 80th anniversary of the republic [12].

ASSOCIATED TERRITORIES

Although numerous stamps reflect the invasion and occupation of Turkish territory that now forms part of Greece, Albania, Romania, Bulgaria and Russia, the process was reversed in 1898 when the Turks invaded Thessaly, a Greek province. Five octagonal stamps showing the railway bridge at Vardar were used by Turkish troops before they evacuated most of the area, which reverted to Greece [14].

In 1919 the French occupied Cilicia, formerly the *vilayet* (province) of Adana, and overprinted Turkish stamps [13] with the name and initials "T.E.O." for *Territoires Ennemis Occupés* (Occupied Enemy Territories). The territory reverted to Turkey in October 1921. In 1923 the French granted autonomy to the *sanjak* of Alexandretta and overprinted Syrian stamps for the purpose. When they planned to hand this Turkish enclave to Syria in 1938, the inhabitants rose in revolt. Following a plebiscite it became the autonomous republic of Hatay. Turkish stamps were overprinted in 1939 [15] before its re-incorporation into Turkey in June 1939.

FOREIGN POST OFFICES

For many years up to the outbreak of World War I the external posts of the Ottoman Empire were run by various foreign powers. Stamps surcharged in Turkish currency or inscribed "Levant" or the name of a town were used at the various foreign post offices.

Austria-Hungary maintained a number of offices in Constantinople, Smyrna and those parts of the Balkans that were under Turkish rule. Stamps of Lombardy and Venetia were introduced in 1867, but from 1880 Austrian stamps surcharged in paras or piastres were used [16]. The British offices used ordinary British stamps, identifiable by their cancellations, but from 1885 to 1914 stamps were surcharged in Turkish currency [17]. France not only had a general issue, similar to contemporary French stamps but engraved with the name "Levant" [18], but also overprints for use at individual offices. German stamps surcharged in Turkish currency were adopted in 1870 [19].

The Italian post offices began with a general issue inscribed "Estero" (foreign) but from 1902 Italian stamps were overprinted with the name of the individual office and surcharged in Turkish currency [20]. Russia also favoured individual stamps for each of its 13 offices as well as a general series for the Russian Company for Steam Shipping and Trade, known by the abbreviation ROPiT. The British post offices were reopened in 1919–21, while Poland and Romania also operated post offices in this period.

Below: This Syrian stamp was overprinted by the French for use in the sanjak *(region) of Alexandretta.*

Typewritten Stamps

Probably the oddest stamps to emerge during World War I were those produced by Lieut. Commander Harry Pirie-Gordon DSC, RNVR, who commanded a detachment of the Royal Navy that occupied the island of Cheustan, or Makronisi, in the Gulf of Smyrna for a few weeks in 1916. During that period the commander produced his own stamps on the office typewriter, inscribed "Long Island" (a translation of the Turkish and Greek names), with the royal monogram "G.R.I." at the top and denominated in sterling.

11

12

13

14

15

16

17

18

19

20

1

2

3

4

5

6

7

8

9

10

11

12

ITALY

Like Germany, 19th-century Italy was divided into a number of separate kingdoms and duchies, while Lombardy and Venetia, the South Tirol and Italian-speaking districts north of the Adriatic were in Austrian hands. From the 1830s Giuseppe Mazzini's Young Italy movement encouraged the idea of unification. After defeat against Austria in 1848–9, Mazzini's followers started the second War of Independence in 1859, aided by Giuseppe Garibaldi. By the end of 1860 southern Italy was unified under Victor Emmanuel II of Sardinia, though Lombardy and Venetia remained in Austrian hands until 1866 and Rome was garrisoned by the French until 1870.

Left: The battles of Magenta (appropriately depicted on a magenta-coloured stamp of 1959) and Solferino (whose carnage inspired Henri Dunant to found the Red Cross) were two of the great conflicts in the war that unified Italy.

ITALIAN STATES

Before 1860 the various states issued their own stamps. Modena and Parma [1] were duchies under Austrian rule, while Naples [2] and Sicily [3] formed the Kingdom of the Two Sicilies, ruled by Ferdinand II, nicknamed "King Bomba" from his habit of bombarding his unruly subjects from time to time. Since 754 the Pope had ruled Rome and the surrounding territory, known variously as the States of the Church or the Papal States [4]; it included the Romagna extending to the Adriatic coast [5]. The grand duchy of Tuscany [6] fell to the liberators in August 1859 and latterly had stamps featuring the arms of Savoy as a prelude to unification with Sardinia [7], whose ruler eventually became king of Italy. Stamps with his embossed profile were issued in the Neapolitan Provinces [8] following the unification of Italy, pending the introduction of lire currency there.

THE RISE OF FASCISM

Italy made further territorial gains, siding with Prussia against Austria in 1866 and winning Lombardy and Venetia, taking advantage of the Franco-German War of 1870 to drive the French garrison out of Rome, and also acquiring the South Tirol, Trieste and other Austro-Hungarian areas [9] at the end of World War I. However, widespread discontent in the aftermath of the war led to the rise of fascism led by Benito Mussolini.

Mussolini's Blackshirts marched on Rome [10] in October 1922, and he became prime minister and subsequently dictator under the title of Il Duce ("the leader"). He was the role model for Hitler, although by World War II he was the junior partner in the Axis alliance [11]. In 1943 Victor Emmanuel III dismissed him and had him imprisoned when Italy changed sides. The Germans rapidly overran northern Italy, freed Mussolini and installed him as head of a puppet state known as the Italian Social Republic [13], which was overthrown by partisans in 1945.

POST-WAR REPUBLIC

Allied troops landed in Sicily in July 1943 and on the Italian mainland in September. In the occupied areas stamps produced in Washington [14] were issued by the Allied military government. Control was handed over to the king but in June 1946 Italy became a republic. The last of the royalist stamps [15] symbolized freedom, enlightenment, peace and justice and continued in use till 1948. A later series, known as *la Sircusa* because it

Commercial Advertising
Stamps of the 1901–22 series portraying Victor Emmanuel III were released in 1924 with commercial advertisements printed on labels. There were no perforations between the stamps and the labels, so that the public were encouraged to advertise various products every time they posted a letter.

was based on an ancient Greek coin of Syracuse, was adopted in 1953 and continued until 1980. On two occasions it was incorporated in stamps urging Italians to pay their taxes [12]. It was followed by a series featuring some of the many castles of Italy [16].

More recent special issues have been produced by intaglio or photogravure at the Mint in Rome [17]. Many Italian stamps are inspired by the sculpture of the Roman Empire, a legacy from the fascist period, rather than the influence of the Church, and religious themes are usually restricted to Old Master paintings, such as the stamps celebrating the 450th anniversary of the death of Raphael [18].

SAN MARINO AND THE VATICAN

The tiny landlocked republic in north-eastern Italy, independent since the fourth century, began issuing its own stamps in 1877. By the 1900s they were its principal source of revenue and became immensely popular worldwide because of their wide-ranging topics. They included a set of 20 in memory of Franklin D. Roosevelt in 1947 [19]. Numerous sets since the 1950s have catered to the thematic market.

San Marino was very much in the forefront of developments in philately, pioneering long sets devoted to popular themes such as sports, flowers, birds, veteran cars, vintage aircraft [20] and ancient ships, as well as more esoteric subjects ranging from medieval tournaments to dinosaurs. It was also one of the first countries to issue stamps in support of the Olympic Games (1955–6) and led the way in illustrating Disney characters. More recently it has produced sheetlets for Italian operas, comic strips and science fiction. Joint issues with other countries are now common, but San Marino and Italy scored another first in 1994 with a miniature sheet containing a pair of L750 stamps (one from each country) showing St Mark's Basilica in Venice. The stamps were arranged in the sheet upside down in relation to each other, giving the impression of a reflection in the water. An inscription on the back limited the validity of each stamp to the appropriate country.

The Vatican City State was created in 1929, giving the Pope temporal powers including the right to issue stamps [21]. Not surprisingly, the vast majority of these have had a religious theme, celebrating popes, saints and the achievements of the Catholic Church down through the ages. In recent times, however, they have also addressed social and political issues of global concern, such as aid for the refugees of the world's trouble spots.

Below: In 1999 the Vatican issued this stamp to raise money for refugees from Kosovo in war-torn former Yugoslavia.

13

14

15

16

17

18

19

20

21

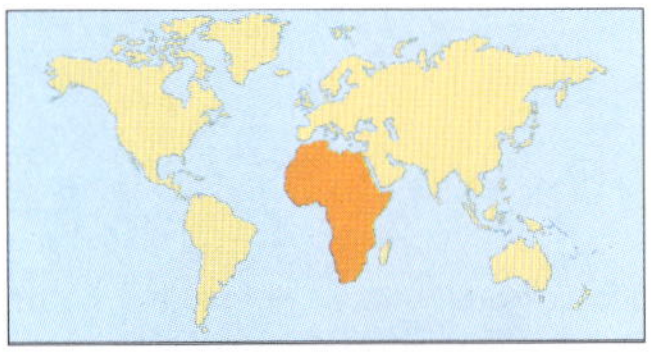

AFRICA

Africa was the last inhabited continent to adopt adhesive stamps, beginning with the celebrated Cape of Good Hope triangulars in 1853. Natal introduced stamps in 1857 but other states did not follow suit until the 1860s. By 1870 distinctive stamps were appearing in some Spanish colonies.

SPANISH AFRICA

As well as the Spanish-protected zone of Morocco, Spain acquired a considerable amount of territory in north-west Africa. However, most of this was in parts that were of little or no interest to the other European powers, mainly in the Sahara desert regions but also around the Gulf of Guinea.

Left: A general issue of stamps inscribed "Spanish West Africa", for use in Ifni and Spanish Sahara, was in use from 1949 to 1951. A portrait of General Franco was inset in designs featuring the scenery of the area.

GULF COLONIES

Spain's oldest colony was the offshore island of Fernando Poo in the Gulf, which it acquired from Portugal in 1778. From 1827 to 1834 Spain leased it to Britain as a naval base for the suppression of the slave trade. A British consulate was opened there in 1849 and a postal agency in 1858, using ordinary British stamps identifiable by the postmarks. This closed in 1877. Fernando Poo opened a Spanish post office in 1868 and issued a stamp portraying Isabella II (reproduced on a centenary stamp [1]) but it was soon withdrawn and from then until 1879 the stamps of Cuba were used instead.

From 1879 to 1960 the stamps of Fernando Poo consisted of contemporary Spanish stamps overprinted or inscribed thus. It was not until the creation of two Spanish overseas provinces in July 1959, one of which consisted of Fernando Poo and the island of Annobon, that distinctive stamps first appeared. The stamps were inscribed with the provincial name in letters smaller than those of the country name [2]. In October 1968 Fernando Poo joined Rio Muni to form the Republic of Equatorial Guinea.

Spain acquired the three islands of Elobey, Annobon and Corisco [3] from Portugal in 1778. Annobon is in the Atlantic south of the then Portuguese colony of St Thomas and Prince Islands; the other two are off the coast of Gabon. Spain established a protectorate over a part of the mainland of Guinea, also known as Rio Muni, in 1885, and from 1909 to 1960 the islands were joined with Fernando Poo and Spanish Guinea. Keytype stamps were used in "Spanish Continental Guinea" from 1902 to 1909 [4].

In that year both continental territory and offshore islands were combined as the Spanish Territories of the Gulf of Guinea, and stamps thus inscribed were then introduced [5]. Royal portraiture was superseded by pictorial designs from 1924 onwards [6]. The much shorter title of "Spanish Guinea" was adopted in 1949 [7] and continued until 30 July 1959, when the territory was divided into the overseas provinces of Fernando Poo and Rio Muni, covering the offshore islands and the continental portion respectively. Rio Muni issued stamps from 1960 to 1968, most issues being for Stamp Day [8] or Child Welfare [9].

1

2

3

4

5

6

7

8

9

Movie Stars

Typical of modern issues from the Republic of Equatorial Guinea are the stamps of 1996 honouring Marilyn Monroe, Elvis Presley and James Dean.

SAHARAN TERRITORIES

In 1885 Spain established a protectorate over the basin of the Rio de Oro (river of gold) in north-west Africa, just south of Morocco. The territory was administered from the Canary Islands and used ordinary Spanish stamps until 1905, when the keytypes were introduced [10]. The Rio de Oro region was renamed Spanish Sahara in 1924. In 1920 Spanish troops had occupied La Aguera on Cape Blanco with the intention of building an airfield for a projected route to Latin America, and for this stamps of Rio de Oro were overprinted accordingly [11]. The district was incorporated in Spanish Sahara in 1924.

In 1916 Spanish troops occupied Cape Juby at the southern end of Morocco. Stamps of Rio de Oro, Spain or Spanish Morocco were overprinted at various times [12]. Cape Juby was incorporated in Spanish Sahara in 1950 but ceded to Morocco in 1958.

Ifni was a Spanish enclave on the Moroccan coast from 1860 onwards. Before stamps were introduced in 1941, mail was franked by rubber stamp. Spanish stamps overprinted "Territorio de Ifni" [13] were used until 1950, when distinctive stamps were adopted. As in Rio Muni, most later stamps were issued for Child Welfare [14] or Stamp Day [15]. On 30 June 1969, Ifni was returned to Morocco.

Spanish Sahara started off with a distinctive series in 1924 [16] but thereafter relied on overprinted Spanish stamps until 1943, when attractive pictorials were resumed [18]. In 1975 Spain decided to relinquish the territory and it was divided between Morocco and Mauritania, but this was resisted by the Polisario movement, which proclaimed an independent Arab republic and has since issued stamps in areas under its control.

EQUATORIAL GUINEA

The Spanish colonies became the independent Republic of Equatorial Guinea in October 1968 and distinctive stamps were introduced the following year [17]. At first stamps with designs relevant to the country were issued [19] but since the early 1970s they have been frankly thematic and international in scope.

Below: In 1994 Equatorial Guinea issued this stamp portraying Neil Armstrong, Buzz Aldrin and Michael Collins to commemorate the first landing of men on the Moon.

10

11

12

13

14

15

16

17

18

19

1

2

3

4

5

6

7

8

9

10

11

NORTH AFRICA

The four countries of North Africa represented the furthest extent of Turkish rule from 1518 until the early 20th century, by which time they had become semi-independent and wholly lawless. They were the haunt of the Barbary pirates who preyed on Mediterranean shipping. European inroads began with the French invasion of Algiers in 1830 to extirpate piracy, leading to the direct annexation of Algeria in 1848 after a protracted and costly colonial war. The suppression of piracy led to the French protectorate over Tunis in 1881, although the Bey of Tunis remained as nominal ruler. As a result of the Italo-Turkish War of 1911 Libya fell to the Italians, and the following year France and Spain partitioned Morocco into protected zones, with Tangier as an international free port. Both powers had considerable difficulties with rebellious tribes. All but Morocco suffered the ravages of World War II and long, bitter conflict to attain independence in the 1950s.

Left: The North African campaign of 1942–3 was largely fought on Tunisian soil. Its liberation from German occupation was celebrated by a stamp of 1943 showing British, Free French and American soldiers.

ALGERIA

Ordinary French stamps were used until 1924 when Algeria was granted a measure of autonomy, and stamps were overprinted "Algerie" [1] pending a distinctive issue [2]. Administered by the Vichy French regime, the country was invaded by Allied forces in 1942; after the liberation stamps including the name of the French Republic were issued in 1944 [3]. Algeria continued to have its own stamps [4] until 1958, when it was again incorporated in France following the outbreak of rebellion in 1954. When the Algerians won their independence in 1962 French stamps were locally overprinted before distinctive stamps were resumed. Many stamps since then have referred to the struggles of that period [5], alternating with issues featuring landmarks [6] and the wide variety of scenery.

MOROCCO

By the late 19th century the Sherif of Morocco was virtually independent, but the strategic importance of his country led to it falling prey to rival European powers. The Agadir incident in 1911, involving the gunboat *Panzer*, almost triggered off a full-scale war between Germany and France. Britain [7], France, Spain and Germany all had their own postal services handing overseas mail, while internal services were operated by the Sherifian Posts [8].

After Morocco was partitioned between France and Spain in 1912 Tangier had its own postal services run by Britain [9], France and Spain [10]. The stamps used in the French and Spanish zones followed the styles of these countries but featured local scenes [11–12]. In 1956 both powers relinquished their protectorates and Morocco became a wholly independent kingdom [13]. Since then stamps have portrayed Muhammad V or his son Hassan II, interspersed with landmarks [14], scenery and wildlife [15].

LIBYA

Under Italian rule overprinted stamps were followed by distinctive designs that tended to highlight Libya's Roman history [16]. During World War II British stamps were overprinted "M.E.F." (Middle East Forces) for use in North Africa [17]. Later, similar overprints were produced for use in

Tripolitania. The French invaded Libya from the south and occupied Fezzan and Ghadames [19]. In 1949 Britain recognized the leader of the Senussi tribe as Amir of Cyrenaica and stamps thus inscribed appeared in 1950. In December 1951 Cyrenaica united with the states of Tripolitania, Fezzan and Ghadames to form the kingdom of Libya. It was the first country to achieve independence through the United Nations.

Stamps of Cyrenaica were overprinted, with the denominations in military administration lire [18]. Libya's stamps continued in the Italian tradition but increasingly espoused Islamic solidarity. In 1969 the monarchy was overthrown by a military coup that brought Colonel Gaddafi to power. Stamps of the Libyan Arab Republic (LAR) have boasted of its military preparedness to withstand western attempts to subvert the regime.

Below: Libya celebrated the centenary of the Universal Postal Union in 1974 with this stamp (top) showing a post-rider and Concorde to contrast mail communications old and new. A stamp (bottom) from Tunisia marked the fifth annual week promoting the health of schoolchildren in the Maghreb (Arab region of North Africa).

Surreal Stamps

A characteristic of Tunisian stamps in the early years of the republic was their surreal quality, largely as a result of the work of one designer, Hatem Elmekki. Contrasting with the dour portraits of President Bourguiba, Elmekki's designs ranged from the whimsical to the bizarre and continued to flourish for almost 40 years.

TUNISIA

The French took over this Turkish province in 1881, recognizing the Bey of Tunis but establishing a regency because the region was on the verge of economic collapse as a result of the suppression of piracy, its main source of revenue. Stamps gave an outward semblance of independence [20] but it was not until 1955 that France bowed to nationalist agitation and granted it [21]. The following year the monarchy was abolished and Tunisia became a republic, one of the more moderate and westernized of the Arab states.

Tunisia pursues a moderate new issue policy, averaging about 30 stamps a year. Most are singles focusing on matters of national and international importance; their symbolic or allegorical motifs show the pervasive influence of Hatem Elmekki. Occasional stamps portray famous Tunisians, including women (such as the singer Saliha) which is relatively unusual in Muslim countries. Since 1997 short sets have reproduced paintings by indigenous artists, while a few sets of three or four stamps have adopted a thematic line, featuring horses, reptiles, shells, musical instruments and ancient ruins.

12

13

14

15

16

17

18

19

20

21

1

2

3

4

5

6

7

8

9

10

11

EGYPT AND SUDAN

The present-day Arab Republic of Egypt day is a world removed from the great pharaonic civilization of the Nile that was flourishing by 4000 BC when the upper and lower kingdoms of Egypt were united. After 525 BC Egypt was dominated by foreign powers from the Persians to the Turks, but was running its own affairs when the British became involved in the Suez Canal in 1869 and seized control in 1882. Although still nominally under the Ottoman Empire, Egypt became a British protectorate in 1914 following the outbreak of World War I. This arrangement continued until 1922, when it was declared an independent kingdom. The monarchy was abolished in 1952 and Egypt became a republic.

To the south, and three times the size of Egypt, lay Sudan, which Mohamed Ali, Pasha of Egypt, conquered in 1822. The Egyptians were driven out of Sudan by the Mahdist revolt of 1881, but the country was reconquered in 1899 and declared an Anglo-Egyptian condominium.

Left: A set of three stamps marked the signing of the Anglo-Egyptian Treaty of 1936. Ramsay Macdonald, British Prime Minister in 1924 and 1929–35, chaired the conference and is depicted at the top of the table; the future prime minister Anthony Eden sits beside him.

FROM KHEDIVE TO KING

When Egypt adopted stamps in 1866, they were totally oriental in appearance with Arabic inscriptions [1], but the Great Pyramid became the motif of all stamps from 1867 to 1914 [2]. Egypt was then ruled by a khedive (viceroy) for the sultan in Constantinople, but when it became a British protectorate in 1914, the khedive became a sultan in his own right. As well as the obligatory pyramids, stamps of this period showed other ancient monuments [3]. Sultan Ahmed Fuad became king on 15 March 1922, and stamps portraying him were produced by Harrison and Sons of London in 1923, using photogravure for the first time [4].

KINGDOM OF EGYPT

The kingdom lasted three decades, during which various special issues drew inspiration from the pharaonic period [5]. A stamp of January 1938 celebrated King Farouk's wedding to Princess Farida of Iran [6] while a similar stamp, with a wedding group substituted, celebrated the king's 18th birthday a month later. Farouk had ambitions to throw off British influence. He ejected their troops from the Nile delta in 1947 and confined them to the Canal Zone, then abrogated the treaty regarding Sudan in 1951, signalled by overprinting the stamps in Arabic to signify that he was king of both Egypt and Sudan [7]. From 1932 to 1941 special stamps were used by the British forces in Egypt [8–9].

ARAB REPUBLIC

Farouk was forced to abdicate in 1952 and a military junta proclaimed a regency for the infant Ahmed Fuad II, then declared a republic. The Farouk stamps were overprinted with bars to blot out his face [10]. After the Anglo-French Suez venture of 1956 the spelling of Egyptian stamps was changed from French [11] to English, although the Egyptians maintained that it was American [12]. Colonel Nasser merged Egypt with Syria in 1958 to form the United Arab Republic. It was shortlived but Egypt retained the title of UAR until 1971, when "Egypt Arab

Hollow Victory

Nasser nationalized the Suez Canal in September 1956, prompting the British and French to invade Egypt. Although the brief campaign was a military success, the Allies were forced to evacuate the country when the USA and USSR (in a rare Cold War truce) joined in condemning the action and threatening sanctions. Egypt celebrated its "victory" with a stamp showing soldiers and civilians, shoulder to shoulder, resisting the enemy invasion.

Republic" [14] was chosen. Modern Egyptian stamps continue to draw heavily on pharaonic images, contrasting them with modern buildings and logos reflecting the importance of Cairo as a global conference centre [15].

SUDAN

The reconquest of Sudan by an Anglo-Expedition army commanded by General Kitchener (Later Field Marshal Lord Kitchener of Khartoum) began in 1896 and was completed in 1899. The first stamps, issued in 1897, were Egyptian stamps overprinted [16], followed by a series depicting a camel postman [13]. This design was produced by E.A. Stanton, then a *bimbashi* (captain) in the khedive's army but later a colonel in the British Army and one of Britain's foremost philatelists. He persuaded the sheik of the Howawir tribe to pose with straw-filled sacks to represent mailbags. The bags were optimistically inscribed "Khartoum" and "Berbera", although these towns were still in enemy hands at the time. So popular did the image become that it remained on stamps until the 1950s and then became the national emblem on Sudanese coins. An interlude in 1941 used a palm tree design [17] but the camel postman was restored in 1948 for the entire definitive series. Even when pictorial motifs were adopted in 1951 the camel postman was retained for the 50p top value.

The statue of General Gordon, murdered by the Mahdists in 1885, was the subject of the airmail series of 1931 [18], while a set of nine, released in 1935, marked the 50th anniversary of his death [19]. Self-government in 1954 was celebrated by three stamps showing the camel postman. Two years later Sudan became an independent republic, with stamps showing the wings of hope over a map [20].

In 1969 a pro-communist democratic republic was proclaimed [21]. Although this totalitarian regime was overthrown in April 1985 and an ordinary republic established [22], the country has been torn apart by ethnic and religious trouble in recent years.

SUEZ CANAL

During the late 19th century, France, Britain, Greece, Italy and Russia operated post offices in Egypt, but only the first of these issued stamps specifically inscribed or overprinted for use in Alexandria and Port Said. French involvement was largely concerned with the construction of the Suez Canal, begun in 1859 and completed ten years later. Stamps printed in Paris were used in connection with a mail service operated by the Suez Canal Company between July and the end of August 1868 [23].

Below: This French stamp of 1899 was overprinted for use at Port Said (left), and in 1902 French stamps were engraved for use at Alexandria (right).

12

13

14

15

16

17

18

19

20

21

22

23

ART AND ARCHITECTURE OF THE PHARAOHS IN STAMPS

The art and architecture of ancient Egypt is extraordinary and without parallel anywhere in the world. The tombs of the pharaohs are masterpieces of engineering that defy rational explanation and we still marvel at the methods used to raise such gigantic blocks of stone with such precision. The pyramids were one of the seven wonders of the ancient world, and it is small wonder that they have appeared on numerous Egyptian stamps since 1867.

Ranking in iconic stature with the pyramids is the colossal statue of the Sphinx nearby, which is often depicted in the foreground of stamps featuring the tombs. Although these famous structures are among the largest and oldest in the world, Egypt boasts many other architectural masterpieces, such as the great temple at Karnak, built by Seti I and Rameses II.

When the temples of Abu Simbel were threatened with inundation following the construction of the Aswan Dam in the 1960s, UNESCO mounted a worldwide appeal to raise the funds to have the temples dismantled and moved to higher ground. This provoked a flood of stamps from all over the world in its support. Egypt returned the compliment with stamps showing aspects of the temples with the UNESCO emblem alongside.

The Sphinx and the gigantic seated figures of Abu Simbel are prime examples of architectonic sculpture that have never been surpassed, but dynastic Egypt also produced countless life-sized statues, heads and busts, from the exquisite head of Nefertiti, painted to re-create her fabled beauty, to the gold mask of Tutankhamun, the boy pharaoh. The discovery of his spectacular tomb in 1922 was one of the most important landmarks in archaeology and it has been the subject of many definitive and special issues. The 50th anniversary of the find was celebrated by issues from Britain to Bhutan.

Not as spectacular, perhaps, but of immense importance to the emerging science of Egyptology, was the Rosetta Stone, whose parallel inscriptions in Greek and Aramaic enabled Jean-François Champollion to decipher hieroglyphics. This remarkable stone document was discovered during Napoleon's expedition to Egypt in 1798. When the French were defeated in 1801 the stone was handed over to Britain and is now in the British Museum, whose collection of Egyptian antiquities is second only to that of the Cairo Museum. The 150th anniversary

Below: A British stamp of 1972, marking the 50th anniversary of the discovery of Tutankhamun's tomb.

Left (clockwise from top): Egyptian stamps issued to mark the centenary of the opera Aida *in 1971, the International Conference on Population and Development, 1994, and the Cairo Statistical Congress, 1927, showing a statue of Amenhotep.*

Right (clockwise from top): Egyptian stamps featuring a gold chair back from Tutankhamun's tomb, 1972, Imhotep, god of medicine, 1928, and the World Under-17s football mascot, 1997.

Above: Queen Nefertiti (1953) and Rameses II (1957) flanking a stamp of 1985 showing a slave kneeling with a tray of fruit, taken from a fresco.

Left: The souvenir sheet released by Egypt in 1972 to celebrate the 50th anniversary of the discovery of Tutankhamun's tomb shows his richly gilded second mummiform coffin.

Right: The elaborate court dress of a pharaonic messenger depicted on one of the annual issues for Post Day (1969).

Above: Champollion and the Rosetta Stone on a stamp of 1972 marking the 150th anniversary of his translation of Egyptian hieroglyphics.

Above: Edfu Temple, depicted on an airmail stamp of 1985. Others in this series featured the pyramids of Giza and the colossal statue of Akhenaton.

Above: The Eye of Horus, flanked by the goddesses Nekhbet and Wadjet, on stamps for the 15th Ophthalmological Congress, held at Cairo in 1937.

of Champollion's breakthrough was celebrated by both Egypt and France in 1972. His discovery, and the booty brought back to Europe, triggered off a craze for all things Egyptian. It influenced everything from furniture to jewellery design in early 19th-century Europe. In the 1920s and 1930s, following the discovery of the boy pharaoh's tomb, there was an astonishing revival of Egytian style, which greatly influenced Art Deco.

The art of the pharaohs also exerted a tremendous influence on the development of Egyptian nationalism in the 19th century. Khedive Ismail commissioned Giuseppe Verdi to write the opera *Aida*, set in ancient Egypt, for the opening of the Cairo Opera House in 1871; stamps marking its centenary depicted the opera's victory parade.

Egypt has been adept at harnessing pharaonic imagery to all manner of modern subjects. This fashion began when the statue of Amenhotep was used for the Statistical Congress stamps of 1927, while Imhotep graced stamps the following year for the Medical Congress in Cairo. The sacred Eye of Horus was an appropriate motif for the stamps of 1937 for the 15th World Ophthalmological Congress in Cairo.

These stamps set the trend for numerous more recent issues. In particular, wall paintings of the 18th dynasty from the tombs at Thebes have provided a virtually inexhaustible source of pictures for the annual Post Day stamps. In one case, using a theme within a theme, pharaonic costumes were set within a frame derived from the great temple at Karnak.

Even events such as the Olympic Games have been given the pharaonic treatment. No matter what the topic or occasion, Egypt can invariably find a motif from pharaonic figurative or decorative art that is appropriate. The ceremonial headdress of the pharaohs has become almost a national symbol and has even lent itself to cartoon treatment, as in the mascot devised for the World Football Championships for Under-17s, held in Egypt in 1997.

1

2

3

4

5

6

7

8

9

FRENCH WEST AFRICA

The French colonies and protectorates in Africa were grouped into two large administrative units from 1944 until the various components became independent republics in the 1950s. They formed a vast area south of the Sahara that comprised Dahomey, French Guinea, French Sudan, the Ivory Coast, Mauritania, Niger, Senegal and Upper Volta. There was also a certain amount of adjustment territory. French Sudan was abolished in 1899 and its land was parcelled out among Senegal, Guinea, Ivory Coast, Dahomey, Senegambia and Niger, but it was reconstituted in 1921 and eventually merged with Senegal to form Mali.

Left: A stamp from the republic of Guinea shows a map of Africa with the four countries of the OERS (an organization of states bordering on the River Senegal) highlighted. This reflects the solidarity of the former colonies in French West Africa.

UNDER FRENCH RULE

Separate issues for the French colonies were replaced in 1944 by a single series inscribed "Afrique Occidentale Française" (French West Africa). They continued until 1958–9 [1] when they were superseded as the various colonies achieved independence. Before 1944 the various territories had their own stamps, mainly using one or other of the French colonial keyplate designs [2; 4–5] with the West African name as part of the permanent motif and the individual name added to the inscription. Later issues were distinctive to each territory. They were originally printed typographically in rather garish two-colour combinations [6], but intaglio was later used with the overall name reduced to the initials "AOF" [3; 7–8]. In general, these stamps provided a good insight into the scenery, landmarks, fauna and flora, tribal customs and culture of the region, yet had a distinctly French character.

INDEPENDENCE

The transition from colony to independent republic was achieved smoothly after the advent of the Fifth Republic under de Gaulle in 1958. At first the various colonies and protectorates became republics within the French Community and this was reflected in the stamps of the period, which, for the most part, continued to be engraved and recess-printed at the Institut de Gravure in Paris.

The concept of a community of independent republics, modelled on the British Commonwealth, gradually disappeared, and the various countries went their separate ways. The political changes of the 1960s are charted by the switch to multicolour photogravure or lithography, as well as a number of name changes. Dahomey [9] became a popular republic in November 1975 and changed its name to Benin but a political change in 1990 led to the "popular" being dropped [10]. At the beginning of the 20th century Benin had been the name of a coastal strip that briefly had its own stamps before being absorbed by Dahomey.

The Ivory Coast [11] retained its colonial name after the attainment of independence in 1960, astonishingly as the name reflected the traditional trade in ivory, now highly illegal. The federation of Mali was formed in April 1959 by a merger of the former French Sudan and Senegal [12]. It had become independent within the French Community on 20 June 1950, but broke up when Senegal seceded two months later and resumed its own stamps [13]. Sudan, retaining the name

Trust Territory

Following the independence of the French trust territory of Cameroun in January 1960, the United Nations ordered a plebiscite to be held in the British Cameroons, which used the stamps of Nigeria. The northern district voted to join Nigeria but the south opted to ally itself to France. Nigerian stamps overprinted "Cameroons U.K.T.T." (United Kingdom Trust Territory) were in use from October 1960 until 30 September 1961, when the Southern Cameroons became part of the Republic of Cameroon.

Mali, left the French Community. While its ties with France remain strong and are reflected in many of its stamps since 1960, Mali has increasingly pursued an independent line, paying tribute to world personalities [14] and events.

The Islamic Republic of Mauritania [15] was created as an autonomous state within the French Community in November 1958 but became fully independent and left the Community two years later. The Republic of the Niger was granted autonomy within the French Community in December 1958, but became a wholly independent republic in August 1960 [16]. Its stamps followed the same pattern as other former French West African colonies. Upper Volta [17] changed its name in August 1984 to Burkino Faso.

Below: A white-collared kingfisher appeared on one of Burkino Faso's stamps devoted to aquatic birds, 1988.

FORMER GERMAN COLONIES

Germany joined in the scramble for Africa in 1884 and annexed territories in West Africa under the names of Kamerun (Cameroon) and Togogebiet (Togo). Overprinted German stamps were followed by the Yacht keytype stamps. Following the outbreak of World War I both territories were rapidly overrun by Anglo-French forces.

The French overprinted stamps of Gabon and Dahomey for use in the respective territories, while Britain overprinted stamps of Kamerun with "C.E.F." (Cameroon Expeditionary Force) with values surcharged in sterling. The British zones of Cameroon and Togo were incorporated in Nigeria and the Gold Coast, using the stamps of those countries, whereas the French made separate issues for Cameroon and Togo. Togo subsequently became an independent republic. Following a plebiscite under UN supervision the French and British parts of Cameroon combined to form a federal republic, with stamps inscribed bilingually.

Below: Andrea del Sarto's Virgin and Child *is one of many religious paintings on Christmas stamps from Cameroon.*

10

11

12

13

14

15 16

17

FRENCH EQUATORIAL AFRICA

Located on the western side of central Africa, French Equatorial Africa consisted of four self-governing dependencies, Middle Congo, Ubangi-Shari, Chad and Gabon, covering an area of almost 2.6 million sq km/1 million sq miles but with a population of only about two million. France's initial intention was to establish a few coastal trading posts to combat the slave trade, but in the "scramble for Africa" it acquired Gabon and the Middle Congo between 1885 and 1891, and between 1894 and 1897 Chad and the Ubangi basin were annexed. The four colonies, united in 1910, became overseas departments in 1946. In 1956 they became autonomous republics within the French Community and attained total independence in 1960.

1

2

3

4

5

6

7

8

9

10

Left: In 1952 this stamp celebrated the centenary of the birth of Pierre Savorgnan de Brazza, a Brazilian who became a French citizen in 1874, joined the navy and served in Gabon, whence he explored the hinterland north of the Congo and founded the trading post Brazzaville, now the capital of the Congo Republic.

UNDER FRENCH RULE

The frequent permutations and combinations of colonial administration under the French are reflected in the complex stamps of this region. General issues for use throughout Equatorial Africa appeared from 1937 [1] to 1961 [2], with a series printed for the Free French in London during World War II [3]. At other times the various territories had distinctive stamps. Stamps inscribed for French Congo were in use from 1891 until 1906. At first the French Colonies general issues were overprinted, then the colonial keytype series was engraved with the name [4], followed in 1900 by a pictorial set showing a stalking leopard [5]. Gabon issued its own stamps (1886–9) then formed part of French Congo (1889–1904) until it became a separate colony with its own stamps again [6].

After the break-up of French Congo in 1906, distinctive stamps were adopted by Middle Congo showing an enlarged version of the leopard design [8]. Stamps of this series, in different colours, were overprinted for use in Chad [9]. In 1915 Chad was joined to Ubangi-Shari and stamps were accordingly overprinted [10]. In 1922 they became separate colonies again and resumed distinctive stamps [11]. The stamps of Ubangi-Shari were reissued in 1924 with an additional overprint "Afrique Equatoriale Française" and these continued until 1937, when the general issues for the whole of Equatorial Africa were introduced.

INDEPENDENT STATES

All four territories opted to become republics in 1958. Their history since then has been turbulent, with revolutions and military coups or uprisings often suppressed with the aid of French troops. By the 1990s, however, greater stability gradually developed.

The restrained intaglio of the 1960s gradually gave way to exuberantly coloured stamps, usually printed by photogravure or, more recently, offset lithography. There is no common thread running through them, certainly not one that reflects the character or cultural heritage of the upper Congo basin. Rather they have succumbed to the desire to use their stamps as a means of raising hard currency overseas, hence their apparent penchant for stamps portraying American presidents or the British royal family.

Chad became a republic within the French Community on 28 November 1958. Although it is now a fully independent sovereign state it retains close ties with France, reflected in the many stamps that are not only printed there [12] but feature French personalities, notably a lengthy series of 1971–3 portraying the kings and queens of France from the Middle Ages onwards. Other series have reproduced French works of art [13], contrasting with the issues of local interest such as those featuring wildlife [14].

As a sovereign state Gabon has also retained its colonial name. Its progress from autonomy within the French Community to full independence is reflected in its stamps, which have successively portrayed Leon Mba as prime minister [7] and then as president.

Middle Congo became the Republic of Congo [15], often referred to as Congo (Brazzaville) to distinguish it from the former Belgian Congo, which was known as Congo (Leopoldville) and later Congo (Kinshasa). In 1970 it adopted the title of Popular Republic of the Congo [16], when its former Belgian counterpart assumed the title of the Democratic Republic, but since 1991 it has been simply Congo.

An interesting feature of many of these former French colonies was their preference for triangular stamps to denote postage due. Unlike postage dues in most other parts of the world, noted for their monotonous uniformity, the former French territories favoured pictorials for this purpose with distinctive themes, such as different modes of mail transportation.

The biggest change of all came when Ubangi-Shari chose the name of the Central African Republic on attaining independence [17]. Its early stamps were recess-printed in Paris and clung to traditional art and handicrafts or distinctive fauna and flora, but by 1970 many issues had become highly politicized under the tyrannical rule of Jean Bedel Bokassa. A former French sergeant, he had become commander-in-chief in 1963 and overthrew President David Dacko in 1965, making himself life-president and then proclaiming himself emperor in December 1976. For two years the poorest country in Africa was an empire, but reverted to its republican title [18] when Bokassa was overthrown in 1979. One of the more prolific stamp-issuing countries of Africa, it produced numerous stamps with little or no relevance to Africa, far less to the republic itself.

Renaissance Man

Albert Schweitzer (1875–1965), theologian, philosopher and musician, and one of the greatest exponents of Bach's organ works, took up medicine at the age of 30 and in 1913 left Europe to establish a hospital to combat leprosy and sleeping sickness at Lambarene in Gabon. This stamp, originally released in 1960, was overprinted in 1963 to celebrate his golden jubilee in Africa. Note the view of Lambarene (left) and the organ with Bach's music, an important secondary motif for collectors of the musical theme.

Below: Typical of the flamboyant stamps issued by the short-lived Central African Empire in the 1970s is this stamp commemorating the Graf Zeppelin *flight to Chicago of 1933.*

11

12

13

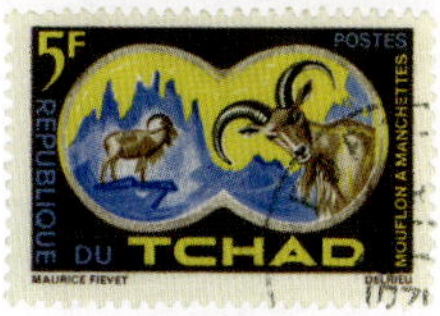

14

15

16

17

18

THE HORN OF AFRICA

This vast region in the north-east corner of Africa includes Ethiopia, a country whose civilization dates from biblical times and which extended its sway over many neighbouring tribes until the late 19th century, when the British, French and Italians began nibbling at the edges of its territory. Today, the region consists of Ethiopia, Eritrea, Djibouti and Somalia.

Left: Haile Selassie, Conquering Lion of Judah and Emperor of Ethiopia, was driven out by the Italians in 1936 but was restored in 1941 following the British liberation. Stamps portraying the emperor in ceremonial robes were issued in March 1942. The basic stamps were printed in India and the values added in Khartoum, Sudan – a unique example of stamps produced in two countries for use in a third.

1

2

3

4

5

6

7

8

9

FRENCH TERRITORIES

The French were the first European power to establish a toehold in the Horn of Africa, by acquiring the port of Obock on the Red Sea coast in 1892. French colonial keytypes were used until in 1894 Obock got stamps of its own – some of the strangest of all time [1]. In 1893 the French acquired the much more important seaport of Djibouti, whose stamps were modelled on those of Obock, printed on lined paper, imperforate but with simulated perforations surrounding the designs [2]. These issues were replaced in 1902 by a series for the French Somali Coast [3]. A Free French series during World War II had the name "Djibouti" larger than the country name, on a locomotive symbolizing the railway line that linked Ethiopia to the coast [5].

In the 1960s, Somali agitation for the inclusion of the French territory in the republic led to a plebiscite in 1966 by which the people voted to remain French, but the country name was then changed to French Territory of Afars and Issas [6] to distance it from Somalia. In 1977 it became the independent republic of Djibouti [7].

ITALIAN TERRITORIES

In 1893 the Italians seized territory in the Horn of Africa and named it Eritrea, derived from the ancient name for the Red Sea. Overprinted Italian stamps [8] were followed by distinctive designs [10]. From Eritrea the Italians mounted an invasion of Ethiopia but were decisively defeated at Adowa in 1894. Nine years later, however, Italy gained a port on the Somali coast. Stamps inscribed "Benadir" (Arabic for port) were issued in 1903 [9]. Stamps inscribed "Somalia" were introduced in 1916 [11]. In 1925 Britain ceded a tract of Kenya west of the Juba River. Italian stamps overprinted "Oltre Giuba" (beyond the Juba) were issued pending a distinctive series featuring a map of the area [4]. Jubaland was incorporated into Somalia in 1926.

Italy was revenged for Adowa in 1936 when its forces invaded and occupied Ethiopia. Stamps inscribed "Etiopia", portraying Victor Emmanuel III, were soon followed by those inscribed "Africa Orientale Italiana" (Italian East Africa). In 1940 Italy declared war on Britain but by 1941 British troops had not only occupied Somalia and Eritrea but also liberated Ethiopia. British stamps overprinted "E.A.F." (East African Forces) were used in the former Italian territories [12], followed by stamps overprinted for Eritrea or Somalia under British military administration [13] and latterly under civil administration [14]. Somalia reverted to Italy in 1950 as a UN trust territory but gained its independence in 1960.

A Hard-won Struggle

Within ten years of their incorporation in Ethiopia, the Eritreans had risen in revolt and started a war that lasted 30 years. Two years before its independence was finally recognized by the world at large, Eritrea established a postal service, complete with stamps, in 1991. Stamps inscribed in English but printed in Italy reflect the support given to the new country by its former colonial rulers.

BRITISH TERRITORIES

British penetration of the area began in the 1880s as part of the Anglo-Egyptian Sudan, and Indian stamps were used until 1903 when the protectorate was transferred from India to the British government. Indian stamps overprinted "British Somaliland" [15] were used pending a supply of stamps more correctly inscribed "Somaliland Protectorate" [16]. Pictorial stamps were introduced in 1938 and continued until 1960, when the protectorate joined the newly formed Somali Republic [17].

ETHIOPIA

One of the oldest civilizations in Africa, Ethiopia was ruled by emperors who claimed descent from Solomon and the Queen of Sheba. The country retained its unique Coptic Christian culture and held aloof from the outside world until the late 19th century. It emerged from its isolation under Emperor Menelik II, portrayed on the stamps introduced in 1894. The country continued to make progress under his daughter, the Empress Zauditu (Judith) and her successor, Prince Ras Tafari, who was crowned emperor, with the title Haile Selassie, in 1930.

Many Ethiopian stamps of the early 20th century portrayed the members of the imperial family, along with exotic wildlife. Haile Selassie [18] reigned twice (1930–6 and 1941–74), steering his vast country into the modern world. Accusations of corruption levelled at the emperor, together with strikes and economic hardship arising from a severe drought, led to the abolition of the monarchy following a military coup, and Ethiopia became a republic [19]. In 1976 the ruling military junta proclaimed Ethiopia a socialist state, but in 1991, following a change of regime, Ethiopia emerged as a federal republic. Oddly, none of these political upheavals was reflected in any change of title on the stamps.

As a result of the new constitution of 1991 the province of Eritrea, which had fought a long and bitter civil war, was formally granted autonomy, and in 1993, following a plebiscite, it voted for outright independence from Ethiopia. Distinctive stamps appeared in 1991 to celebrate autonomy and the 30th anniversary of the armed struggle, followed by definitives showing the national flag and map. Most Eritrean stamps have been printed in Italy, the former colonial power.

Below: In 1995 Eritrea issued a set on the theme of the Council for Mutual Economic Assistance in Africa. The top value shows the emblems and flags of the member countries.

10

11

12

13

14

15

16

17

18

19

1

2

3

4

5

6

7

8

9

10

11

EAST AFRICA

This region, now comprising the republics of Kenya, Uganda and Tanzania, was colonized by the British in the 1890s and absorbed the former German East Africa (Tanganyika) during World War I. The postal services of this new British East African territory (later renamed the East African Posts and Telecommunications Corporation) were unified, although the component countries had political autonomy. This situation continued for some years after all three countries became independent republics within the Commonwealth. Nationalism developed rapidly after World War II in the "wind of change" that was blowing across the African continent. Kenya won its independence in 1963 after a long period of guerrilla warfare, and the other two republics soon followed.

Left: The architect of Kenyan independence was Jomo Kenyatta. Imprisoned by the British during the Mau Mau campaign in the 1950s, while in detention he was elected president of the national Kenya Africa Union party, becoming prime minister in 1963 and president of the republic a year later. His moderate policies and statesmanship conciliated the white community and made Kenya one of the most stable countries in Africa.

KENYA, UGANDA AND TANGANYIKA

East Africa was opened up by the Imperial British East Africa Company, which issued its own stamps [1] from 1890 to 1895, when it was taken over by the British government. In the same period a protectorate was proclaimed over Uganda, whose stamps featured a portrait of Queen Victoria by Baron Heinrich von Angeli [2]. The postal services of both territories were combined in 1903 and stamps portraying Edward VII [3] were introduced; the same frames were later used for stamps showing George V. The neater title of Kenya and Uganda was adopted in 1922 when British East Africa was transformed from a protectorate into a crown colony [4]. The former German colony of Tanganyika joined the postal union in 1935 and stamps bearing the names of all three countries were issued from then onwards.

It is important to note that, although collectors refer to this group as "Kenya, Uganda and Tanganyika" (KUT), the authorities were at pains to vary the order of the inscriptions so that no single territory assumed a dominant position. The inaugural series was in the prevailing colonial fashion for bicoloured pictorials, with a portrait of George V inset, and the series was reissued in 1938 with the portrait of George VI substituted [5]. Stamps bearing the names of the three countries [6] continued until the 1960s, after they had become independent politically and even had their own stamps. From 1965 to 1975 stamps inscribed with the names of Kenya, Uganda and Tanzania were produced by the East African Posts and Telecommunications Corporation [7].

KENYA

Achieving independence in December 1963, Kenya became a republic a year later. The inaugural series inscribed "Uhuru" (Swahili for "independence") showed a mixture of subjects [8] but stamps since then have favoured natural history [9–10], handicrafts [12] and other subjects likely to attract tourists. They have also featured many universal organizations, such as Rotary, whose founder Paul P. Harris was portrayed on a stamp of 1994 for the 50th anniversary of the Mombasa club [11].

UGANDA

Distinctive Ugandan stamps were re-introduced in 1962, beginning with a set marking the centenary of the discovery of the source of the Nile [13]. Recess-printed, with a profile of Elizabeth II, these stamps were a far cry from the gaudy issues of later years, although the tyrant Idi Amin did not leave his mark on Ugandan stamps.

In later years stamps had a global outlook [14] but more recently Uganda has jumped on the thematic bandwagon with numerous sets – including the ever-popular Disney stamps [15] – aimed at collectors.

TANZANIA

Germany colonized Tanganyika in the 1890s and issued stamps inscribed "Deutsch-Ostafrika" [16] from 1893 to 1916, when the colony was occupied by British imperial forces. In this period stamps of the Indian Expeditionary Force were overprinted for use by troops on Mafia Island [17] blockading the Rufiji delta. From November 1917 German East Africa was under British administration and used stamps of East Africa and Uganda overprinted "G.E.A." [18]. Distinctive stamps featuring a giraffe [19] were introduced in Tanganyika in 1922 and continued until 1935, when the unified series was adopted. Though it was the last of the three countries to join the Commonwealth, Tanganyika was the first to gain independence, in 1961. Pictorial stamps inscribed "Uhuru" were issued in December that year.

Below: Lions of the Serengeti featured on one of Tanganyika's independence set of 1961 (left), and Sultan Kalif bin Harub on the Zanzibar definitive series of 1952 (right).

Missionary Mail

Uganda in the late 1880s was in a religious ferment as Muslim, Catholic and Protestant factions fought each other for converts. After the Anglo-German agreement of 1890, in which Britain exchanged Heligoland for a free hand in Uganda and Zanzibar, British influence increased and its missionaries were able to continue their work unhindered. One of these, the Reverend Ernest Millar at Mengo, organized the first postal service in March 1895, using sermon paper to produce stamps of a very basic design on his typewriter. Gum was supplied by the resin of a nearby tree.

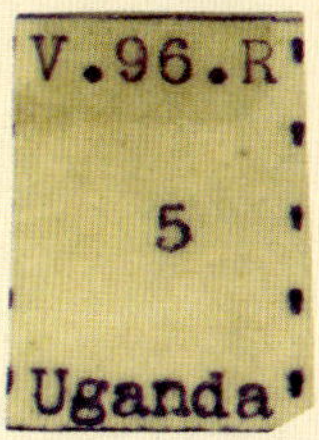

The offshore island of Zanzibar, formerly centre of the Arab slave trade in Africa, had been a British protectorate since 1895 and originally used Indian stamps suitably overprinted. Later issues portrayed the sultans, dhows and distinctive Arabic architecture of the island. It gained full independence in December 1963 but only a few weeks later an African-inspired revolution toppled the sultan. Shortly afterwards Zanzibar joined Tanganyika to form the United Republic of Tanganyika and Zanzibar, soon shortened to Tanzania, but continued to issue its own stamps until 1967. During this period, despite the apparent unity represented by the stamps, Zanzibar was very much a law unto itself, with a Marxist regime that had its stamps printed in the German Democratic Republic and used strident images on them to promote its extreme left-wing politics [20].

12

13

14

15

16

17

18

19

20

1

2

3

4

5

6

7

8

9

10

11

CENTRAL AFRICA

A British expedition sponsored by the imperialist and financier Cecil Rhodes led the "scramble for Africa" in the late 1880s and resulted in the annexation of 1.25 million sq km/0.5 million sq miles of southern and central Africa in the name of the British South Africa Company. Out of Rhodes's ambition to create a British empire that stretched from the Cape to Cairo came the Bechuanaland protectorate (now Botswana in southern Africa) and three countries, formerly Northern and Southern Rhodesia and Nyasaland, but now known as Zambia, Zimbabwe and Malawi respectively.

Left: Cecil Rhodes made a fortune from the Kimberley diamond mines before entering politics and becoming prime minister of Cape Colony. At the same time his imperial ambitions led him to found the British South Africa Company as well as endowing Rhodes scholarships for Americans, Germans and colonials at Oxford University.

COMPANY RULE

Stamps inscribed "British South Africa Company" were introduced in 1892 [1], followed by two later sets also featuring the company arms. A shortage of stamps during the Matabele rebellion of 1896 was met by overprinting stamps of the Cape of Good Hope [2]. Although stamps continued to bear the company name until 1909, the name "Rhodesia" was adopted in 1895. Cecil Rhodes thus joined the elite band of those, including Amerigo Vespucci, Christopher Columbus and Simon Bolivar, who had countries named after them, the only difference being that he chose the name himself.

Sadly Rhodes did not live long enough to see his name on the stamps for he died in 1902, worn out by his exertions in the defence of Kimberley during the Boer War. In April 1909 existing stamps of the British South Africa Company were overprinted "Rhodesia" [3], pending a supply of stamps with this name engraved at the foot, although the company name continued to appear at the top. The inaugural series of 1910 is popularly known as the Doubleheads, on account of its side-by-side portraits of George V and Queen Mary. This bicoloured series was not only very beautiful but also rich in its philatelic variety. It was superseded by the Admirals, so-called because the series portrayed the king in naval uniform.

Further north, an expedition led by Sir Harry Johnstone occupied Nyasaland in 1893 to prevent the Portuguese from joining Angola to Mozambique. Sir Harry not only founded British Central Africa but even designed its stamps [4]. Stamps of this territory included a provisional issue in 1898 that utilized the upright oval designs normally embossed on cheques to create 1d stamps during a shortage of that denomination.

COLONIAL RULE

Following a proposal in 1923 by the British government to detach the main area of white settlement from company territory and join it to South Africa, the white settlers voted to become a separate crown colony with self-governing status. In 1924, therefore, the company's territories were divided into Northern and Southern Rhodesia and thereafter used stamps thus inscribed.

In both territories definitives portrayed the reigning monarch [5]. The Victoria Falls featured in several issues of Southern Rhodesia, including sets celebrating the silver jubilee of George V in 1935 [7] and the coronation of George VI in 1937. British Central

Illegal Stamps

The regime of Ian Smith in Rhodesia defied the British government by the illegal act of UDI (unilateral declaration of independence). When a stamp celebrating this event was issued, the British declared it invalid for postage, and any mail arriving in the UK with such stamps affixed was treated as unpaid and surcharged accordingly.

Africa was renamed the Nyasaland protectorate in 1907, and stamps portraying the reigning monarch were subsequently produced. A first tentative essay in pictorialism was the series of 1934, which showed a leopard on a rock, derived from the badge of the protectorate, with the profile of George V inset. The same motif, with a profile of George VI, was in use from 1938 to 1944 but then gave way to pictorial definitives [8]. In Northern Rhodesia small-format stamps managed to combine royal portraiture with a vignette of African wildlife [6].

FEDERATION

With the intention of creating an independent dominion, the three British territories in central Africa formed a federation in 1954 and introduced a joint issue of stamps inscribed "Rhodesia and Nyasaland" [9], followed by a small-format pictorial series [10]. Political disagreements emerged between the predominantly black countries and Southern Rhodesia, so this merger proved unworkable. When the federation broke up in 1964 each country resumed its own stamp issues. The only thing they had in common was a penchant for small horizontal stamps, but whereas Southern Rhodesia [12] and Nyasaland [14] favoured a wide variety of subject, Northern Rhodesia produced a standard design showing the national emblem [13].

CHANGES OF NAME

Both Nyasaland and Northern Rhodesia attained independence in 1964 and reverted to names long used by their indigenous peoples. Thus Nyasaland became Malawi and Northern Rhodesia was renamed Zambia. Both celebrated their independence with stamps: Malawi portrayed Hastings Banda and the sunrise [11] while Zambia chose jubilant dancers [16]. Definitives under the new names continued existing patterns [15].

Most Zambian stamps since 1964 have been designed by Gabrielle Ellison [17]. This has given them an integrity that the stamps of many other African nations now lack, and until very recently they concentrated on subjects specific to the peoples of the country and their way of life, with attractive genre scenes [18–19]. Another unifying element in many stamps was the incorporation of a band of metallic ink alluding to the copper industry.

Southern Rhodesia merely dropped the "Southern" and retained the name of its founder, becoming a bastion of white supremacy. While affirming allegiance to the Crown, as exemplified in its Churchill stamp of 1965 [20], it was drifting apart from the mother country. In November that year it unilaterally declared independence. Stamps with an "Independence" overprint were followed by definitives omitting "Southern" [21]. Black majority rule eventually prevailed and in 1980 Rhodesia changed its name to Zimbabwe [22]. Stamps since then have either been thematic, with the usual themes of fauna and flora, or have highlighted the apparent technological progress of Zimbabwe [23]. In place of a portrait, these stamps feature the secretary bird, its national emblem, carved in soapstone.

12

13

14

15

16

17

18

19

20

21

22

23

1

2

3

4

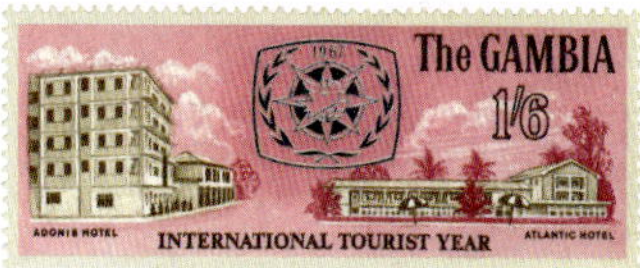

5

6

7

8

9

10

11

WEST AFRICA

Four of the five countries on the west coast of Africa south of the Sahara were formerly British colonies, while the fifth, Liberia, shares with the others a common language (English) and a parallel history. Sierra Leone (1787) and Liberia (1822) were created by Britain and the USA respectively as homes for freed slaves, while the Gambia was, from 1808, a base for the Royal Navy in pursuit of slave-traders. The Gambia formed part of Sierra Leone until 1843, when it became a separate colony with a protectorate extending inland along the banks of the Gambia River.

The Gold Coast, which was first settled in 1821, was likewise administered by Sierra Leone until 1886. Nigeria first came under British influence in 1853, when a base was established at Lagos for the suppression of the slave trade. Later protectorates were proclaimed over the Oil Rivers and the Niger Coast. A chartered company penetrated the hinterland, which, in 1900, was formed into the separate colonies of Northern and Southern Nigeria; these were united in 1914.

Liberia had the distinction of being the first black African independent republic and it was from there that the concepts of nationalism and independence spread to the Gold Coast, the first of the British colonies to break away and become a dominion in 1957, assuming the name Ghana from an ancient African empire of that name.

Left: Dr Kwame Nkrumah (1909–72) was prime minister of Ghana from 1957 to 1960 and president from then until 1966, when he was ousted by a military coup while on a visit to China. Educated at Lincoln University in the USA, he is shown here posing in front of the Lincoln Memorial in Washington, DC.

THE GAMBIA

The first stamps are known as the Cameos, from the embossed profile of Queen Victoria [1]. From the 1920s pictorial stamps were recess-printed in the restrained two-colour settings fashionable until after World War II [3], giving way to multicolour photogravure with definitives following a single theme [4]. Since independence the Gambia has developed as a popular tourist destination [5]. It achieved autonomy in 1963, independence in 1965 and became a republic within the Commonwealth in 1970 [6].

GHANA

The first stamps of the Gold Coast were issued in 1875 and thereafter followed the prevailing colonial fashions for royal portraits. In 1928, however, it became the first British colony to adopt photogravure, for a small-format series featuring Christiansborg Castle, a former Danish trading post in Accra, the capital [2]. Later definitives (1938–58) were recess-printed and reflected the British influence on the country [7]. Under Kwame Nkrumah [8], Ghana soon adopted an independent policy championing non-alignment and the cause of African freedom and unity [9], ideals maintained by his successors.

SIERRA LEONE

Sierra Leone introduced stamps in 1859, the first territory in West Africa to do so. They were confined to royal portraiture until 1932 when pictorial definitives were adopted [10–11]. Intaglio was employed from then until after independence was achieved in

1961. Since then a high proportion of the stamps have been colourful and exciting but seldom relevant to the country itself.

NIGERIA

Stamps were introduced at Lagos in 1874, portraying Queen Victoria [12]. Separate issues were discontinued in 1906 when Lagos joined Southern Nigeria. Ordinary British stamps were used in the Oil Rivers region pending the introduction of stamps overprinted after the territory was declared a protectorate in 1892 [13].

The protectorate was extended into the hinterland and renamed the Niger Coast Protectorate in May 1893, adopting stamps portraying the elderly Victoria the following January [14]. In 1900 Southern Nigeria was declared a crown colony and protectorate [15], while Northern Nigeria became a protectorate [16]. In January 1914 they were amalgamated to form Nigeria [17], which became an independent federation in 1960. Most stamps since then have been printed by the Nigerian Security Minting and Printing Company [18–19].

In 1967 the eastern region seceded from the federation under the name of Biafra and distinctive stamps were issued in 1968–9 before the area was overrun by federal forces. The stamps celebrating the first anniversary of independence depicted atrocities allegedly committed by the Nigerian army.

Below: Few charity stamps are as specific as this one from Liberia, which names a particular charity and shows Seán Devereux in action.

Free-form and Self-adhesive

Sierra Leone made philatelic history in 1964 when it produced the world's first self-adhesive stamps, die-cut in the shape of the country itself, with commercial advertisements on the backing paper.

LIBERIA

The first stamps appeared in 1860 and featured the seated figure of Liberty alongside a sailing ship, uncannily like the reverse of the British copper coinage of the period. By the 1880s pictorial designs were featuring scenery, wildlife and native types as well as presidential portraits in the American style. From 1894 onwards stamp designs [20] leaned heavily on the famous Cape Triangulars. Separate stamps for registered mail [21] were produced from 1893 to 1923, many bearing the names of individual towns. The earlier stamps even provided a space for the manuscript insertion of the registration serial number, but by 1919 a more pictorial approach had been adopted.

By the 1930s Liberia had virtually become the private fief of the Firestone Rubber Company and many stamps from then onwards had an American slant. The very prolific issues since the 1980s seldom allude to the chronic civil wars affecting the country, but more often express its indebtedness to the USA [22]. Although it is not a member of the Commonwealth, Liberia has even participated in colonial omnibus issues commemorating the British royal family.

12

13

14

15

16

17

18

19

20

21

22

PORTUGUESE AFRICA

The Portuguese had a head start on all other European nations in opening up the "Dark Continent". In the 15th century their seamen, encouraged by Prince Henry the Navigator, pushed far down the west coast of Africa, establishing the trading posts that would become the nuclei of colonies. In 1498 Vasco da Gama rounded the Cape of Good Hope and sailed up the east coast of Africa as far as Mombasa, Kenya, before striking east to India. The major Portuguese territories in West Africa ranged from Cape Verde in the north-west to Guinea and the Congo in the centre and Angola in the south. On the east coast the main colonies were in Mozambique and Nyassa. The rise of nationalism in the 1960s led to long-running warfare on both sides of the continent before Portugal granted independence in 1975. With the exception of Portuguese Guinea (now known as Guinea-Bissau), the former colonies have not changed their names since the grant of independence.

Left: Stamps for general use in the Portuguese colonies and protectorates in Africa were issued in 1898 for the quatercentenary of Vasco da Gama's discovery of the sea route to India.

1

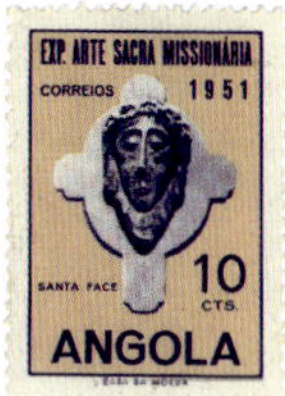

2

3

4

5

6

7

8

9

10

ANGOLA

The earliest stamps of Angola, introduced in 1870, conformed to the prevailing keyplate types used throughout the colonial empire, only the name and currency being distinctive. Even as late as the 1930s special issues followed an omnibus pattern [1], but in the 1950s special issues [2] and individually styled definitives were coming into use. The first multicoloured set appeared in 1955 and featured a map of the colony [3]. Since independence, stamps of Angola have adopted a more frankly thematic approach, although few issues have been as minimalist as the birds series of the 1990s [5]. A set of 2000 featured post offices around the country [6]. The Portuguese Congo, now the province of Cabinda north of the River Congo, had its own keytype stamps [4] from 1894 to 1920, when it was absorbed by Angola.

CAPE VERDE

The Cape Verde archipelago consists of ten islands off the west coast of Africa. Discovered in 1456, they were colonized four years later by Diogo Gomes. They became a Portuguese overseas province in 1951 and an independent republic in 1975. Standard colonial designs [7–8] were used until 1948 and new issues since then have been relatively moderate. The first full-colour stamps appeared in 1952, appropriately honouring the Portuguese navigators who used the islands as a staging post [9]. Tourism, wildlife and concern for the environment are recurring themes of more recent stamps [10].

GUINEA

The first stamps of Guinea consisted of those of Cape Verde overprinted in 1881. Thereafter, stamps of the keyplate types were inscribed for use until 1946, when a pictorial definitive series was adopted. In the 1960s stamps became more colourful and included an eye-catching diamond-shaped set devoted to indigenous snakes [11].

A revolt led by Amilcar Cabral against colonial rule erupted in 1963 and a decade later the republic of Guinea-Bissau was proclaimed. Its independence was recognized by the revolutionary government in Lisbon a year later, the first step towards the granting of independence to all the

Sir Rowland Remembered

St Thomas and Prince marked the centenary of Rowland Hill's death in 1979 with a set reproducing earlier stamps alongside the portrait of the great postal reformer.

other African colonies. Stamps since then have been predominantly thematic in nature, from fire engines [12] to cats and dogs [13].

MOZAMBIQUE

At one time the provinces of Inhambane [14], Quelimane, Tete [18] and Zambezia had their own stamps in the prevailing keytypes. Lourenço Marques, Mozambique's chief port, also issued colonial keyplate stamps, as well as a solitary stamp in 1952 [15]. During World War I Portuguese troops invaded German East Africa and occupied the district of Kionga; stamps of Lourenço Marques were overprinted for use there [20].

Separate issues were made by two chartered companies for territory under their control. The Mozambique Company was chartered in 1891 and issued stamps featuring the company arms, followed by pictorial definitives in 1918 [16] and a series designed and printed in England in 1937 [17]. The Nyassa Company was chartered in 1894. Pictorial stamps appeared in 1901, followed by a series of 1921 [19], both printed by Waterlow of London. Nyassa reverted to Mozambique in 1929. The stamps of Mozambique proper followed the colonial pattern, apart from some charity tax stamps during and after World War I, until 1944. Even thereafter, most issues formed part of the Portuguese colonial omnibus series, but from 1951 attractive thematic sets appeared [21]. A restrained issue policy has been pursued since the country's independence. In 1995 Mozambique became a member of the Commonwealth.

ST THOMAS AND PRINCE

These two islands in the Gulf of Guinea were discovered by the Portuguese in 1471 and were used as a penal colony from 1493 onwards, accommodating common criminals as well as Jewish children forcibly taken from their parents and baptized. By the mid-16th century the islands were covered with sugar plantations. Continual raiding by the French and Dutch destroyed the islands' prosperity in the 17th and 18th centuries and the colony began to recover only after the introduction of cocoa cultivation in 1890.

The islands used the various Portuguese colonial types from 1870 to 1948, but in 1951 they attained the status of an overseas province with considerable autonomy, and a more liberal policy was inaugurated. Although many of the stamps in the ensuing period honoured Portuguese explorers and politicians there were also sets featuring wildlife, ships, military uniforms and other popular subjects.

The islands became a wholly independent republic on 12 July 1975. Since 1977, however, the country has produced prolific "bandwagon" issues of little indigenous relevance.

Below: Stamps portraying President Carmona of Portugal (left) were released to mark his visit to the African colonies in 1970. Even before joining the Commonwealth, Mozambique celebrated British events (right).

11

12

13

14 15

16 17

18 19

20 21

SOUTHERN AFRICA

Three countries adjoining, or even landlocked within, South Africa were formerly known as the High Commission Territories because they continued to be administered by the British High Commissioner in South Africa after that country became an independent dominion in 1910 and subsequently a republic outside the Commonwealth. Lesotho (formerly Basutoland) and Swaziland are enclaves within South Africa, while Botswana (formerly Bechuanaland) lies between South Africa and Zimbabwe.

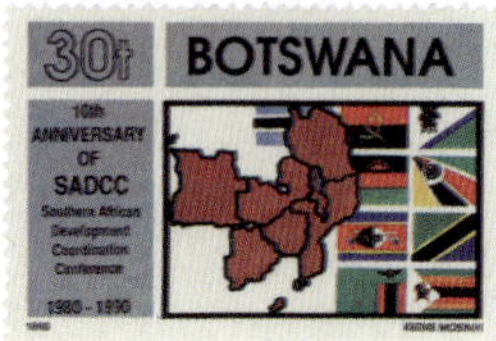

Left: The position of these three countries in relation to South Africa and their other neighbours was vividly illustrated by this stamp of 1990, which celebrated the tenth anniversary of the Southern African Development Coordination Conference and showed the countries' boundaries and flags.

1

2

3

4

5

6

7

8

9

10

BRITISH INVOLVEMENT

The British developed an interest in the essentially tribal territories of southern Africa in the second half of the 19th century. British Bechuanaland was declared a crown colony in 1885 and at first used the stamps of the Cape of Good Hope with a distinctive overprint [1]. Two years later British stamps, similarly overprinted, were adopted and continued to be used in that region until 1895, when it was annexed by the Cape and subsequently became part of South Africa.

Tribal territory to the north of British Bechuanaland was made a protectorate in 1888. The British stamps that had previously been overprinted for use in British Bechuanaland were now additionally overprinted with the word "Protectorate" to denote their use in this area [2]. British stamps overprinted "Bechuanaland Protectorate" continued to be used there until 1932, when a series portraying George V showed cattle at a water-hole [3]. The "thirsty cattle" design was subsequently used for the definitives of George VI and Elizabeth II until 1961. Even the stamps celebrating the 75th anniversary of the protectorate showed thirsty cattle flanked by Queens Victoria and Elizabeth [5]. Sterling currency was replaced by South African rands and cents in 1961. At first, existing stamps were overprinted pending a pictorial series featuring birds [4]. Most countries hail independence with a sunrise but here again the importance of water in a semi-arid region was reflected in the stamps of 1965 marking internal autonomy [6].

Up to 1933 Basutoland used the stamps of South Africa distinguishable only by the postmark, but in that year it followed Bechuanaland with a series portraying George V over a picture of a crocodile and the Drakensberg Mountains [7]. This motif was retained for the George VI series but in 1954 a pictorial series with different themes was adopted. All three territories adopted South African decimal currency in 1961. The inauguration of the Basuto National Council in 1959 was marked by three stamps and for the first time the indigenous name of "Lesotho" was inscribed alongside the European name [8].

BOTSWANA

Bechuanaland became an independent republic in 1966 and adopted the older form of the name. Early issues, such as the set of 1970 marking the centenary of the death of Charles Dickens [9], reflected continuing cultural ties with Britain. Later stamps, however, faithfully recorded every aspect of the life and culture of the country, from occupations [10] and dress to the distinctive fauna [11] and flora [12] of the region. The countries of Southern Africa have enjoyed relative stability since independence, with strict observance of democratic principles [14].

LESOTHO

The kingdom of Lesotho has been ruled since gaining independence by Moshoeshoe II, apart from a five-year period (1990–5) when he was deposed and replaced by King Letsie, who later abdicated in his favour. Moshoeshoe II was portrayed on the 1988 definitives showing birds [15]. Latterly Lesotho has veered away from traditional subjects and become more aware of the themes that sell well, though there is no doubting the genuine feeling of affection in the country for the late Diana, Princess of Wales [13].

SWAZILAND

The tribal kingdom of Swaziland was placed under the joint protection of Britain and the South African Republic (Transvaal) in 1890 and stamps of the latter, overprinted "Swazieland" (*sic*) were then introduced [16]. Britain handed over sole control to the Transvaal in 1894 and ordinary stamps of that country (and later of South Africa) were used until 1933. Stamps portraying George V flanked by shields over a map of the country and mountain scenery [17] were then introduced and, as in the other territories, remained in use until the 1950s, with a portrait of George VI substituted.

In 1967 Swaziland became a protected state and stamps portraying Sobhuza II marked the occasion [18]. Full independence was granted the following year. Since then stamps have retained their primary interest in Swazi subjects, with portraits of Sobhuza II and his grandson, Mswati III.

Unusually, many of the early issues following the attainment of independence were lithographed in Bogota, Colombia, breaking with the usual tradition of obtaining stamps from the British security printers. Stamps from 1968 onwards chronicled Swaziland's entry into the United Nations and its membership of the Commonwealth. Material progress was the subject of the annual independence anniversary sets. At the same time the British connection was continually emphasized (especially in the Apartheid era in neighbouring South Africa), with stamps honouring the queen's silver jubilee [19], the Duke of Edinburgh's Award Scheme and Princess Diana, among other subjects.

Below: Swaziland stamps show a Kudu horn trumpet (top) and publicize the national AIDS campaign (bottom).

Royal Tour

In 1947 the British royal family toured Southern Africa and stamps celebrating their visit were issued by the various countries. The High Commission Territories had an omnibus issue, each releasing a set of four stamps in standard designs.

11

12 13

14

15

16 17

18

19

1

2

3

4

5

6

7

8

9

10

11

12

SOUTH AFRICA AND NAMIBIA

The Union of South Africa was created in 1910 as an amalgamation of two British colonies (Cape Colony and Natal) and two Boer republics (the South African Republic, or Transvaal, and the Orange Free State). The passage around the coast was discovered by the Portuguese in 1498 but it was the Dutch who settled the Cape in the 17th century. Cape Colony was captured by the British during the Napoleonic Wars and it was to escape from British rule that the resident Dutch farmers (the Boers) trekked northwards from 1836 onwards, creating a number of ephemeral states that eventually formed the Transvaal and Orange Free State.

The discovery of gold and diamonds in these areas led to British attempts to take them over. The Transvaal was briefly annexed but won its independence in the first Boer War (1880–1), but the second Boer War (1899–1902) resulted in British victory. A resurgence of Afrikaner nationalism in the 1940s and 1950s led to South Africa becoming a republic and leaving the Commonwealth in 1961. In the ensuing years the policy of apartheid (literally, "separateness") was pursued relentlessly, and several African "homelands" were established as part of the process. It ended in 1993 with the election of Nelson Mandela, recently released from prison, as president. On 1 June 1994, South Africa rejoined the Commonwealth.

Left: One of the truly great men of the 20th century, Nelson Mandela spent 26 years in prison for political offences, directing the African National Congress campaign of defiance against the Afrikaner regime. His magnanimity did much to unite black and white.

COLONIAL TIMES

The Cape of Good Hope was the first part of Africa to issue stamps: its famous Triangulars, introduced in 1853 [1], showing the seated figure of Hope. Later stamps showed the standing figure of Hope [2] and a view of Table Bay with the colonial arms [3]. Natal followed suit in 1857. Its first stamps, embossed on coloured paper, were followed by a series bearing the Chalon portrait of Queen Victoria [4].

The Transvaal, then known as the South African Republic, adopted stamps in 1869 [5], later stamps being printed in Holland [6]. Stamps portraying Victoria were briefly used in the Transvaal when the British took over to rescue it from bankruptcy. The Orange Free State introduced stamps in 1866 and from then until 1902 the orange tree emblem was used exclusively [7].

Following the second Boer War, the Orange Free State and the South African Republic came under British administration, with their names changed to the Orange River Colony [8] and the Transvaal [9]. Separate issues were made by the short-lived Boer states of Stellaland and the New Republic as well as for the tribal areas of Griqualand West and Zululand [10].

SOUTH AFRICA

The former Boer republics and the two British colonies came together in August 1910 to form the Union of South Africa with dominion status. Pending the introduction of a unified definitive series in 1913 [11], stamps of the four provinces could be used throughout South Africa and collectors now prize examples of these "interprovincials" with legible postmarks of provinces other than the territory of original issue. The opening of the Union parliament in November 1910 was celebrated by a large stamp portraying George V in ceremonial robes, with the emblems of the provinces in the corners. Like the definitives, this stamp was inscribed in English and Dutch, but from 1925 onwards Afrikaans replaced Dutch. A few stamps from then onwards were inscribed in both languages but in general stamps from 1926 were issued in bilingual pairs, inscribed alternately in English or Afrikaans [12]. This ceased in 1952 and from then until the 1970s inscriptions were provided in both languages [13]. From 1966 design was greatly improved by the reduction of the country name to its initials, "RSA" [15], following its change of status to a republic. Interestingly, the name "South Africa" with its Afrikaans equivalent returned to favour in 1993.

A pictorial series was introduced in 1926 and continued for a quarter of a century, undergoing numerous changes of printing and providing a rich field for philatelic study. Originally printed in England by letterpress, stamps were later produced in Pretoria using an early form of rotary photogravure. Apart from a few airmail sets the vast majority of South African special issues from 1938 onwards were charity sets marking the anniversary of the Boer trek of a century earlier. Although these stamps were increasingly nationalistic, they were balanced by stamps celebrating British royal events, from the silver jubilee of 1935 to the royal visit of 1947 [12] and the coronation in 1953. Many stamps from 1961, when South Africa declared itself a republic and left the Commonwealth, reflected the politics of the period, giving way to a more liberal policy since 1993.

BLACK HOMELANDS

Apartheid was taken to its illogical conclusion by the Bantu Homelands Constitution Act, passed in the 1970s, which established a series of "black homelands". These were theoretically independent states within the frontiers of South Africa, but the intention was that black workers could be deported back to them at will and were therefore denied the full rights of citizenship within the republic itself. This system never achieved international recognition but the stamps of the homelands were accepted as valid on mail.

Bophuthatswana [16], Ciskei [17], Transkei [18] and Venda [19] issued stamps, beginning with Transkei in 1976, while Venda did not join in until 1981. All four homelands ceased to exist in April 1994 when they were reincorporated in the republic.

Africa's First Commemorative Stamp

The honour of producing Africa's first commemorative, in 1895, fell to the Transvaal, which issued a stamp celebrating the introduction of a 1d postage rate. The national arms were flanked by a mail coach and a mail train.

NAMIBIA

Formerly German South West Africa, using the German keyplate stamps, this territory was occupied by Union forces in World War I and was subsequently mandated to South Africa. South African stamps overprinted "SWA" were often used, although distinctive stamps also appeared, including the pictorial definitive series from 1931 onwards [14]. The territory gained independence in March 1990, taking its name from the Namib desert. Its stamps at first portrayed President Sam Nujoma, the map and flag [20]; more recently scenery [21] has featured.

13

14

15

16

17

18

19

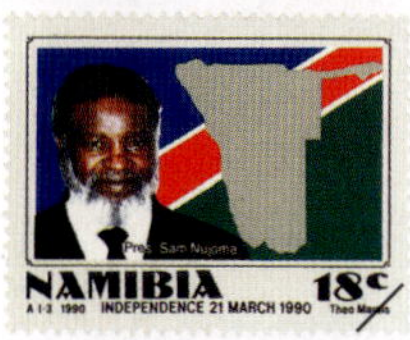

20

21

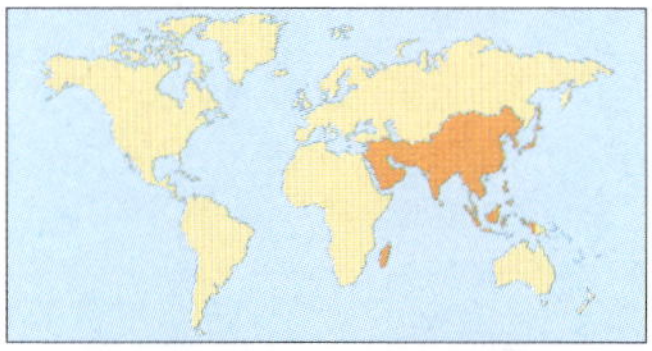

ASIA

The first adhesive stamps in Asia were used in the Indian province of Scinde (now part of Pakistan) in 1852, preceding the general issue of India by two years, but in some other regions progress was slow. Afghanistan and Persia both released stamps in 1870; Japan joined in 1871 and China in 1878.

LEBANON, IRAQ AND SYRIA

The three countries lying between Turkey and Arabia and stretching from the Mediterranean to the Persian Gulf have a common history and culture, diverging in only one respect. Having been part of the Ottoman Empire until 1918, Lebanon and Syria were mandated to the French while Iraq was mandated to Britain. As well as the resulting use of French or English in their stamps, each of the three countries adopted the form of government used by the controlling power, so Lebanon and Syria became republics whereas Iraq was a kingdom. Ironically, the Emir Faisal of the Hejaz, who had led the Arab Revolt against the Turks with the aid of Colonel T.E. Lawrence (Lawrence of Arabia), was originally installed as king of Syria, but he was promptly ejected by the French and consequently the British made him king of Iraq instead.

Left: Between February 1958 and September 1961 Syria was joined with Egypt to form the United Arab Republic (UAR). Stamps thus inscribed were used in both countries, distinguishable only by the currency – milliemes in Egypt and piastres in Syria.

LEBANON

The French added a considerable area, including Beirut, now the capital, to the traditional territory of Lebanon. Under the name "Grand Liban" (Greater Lebanon) stamps were introduced in 1924. At first contemporary French stamps were overprinted [1], followed in March 1925 by distinctive stamps [3]. The Lebanese Republic was proclaimed by the French in May 1926. The previous stamps were overprinted accordingly [2] and included overprints for airmail in 1928 [4].

The salient feature of Lebanese stamps has been the depiction of landmarks that date from Greek, Roman and Crusader times [5], a feature shared with those of Syria and Iraq. Definitive issues from 1937 onwards depicted the country's cedar trees, prized for their timber since classical times [6–7]. In 1941 Lebanon became an independent republic, following a takeover by the Free French from the Vichy administration, and most stamps since then have been simply captioned "Liban" [8–9].

IRAQ

Soon after the outbreak of World War I British and Indian troops occupied the port of Basra, at the head of the Persian Gulf, to protect the oil pipeline. From there they advanced up the rivers Euphrates and Tigris. Turkish stamps were issued for the occupation of Baghdad (1917) and Mosul (1918), followed by overprints for Iraq as a whole [10]. In April 1920 the League of Nations granted a mandate to the British, who installed the Emir Faisal of Syria as King Faisal I of Iraq. The British mandate expired in 1932 and thereafter Iraq was a completely independent republic. Later stamps

1

2

3

4

5

6

7

8

9

Tradition Triumphant

The vast majority of Syrian stamps in recent years have maintained the tradition of blending military symbolism and portraits of President Hafez al-Assad with images drawn from the region's long and colourful history. A series of 1980 illustrated tales from the *Arabian Nights*, including Sinbad the Sailor (curiously captioned as Sindibad).

portrayed King Ghazi who, when he was killed in a car crash in 1939, was succeeded by his four-year-old son Faisal II [11]. Later definitives showed the boy king grown to manhood.

Faisal II's reign was brutally terminated when he was murdered on 14 July 1958. Stamps portraying him were overprinted to signify the republic [12] that installed General Karim Kassem, leader of the coup, as president [13]. Kassem eventually came to a sticky end when he was overthrown by Colonel Salem Aref in 1963. He in turn was ousted by the revolution of 1968, masterminded by Saddam Hussein, who had fled to Egypt after attempting to assassinate Kassem in 1959. Most stamps of Iraq in this turbulent period glorified the army [14–15], a trend that increased during the Saddam regime.

SYRIA

In 1919, following the Arab Revolt, the entire area of Syria and Lebanon was assigned to the French, who issued stamps overprinted to signify their military occupation [16]. A mandate by the League of Nations came into effect in September 1923, and stamps inscribed "Syrie" were then introduced, of which the vast majority featured landmarks from Greek, Roman and Crusader times [17; 19]. In 1934 Syria became a republic under French control. Separate issues were made for the territory of the Alawites [18], which became the Republic of Latakia in 1930 but was absorbed by Syria in 1937 when the latter became a wholly independent republic.

The later history of Syria is one of revolutions and military coups. In 1958 Syria joined with Egypt to form the United Arab Republic and stamps were overprinted "UAR" pending the release of stamps thus inscribed. The union was dissolved in September 1961 and since then stamps have been inscribed for the Syrian Arab Republic, often denoted simply by the initials SAR.

Below: Syrian stamps were overprinted for use in Latakia in 1930 (top); the revolution of 30 March 1949, was celebrated by stamps portraying President Hushi el-Zaim (middle); and stamps were overprinted "UAR" in 1958 following Syria's union with Egypt (bottom).

10

11 12

13

14

15

16

17 18

19

MIDDLE EAST

The land at the eastern end of the Mediterranean was part of the Ottoman Empire until World War I. The Egyptian Expeditionary Force (EEF) under General Allenby advanced along the coast and took Palestine, while T.E. Lawrence organized the Arab Revolt, which liberated much of Arabia and the land east of the Jordan. Britain was granted a League of Nations mandate over Palestine and Transjordan. The British mandate over the latter ended in March 1946 when it became an independent kingdom. The mandate in Palestine ended on 14 May 1948, the day the State of Israel was proclaimed.

Left: Stamps of the EEF were overprinted in Arabic alone (far left), or in Arabic, Hebrew and English, for use in Transjordan and Palestine respectively.

1

2

3

4

5

6

7

8

9

10

JORDAN

Abdullah, son of the king of the Hejaz (later part of Saudi Arabia), was made Emir of Transjordan, becoming king when the mandate ended. Stamps of Saudi Arabia were overprinted in 1924 to signify "Government of the Arab East AH 1343" [1] while Abdullah's portrait appeared on stamps of 1927–44 [2]. When the British withdrew from Palestine the neighbouring Arab states declared war on the infant Jewish state. Jordan gained territory on the west bank of the river (including part of Jerusalem) and as a result the country was renamed the Hashemite Kingdom of Jordan. Abdullah's son Hussein succeeded in 1952 [3] and played a prominent part in the Arab League [4], where he was a useful counter to Egypt's Nasser (who tried several times to have him assassinated).

Many Jordanian stamps from the 1960s onwards were printed by Harrison's of England [5]. An interesting feature of the stamps after 1964 was their emphasis on Jordan's custody of the Christian holy places, notably the set of 14 in 1966 showing the Stations of the Cross [15]. Jordan played a major role in defusing tension in the Middle East. A set of ten devoted to Builders of World Peace (1967) included Pope John XXIII and Presidents Kennedy and Johnson as well as Hussein himself [6].

PALESTINE

During the British mandate, stamps featuring prominent landmarks such as King David's Citadel and the Dome of the Rock [9] were issued. The Hebrew version of the name Palestine terminated in the letters *aleph yud*, meaningless to anyone but the Jews, who realized that they were the initials of Eretz Yisrael (land of Israel). Yet when the first stamps of Israel appeared in May 1948 [8] they were merely inscribed "Do'ar Ivri" (Hebrew Post). By the time the Jewish New Year was celebrated that September, the inscription "Israel" was in use.

During the war of 1948 both Jordan and Egypt seized parts of Palestine, on the West Bank and the Gaza Strip respectively, and overprinted stamps for use in their occupied territories [10–11]. Egypt later released a number of stamps inscribed specifically for Palestine [7]. An Indian stamp overprinted "UNEF" (United Nations Emergency Force) was used by peacekeepers in Gaza. Victory in the Six Day War (1967) gave Israel possession of both territories.

ISRAEL

Although Israeli stamps are inscribed in Arabic as well as Hebrew, no stamps portrayed an Arab Israeli until 2004. The vast majority of Israeli stamps have either emphasized the country's military might [12] or drawn heavily on Jewish culture, often from Europe. A very few have portrayed Britons who played a part in the creation of the state, such as Lord Balfour or Orde Wingate [16]. Several issues have extolled the bravery of women, including Haviva Reik, a British agent killed by the Gestapo.

A unique feature of Israeli stamps is the tabs along the bottom row of the sheet, which often bear an apt Biblical quotation, as seen in the issue marking the 50th anniversary of the Balfour Declaration [14], or form an extension of the design of the stamp.

THE PALESTINE AUTHORITY

Control of Gaza and Jericho passed from Israel to the Palestinian Authority under Yasser Arafat in May 1994 and stamps printed in Berlin have been used there ever since. The first series was denominated in mils, the currency of Palestine up to 1948, but later issues have been valued in fils, the currency of Jordan. Most Palestinian stamps have, as in Jordan [15] previously, emphasized the Christian aspects of the Holy Land [17]. Stamps are regularly issued for Easter and Christmas [13].

Below: Israel issued a stamp in 1994 to mark the centenary of the "Dreyfus Affair". It shows the public disgrace of Captain Dreyfus, who was wrongfully convicted of treason. Emile Zola, whose newspaper article exposed French anti-semitism, appears on the tab below.

A League of Their Own

In 1964 the first Arab League Summit was hosted in Cairo. The League was created in 1945 to progress mutual economic and cultural aims in the Arab World. For the Summit, Jordan issued stamps bearing its opening date and portraying King Hussein of Jordan with a map of Palestine as it was in 1920. Concerns about the fate of Palestine were a major topic of discussion at the Conference.

Personalities featured on Palestinian stamps include Mother Teresa and the German politician Hans-Jurgen Wischnewski, who have appeared on annual issues made under the title of Friends of Palestine, invariably portrayed with Yasser Arafat.

Below: Every year Israel remembers its war dead with a stamp showing a different war memorial.

11

12

13

14

15

16

17

1

2

3

4

5

6

7

8

9

10

ARABIA

Four-fifths of the Arabian peninsula is occupied by Saudi Arabia, an absolute monarchy created in 1932 by Abdul Aziz Ibn Saud, Sultan of Nejd, who conquered most of eastern and central Arabia in 1923 and then occupied the kingdom of the Hejaz in 1924–5. The combined territories were renamed by him seven years later. To the south lay the kingdom and imamate of the Yemen. The whole of Arabia was nominally under Turkish rule but it broke up in the aftermath of the Arab Revolt during World War I. At the south-western tip of Arabia lay Aden, a British crown colony since 1839, together with the eastern and western Aden protectorate comprising a number of small sultanates. In 1963 they became the Federation of South Arabia, but four years later left the Commonwealth to form the Yemen People's Democratic Republic in November 1967.

Left: The designs for the first stamps of the Hejaz in 1916 were suggested by Lawrence of Arabia and were derived from carvings on doors or prayer niches in Cairo mosques, or stucco work over the entrance to Cairo railway station. The stamps were printed at the Survey of Egypt, Cairo.

SAUDI ARABIA

The ruler of the Hejaz was Hussein, Emir of Mecca, in whose reign stamps were introduced by T.E. Lawrence. True to Islam, they were non-figurative and relied heavily on quotations from the Koran [1]. In 1923 the Wahabis of Nejd, under Ibn Saud, began rapid expansion. In 1925 Hussein was forced to abdicate and go into exile in Cyprus, but his son Faisal was later made king of Transjordan. In 1924–5 the Wahabis of Nejd invaded and took over the Hejaz. Stamps for the joint territories showed the *toughra* of Ibn Saud [2]. Early Saudi Arabian stamps continued this tradition [3] but by the mid-1940s pictorialism was making a tentative appearance [4]. Pictorial definitives since 1960 have included the cartouche of the monarch in lieu of a portrait [5]. The first portrait stamp marked the installation of King Faisal in 1964 [7]; since then the palm tree and crossed swords emblem has usually been the only form of identification [8].

YEMEN

Imam Yahya became the spiritual ruler of the Yemen in 1904 and transformed it into a monarchy in 1918 when Turkish rule was overthrown. Stamps were introduced in 1926 and were non-figurative until 1946 [9], but a scenic definitive series appeared in 1951 [6] and thereafter stamps followed the western tradition. His successor, Imam Ahmed, died in September 1962 and his son Mohammed al-Badr proclaimed himself imam, but his palace was bombarded and rebels proclaimed a republic. The imam escaped to the mountains of the north-west and for several years there were two rival states: the Mutawakelite kingdom [10] and Yemen Arab Republic, often abbreviated to YAR on its stamps [11].

SOUTH ARABIA

The nucleus of South Arabia was the seaport of Aden at the south-western tip of the peninsula. It was originally occupied by the British in 1839 and used as a base to stamp out piracy, but following the opening of the Suez Canal in 1869 it became an important coaling station. It used Indian stamps, identifiable by their postmarks, until 1937, when a series featuring an Arab dhow flanked by curved daggers was introduced [12]. The series was reissued in 1939 in an elongated format

Opposing States with a Common Goal

The royalist and republican factions in the Yemen fought a ferocious civil war, but both had an eye to the main chance when it came to stamps, often commemorating the same events and personalities. This common purpose was vividly demonstrated by the stamps issued by both sides in 1964 in memory of the late John F. Kennedy.

to incorporate a portrait of George VI, with other vignettes added. An entirely new pictorial set portraying Elizabeth II appeared in 1953–63 and was reissued in 1964 overprinted to mark the grant of a revised constitution that paved the way for the creation of the Federation of South Arabia. In the colonial period Aden produced no distinctive commemoratives but issued a number of sets in the prevailing colonial omnibus designs.

Aden controlled the eastern and western Aden protectorates, several of which issued stamps. Initially these consisted of the Kathiri State of Seiyun [14] and the Qu'aiti State of Shihr and Mukalla [15], but the latter changed its name to Hadhramaut in 1955 [13]. In 1966 both states began issuing multicoloured stamps following prevailing fashions for Churchill [16], the Olympic Games and the World Cup. The Mahra State of Qishn and Socotra and the State of Upper Yafa briefly had stamps in 1967 showing their state flags [17], but these states were taken over by the National Liberation Front on 1 October 1967, and their stamps withdrawn from use.

The stamps of Aden and its protectorates were gradually phased out from 1963, being superseded by issues of the Federation of South Arabia [18]. Apart from the definitive series featuring the national flag or federal crest, the special issues of the federation were confined to the various colonial omnibus issues, from the Red Cross series of 1963 to the UNESCO anniversary set of December 1966, on which the queen's portrait was replaced by the federal emblem.

The federation became wholly independent in 1967, taking the name of the People's Republic of Southern Yemen [19]. Its title was changed at the end of 1970, when the word "Southern" was dropped and the style was changed to the Yemen People's Democratic Republic or People's Democratic Republic of Yemen [20]. The Yemen PDR and YAR amalgamated in May 1990 and since then stamps have been inscribed "Republic of Yemen".

Below: Stamps inscribed simply "Republic of Yemen" celebrated the merger of the two Yemeni republics in May 1990.

11

12

13

14

15

16

17

18

19

20

GULF STATES

A number of small states on the western side of the Persian Gulf, nominally under Turkish rule, came under British influence in the 19th century. Bahrain, Kuwait and Muscat had Indian post offices to facilitate external trade but following the establishment of the dominion of India in 1947 control of the Gulf post offices passed to Britain. In the 1960s the sheikhdoms introduced local posts and eventually also took over their external mails. Britain continued to give military aid, both in quelling local rebellions and in dealing with aggression from Iraq.

Left: Following the Iraqi invasion and occupation of Kuwait in August 1990, an international coalition liberated it in February 1991. The first stamps of Kuwait, released in May, celebrated the liberation.

1

2

3

4

5

6

7

8

9

10

COLONIAL ISSUES

Bahrain [1], Kuwait and Muscat [2] used Indian stamps suitably overprinted until 1947, when British stamps overprinted and surcharged in Indian currency [3] were substituted. British stamps with no name but denominated in annas and rupees [4] were used in Qatar.

INDEPENDENT STATES

Bahrain took over its own postal services in 1966, most stamps from that date including a portrait of the ruler Shaikh Isa bin Sulman al-Khalifa [5]. The usual range of popular themes is covered but a strong feature is the chronicling of the material progress of the state, especially public projects [6].

Kuwait assumed responsibility for its postal services in 1959 and stamps have since followed a pattern very similar to that of Bahrain. Portraits of the rulers [7] tend to be confined to the definitive issues, while a poster style is used for an extraordinary range of stamps released for Mother's Day, Family's Day [8] and many other annual events.

The sultanate of Muscat and Oman began issuing its own stamps in 1966, using the state emblem in lieu of the ruler's portrait in strict observance of Koranic law [9]. When Sultan Qabus succeeded in 1970 he decided that the name of the country should be shortened and since then stamps have been inscribed "Sultanate of Oman" [10]. He had no compunction about using his portrait.

Overprinted British stamps were used in Qatar until 1963. Distinctive stamps were issued from 1961 for internal mail, and were later extended to overseas mail. The majority portray the ruler alongside subjects that range from the extraordinary progress of the sheikhdom to international events [11].

UNITED ARAB EMIRATES

The southern coast of the Gulf was formerly known as the Pirate Coast. The British took strenuous measures to stamp out piracy and concluded a treaty with the ruler of Dubai to extend British influence in the Gulf. From this arose the collective name of the Trucial States for the seven sheikhdoms and emirates. British stamps surcharged in Indian currency were also used in Dubai till 1961, when stamps inscribed "Trucial States" were introduced [12]. In 1963 Dubai took over responsibility and began issuing stamps bearing its own name [13]. Later issues charted the phenomenal rise of Dubai as an oil-rich international trading centre [14].

Distinctive stamps spread to the other states in 1963–4 and over a seven-year period output assumed piratical proportions. The stamps

Big is Beautiful

Sharjah was not only prodigal in its own right but churned out numerous "regional" stamps for its dependency Khor Fakkan. Like the other Trucial States, Sharjah had a penchant for Americana, but outdid them all with this triptych for the New York World Fair in 1964.

shown here represent the more legitimate end of the spectrum, but by 1970 the various rulers had signed agreements with philatelic agents (some with two different agents simultaneously) and stamps poured off the world's presses at an astonishing rate, covering all the fashionable topics of the period but especially reproductions of European paintings (many of them

Below: A scene from the film Casablanca *featured on a stamp of 1969 from Umm al Qiwain (top). Mosques and desert forts are perennial subjects for stamps of the United Arab Emirates (bottom).*

nudes that would have been frowned upon had any of these stamps ever appeared in their respective states).

At their best, the stamps of Abu Dhabi showed the traditional way of life. One of Ajman's earliest sets celebrated the centenary of the Gibbons catalogues [15]. Few of Fujeira's unduly prolific stamps after 1966 have attained catalogue status [16]. From the assassination of the Kennedy brothers onwards, all of the Trucial States produced a prodigious number of stamps devoted to Americana. Ras Al Khaima's Apollo XI set was one of the few issues in the world to portray President Nixon [17]. In Umm al Qiwain the gift of a 16mm projector was sufficient to trigger off a set of 48 stamps featuring stills from famous films.

This philatelic whirlwind ended in 1973, when the seven states combined to form the United Arab Emirates, whose stamp policy has been a model of conservatism, combining traditional scenes with issues publicizing a wide range of international conferences.

At first Harrison and Sons in England enjoyed a monopoly of stamp production, but from 1984 onwards contracts were awarded to many other printers, from Questa and De La Rue to Enschede of Holland and Cartor of Normandy. Very occasionally they are lithographed at the Oriental Press in Bahrain, but are invariably designed locally, with a penchant for symbolism.

11

12

13

14

15

16

17

1

2

3

4

5

6

7

8

9

AFGHANISTAN AND IRAN

The neighbouring Islamic republics of Afghanistan and Iran lie in southwest Asia. Afghanistan is completely landlocked whereas Iran, lying to the west, has access to the Caspian Sea (north) and the Persian Gulf (south). Iran, three times the size of Afghanistan with more than three times its population, was one of the world's great empires from the 6th to the 4th centuries BC, and in the 20th century, when the country changed its name from Persia to Iran, attempts were made to capitalize on its ancient glories. Afghanistan, by contrast, was always a relatively poor country, its mountainous terrain making communications difficult and encouraging division. Afghanistan was, in fact, conquered by Darius I of Persia and subsequently endured conquest by Alexander the Great, Genghis Khan, Tamerlane, the Mughals and the British, though none of them ever succeeded in controlling it for long, as the Russians learned to their cost in the 1980s. The great Persian Empire had been in decline for many years when an obscure Cossack captain seized power in 1925 and began its transformation. The work was completed by his son, the last Shahinshah.

Left: In 1970–1 Iran celebrated the 2,500th anniversary of the Persian Empire with no fewer than eight sets of stamps harking back to the glories of Darius and Xerxes. The final issue glorified the Pahlavi era, portraying Shah Mohammed Riza at the height of his power.

AFGHANISTAN

The kingdom of Afghanistan was instituted in 1747, although the writ of the Amir did not run beyond Kabul. In 1871 Amir Sher Ali set up a postal service using circular stamps with the head of a lion surrounded by a Farsi text [1]. Similar stamps, introduced in 1877, were printed in different colours according to the province in which they were used. The stamps were among the most primitive in the world well into the 20th century, a circular armorial design being used for official correspondence [2]. A scenic definitive series was released in 1939–47 [3].

Crudely typographed or lithographed stamps continued until 1958, when the State Printing Works was granted a contract to produce stamps by photogravure [4]. Even so that year's Atoms for Peace stamps plagiarized stamps issued previously by the USA. An agreement with a philatelic agency in the USA in 1961 resulted in a deluge of stamps from Afghanistan over the ensuing three years [5]. Since then they have been much more restrained and generally thematic in content [6]. Annual issues marked "Pakhtunistan Day" are part of a propaganda exercise to wrest the land of the Pathans from neighbouring Pakistan [7].

In 1975 King Mohamed Zahir Shah was deposed and Afghanistan was declared a republic [8]. In 1978 Afghanistan became a Democratic Republic [9], a move that provoked Soviet invasion the following year and led to a war lasting until 1987. In that year Afghanistan became a republic again but as the Russians withdrew the Taliban regime took over. In more recent years, before the US invasion, Afghanistan's stamps had taken on a much more commercial tone, as seen in the stamps sponsored by the Ferrari motor company in 1999 [10].

PERSIA

The earliest stamps of Persia, introduced in 1868, were almost as primitive as those of Afghanistan. Although they were engraved by Albert Barre of Paris, they were printed in Tehran and the resulting impressions were very coarse [11]. Portraits of the Shah appeared from 1876 onwards, when stamps were printed in Vienna and later by Enschede of Haarlem [12]. Fine European printing contrasted with the numerous issues produced locally and their bewildering array of provisional overprints [13]. The coronation of Shah Ahmed in 1915 was celebrated by 51 stamps, the higher values with metallic gold frames [14].

Mutilation Cancellation

Until the early 20th century the stamps of Afghanistan were cancelled by the postmaster or letter receiver by tearing a chunk out of them before mail went forward to its destination.

IRAN

In October 1925 cavalry captain Riza Khan Pahlavi deposed Shah Ahmed Mirza and seized power; in December he was crowned Shahinshah of Persia and immediately began modernizing the tottering empire. Two-colour photogravure was adopted for the airmail series of 1930 [15] and stamps generally adopted a more westernized character. In 1935 Shah Riza changed the name of the country to Iran, an ancient term literally meaning "land of the Aryans". Despite westernization, Iranian stamps went through a phase when they were inscribed entirely in Farsi, including the set of 1939 celebrating the marriage of Crown Prince Mohammed Riza to Princess Fawzieh, sister of King Farouk of Egypt [16].

Shah Riza intrigued with Nazi Germany and was ousted in favour of his son in 1941. From the late 1940s the stamps of Iran contrasted the glories of the ancient empire of the Medes and Persians with the achievements of the Pahlavi regime in modernizing such a vast and disparate country. On the whole, however, the stamps of the reign of Shah Mohammed looked back to ancient Persia, culminating in a veritable orgy of celebration for the 2,500th anniversary of the empire [17]. Stamps of 1968 marked the centenary of the first stamps with reproductions of the lion and sun design [18].

In January 1979 the Shah went to America for medical treatment and in his absence Ayatollah Khomeini returned from exile and began the revolution that transformed the westernized empire into a fundamentalist Islamic republic. Stamps in the era of the ayatollahs reflected their uncompromising religious fanaticism.

Below: Many Iranian stamps celebrated the 2,500th anniversary of the Persian Empire (top) and a stamp of 1979 (bottom) designed by children, marked the International Year of the Child.

10

11

12

13

14

15

16

17

18

1

2

3

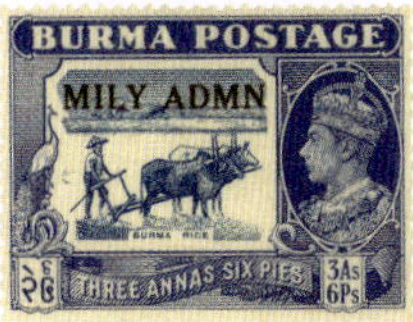

4

5

6

7

8

9

10

BANGLADESH, PAKISTAN AND BURMA

These three countries have had a common history, having been part of British India for very many years. The territories of Bangladesh and Pakistan came under the dominion of the Mughal emperors in the Middle Ages and thus passed into the hands of the East India Company in the 19th century. Burma was also part of British India, of which it was the largest province as well as the most easterly. It had been a powerful kingdom in its own right, but when its king invaded Bengal in 1825 the British retaliated and annexed Lower Burma in 1926. Two further Burmese wars, in 1852 and 1885, led to the entire country coming under British rule. It was granted autonomy in 1937, suffered Japanese occupation in 1942 and after liberation in 1945 adopted a nationalist government that attained full independence in 1947 and left the Commonwealth. Pakistan was created in the same year and consisted of the two predominantly Muslim parts of British India. However, as these were separated by India and ethnically different from each other, it was inevitable that they would split up. When West Pakistan resisted the secession of East Pakistan and tried to put down the revolt, the Indian Army intervened on the side of the rebels, whose independence as Bangladesh was confirmed in 1971.

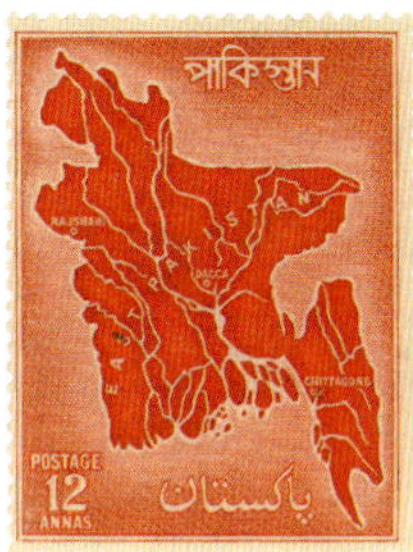

Left: Stamps of 1955–6 showed maps of West and East Pakistan, the latter marking the first session of the Pakistani parliament in Dacca, the capital of Bengal. This was the region that seceded in 1970–1 to form Bangladesh. Stamps were usually inscribed in English and Arabic but this set was exceptionally inscribed in Bengali instead of English in an attempt to appease Bengali nationalism.

BURMA

Ordinary Indian stamps were used in Burma until April 1937, when it was separated from India and placed under direct British administration. Indian stamps were then overprinted for use there [1] pending a distinctive series released in 1938–40 [2]. Burma was the only country in the British Empire to celebrate the centenary of adhesive postage stamps, with an overprinted stamp issued in May 1940 [3].

The Japanese invaded Burma in 1942 and blotted out the portrait of George VI with a peacock emblem. In 1943 they set up a puppet government, which issued its own stamps. At the end of World War II the country was placed under military administration [4] prior to the creation of the Union of Burma as a completely independent state [5]. While very few stamps were released in the ensuing years, they tended to emphasize the unique character of the people [6].

Following a referendum in December 1973 the military junta that had seized power in 1962 made way for a one-party socialist republic. Stamps with inscriptions reflecting this change were in use from 1974 [7] until the government changed the name of the country in 1990: "Myanmar", which had always been used in Burmese script, was adopted as the western form as well [8]. The country now holds the world record for the fewest new stamps, only about 20 having been issued since 1990, usually for the anniversary of independence.

Martyrs for the Cause

In 1991 Bangladesh celebrated the 20th anniversary of independence by embarking on a long series of stamps portraying Martyred Intellectuals – doctors, lawyers, politicians and teachers who lost their lives when Pakistan attempted by force to prevent the secession. These stamps were issued in sheets of ten different designs. A total of 240 different stamps were released, 30 at a time, up to 1999.

PAKISTAN

When the Islamic Dominion of Pakistan was created in August 1947 overprinted Indian stamps [9], many of them handstruck locally, were in use pending the supply of distinctive stamps in 1948 [10], recess-printed by the new Pakistan Security Printing Corporation, which has been responsible for the vast majority of stamps ever since. One of the earliest special issues marked the centenary of the Scinde Dawks, Asia's first stamps [11], as the formerly Indian province of Scinde now forms part of Pakistan.

In 1956 Pakistan became an Islamic republic [12] and thereafter stamps became more Muslim in character and content. By the early 1960s stamps were inscribed in English, Bengali and Urdu in a bid to placate the secessionist tendencies of East Pakistan [13]. A recurring theme was the quarrel with India over Kashmir, which had a mainly Muslim population but had remained in Indian hands [14]. From time to time the philatelic propaganda campaign has erupted into border incidents that have almost brought India and Pakistan to open warfare. More recent stamps have reflected Pakistan's involvement in world affairs, including an issue publicizing its expedition to Antarctica [15]. One thing Pakistan has in common with India is a policy of issuing mainly single stamps, often portraying personalities little known by the rest of the world, although a 1990s series celebrated Pioneers of Freedom.

BANGLADESH

In time-honoured fashion the new country made use of overprinted Pakistani stamps before adopting distinctive stamps. The first series of these, issued in July 1971, showed a map of the new country [17] and portrayed the leader of the struggle for independence, Shaikh Mujibur Rahman [16]. Over the past 30 years the stamps of Bangladesh have been printed as far afield as Vienna and Melbourne. Many of them provide public service messages to the population [18] but the majority emphasize the distinctive cultural heritage of the country [19].

Below: The Bagha mosque of Rajshahi (top) was part of the 1997 Historic Mosque set, and a 2000 stamp (bottom) marked the tenth anniversary of the uprising for the restoration of democracy.

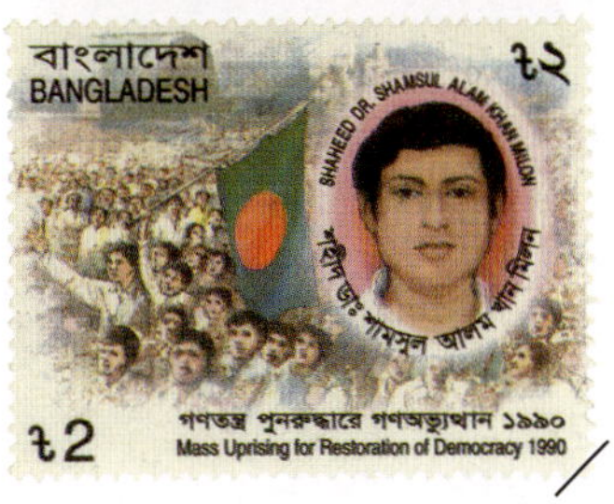

11

12

13

14

15

16

17

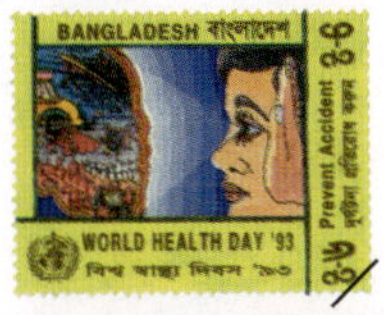

18

19

1

2

3

4

5

6

7

8

9

10

11

12

INDIA

The subcontinent of India has fostered civilizations for thousands of years and is home to almost a billion people of many languages, cultures and religions. The only factor common to all educated Indians is the English language, but in the scramble for India the British were late starters. The Portuguese got there first, in 1498, followed by the French and the Danes. The British founded the Honourable East India Company in 1600 to trade with India and the Far East, establishing its first settlement at Surat in 1612. Bombay was ceded by Portugal as part of Catherine of Braganza's dowry when she married Charles II in 1662. By 1700 Britain also had control of Madras and further expansion came at the expense of the French, who were defeated by Robert Clive in 1757. Over the ensuing century the East India Company gained control of the whole of India by bribery or force, ruling directly or through the feudatory princes. The Sepoy Mutiny (1857) led to the administration of India being handed over to the imperial government.

Indian nationalism grew after World War I, under the charismatic leadership of M.K. Gandhi. Britain agreed to independence in principle in 1931 but implementation was delayed by disagreement between the Hindu and Muslim factions. India eventually gained independence in August 1947, but was partitioned between India and Pakistan, with great bloodshed and ethnic cleansing, creating the greatest upheaval of population.

Left: Mohandas Karamchand Gandhi, architect of Indian independence, was assassinated by a Hindu fanatic on 30 January 1948, because he had failed to prevent the secession of Pakistan. The first of many stamps portraying him were released on 15 August 1948, the first anniversary of India's independence.

BRITISH INDIA

In 1852 India had the distinction of issuing the first stamps in Asia, the Scinde Dawks (derived from the name of the province and *dawk*, the Hindi word for posts). They were embossed and bore the emblem of the HEIC [1]. Stamps for the whole of India were introduced in 1854 [2] and from 1855 to 1926 were printed by De La Rue in England [3]. The inscription "East India" continued in use until 1877, when India was declared an empire with Victoria as Empress. Later definitives portrayed the reigning monarch [4] until 1947 and included the George VI series showing the many forms of mail transport in use [5]. India's first commemorative stamps appeared in 1931 to celebrate the inauguration of New Delhi as the nation's capital [6].

REPUBLIC OF INDIA

A set of three stamps was released on the day independence was proclaimed. The communal violence, which created an immense refugee problem, induced the Indian government to issue compulsory tax stamps in aid of refugee relief [7]. The same device was used in the 1970s to help refugees from the former East Pakistan.

Most definitives, such as those publicizing the Five Year Plan of 1955 [8], have retained the small size used under the British Raj. When the currency was decimalized in 1957 stamps showing the map were released [9]. Later sets were often didactic, educating the Indian public by focusing on social and economic matters from good husbandry to family planning. The latest series portrays prominent figures [10].

Most special issues are single stamps portraying historic personalities. Relatively few, such as Nehru [11], are known outside India. Subhas Chandra Bose was the leader of the Free India movement [12] who collaborated with the Japanese during World War II. The conquest of Everest in 1953 was marked by stamps showing the mountain, but it has also featured in several later issues [13]. Very few non-Indians have been portrayed, although they include Lord Mountbatten (the last Viceroy), Annie Besant (the founder of the theosophist movement), Abraham Lincoln [14] and Martin Luther King [15]. Philatelic tributes to the great and good of the past [16], as well as the religions and mythology of the subcontinent [17], are aimed at making Indians more aware of their diverse cultural heritage.

HIMALAYAN KINGDOMS

Nepal, the world's only Hindu kingdom, was welded into a single state in the late 18th century when the Gurkha ruler conquered a number of independent mountain principalities. Nepal had its own stamps from 1881 [18] but they were confined to internal mail until 1959, when Nepal joined the Universal Postal Union, and until then Indian stamps were used on mail going abroad. Everest, which lies partly in Nepal, features prominently on the modern stamps [19].

The kingdom of Bhutan also had stamps for internal use [20] until 1969, when it joined the UPU. Even before that date, however, it had embarked on prolific issues aimed at the international philatelic market.

EUROPEAN COLONIES

In the 17th and early 18th centuries France rivalled Britain for possession of India, but by the Treaty of Paris, which ended the Seven Years War, France relinquished all her territory except for Pondicherry and four other small outposts. These constituted the French Indian Settlements until 1954 when they were taken over by the Republic of India. The French colonial keytypes, suitably inscribed, were introduced in 1892, followed by bicoloured pictorials in 1914 showing the god Brahma and a temple near Pondicherry. These stamps were overprinted "France Libre" in 1941 when the settlements joined the Free French, and subsequently a set of stamps produced in England was released [21]. A postwar series featured various Hindu deities.

The Portuguese territories of Goa, Damao and Diu on the west coast were all that remained of the territory acquired by Portugal from 1510 onwards, following Vasco da Gama's discovery of the sea route to India. Distinctive stamps, designed and printed in Goa, were introduced in 1871, and the local issues were superseded by colonial keytypes from 1877 to 1945, followed by a set portraying historic figures [22]. Portuguese stamps were withdrawn in 1961 when the territory was annexed by India.

World Leader in Gimmickry

Bhutan has produced more innovations in stamps than the rest of the world put together, including the first scented stamps (with flower motifs), stamps printed on textiles or steel plates, and even talking stamps in the form of phonograph records that play the national anthem. It also pioneered 3D stamps (see below), either laminated prismatic stamps or plastic stamps in high relief.

13

14

15

16

17

18

19

20

21

22

INDIAN STATES

In prewar India the British Raj ruled almost 400 million people, a fifth of the world total at that time. It was the most amazing mix of humanity, with 203 languages, many different ethnic groups and a dozen major religions. The British administration was divided into 17 provinces but the number of states ran to four figures. Some of the states were larger than many European countries, with their own armies; others were little more than tribal groups headed by chieftains.

More than 40 states had their own distinctive postage stamps at one time or another, a mere drop in the ocean compared with those that had revenue stamps. Surprisingly, two of the largest states, Mysore and Baroda, did not have their own postage stamps, being content to use the facilities of the British Indian postal service.

Left: Charkari began with crudely printed stamps in 1894 but pictorials were in use from 1931 to 1948, when the state became part of Vindhya Pradesh.

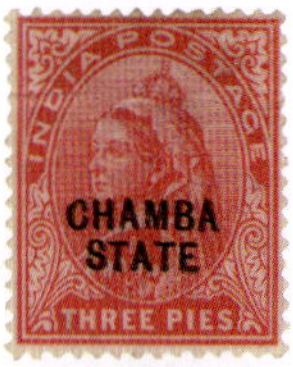

1

2

3

4

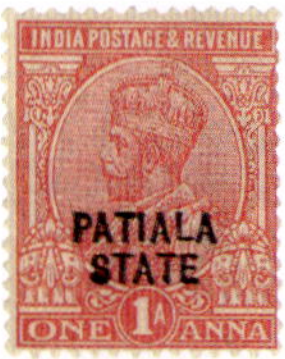

5

6

7

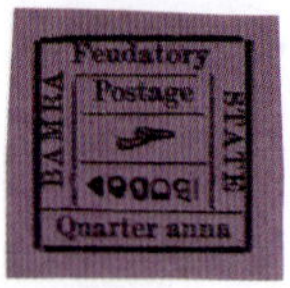

8

9

10

11

12

13

CONVENTION STATES

Collectors divide the stamps of the states into two separate categories. The Convention States were those that signed postal conventions with the imperial administration, whereby the latter supplied them with Indian stamps overprinted for use in their states. These stamps were valid for postage within the state, to other convention states and anywhere within British India. The various conventions were negotiated between 1884 and 1887. The stamps of Chamba [1], Gwalior [2], Jind [3], Nabha [4] and Patiala [5] were still in use at the end of 1950, when they were replaced by the issues of the Republic of India. Faridkot [6] was the last state to adopt this system (1887), having previously issued its own stamps, and it was the first to abandon them, in 1901.

FEUDATORY STATES

The stamps issued by the princely states were valid only for postage within each state, except in a few instances. Stamps of Cochin [15], for example, were also valid on mail to neighbouring Travancore [39] and vice versa. Indeed these two states combined in 1949 and their joint stamps were then valid for mail throughout India and abroad [35]. Only one state in what later became Pakistan – Las Bela [29] – issued stamps in the imperial period, but one other began issuing stamps after the subcontinent broke up.

The stamps of the Feudatory States ranged from the extremely crude issues of Bhor [11], struck by hand, to the elegant stamps of Jaipur and Saurashtra [38]. They were printed by every method, including a high proportion of the very few printed by the halftone process [12; 20]. As many stamps have inscriptions only in their indigenous language they are identified here.

Alwar [7] issued stamps from 1877 to 1902, while the typeset stamps of Bamra [8] were in use from 1888 to 1895. Barwani did not commence until 1921 [10] but continued until the state was absorbed by Madhya Bharat in July 1948. Bhopal had ordinary stamps from 1872 to 1902 but continued to issue "Service" stamps for official mail until 1949 [9]. The handstruck stamps of Bhor [11] appeared in 1879, while Bijawar's issues were confined to 1935–41 [12]. Bundi's stamps ran from 1894 to 1948 and ranged from extreme primitives to the last set, typeset by the *Times of India* [13]. Bussahir's stamps from 1895 to 1900 were overprinted with a security

Briefly Independent

Bahawalpur was independent between the partition of India on August 15, 1947, and joining Pakistan on October 3. No fewer than 46 stamps were issued in that period. Bahawalpur also had stamps for official mail from 1945, which remained valid until 1953.

monogram [14], as were those of Dhar in 1887–1900 [16]. Dungarpur had stamps from 1933 to 1947. Duttia (or Datia) had armorial stamps from about 1894 to 1920 [17]. Faridkot had very primitive stamps in 1879–86 [18] before adopting the Convention States' issues. Hyderabad's stamps ranged from 1869 to 1949 [19], but Idar's postal issues were confined to 1932–44 [20].

Indore or Holkar produced stamps from 1886 to 1948 [21], while Jaipur issued them from 1904 to 1949, both states ranging from the crude to the sophisticated. The stamps of Jammu and Kashmir from 1866 to 1894 [22] were non-figural. Jasdan's 1a stamps of 1942–7 featured the sun [23], while Jhalawar's stamps of 1886–1900 showed a dancing nymph [24].

Other states were Jind in 1874–85, Kishangarh in 1899–1949 [28], Morvi in 1931–48 [30], Nandgaon in 1891–4 [31], Nawanagar in 1877–93 [26], Orchha in 1913–48 [34], Poonch in 1876–88 [27], Rajpipla in 1880 [32], Shahpura in 1914–48 [36], Sirmoor in 1878–1901 [37], Soruth in 1864–1913 [33], when it became Saurashtra [38], and Wadhwan in 1888–94. Cochin from 1892 [15] and Travancore from 1898 [39] united to form Travancore-Cochin [35] in 1949.

14

15

16

17

18

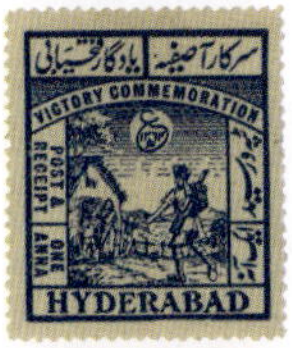

19

20

21

22

23

24

25

26

27

28

29

30

31

32

33

34

35

36

37

38

39

1

2

3

4

5

6

7

8

INDIAN OCEAN

Dotted around the Indian Ocean are a number of archipelagos and individual islands, all of which are, or were, colonized by Britain or France. Some, like Sri Lanka, have a civilization dating back thousands of years, which saw the Portuguese and the Dutch come and go before falling into British hands. At the other end of the ocean, Mauritius was settled by Arabs and Malays before passing to the Dutch, then the French, before it fell to Britain during the Napoleonic Wars. Madagascar was contested by Britain and France before the latter triumphed. Other islands were gradually snapped up by the two major colonial powers in the 19th century. Relatively undeveloped, their mainstay was fishing and coconut cultivation until the advent of tourism in more recent years.

Left: Sri Lanka, formerly Ceylon, is arguably the foremost preserver of Buddhism, as reflected in numerous stamps. This one of 1959 marks the inauguration of the Pirivena universities.

SRI LANKA

Formerly Ceylon, Sri Lanka was taken from the Dutch in 1802 and became a British crown colony, adopting stamps in 1857. They followed the prevailing British colonial patterns, using various portraits of Queen Victoria until 1900. Following the switch from sterling to a decimal system based on the rupee in 1872, Ceylon acquired an unenviable reputation for its enormous number of provisional surcharges throughout the 1880s and 1890s. After the Edwardian series the colonial keytypes were adopted for the stamps of George V, followed by scenic pictorials in 1935 with the king's portrait inset. The same designs were retained under George VI with his portrait substituted [1].

Although Ceylon became a dominion in 1948, ties to the British Crown remained strong, exemplified by stamps for the coronation and royal visit of 1954 [2]. It became the Republic of Sri Lanka in May 1972, and most stamps since that time have featured local personalities and institutions, with a strong Buddhist flavour [3–4].

MAURITIUS AND DEPENDENCIES

Although to this day French influence has remained strong in the language and customs of Mauritius, it was one of the few British colonies to celebrate the diamond jubilee of Queen Victoria with stamps [5]. After achieving self-government in 1967 the island became a republic within the Commonwealth in 1992 [6]. It continues a modest policy regarding new issues, which publicize tourism and an unchanging way of life [7–8].

The Seychelles were formerly a dependency of Mauritius and used its stamps, distinguishable only by their postmark, until they adopted distinctive stamps in 1890. Many stamps issued since gaining independence in 1975 have featured the wildlife of the islands, a major tourist attraction [9]. The Seychelles Outer Islands (Les Iles Eloignés Seychelles), comprising several outlying islands, had their own stamps from 1980 to 1992 and were served by a ship acting as a floating post office. During that period three different forms of the name in the local phonetic patois were tried.

The Chagos archipelago, formerly administered by Mauritius, became a separate crown colony in 1965 under the name of the British Indian Ocean Territory [10]. It included the Seychelles Outer Islands, but when the Seychelles became independent these outliers reverted to them.

World's Most Expensive Stamps

Only 500 of each of the Mauritius Post Office stamps were printed by James Barnard in 1847 and barely a dozen of each survive today. Not only are they among the world's most valuable stamps but they were also the most expensive to produce, as Barnard was paid more than their total face value for the engraving and printing.

MALDIVE ISLANDS

Lying to the south of Ceylon (Sri Lanka), this archipelago was a British protectorate and used stamps of Ceylon suitably overprinted before adopting distinctive stamps in 1933. In 1953 it briefly became a republic, but reverted to a sultanate later the same year. Since then it has become one of the most prolific stamp-issuing countries in the world. The vast majority of Maldives stamps have no bearing on the islands but are aimed at the world philatelic market [11–12].

MADAGASCAR AND DEPENDENCIES

An independent kingdom until the late 19th century, Madagascar's mail services were operated by the British consul (overseas post) and a syndicate of businessmen (inland mail), both using distinctive stamps [13]. These posts were suppressed by the French when they subjugated the island in 1895. French colonial stamps [15] were in use from then until 1958, when Madagascar attained independence as the Malagasy Republic, but it reverted to its original name in 1992. Since then, like the Maldives, it has gone overboard on stamps that are more relevant to the USA than to the Indian Ocean, including a lengthy series cashing in on the *Titanic* craze.

North-west of Madagascar lies the Comoro archipelago. Each island in the group at first issued its own stamps, using the French colonial standard design with the name at the foot [14], but a general series was substituted in 1950 [16]. When the Comoros became an independent state, Mayotte was detached and became an overseas department of France. French stamps were used until 1997, when distinctive stamps were adopted.

Réunion, east of Madagascar, had its own stamps as long ago as 1852 but from 1891 used the French colonial keytypes. It used distinctive stamps from 1907 [17] as well as a Free French issue during World War II. Réunion became an overseas department of France after the war and the majority of its stamps were French, inscribed or overprinted in colonial francs. In 1975 it adopted the French metropolitan currency and separate stamp issues were then discontinued.

Below: The stamps of present-day Mayotte reflect the exuberance of the people (top). The Free French stamps of Réunion showed local produce (bottom).

9

10

11

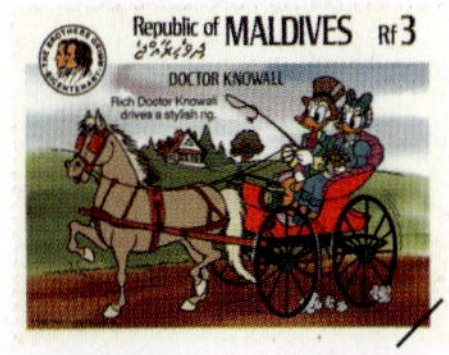

12

13

14

15

16

17

1

2

3

4

5

6

7

8

9

10

11

INDOCHINA

The French conquered Indochina in the late 19th century, the name being given from 1888 onwards to the colonies and protectorates of Cochin-China, Annam and Tongking (Vietnam) and Cambodia, to which were later added Laos (1893) and Kouang-Tcheou (1900). With an area greater than France itself, inhabited by peoples of diverse races with civilizations dating back many centuries, it is not surprising that colonial rule was resisted to a greater or lesser degree.

Resistance was greatest in north and central Vietnam, where Nguyen Ai Quoc (later known as Ho Chi Minh) campaigned for independence from the 1920s. Japan occupied Indochina in 1942–5 but allowed the Vichy administration to continue. During this period anti-Japanese resistance was organized by Ho. When French power was restored in 1945 France created the United States of Indochina, giving limited autonomy to each region. The Viet Minh waged war to unite the Vietnamese regions. In 1950 France tried to retain overall power in the area by giving greater autonomy to Vietnam and the kingdoms of Cambodia and Laos, but by that time its action was too little and too late.

Left: Ho Chi Minh (1892–1969), prime minister (1954–5) and president (1955–69) of North Vietnam, led the Viet Minh resistance movement from 1941 against the Japanese and later the French. "Uncle Ho" was also the driving force in the war between North and South Vietnam in the 1960s.

CAMBODIA

The French had produced stamps showing indigenous subjects for the whole of Indochina from 1889 to 1945 [1–2]. Stamps for the independent kingdom of Cambodia were introduced in 1951. King Norodom Sihanouk abdicated in 1955 in favour of his father Norodom Suramarit [3] but continued as president of the council of ministers. Stamps from this period concentrated on Cambodian culture [4]. When Suramarit died in 1960 Sihanouk refused the crown but ruled as chief of state. In 1970 he was deposed by the Khmer Rouge communist rebels, who established the Khmer republic [5] under Lon Nol.

In turn Lon Nol was overthrown by Pol Pot, who created Democratic Kampuchea. He abolished money, public transport and the postal service as well as murdering countless thousands of his own people. The country was liberated by Vietnamese forces, and the People's Republic of Kampuchea was proclaimed in 1969. The stamps of the ensuing period were apolitical and strongly thematic [6], a policy continued after the Vietnamese withdrawal in 1989 and reversion to the name of Cambodia [7]. The kingdom was restored, with Norodom Sihanouk once more on the throne.

LAOS

Compared with that of its neighbours, the history of Laos since independence in 1951 has been relatively stable. It remained a kingdom until 1975, when King Savang Vatthana abdicated and the Pathet Lao rebels proclaimed a people's democratic republic. Under the monarchy, most stamps were produced in France, mainly by intaglio [8] but latterly in multicolour lithography [9]. In the republican period they have been predominantly thematic [12].

VIETNAM

The Vietnam Democratic Republic was proclaimed by Ho Chi Minh [13] at Hanoi in September 1945 and was initially recognized by France, but relations deteriorated and erupted into guerrilla warfare. By 1947 the Viet Minh had withdrawn to northern Tongking [10]. In 1951 the French created Vietnam as an independent state within the French Union [11] but gradually the Viet Minh fought back. After they had decisively defeated the French at Dien Bien Phu in 1954 [14] a conference in Geneva partitioned the country at the 17th parallel.

The stamps of North Vietnam were extremely political, either attacking the USA directly for its support of the South, or praising those who protested against American policy, such as Norman Morrison, a Quaker who burned himself to death. Stamps supported Cuba and mourned the Marxist leader of Chile, Salvador Allende [15]. Separate issues were made in 1963–76 by the National Front for the Liberation of South Vietnam and these, if anything, were even more virulently anti-American [16]. By contrast, the stamps of South Vietnam highlighted the plight of refugees from the North [17] or promoted the solidarity of its allies in the long-drawn-out war.

Following the American withdrawal in 1975 the country was re-unified under the name of the Socialist Republic of Vietnam. Since then stamps have simply been inscribed "Viet nam" and have been devoted to the usual range of popular subjects.

Below: A set of four stamps was issued by South Vietnam in 1968 to express thanks for international aid (top). Many recent issues of Vietnam feature wildlife (bottom).

Shooting Down the Enemy

During the Vietnam War the US Air Force carried out numerous air raids on North Vietnam and areas of the South controlled by the Viet Cong. A recurring theme of stamps in this period was the shooting down of American planes, often showing downed fliers as prisoners or anti-aircraft batteries in action, with the latest score.

KEEPING THE PEACE

In August 1954 the International Control Commission for Indonesia was created by the Geneva Declaration. It was chaired by India, regarded as the leading power among the neutral nations of the world, with Canada and Poland as the other members. Joint inspection teams of service personnel were provided with 1949 Indian definitives overprinted in Hindi, for separate use in Cambodia [18], Laos [19] and Vietnam. In 1960 the map series was overprinted for use in Laos and Vietnam [20]. They were replaced in 1965 by stamps overprinted "ICC" for use throughout Indochina [21].

12

13

14

15

16

17

18

19

20

21

1

2

3

4

5

6

7

8

9

10

11

12

CHINA

The world's largest country, China is inhabited by a quarter of the human race. The Manchu dynasty, which had ruled China since 1644, was overthrown by Sun Yat-sen in 1911 but the republic barely survived the trauma of World War I. Central government collapsed in the 1920s as China was polarized between communism and nationalism, led by Mao Zedong and Chiang Kai-shek respectively. Breakaway provinces were ruled by warlords and the country was on the brink of anarchy. From 1931 onwards it was also prey to the aggression of the Japanese. At the end of World War II the Japanese returned Taiwan (which it had seized in 1895) just in time to provide the nationalists with a home after they were ousted from the mainland. The People's Republic of China was proclaimed in September 1949.

Left: Mao Zedong, the red flag and a military parade in Beijing were potent symbols used on many stamps from 1949 onwards.

EARLY POSTAL SERVICES

Although the Chinese emperors had a very sophisticated communications network for thousands of years, there was no countrywide postal service open to the public before 1897. The first stamps were issued in Shanghai in 1865, and were later overprinted to commemorate 50 years of international settlement [1]. The various towns with international communities under the terms of the Treaty of Nanking (1842) followed suit, and distinctive stamps were issued by Amoy, Chefoo [3], Chinkiang, Chungking, Foochow, Hankow, Ichang, Kewkiang, Nanking, Wei Hai Wei and Wuhu.

Several foreign powers operated postal agencies in China to facilitate the handling of overseas mail. Following the murder of German missionaries in Shantung, Germany occupied the port of Tsingtao and subsequently acquired a 99-year lease of Kiaochow, which had its own stamps [2], until the outbreak of World War I, when it was captured by the Japanese.

In 1863 Robert Hart was appointed Inspector General of the Imperial Customs and it was under this department that a new postal service was introduced in 1878 [5]. Knighted in 1882, Sir Robert went on to organize the Chinese Imperial Post in 1897. The last issue of the empire appeared in 1909 and celebrated the first anniversary of the accession of the baby Emperor Hsuan T'ung. Appropriately it depicted the Temple of Heaven in the Forbidden City [4]. Deposed in 1912, Hsuan T'ung continued to live in the Summer Palace in seclusion but in 1932 he was plucked from obscurity by the Japanese to rule Manchukuo (formerly Manchuria) under the title of Kangde. Stamps of the puppet empire were issued from 1932 until 1945 [6].

NATIONALIST REPUBLIC

The first special stamps of the republic appeared in December and portrayed Sun Yat-sen, who had engineered the overthrow of the Manchu dynasty. Subsequently he appeared on most of the definitive sets down to 1949 [9]. An airmail series introduced in 1932 showed the Great Wall of China [7]. In addition to the mainstream issues of the republic, stamps were overprinted or surcharged for use in many of the provinces where the yuan fluctuated in value. From 1927, when war between

Gymnastics by Radio

A set of 40 stamps was issued in 1952 to illustrate a radio gymnastics programme, and everyone was expected to practise daily.

nationalists and communists broke out, there were many local posts in areas under communist control.

War with Japan erupted in 1931 and escalated in the ensuing decade. The value of the yuan plummeted [8], as shown by the inflated value of this stamp, and China suffered hyperinflation from 1946 until the nationalists withdrew from the mainland three years later [10].

COMMUNIST INSURGENCE

By 1937 the Japanese had occupied most of China but both communists and nationalists put up a strong resistance. The communist guerrilla armies operated in Japanese-held territory and organized a somewhat nomadic postal service, with many issues that fluctuated as the tide of war ebbed and flowed. These stamps are among the most complex in the world, issued by armies constantly on the move rather than associated with postal services in the accepted sense. Often crudely designed and printed under difficult conditions, they include many rarities.

As the communists gained control of many provinces after the defeat of Japan in 1945 postal services became more settled, and separate issues that read like the points of the compass appeared in different parts of China. Nevertheless, there were still many different issues, including seven in North-east China and ten in North-west China alone. Typical of these provincial stamps of 1945–9 were motifs of Mao Zedong and banner-waving troops [11–14]. Even after the proclamation of the People's Republic in 1949, separate stamps continued in North-east China because of the different value of money there.

PEOPLE'S REPUBLIC

The earliest definitives showed the Gate of Heavenly Peace in Beijing [15] or Chairman Mao [16], both themes that recurred frequently. Special issues reflected the rhetoric of the period, celebrating the 25th anniversary of the People's Liberation Army [17] and inauguration of the New Constitution [18]. The currency depreciated during the early 1950s but in 1955 it was reformed. In the ensuing period a more thematic approach crept in, gradually replacing endless Five Year Plan sets and portraits of communist heroes with sets reflecting the arts and crafts of old China [19]. During the Cultural Revolution (1965–71) quotations from Mao's little red book predominated [20]. Since the 1980s, recurring themes have been history and culture, among them stamps illustrating scenes from folk tales and Chinese classics. China's spectacular material progress since the 1990s has also been recorded [21].

Below: Supporting the Front *by Cui Kaixi featured on a 1998 stamp for the 50th anniversary of the Liberation War (top) and spectacular scenery is shown on a stamp of 2004 (bottom).*

13

14

15

16

17

18

19

20

21

LUNAR NEW YEAR

The Chinese calendar is based on the phases of the Moon and can be traced back 2,000 years to the time of the Eastern Han dynasty. The vast majority of China's predominantly rural people were illiterate, so astronomers worked out a dozen animal signs as readily identifiable symbols for the months, and these were also employed to describe the 12-year cycle of the years.

In Chinese culture the animal emblems are associated with the 12 earthly branches, representing nature or destiny. When combined with the five celestial stems or main elements – gold, wood, water, fire and earth – they produce a 60-year cycle known as a *chia-tzu*. Long after the construction of the calendar, the zodiac came to be applied to casting horoscopes, the reasoning being that every person born in a particular year would exhibit broadly similar character traits, governing their lives and affecting their future.

The 12-year cycle begins with the Rat (*Tzu*), which is followed by the Ox (*Chou*), Tiger (*Yin*), Rabbit (*Mao*), Dragon (*Chen*), Snake (*Szu*), Horse (*Wu*), Ram (*Wei*), Monkey (*Shen*), Rooster (*Yu*), Dog (*Hsu*) and Pig (*Hai*). These are the animals believed to have been especially loyal to the Lord Buddha. According to Chinese folklore, their order of precedence in the zodiac follows the sequence in which they responded to the Buddha's summons to his power conference.

LUNAR NEW YEAR STAMPS

Although stamps marking the Lunar New Year were issued by Japan as long ago as 1936, this is a theme that developed only gradually from the 1950s onwards. By the 1980s they were regularly released by Japan, Korea, Taiwan, Hong Kong, Macao and Singapore, invariably featuring the relevant animal in the Chinese zodiac. In recent years Japan's Lunar New Year stamps have been issued in two versions: a pair for ordinary postal use, and a matched pair in a longer format with serial numbers that are entered in a draw, the prizes being special miniature sheets.

In almost 70 years the Lunar New Year has spawned a formidable array of stamps, booklets, pre-stamped postcards and souvenir covers. Until fairly recently these were quite compact and manageable, being confined to the

Left: A rat and a snowman were shown on the New Year stamp from South Korea in 1995.

Below: Travelling pigs appeared on South Korea's stamp for the Year of the Pig, late 1994; the Hong Kong series (January 1995) showed pottery pigs.

Below: A stylized monkey is shown on a Macao stamp for the Year of the Monkey (2004); the 33c US stamp by Yuan Lee marked the Year of the Rabbit in 1999.

Below: Courting pigs from French Polynesia marked the Year of the Pig, 1995; Yuan Lee designed this 37c US stamp for the Year of the Goat, 2003.

Above: To mark the Year of the Dragon (2000) Micronesia released this $2 miniature sheet (left), reproducing a traditional Chinese image. Japan uses miniature sheets (right) as prizes in its annual New Year lottery.

countries of South-east Asia, but in the past few years the concept has spread like wildfire.

GOING WORLDWIDE

The United States, which has the largest Chinese population outside Asia (about six million), started the ball rolling with a 29c stamp in December 1992 to mark the Year of the Rooster (1993) and this has since become the theme for an annual issue. It spread to Canada in 1997 when the Year of the Ox was marked by a 45c stamp accompanied by a miniature sheet in the shape of a Chinese fan – this was a major innovation, as miniature sheets up to that time had invariably been rectangular in shape.

In recent years the concept has spread to every part of the globe, yielding Lunar New Year stamps as far afield as Ireland, the Marshall Islands and the Netherlands Antilles, and from Sweden to New Zealand and South Africa. Among the most attractive, and certainly most humorous, are those designed by Victor Ambrus for Jersey in the Channel Islands. They are in the form of £1 miniature sheets with the appropriate motif projected into the sheet margins. The Republic of China (Taiwan) has been issuing Lunar New Year stamps since 1969 (Year of the Dog). Latterly these issues have taken the form of two stamps showing different artistic interpretations of the appropriate animal.

Sweden seems about as unlikely a country as any to celebrate the Lunar New Year, but in recent years the event has been cleverly combined with tributes to children's literature. New Zealand likewise adopted an oblique approach to the Lunar New Year. In 1997 a set of six stamps featured different breeds of cattle, but the interpane gutters included the Chinese zodiacal symbol for the Year of the Ox. This established a precedent that is now followed every year.

For some years Ireland has produced stamps early in the year, primarily for Valentine's Day greetings. In January 1995 a booklet of four 32p stamps depicted various symbols of love, but the stamps were released simultaneously as a miniature sheet celebrating the Year of the Pig, with appropriate motifs and symbols for the Lunar New Year in the sheet margin. This established a pattern that has been maintained ever since.

A number of issues from the countries in the Inter-Governmental Philatelic Corporation group have also celebrated the Lunar New Year. These made their debut in May 1994, well into the Year of the Dog, and consisted of a number of sets depicting different canine breeds, but these stamps incorporated a tiny symbol in one corner inscribed "Year of the Dog", flanking the appropriate Chinese symbol.

More relevant were the issues of April 1995, designed by the leading Chinese-American artist Yuan Lee and featuring different aspects of pigs. Recent issues have tended to be more modest, confined to sheetlets of four and a matching souvenir sheet, with artwork by Yuan Lee predominating.

Below: One of the four stamps issued by Hong Kong for the Year of the Horse in 1990 (top) and the stamp from French Polynesia for the Year of the Dragon in 2000 (bottom).

1

2

3

4

5

6

7

8

9

CHINESE TERRITORIES

In addition to China proper there are a number of territories that were at one time part of China (such as Mongolia) or, conversely, were European colonies but have now reverted to China (Hong Kong and Macao). Tibet, once autonomous, has been absorbed by the People's Republic, whereas Taiwan, which was occupied by Japan from 1895 to 1945, later became the refuge of the Chinese Nationalists and survives to this day under the name of the Republic of China. The former British and Portuguese colonies of Hong Kong and Macao have enjoyed phenomenal economic growth in recent years; though now part of China again they are guaranteed autonomy for 50 years.

Left: The high-rise commercial buildings of Victoria, Hong Kong's capital, include several of the tallest structures in the world. Set against this background, the Peak Tram, opened in 1888, continues to transport tourists and commuters alike.

HONG KONG

In 1839 the Chinese tried to suppress the opium trade from India, but Britain retaliated and in 1841 forced China to cede Hong Kong island, which thereafter became the centre of drugs trafficking. The Kowloon peninsula was ceded in 1860 and a 99-year lease on the New Territories was granted to Britain in 1899. When it expired in 1997 Hong Kong's status was no longer viable and it was returned to China. Since then it has been a special administrative region and retains its own currency and stamps.

Hong Kong adopted stamps in 1862 and for almost a century most definitives were identical apart from the monarch's portrait. Although it actually produced the first commemorative stamp in Asia – the 2c definitive overprinted in 1891 to celebrate the 50th anniversary of British rule – a further half century would elapse before the first distinctive series appeared. This was a set of bicoloured pictorials marking the centenary of the colony in February 1941 [1], shortly before it was occupied by the Japanese.

Hong Kong participated in the various colonial omnibus issues from 1935 to 1966, an exception being the Victory pair of 1946: these utilized a design sketched by W.E. Jones in a Japanese prison camp, showing a phoenix rising from the flames to symbolize the eventual re-emergence of Hong Kong after enemy occupation. Royal events, such as the wedding of Charles and Diana in 1981, and a visit of 1989 [3], were also covered.

Postwar commercial development and the influx of refugees from the People's Republic of China totally transformed the crown colony. Many stamps of this period presented a view of Hong Kong as a little bit of Britain in the Far East, with features such as Georgian pillar-boxes [2], but increasingly its Chinese heritage came to the fore. Numerous sets of recent years have featured costumes [4] and other aspects of the applied and decorative arts. Tourism is a major subject, reflected in scenery and local events such as the dragon boat races [7]. Since 1997 stamps have been inscribed "Hong Kong China", including a set celebrating the centenary of its waterfront trams [5]. The People's Liberation Army [8] took over the former British bases but generally keeps a low profile.

MACAO

The oldest European settlement in the Far East, Macao was settled by the Portuguese in 1557. As Portuguese colonial power declined in the 19th century Macao became a backwater, preserving its distinctive Iberian architecture. In 1999 it became a special administrative region of China and, like Hong Kong, retains its own stamps and currency. The early stamps from 1884 conformed to the Portuguese colonial designs, and distinctive motifs did not appear until the 1930s. After World War II they became much more colourful and thematic [6], but have latterly concentrated on indigenous art and culture, with numerous sets featuring the rapidly vanishing way of life [11]. Recent stamps, inscribed "Macau China", include a pair celebrating the first Chinese astronaut [9].

TAIWAN

The early issues of the Republic of China (ROC) were often inscribed entirely in Chinese, even when they related to international organizations [10], but later the name was rendered in English. When the nationalists fled from the mainland they took the vast bulk of the Chinese art treasures from Peking (Beijing) and these have been a fertile source of stamp illustrations ever since [12]. Many stamps from the 1960s to the 1980s highlighted Taiwan's siege mentality, but in the more relaxed atmosphere of recent years the emphasis has shifted to nostalgia, as in the old railway station series [13], and a revival of the penchant for illustrating the arts [14] and customs such as puppetry [15], folk tales [16] and children's pastimes [18].

Below: Damdinsuren's Camel Caravan *was one of several paintings on a 1969 Mongolian set for the tenth anniversary of the Co-operative Movement.*

Boxer Rebellion

When the Boxer rebellion laid siege to the foreign legations in Peking (1900), twelve countries, including the USA and Japan, formed a coalition to relieve them. Indian stamps overprinted "C.E.F." were used by the China Expeditionary Force which quashed the uprising.

MONGOLIA AND TIBET

Landlocked in central Asia, between Russia and China, is Mongolia, one of the oldest countries in the world. When at the height of its power in the 13th century Mongolia, under Genghis Khan, conquered the whole of China and expanded as far west as Poland and Hungary. After the Manchus conquered China in 1644 they absorbed Mongolia in 1681.

Following the Chinese revolution of 1911, Mongolia asserted its independence, which it attained in 1921 under the leadership of Sukhe Bator [17]. A people's republic from 1924, it overthrew its communist regime in 1990 and became the State of Mongolia. Since the 1930s, stamps have been an important source of hard currency.

Tibet was at various times tributary to China and its earliest stamps were those of China overprinted. Distinctive stamps appeared in 1912 and continued until 1950, when the Chinese invaded and annexed Tibet. The world's only theocracy has struggled ever since to regain independence, and stamps portraying the Dalai Lama and showing monasteries and the Potala Palace in Lhasa [19] have been produced by the government in exile.

10

11

12

13

14

15

16

17

18

19

1

2

3

4

5

6

7

8

9

10

11

KOREA

As a kingdom, Korea dates its origins to 2333 BC, and this is the starting point of its calendar. The country's history is well documented from 57 BC. The Yi dynasty had an unbroken record from 1392 until it was overthrown in 1910. In 1637, however, Korea was defeated by the Manchus and was a tributary of China from then until 1895. It was completely cut off from the outside world until 1876, when it was compelled to allow trade with Japan. In 1897 King Kojong proclaimed an empire. In 1905 Japan took over the postal service and five years later forced the emperor to abdicate. Korea was then annexed and remained part of the Japanese empire until 1945. Shortly before the war ended Russia declared war on Japan, and Soviet troops invaded North Korea. This proved to be the opening round of a conflict that has lasted ever since. The country was divided into Soviet and American zones of occupation by a line drawn across the peninsula at the 38th parallel.

Left: One of many tributes to its allies in the Korean War, a miniature sheet portraying General MacArthur and the Korean, UN and US flags was issued by South Korea in 1965.

UNITED KOREA

A postal service was introduced in November 1884 but a riot at the post office in Seoul a few weeks later led to the suspension of the service and the gradual infiltration of Japanese agents. The first stamps [1] are plentiful in mint condition but of the greatest rarity used, which is hardly surprising since they were in use for such a short time. A second attempt, in 1895, was more successful. The last series was designed and printed in Paris and bore the name of the Korean Empire in French. Under United States military government in 1945, distinctive stamps were revived [2].

SOUTH KOREA

The Republic of Korea, under Syngman Rhee, was proclaimed in August 1948, but in June 1950 it was invaded from the north. By September the enemy had overrun most of the country, but an American-led UN force landed at Inchon and the war raged back and forth for two years. Eventually a truce was reached and a demilitarized zone established, initially patrolled by Indian troops, who had their own stamps [3]. Many of the stamps of South Korea since that time have referred to the war [4] and paid tribute to the USA for its support [5].

President Rhee was elected to a fourth term in 1960 but ousted by a military coup a month later [6]. By the 1970s South Korea was enjoying unprecedented prosperity and this is reflected in the stamps, which were not only well designed and printed but covered a wide range of topics, from fauna and flora [7] to cartoons [9] and comic book characters [10]. South Korea enthusiastically embraced the American way, from Boy Scouts to Lions Clubs [11], but its unique culture was not forgotten [12]. High-speed trains [13], motor manufacture and jet liners are recurring definitive themes. The country gained international prestige by hosting the Olympic Games (1988) and the football World Cup (2002), both marked by numerous stamps.

Cult of the Personality

The overriding theme of North Korean stamps has been the glorification of the Comrade Great Leader Kim Il Sung and now his son and successor Kim Jong Il. Not content with merely portraying these figures, the stamps incessantly depict them as role models and paragons of every virtue, in scenes that range from showing the peasants how to plant their crops to exhorting the factory workers to even greater efforts. Every other issue from the North seems to portray the two Kims.

12

13

14

15 16

17

18

19 20

NORTH KOREA

The polarization of the two Koreas is vividly demonstrated in their stamps. The Russian occupation ended in September 1948 with the institution of the Korean People's Democratic Republic. The stamps of this period were often crude imitations of contemporary Soviet designs, and they included numerous references to the war, especially when it was going well for the communists [8]. Whereas the stamps of the South clung to the Korean chronology, the North adopted the Christian calendar. Many stamps alluded not only to victories and anniversaries of the Korean War but also commemorated earlier conflicts, from strikes and demonstrations [15] to outright guerrilla warfare against the Japanese [14].

More peaceful subjects began to appear in the late 1960s [16] but the onset of the Vietnam War gave North Korea more scope for its ongoing hatred of America. Anti-American propaganda included a stamp showing a monster in a GI helmet being skewered by bayonets [17]. In more recent years propaganda against the South has increased [18] although at the same time greater attention is given to popular themes [19]. Even UNICEF (if not the UN itself) gets some credit for relieving child poverty [20].

Below: This North Korean stamp was issued in 1998 to mark the 75th anniversary of Kim Il Sung's "250-mile journey for national liberation".

1

2

3

4

5

6

7

8

9

10

11

JAPAN

According to legend the empire of Japan was founded in about 600 BC by Jimmu Tenno, who was a descendent of the great sun goddess Amaterasu. All the emperors from that time until now have been in direct descent and their status as living deities explains why they are never portrayed on Japanese stamps, for to deface them with a postmark would be an act of sacrilege. Although the Portuguese first visited Japan in 1542 and Dutch traders subsequently got a toehold on Deshima, all foreign contacts were banned from 1630 until the visit of Commodore Perry of the US Navy in 1853. For 250 years the emperor was little more than a figurehead, while real power was vested in the shoguns, the xenophobic leaders of the military caste, but under Emperor Meiji, who ascended to the throne in 1868, Japan rapidly industrialized, the shogunate was abolished and the country adopted western dress, technology and warfare, as well as a postal system, complete with stamps.

Left: The founder of the modern postal service was Baron Maeshima, who has been portrayed on many definitive stamps and special issues since 1946.

EARLIEST STAMPS

Four stamps covering the basic postal rates, denominated in mon, were introduced in April 1871 [1], but a few months later the currency was decimalized, based on the yen of 100 sen. Japan was not slow to introduce special issues: the first, in 1894, celebrated the emperor's silver wedding with a motif of cranes (symbolic of fidelity and long life). Victories over China in 1895 and Russia in 1905 were celebrated by stamps [2], while the battleships *Katori* and *Kashima* were featured on stamps issued in 1921 to celebrate the return of Crown Prince Hirohito from a tour of Europe [3].

WORLD WAR II AND ITS AFTERMATH

Japanese militarism gathered momentum in the 1920s and 1930s. Censured for its invasion of China in 1931, Japan left the League of Nations and formed an alliance with Nazi Germany. Rivalry with the USA in the Pacific led to the unprovoked attack on Pearl Harbor in December 1941, the start of Japan's own "lightning war" in the Pacific. The first anniversary of that "day of infamy" was celebrated by stamps showing the air raid on Pearl Harbor and Japanese tanks in action at Bataan in the Philippines [4]. Although the tide turned at Midway in 1942 it took three long, hard years, and the use of two atomic bombs to destroy Hiroshima and Nagasaki, to bring Japan to its knees. Wartime definitives reflect the militaristic outlook of the period, but in the immediate aftermath stamps were poorly printed, often without perforations, because the usual printing works had been destroyed [5].

MODERN JAPAN

In contrast with the bellicose nature of the years up to 1945, postwar Japan concentrated on conquering the world markets, developing especially in the fields of electronics and the automotive industry. The vast majority of stamps are printed in photogravure, latterly in full colour. Definitives concentrate on antiquities, fauna and flora [6]. Since 1936 Japan has produced hundreds of stamps extolling the beauties of its many national parks [7]. Stamps have also been produced for New Year greetings, while annual issues of more recent

Letter Writing Day

To encourage Japanese children to write more letters, stamps in many different shapes have been designed by the Dutch artist Dick Bruna in recent years.

times have been aimed at popularizing letter writing, especially to pen-pals abroad [8]. Stamps are captioned only in Japanese [9], which creates difficulties for foreign collectors lacking a fully illustrated catalogue, but in compliance with Universal Postal Union regulations the country name "Nippon" has been inscribed in the Roman alphabet since 1966 [12]. The vast majority of Japanese stamps concentrate on the unique culture of the country, including its architecture, costume [10], theatre [11], art and music. However, western influences shine through in sport [13] and, of course, in technology [15]. For the Millennium Japan began a series of ten sheetlets (one for each decade of the 20th century) and has since produced similar sheetlets for the UNESCO World Heritage Sites in Japan, art treasures, and popular cartoon and comic-book characters.

Japan is divided into 47 administrative regions known as prefectures. In 1990 it released a sheet of 50 stamps to publicize the PhilaNippon international philatelic exhibition of 1991. Three non-postal labels advertised the exhibition but the rest of the sheet consisted of 47 stamps of the ¥62 denomination, each featuring a different flower associated with a particular prefecture, from the sweet briar of Hokkaido to the coral tree of Okinawa. This sheet was analogous to the sheets of 50 that have been issued by the United States since 1976, featuring the flags, birds and flowers of the 50 states. Japan, however, took the concept a stage further in April 1989 when the first batch of stamps pertaining to specific prefectures was released. Each prefectural stamp [14] is valid for postage all over the country but is sold only within its own prefecture and the other prefectures in one of the eleven postal regions into which the country is divided. In the main, these stamps are issued in conventional sheets, although some have also been released in booklets of miniature sheets. The number of different stamps fluctuates, from 19 in the inaugural year to 13 in some of the later years. Most of them feature landmarks, scenery and wildlife, but some have been issued to mark a special event.

WARTIME OCCUPATION ISSUES

Between 1942 and 1945, when Japan occupied China, South-east Asia and many of the Pacific islands, it overprinted the stamps of the occupied territories. These are noted elsewhere but a selection of the distinctive stamps of the period is shown here, including stamps for Burma [16–17], Malaya [18], Dutch East Indies [19], North Borneo [20] and the Philippines [21]. After the war Australian stamps were overprinted for the use of British Commonwealth Occupying Forces. In 1945 a US military administration was imposed on the Ryukyu Islands, including Okinawa, and distinctive stamps were used there until 1972 when the islands were handed back to Japan [22].

12

13

14

15

16

17

18

19

20

21

22

INDONESIA AND THE PHILIPPINES

These two large countries of the south-western Pacific have much in common and a parallel history. Both are archipelagos covering vast areas, which made communications difficult and encouraged the development of numerous petty states before they were conquered by European powers – Indonesia by the Dutch and the Philippines by the Spanish. Neither colonial ruler ever exerted full control and there were numerous rebellions. The modern republics have inherited many of these problems. In World War II both were overrun by the Japanese, who exploited latent nationalism. Both are nominally democracies, although in their recent past they have both been subjected to authoritarian rule.

Left: Achmed Sukarno founded the Indonesia National Party in 1927. Imprisoned and exiled by the Dutch, he was given power by the Japanese in 1942 and became president in 1945. In the 1960s luxury hotels contrasted with chaos and poverty and in 1965 an abortive communist coup led to his downfall.

1

2

3

4

5

6

7

8

9

10

11

12

DUTCH EAST INDIES

Portuguese traders discovered the spice islands in the 16th century but it was the Dutch who took over in 1602 and eventually ruled over an archipelago of 13,000 islands spread across 5,000 km/3,000 miles. Stamps were introduced in 1864, bearing a full-face portrait of William III, but from 1870 onwards the Indies, like other European colonies, conformed to the colonial keytypes. In 1902 stamps were overprinted specifically for use in Java [1] and six years later the same series was overprinted "Buiten Bezit" (outer possessions) for the outlying islands.

Airmail stamps were introduced in 1928 and charity stamps for child welfare became an annual feature from 1930 onwards, following the example of the mother country. Other early charity sets raised funds for a leper colony (1931), the Salvation Army (1932) and the YMCA (1933). A pictorial definitive series, with a standard design showing rice cultivation, appeared in 1933, while short sets depicting indigenous peoples and their customs appeared in the 1930s and early 1940s [2].

Although the Netherlands were overrun by the Germans in 1940, the colonial empire continued to function, being administered by the Dutch government in exile. In this period a charity set raised funds for the Dutch forces fighting with the Allies. The Netherlands Indies itself was under Japanese occupation (1942–5) and the nationalists then took over [3], but with the aid of British and Japanese troops Dutch rule was restored in Java. In 1950 the Dutch bowed to the inevitable and handed power over to the nationalists. Stamps portraying Queen Wilhelmina were overprinted "Indonesia" [4].

INDONESIA

A period of chaos followed in which different stamps were issued in Java, Sumatra and Madura and a series printed in Vienna was never put on sale [5], although it was at one time very common on the world stamp market. The various factions united in August 1950 to form the Indonesian Republic [6]. Until 1965 Sukarno, the founder of the country, remained firmly in control [7] but he gradually handed over to General Suharto. In turn Suharto was ousted in 1997, and Indonesia experienced true democracy for the first time in half a century.

The stamps of Indonesia have the usual themes [8] but also endeavour to bring together the country's many different ethnic groups [9]. Tourism is still a major industry, reflected in many sets featuring scenery and wildlife [10].

Separate stamps were issued in 1954–65 for the Riau-Lingga islands, whose currency was tied to the Singapore dollar [13]. After the Dutch handover to Indonesia they held on to West New Guinea and issued distinctive stamps [14], but from 1950 onwards Indonesia laid claim to this territory. To settle the dispute, it was placed under UN administration in 1962 and stamps were accordingly overprinted [11]. It was handed over to Indonesia in May 1963 and renamed Irian Barat, or West Irian [12].

The island of Timor in the Sunda group was partitioned between the Dutch and the Portuguese. Stamps of the Portuguese colonial type were used in east Timor from 1885 to 1975 [15]. Civil war erupted but when the Fretilin faction proclaimed independence Indonesian troops invaded and occupied the area. The oppressive regime was overthrown in 2003 and stamps inscribed "East Timor" are now used.

PHILIPPINES

Fernando Magellan was killed in the Philippine islands in 1521 during his voyage round the world. They were colonized in 1542 and named for the king of Spain. Stamps were introduced in 1854 [16], the last issue, during the Spanish-American War, portraying the young Alfonso XIII [17]. The indigenous population had fought a guerrilla war against the Spanish since 1873 and declared a republic in 1897, with distinctive stamps in 1898–9 [18].

The islands were ceded by Spain to the USA and placed under military administration. US stamps were overprinted [19], but were soon followed by stamps bearing the name of the United States as well as the Philippines. Under the Commonwealth of the Philippines, established in 1935, the islands were granted autonomy. At first the previous pictorial definitive series was overprinted "Commonwealth" [20] and an entirely new series was just in the process of being released in 1941 when the islands were invaded.

After wartime occupation by the Japanese the Philippines became an independent republic in 1946, and the prewar overprinted series was reissued, overprinted "Victory". Many of the stamps from that time hark back to the heroic struggle of the war period [21], including several issues portraying General MacArthur, who was field marshal of the Filipino army from 1935 onwards and returned to liberate the islands in 1944. The modern stamps [22] reflect the unique cultural mixture of the Philippines, an amalgam of Spanish, American and Malay influences and of Catholicism and Islam, as well as the great diversity of landscape.

Good Relations

The close ties that exist between the USA and the Philippines have given rise to numerous stamps over the past century portraying American historical figures, but the Philippines alone produced a stamp showing not just John and Robert Kennedy but the entire Kennedy clan. The contract for the stamps, produced by an American agency with the agreement of the Filipino government, was cancelled at the last moment, and the stamps had no postal validity although they were on sale in the USA.

13

14

15

16

17

18

19

20

21

22

1

2

3

4

5

6

7

8

9

10

11

SOUTH-EAST ASIA

The Malay peninsula at the south-easterly tip of Asia is shared by three countries – Thailand, Malaysia and the tiny island republic of Singapore. Historically and culturally interlinked, their mutual interdependence was formalized when the menace of communism was at its height in the 1970s. Politically, Malaya consisted of three components: the Straits Settlements (a British crown colony consisting of Malacca, Penang and Singapore), the Federated Malay States (Negri Sembilan, Pahang, Perak and Selangor) and the independent states of Johore, Kedah, Kelantan, Perlis and Trengganu, all of which issued their own stamps at various times. A Malayan Postal Union, created in 1934, co-ordinated the postal services and issued postage due labels, but the issues of the various states continued. The Malay states were overrun by the Japanese in 1941–5, and at the end of World War II they came under British military administration until 1948. It was in this period that plans for closer integration and greater autonomy were formulated, leading to the creation of the Federation of Malaya in 1956.

Left: The Association of South-East Asian Nations (ASEAN) has expanded since its formation in 1977, as this 30th anniversary stamp from Brunei, showing the flags of the member states, demonstrates.

SINGAPORE

Founded by Sir Stamford Raffles in 1819, Singapore grew from a fishing village into one of the world's largest ports, a major centre for world trade. With Malacca and Penang, it formed the Straits Settlements, administered by the East India Company, which originally used Indian stamps surcharged in cents [1]. British influence over the Malay peninsula developed in the 19th century and after World War II Singapore was part of the Federation of Malaya [2], but in 1965 it seceded to form an independent republic within the Commonwealth. Its stamps reflect its astonishing urbanization [3], its multi-ethnic character [4] and its military preparedness [5].

MALAYSIA AND BRUNEI

Britain gradually brought the various Malay sultanates under its protection. Some of these were grouped together in the Federated Malay States [6] but each of the unfederated states had its own distinctive stamps [8–9] until the late 1940s. Thereafter uniform designs were used, differing only in the names of the states and the portraits of their rulers [7]. Labuan [10] and British North Borneo [11] combined to form the state of North Borneo [12], which subsequently joined the Malay Federation under the name of Sabah. In 1947, following Sarawak's transfer to the governance of the British colonial administration, its stamps were overprinted with the crowned cipher of George VI, pending a pictorial definitive series in 1950 with a portrait of the king inset. A new series, with Elizabeth II inset, was released in 1955 and continued until 1964, when Sarawak joined the Federation of Malaysia [13].

Stamps inscribed in Malay signified the Federation of Malaya [14], which was unique in having a king elected from the various sultans. The Federation changed its name to Malaysia in 1963. Apart from the states issues the national definitives have featured birds, fruits, fish and, most recently, butterflies [15], augmented by

The Land of the White Rajahs

For ridding his domain of pirates, the sultan of Brunei granted the Englishman James Brooke the title of rajah of Sarawak in 1842. Now a state of Malaysia, Sarawak has had its own stamps since 1869. After Japanese and British military occupation it was returned to the Brooke family in 1946, but the last rajah ceded it to Britain soon afterwards. All three white rajahs were portrayed on the stamps intended for the centenary in 1942 but delayed until 1946 as a result of the Japanese invasion.

short thematic sets ranging from birds of prey to marine life. Many of the recent stamps have shown the extraordinary development of the region, including one of the world's tallest landmarks, the Petronas Towers in Kuala Lumpur, depicted in a stamp marking the inauguration of the Putra light railway system in 1998 [16].

Closely associated with Malaysia is the sultanate of Brunei. Once an insignificant petty state in North Borneo, it is now one of the world's wealthiest countries due to the discovery of oil. Stamps showing a fishing village were current from 1907 until 1952, making them one of the world's longest running series [17]. Even today, Brunei operates one of the most conservative new issue policies in the world, with an average of 20 stamps a year, almost all of which are entirely pertinent to the country itself. Since his accession in 1967 Sultan Sir Hassanal Bolkiah has been portrayed on the vast majority of Brunei's stamps.

THAILAND

A postal service restricted to the royal court functioned in the mid-19th century, but an external service operated at the British consulate in Bangkok from 1858. Straits stamps overprinted "B" were introduced in 1882 [18] but were withdrawn in 1885 when Thailand joined the Universal Postal Union and introduced its own stamps [19]. Stamps bore the name of Siam until 1940, when the present name was adopted. Thailand has strong Buddhist and monarchical traditions, which have featured on numerous stamps [21]. Its military forces are highly trained and well equipped [22]. Most special issues are singles, with occasional longer sets.

JAPANESE OCCUPATION

During World War II the Malay peninsula was under enemy occupation from December 1941 until 1945. The conquerors began by overprinting stamps of the Malayan Postal Union, Malay states, Straits Settlements, North Borneo, Brunei and Sarawak with Japanese characters [20], but in April 1943 they produced a series of pictorials, printed by a Dutch company in Batavia.

Thailand was allied to Japan and was rewarded with the transfer of the northern Malay states (Kedah, Kelantan, Perlis and Trengganu), which had traditionally been under Thai influence. From October 1943 to September 1945 Thailand issued special stamps for use in these states, before they were returned to British administration.

Below: A tin dredger appears on one of the pictorials issued in Malaya during Japanese occupation in 1943 (left). The Thai war memorial featured on the stamps issued in 1944 during the Thai occupation of northern Malaya (right).

12

13

14

15

16

17

18

19

20

21

22

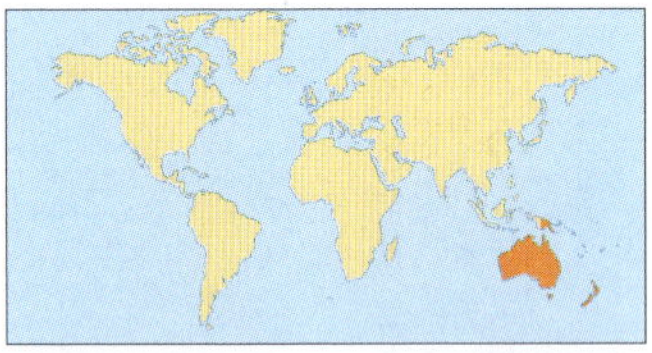

AUSTRALASIA

This term encompasses Australia, New Zealand and their dependencies in the Indian Ocean and Antarctica as well as the islands of the south, central and western Pacific. Adhesive stamps spread to Australia in 1850 and New Zealand in 1855, while the first stamp of New Caledonia appeared in 1860.

1

2

3

4

5

6

7

8

9

10

11

AUSTRALIA

Probably sighted by the Chinese in the early 15th century and visited by the Spanish and Portuguese a century later, Australia was partly explored by the Dutch in the 17th century and charted in 1769–70 by James Cook, who annexed it to the British Crown. It is the smallest continent in the world, and the only one that forms a single country. The British colonized Australia piecemeal and eventually created six colonies, beginning with New South Wales in 1788. Originally allocated to the former territory, Van Diemen's Land (later renamed Tasmania) became a separate state in 1825, followed by South Australia in 1836, Victoria in 1851 and Queensland in 1859. Western Australia was settled by 1829. The British parliament approved a federal constitution in 1900 and the following year the Commonwealth of Australia came into being.

Left: A set of three appeared in 1938 to mark 150 years since the first settlement of New South Wales. All the stamps were of a common design showing the landing at Sydney Cove on January 26, 1788.

AUSTRALIAN COLONIES

Each of the six colonies issued its own stamps, adopting a highly individual approach to the matter. In fact, New South Wales beat the mother country to it by introducing prepaid letter sheets, embossed with the colonial seal, in November 1838, 18 months before Britain adopted the Mulready wrappers. However, adhesive stamps were not introduced in New South Wales until January 1850. From 1851 stamps of New South Wales [1] generally portrayed Queen Victoria, with the exception of the centennial series of 1888. Other colonies followed suit [2–3]. Stamps inscribed "Van Diemen's Land" [4] were used in Tasmania from 1853 to 1857, and in 1899 Tasmania was the only colony to adopt a wholly pictorial definitive series [5]. Victoria likewise favoured portraits [7], whereas stamps of Western Australia [6] featured its emblem, the black swan. The different postal rates in each colony meant that their distinctive stamps continued in use until 1913.

COMMONWEALTH ISSUES

From the outset the issue of stamps was a political tool. Labour were in power when stamps were introduced, hence the national motif of the kangaroo on a map of the country [8], but when the Conservatives returned to power soon afterwards the kangaroo gave way to the king [9]. When Labour returned to power, so did the roo, and so it continued through the 1920s and 1930s. Less controversial was the 6d stamp of 1914 showing a kookaburra [10].

Special issues, which appeared infrequently from 1927 onwards, marked the inauguration of the federal parliament in Canberra and the Sydney Harbour Bridge [11], while the trio celebrating the silver jubilee of George V in 1935 showed him in field marshal's

Australian Innovations

A self-adhesive booklet issued in 2004 took a rather whimsical look at some of Australia's ideas and inventions. These ranged chronologically from Racecam TV sports coverage, introduced in 1979, to the Baby Safety Capsule of 1984 and the world's first polymer banknotes, which were issued in 1988 for the bicentennial celebrations.

uniform mounted on Anzac [12], the horse named in honour of the Australian and New Zealand Army Corps, which had fought at Gallipoli in World War I. Fine intaglio printing continued until the early 1950s. The set honouring Australian Imperial Forces [13] was the only special issue of World War II until February 1945, when stamps marked the arrival of the Duke of Gloucester as governor-general [14]. From 1938 definitives were more pictorial, but continued the tradition of blending wildlife with royal portraits [15]; by the late 1950s less fussy designs were favoured [16].

Stamps for international occasions, such as the 75th anniversary of the UPU in 1949, were given an Australian slant [17]. Monochrome intaglio gave way to multicolour photogravure in the 1960s [19]. Annual stamps mark Australia Day [18] as well as the queen's birthday [20], indicating a strong monarchical feeling despite the rise of republicanism in recent years. Modern stamps reflect the laid-back, often irreverent, attitudes of Australians, whose off-beat humour is often expressed in both definitives and special issues. Not surprisingly, given the nation's many achievements in sport, this remains an immensely popular philatelic theme.

In recent years Australia has adopted a number of technical innovations, such as the use of holograms to convey the impression of Australian opals [21]. In 1994 Australia also led the way in developing self-adhesive stamps, in coils or special booklets. The Melbourne international philatelic exhibition of 2000 introduced personalized stamps, with adjoining labels bearing people's own snapshots, a technique that is now used worldwide. Stamps portraying the Australian gold medallists at the Sydney Olympics were on sale in their home states within 48 hours.

12

13

14

15

16

17

18

19

20

21

TWO HUNDRED YEARS IN STAMPS

While Australia's Aboriginal inhabitants have a history of many thousands of years, Britain's interest began only in the 18th century. About the time that it was losing its empire in what is now the United States of America, it was establishing another in the Southern Hemisphere. The first settlers of the new colony – 750 convicts – arrived in Botany Bay in 1788.

Until 1783 Britain had transported convicts to its American colonies, but robbed of this facility the government looked around for somewhere else to deport them. Then Joseph Banks, the naturalist on James Cook's first voyage to the South Seas in 1769–70, which charted the east coast of Australia, suggested Botany Bay as an ideal site. Late in 1787 HMS *Sirius*, with a flotilla of transport ships, set out from England bound for the land Cook had named New South Wales, from a fancied resemblance to the coastline of Glamorgan. On 26 January 1788, Captain Arthur Phillip and his officers disembarked at Sydney Cove and hoisted the British flag.

This incident would give rise to the world's first commemorative stamps issued by a government postal service: the set labelled "One Hundred Years" by New South Wales in 1888. The 1d stamp showed a view of Sydney a century after that landing, while James Cook was portrayed on the 4d stamp. Interestingly, the 20s stamp portrayed not only Governor Phillip but also Lord Carrington, the governor in 1888. It would be well over a hundred years before Australia next portrayed a living person other than royalty.

None of the later colonies had the opportunity to celebrate their centenaries in this way, as by the time they came round colonial stamps had been superseded by the issues of the Commonwealth of Australia. In 1929 the centenary of Western Australia was marked by a single stamp featuring the state emblem, a black swan. Five years later, the original settlement of Victoria was marked with a set of three showing an Aborigine on the banks of the Yarra gazing in wonder at the city of Melbourne. In 1936 South Australia's centenary was celebrated with a set of three showing the Old Gum Tree at Glenelg flanked by a view of Adelaide in 1836 and the modern thoroughfare of King William Street. Half a century later stamps were issued to mark the

Above: One of four stamps issued jointly by Australia and Britain in 1988 shows an early settler and a sailing clipper.

Left: Two stamps from the second Bicentenary series, with the theme of settlement, show navigator William Dampier and a globe and hand with an extract from Dampier's journal.

Below: A strip of five stamps issued on January 26, 1988, showed the arrival of the First Fleet.

Above: A stamp of 1927 celebrated the opening of the federal parliament in Canberra during that year.

Right: A miniature sheet of 1991 honoured the exploration of Western Australia by George Vancouver in 1791 and E.J. Eyre in 1841.

Above: Sir Edmund Barton and Sir Henry Parkes were portrayed on a se-tenant *pair of 1951.*

Above: The opening of the first federal parliament in Melbourne in 1901 was commemorated on its golden jubilee.

Above: A stamp of 1963 marked the 150th anniversary of the first crossing of the Blue Mountains.

150th anniversaries, and it is interesting to note how radically different artistic styles had become by the 1970s and 1980s.

In 1938 it was time to celebrate the 150th anniversary of the first settlement, with a set of three showing Arthur Phillip and his staff at Sydney Cove. Tasmania had failed to mark its centenary, but made amends with a sesquicentennial set in 1953, which consisted of two small-format stamps of Lieutenants-Governor Collins and Paterson, plus a large-sized 2s of the ships anchoring at Sullivan Cove near Hobart in 1804.

In May 1951 a set of four celebrated the Australian Commonwealth's golden jubilee. Sir Edmund Barton and Sir Henry Parkes, who led the campaign to unify the colonies, were portrayed on two small *se-tenant* stamps, while the federal parliament building in Canberra appeared on the 1s 6d. The 5$^{1}/_{2}$d stamp reproduced a painting by T. Roberts showing the Duke of York (later George V) performing the inaugural ceremony in 1901. Since then many stamps have celebrated the centenaries of services that helped weld the continent into a single nation: the overland telegraph, the mail coaches, the railways and the first internal flights.

From 1968 several booklets portrayed famous Australians, beginning with the balladeer Banjo Paterson and the Aboriginal artist Albert Namatjira. The 75th anniversary in 1976 was marked by a stamp showing the arms of the commonwealth, but since 1978 a stamp has been produced each January 26 to celebrate Australia Day.

As the bicentenary approached in 1988 Australia pulled out all the stops. No fewer than 13 sets of stamps were issued from November 1984, beginning with a set of eight paying tribute to the Aborigines, then charting European exploration, the voyage of the First Fleet in 1787–8, and the early years of the settlement. A joint issue with Britain showed the national flags and people who symbolized the common heritage of the two countries, from Shakespeare to John Lennon and the cricketer W.G. Grace. Joint issues were also made with New Zealand and the USA, using a cartoon treatment.

Australia celebrated the opening of its new parliament building as well as Expo '88 in Brisbane and also released a new definitive series jokily exploring the theme of living together. And, of course, many countries, from Ireland to Israel, also issued stamps in honour of Australia's 200 years.

1

2

3

4

5

6

7

8

9

10

AUSTRALIAN EXTERNAL TERRITORIES

Australia has four dependencies, which are classed politically as Australian external territories. Two are located in the Indian Ocean, one in the South Pacific and one in Antarctica. Christmas Island was originally part of the Straits Settlements and then of the crown colony of Singapore. Occupied by the Japanese in 1942–5, it reverted to Singapore following liberation but was transferred to Australia in October 1958. The Cocos (Keeling) Islands in the Indian Ocean were settled by the Clunies-Ross family in the 1820s, annexed by Britain in 1857 and transferred to Ceylon (now Sri Lanka) in 1878, then attached to the Straits Settlements in 1886. They were transferred to Australia in November 1955. Australian Antarctic Territory consists of a large sector of Antarctica with up to six bases in operation. The stamps of these three territories are provided by Australia Post and can also be used in Australia itself.

Norfolk Island was part of New South Wales from its inception in 1788 and was used as a penal colony for the most hardened convicts. In 1856 it was transferred to Tasmania and in 1914 became an Australian territory. Stamps were introduced in 1947 and, unlike the others, are not valid in Australia itself.

Left: The ties between Tasmania and Norfolk Island were recalled by a pair of stamps in 1969 marking the 125th anniversary of the latter's annexation to what was then Van Diemen's Land.

CHRISTMAS ISLAND

This island got its first stamps cheaply, using the Australian definitive design modified to include different values typographed in black, with the name overprinted [1]. The set of ten definitives sufficed until 1963, when they were replaced by a pictorial issue distinctive to the island, showing a map, scenery and wildlife. The first special issue appeared in 1965 and was part of the Australian omnibus for the 50th anniversary of the Gallipoli landings.

From 1968 onwards stamps included "Indian Ocean" below the island name [2] to avoid confusion with the island of the same name in the Pacific. In more recent years stamps have tended to be confined to subjects of local interest. The few special issues relate mainly to Christmas, either showing totally secular motifs [3–4] or putting a highly individual slant on Santa Claus [5]. Christmas Island now also produces stamps for the Chinese New Year and these rank among the most spectacular of this genre.

COCOS (KEELING) ISLANDS

The only stamp-issuing country with alternative names (one enclosed in parenthesis), the islands used ordinary Australian stamps from 1955 until 1963, when a set of six pictorial definitives was introduced with the usual mixture of map, scenery and local life. Like Christmas Island, their first commemorative was the Gallipoli stamp. In 1979 a local council was established and at the same time the islands were given a greater measure of postal autonomy. Many of the stamps in the ensuing period pictured the birds, marine life [6; 8] and historic ships [7] associated with the group. The islands are of numismatic interest on account of the plastic tokens that passed for money at one time [9]. On 1 January

1994, responsibility for the postal service reverted to Australia. Since then stamps have included "Australia" in the inscription and are valid for postage in Australia, while Australian [10] stamps are also valid in the islands.

NORFOLK ISLAND

The stamps of Van Diemen's Land (Tasmania) were briefly in use in Norfolk Island (1854–5) and examples on cover with the island postmark are of the greatest rarity. Following its transfer to New South Wales, the stamps of that colony were used until 1913, followed by Australian stamps until 1947, when a set showing Ball Bay was introduced. Separate motifs were used for a short set of additional denominations issued in 1953, showing grim landmarks from the period when the island was a penal settlement.

Many subsequent issues have alluded to explorers who visited the island over the centuries [11–12], then a long cavalcade of all the ships that ever touched there [13] and finally the wrecks of ships that foundered there [14]. James

Below: A dog team pulling a sledge was one of the subjects of the Antarctic Scenes set in 1984 (top). A 1979 stamp (bottom) marked the 50th anniversary of Admiral Richard Byrd's flight across the South Pole.

Freeform Stamps

Between 1974 and1978 Norfolk Island issued stamps in the shape of the map, and returned to the idea for the Christmas stamps of 1994, in the form of a scroll.

Cook is a popular subject, with eight issues in just ten years (1969–79) marking the bicentenaries of his voyages [15]. As in Christmas Island, a whimsical approach to Christmas has been used in recent years [16].

AUSTRALIAN ANTARCTIC TERRITORY

A solitary stamp showing a map was introduced by the territory in 1957 [17], followed by a few others from time to time covering basic postage rates. The switch to decimal currency in 1966 heralded an era of multicoloured photogravure or lithographed stamps, released annually and featuring scenery and scientific research [18].

The few commemorative stamps have marked important anniversaries. These have included the Australasian Antarctic Expedition of 1911–14, Captain Cook's circumnavigation of Antarctica in 1772, the first flight over the South Pole in 1929, the Magnetic Pole Expedition of 1909 and various anniversaries of the Antarctic Treaty of 1961. A particularly poignant set was released in 1994 to mark the departure of the last huskies from Antarctica.

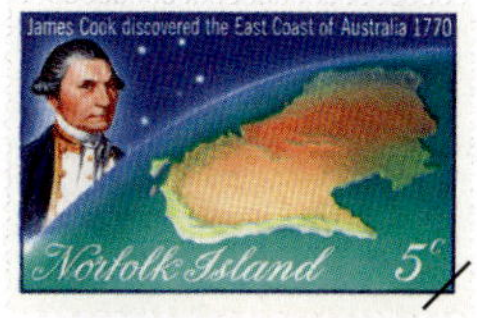

11

12

13

14

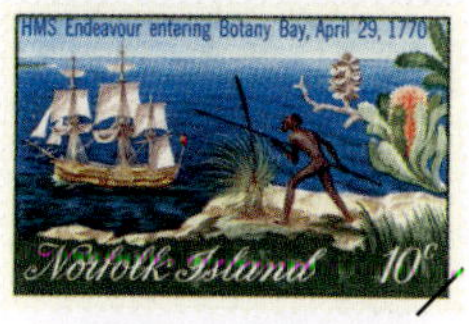

15

16

17

18

1

2

3

4

5

6

7

8

9

10

NEW ZEALAND

Slightly larger than the British Isles but with a 20th of their population, New Zealand is often referred to by the British as the Antipodes (literally, the place lying at the opposite side of the world). Its climate and scenery are similar to those of Britain, if on a much grander scale. The North and South Islands were first populated by the Maori, Polynesians who sailed their canoes across the ocean from Hawaii between the 10th and 14th centuries. The islands were discovered by the Dutch in 1642 and charted by James Cook in 1769. The haunt of whalers in the early 19th century, New Zealand was annexed by the British in 1840, becoming briefly a dependency of New South Wales. It attained self-government in 1852 and, after refusing to join the Commonwealth of Australia in 1901, became a dominion in 1907.

Left: The centennial of annexation was marked by a long series of 1940 charting the country's history from the arrival of the Maori in 1350 onwards. This stamp shows the Treaty of Waitangi being signed by Captain Hobson and Maori chiefs.

EARLY STAMPS

Although a postal service was organized in 1840 it was not until 1855 that New Zealand adopted adhesive stamps. To mark the centenary the original design was revived, with a portrait of Elizabeth II replacing the Chalon portrait of Victoria [1]. Thereafter, most stamps were produced by the Government Printer in Wellington, although the dies were sometimes engraved in Australia. The first 1/2d stamp, introduced in 1873 when a low rate for printed matter was conceded, was a blatant copy of the contemporary British 1/2d stamp.

All stamps until 1898 bore portraits of Victoria, the last series portraying images of the queen from her teens to the Jubilee and Veiled Head portraits of 1887 and 1893 respectively. In 1893 the definitives were issued with advertisements printed on the back and these stamps, popularly known as "Adsons", are much sought-after. In 1898 New Zealand was one of the first colonies to issue pictorial stamps, featuring scenery, wildlife and a Maori war canoe [2]. The advent of the 1d rate to any part of the British Empire was marked by a stamp in 1901 that underwent numerous changes over the ensuing decade before the words "Dominion of" were added, along with a series portraying Edward VII, who also appeared on the 6d [4]. Royal portraiture was the norm for the low values until 1935, when New Zealand returned to pictorials featuring scenery, wildlife and people [3; 7]. Pictorial and portrait definitives alternated until the 1960s.

BRITAIN OF THE SOUTH SEAS

The white settlers of New Zealand were predominantly from Britain and, until the 1960s, regarded that as "home", an attitude reflected in many stamps. A 1920 set marking victory in World War I used motifs from London statuary [5], setting a precedent for the Peace issue of 1946, which included a view of St Paul's Cathedral in the Blitz, with Churchill's assertion, "This was their finest hour" [8]. The Coronation set of 1953 showed not only the Crown Jewels and state coach, but also Westminster Abbey and Buckingham Palace [9]. Special issues also covered local landmarks and even incorporated Maori art in their borders [6], but the overwhelming impression is of stamps that were better at featuring the United Kingdom than British stamps were.

Sir Charles Kingsford-Smith pioneered air routes linking Australia and New Zealand and from 1931 onwards

Health Stamps

New Zealand's world-famous Health stamps began in 1929 with a stamp raising funds for the anti-tuberculosis campaign. It was reissued the following year with the caption altered to "Help Promote Health". Stamps have since been issued annually to raise funds for holiday camps, giving urban children in need the chance of a spell in the country. A recurring theme is the younger members of the British royal family, now extending to the third generation.

special stamps were produced for airmail. Few commemoratives were produced before World War II but the centennial of annexation in 1940 was the pretext for a long set reviewing the country's history and development. A long set of 1946 marked the return to peace, many of the stamps contrasting scenes in peace and war. From 1948 onwards many sets celebrated the centenaries of the settlement of various parts of New Zealand and later the charters of the various towns and cities.

New Zealand began issuing Christmas stamps in 1964, the first stamp appropriately marking the 150th anniversary of the first Christmas sermon, preached by the Reverend Samuel Marsden to a largely Maori congregation in 1814 [10].

MODERN NEW ZEALAND

Britain's entry into the EEC in 1973, and subsequent restrictions on trade between Britain and New Zealand, forced the latter to reassess its position as a country whose chief interests now lay in the Pacific region. This was increasingly reflected in stamps from this time onwards. The definitive series of 1975 portrayed the queen on the 10c stamp but all other values had local subjects [11]. New Zealand sent troops to Vietnam [13] and developed closer ties with other countries of the Pacific Rim. Since 1988 New Zealand has issued a series of circular stamps showing its national bird, the kiwi. Designed in New Zealand, engraved in Canada and recess-printed in Australia, the Round Kiwis have continued intermittently to the present day [12].

RECENT DEVELOPMENTS

Most New Zealand stamps are now lithographed by Southern Colour Print of Dunedin. New Zealand is justifiably proud of the fact that it granted women the vote in 1893 and was the first country to do so [14]. Rugby football has been depicted on numerous stamps since the 1960s, even stamps for individual teams [15]. By contrast with the historical set of 1940 for the centenary, the 150th anniversary triggered off several sets devoted to the country's heritage, followed by the decades of the 20th century [16]. Scenery continues to predominate [18–19], interspersed with sets devoted to historic buildings [20] and antique farming equipment, but recent sets have also poked fun at typically Kiwi phenomena such as hokey-pokey (toffee crunch), jandals (flip-flops or thongs) and fish and chips, or some of the wacky letterboxes that dot the countryside. Special stamps were issued for the Government Life Insurance Department from 1891 to 1989, featuring lighthouses [17].

Below: A Burrell traction engine on a stamp of 2004 was part of a series showing vintage farm machinery.

11

12

13

14

15

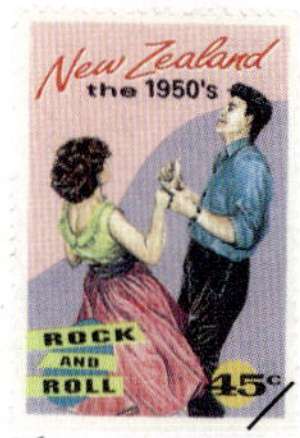

16

17

18

19

20

1

2

3

4

5

6

7

8

9

10

11

12

PNG, NAURU AND VANUATU

New Guinea, the largest of the Pacific islands, was colonized by the Dutch. They annexed the western half of the island to the Netherlands Indies, but the eastern portion was divided between Germany and Britain. German New Guinea was occupied by Australian forces at the beginning of World War I and mandated to Australia in 1921 under the name of New Guinea. British New Guinea, better known as Papua, was under British civil administration until 1942 but came under military rule following the Japanese invasion of the northern coast. In 1945 both parts combined as the Australian trust territory of Papua and New Guinea, shortened to Papua New Guinea, or PNG, in 1972.

The island of Nauru was part of the Marshall Islands but following its occupation by Australian troops in November 1914 it became a British mandate. It was transferred to Australia in 1924 and became an independent republic in 1968. The New Hebrides were jointly ruled by Britain and France from 1906 until 1980, when the condominium became the Republic of Vanuatu and was admitted as a member of the Commonwealth.

Left: The bicentenary of the discovery of the New Hebrides by Captain Cook was celebrated in 1974 by stamps available in both English and French versions and denominated in gold francs.

NEW GUINEA

German keytype stamps were used in the colony of German New Guinea until 1914 [1]. Following the Australian occupation stamps and registration labels of German New Guinea, and stamps of the Marshall Islands, were overprinted "G.R.I." and surcharged in sterling. By March 1915 Australian stamps overprinted "N.W. Pacific Islands" [2] were substituted. Distinctive stamps showing a native village did not appear until 1935 [3]. A long set of air stamps, in denominations from 1/2d to £5, appeared in 1939, mainly for sending packets of gold dust from Bulolo to Rabaul [4].

PAPUA

Stamps of Queensland were used at Port Moresby from 1885 until 1901, when an issue inscribed "British New Guinea" [5] was adopted. Similar stamps, featuring a *lakatoi* (a sailing canoe) but inscribed "Papua", appeared in 1907. Four stamps were issued in 1934 to mark the 50th anniversary of the British protectorate [6] and the following year four definitives [7] were overprinted to celebrate the silver jubilee of George V [8].

PAPUA NEW GUINEA

From 1942 onwards Australian stamps were used in those districts of Papua and New Guinea that had not been overrun by the Japanese, and this situation continued until October 1952, when distinctive stamps bearing the names of both protectorates were introduced following the creation of the Australian trust territory. Up to 1972 stamps included the ampersand in the name [9] but thereafter it was omitted [10]. In September 1975 Papua New Guinea became an independent member of the Commonwealth, but this did not affect the style or content of its stamps, which have tended to focus on the country's flora and fauna [11–13].

NAURU

Following Australian occupation in 1914 stamps overprinted for the North West Pacific Islands were used [2] but when Britain took over administration in 1916 British stamps overprinted "Nauru" were substituted [14]. After Australia acquired the mandate in 1924 stamps depicting the freighter *Century* were used until 1954, when a different pictorial series [16] was introduced. A photogravure series appeared in 1963–5 and was overprinted in 1968 when Nauru became a republic within the Commonwealth [17]. Stamps have been very sparingly issued in recent years and relate to the island [18].

Below: A stamp from a 1994 tourist set of Vanuatu showing fish (top), one from the Hibiscus series of 1995 (middle) and the New Hebrides inter-island stamp of 1897 (bottom).

Myth-making

In 1966 Papua New Guinea issued a set of four stamps illustrating folk art based on local myths. Three years later a second set appeared, but these were in *se-tenant* vertical pairs perforated all round, separated by a very fine line of roulette. The motifs illustrating pagan myths were actually designed by a Christian missionary, the Reverend H.A. Brown.

VANUATU

The stamps of New South Wales and New Caledonia were used in the New Hebrides until 1908 when stamps of Fiji and New Caledonia were overprinted in English and French respectively to mark the Anglo-French condominium [15]. In 1911 two sets of stamps depicting weapons and idols were issued in English and French versions. The British and French symbols flanking the central motif were reversed, depending on the language of the issue [19]. Appropriately, the 50th anniversary of the condominium was marked in 1956 by stamps showing the symbolic figures of Britannia and Marianne flanking a local idol [20]. This dual system continued until 1980 and applied to both definitives and special issues [21]. Aspects of Anglo-French co-operation in other parts of the world, notably the development of the supersonic airliner Concorde [22], were the subject of several issues. A few early issues of Vanuatu were inscribed "Postage" and "Postes" but the English language is now exclusively used for captions on the stamps.

An inter-island mail service was operated by the Australasian New Hebrides Company and issued its own stamps in 1897.

13

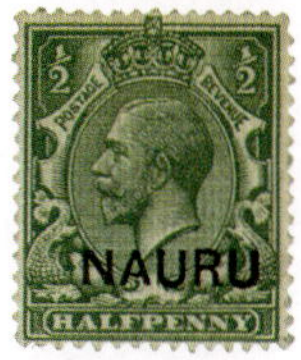

14

15

16

17

18

19

20

21

22

1

2

3

4

5

6

7

8

9

FIJI, KIRIBATI AND TUVALU

The indigenous inhabitants of the native kingdom of Fiji are thought to be a mixture of Melanesians and Polynesians. Incessant tribal warfare induced King Cakobau to cede Fiji voluntarily to Britain in 1874. The import of Indian indentured labourers to work in the sugar and cotton plantations (developed after trade between Britain and the Confederate States was cut off during the American Civil War) eventually led to the native Fijians being outnumbered by Indians, a matter that caused considerable conflict in the 1970s following Fiji's attainment of independence.

The Gilbert and Ellice Islands became a British protectorate in 1892 and a crown colony in 1915. Between December 1941 and November 1943 the Gilberts were overrun by the Japanese and were latterly the scene of some of the bitterest fighting of the Pacific campaign. Self-government was granted in 1971 and five years later the Ellice Islands seceded to form Tuvalu. Subsequently the Gilberts adopted the Polynesian phonetic spelling of their name, "Kiribati".

Left: The Battle of Tarawa in 1943, one of the decisive actions of World War II and the most important event in the history of the Gilbert Islands, has been the subject of many stamps in recent years.

FIJI

The first attempt at a mail service in Fiji was organized by a local newspaper, the *Fiji Times Express*, followed by a nationwide post under the auspices of King Cakobau, whose crowned monogram was featured on the stamps [1]. The monogram of Queen Victoria was substituted after Fiji was ceded to Britain, but subsequently Fiji used the standard colonial keytypes [2].

Pictorial stamps were introduced in 1938, with some denominations reappearing in 1954 with the portrait of Elizabeth II. An entirely new series appeared in 1962–7, with the usual medley of fauna, flora and native customs [3], and this policy was continued with the series of 1968, which was amended for the change to decimal currency in 1969–70. The relatively few special issues tended to commemorate the discovery and exploration of the islands [4].

Since becoming an independent member of the Commonwealth in 1970, with the British monarch as head of state, the stamps of Fiji have become more colourful and issues rather more frequent. Landmarks were the theme of the series of 1979–94 [5] but wildlife continues to be a popular subject [6]. For the annual Christmas stamps, however, from 1996 onwards Fiji switched from Old Master paintings to motifs with a local accent [7].

GILBERT AND ELLICE ISLANDS

This protectorate, later a crown colony, was an artificial creation that linked two widely differing groups of islands scattered across the central Pacific. New Zealand operated postal agencies in Fanning and Washington, two of the Line Islands, and stamps bearing these postmarks are now highly regarded. In 1911 stamps of Fiji were overprinted for use in the Gilbert and Ellice Islands, pending the supply of a series featuring a pandanus pine two months later [10]. This issue was short-lived and from 1912 to 1939 the colonial keytypes portraying George V were employed [11]. A pictorial series appeared in

Man Overboard!

Nowadays, with a much faster pace of stamp issues, design errors are not uncommon. Back in 1938, when stamps might take months to engrave, mistakes were rare, so it was disconcerting to find that two major errors occurred in the Fiji pictorials of that year. Several stamps featured a map of the islands but omitted the important numerals "180", marking the International Dateline. Much more glaring, however, was the 1½d stamp showing an outrigger canoe under full sail with no one at the helm. The stamp was hastily re-engraved and a man inserted.

1939 and continued until 1955 [8]. Apart from the various omnibus sets from 1935 onwards, the islands had no distinctive commemorative stamps until 1964 [9]. Fine intaglio gave way to rather crude lithography in 1965: this series was surcharged in decimal currency [12] and then reissued with values in dollars and cents.

KIRIBATI

Following the break-up of the crown colony of the Gilbert and Ellice Islands at the end of 1975, stamps inscribed "The Gilbert Islands" were used from 1976 to 1979 [13], but when the islands gained independence they adopted the local spelling of their name, Kiribati (pronounced Kiribas). Since then stamps have pursued the same policy as before, apart from bearing the national arms in place of the royal portrait. Although the majority of stamps have continued to reflect the scenery and culture of the islands, Kiribati has participated in a number of international philatelic events and supported them with special stamps. In connection with the 150th anniversary of the Penny Black and the London international stamp exhibition of 1990, Kiribati produced a set reproducing stamps used in the islands from 1912 onwards [14]. Not surprisingly, marine life of the Pacific forms a major source of stamp illustrations [15]. To mark the 15th anniversary of independence Oliver Ball designed a set showing a family silhouetted on the beach [16]. Kiribati has also taken part in a few joint issues, notably the *Sesame Street* series of March 2000.

TUVALU

At first the stamps of Tuvalu, formerly the Ellice Islands, also followed a moderate policy, but since independence in 1978 the tempo has increased from year to year, with an increasing number of "market-led" stamps in more recent years, catering to every passing craze. As in the stamps of Kiribati, the national arms have replaced the queen's profile although the subject matter reflects continuing strong ties with Britain [17–18].

Below: Traditional dancing on a Tuvalu Christmas stamp of 1997 and one of the Dolphin series of 1998.

10

11

12

13

14

15

16

17

18

1

2

3

4

5

6

7

8

9

10

FRENCH PACIFIC ISLANDS

The French became interested in the Pacific in the 19th century, as a result of the voyages of exploration of Bougainville, Durmont d'Urville and others, stimulated by the exploits of James Cook and William Bligh in the late 18th century. Catholic missionaries and traders established churches and trading posts in native kingdoms over which France gradually proclaimed protectorates. New Caledonia, which had been discovered and named by Cook in 1774, was claimed by France in 1853 and became a convict settlement.

Left: The bicentenary of the discovery of the Crozet Islands and Kerguelen in January 1772 was celebrated by a pair of large stamps, engraved in the heroic style favoured by France's most southerly colonial possessions, the Southern and Antarctic Territories.

FRENCH POLYNESIA

The French Settlements in Oceania consisted of the Austral, Society, Tuamotu, Gambier and Marquesas Islands, formed into a single colony in 1903 with Tahiti at its core. The largest of the Society Islands, Tahiti had its own stamps from 1882 to 1915 [1], but a general series for the Oceanic Settlements was also in simultaneous use, beginning with the French colonial keytypes [2] and progressing to distinctive pictorial stamps in 1913 [3]. The introduction of a flying-boat service in 1934 was marked by an airmail stamp [4]. During World War II the islands declared for de Gaulle's Free French and had stamps printed in England [5]. An engraved pictorial series was released in 1948 and continued until 1958 [6].

The inhabitants voted to remain in the French Community and the country was then renamed French Polynesia. Since then stamps have become more colourful, graduating from intaglio [7] to multicolour lithography [8] and, more recently, thermography, a process that is capable of producing a three-dimensional effect, as in the stamps of 1995 depicting black pearls [9]. A self-congratulatory stamp of 2000 publicized the work of the philatelic bureau [10] but as a rule the subjects of the stamps pertain to the islands and their culture. American and European writers and artists inspired by the people and scenery of Polynesia, from Herman Melville to Paul Gauguin, have also been commemorated.

NEW CALEDONIA

The penal colony was garrisoned by French troops and it was one of these, Sergeant Triquerat, who engraved its first stamp with a pin, portraying Napoleon III, in 1860. This piece of initiative was soon suppressed and until 1881 the general series of the French colonies was used, with various surcharges and overprints [11] from then until 1905, when a definitive series featured the kagu, the national bird [12]. A rather garish pictorial series followed in 1928 [13]. The kagu in a stylized version graced the Free French issues of 1942 [14], while a more realistic view of two kagus appeared on the series of 1948 [15]. Stamp policy was liberalized from 1958 onwards, although New Caledonia still prefers restrained intaglio motifs directly related to the country [16].

WALLIS AND FUTUNA ISLANDS

This group of islands to the north-east of Fiji was discovered by Captain Samuel Wallis in HMS *Dolphin* in 1767 during his circumnavigation of the globe. They became a French

Watercolour Stamps

A notable exception to the engraved stamps of the French Southern and Antarctic Territories is the series of miniature sheets released in 1999–2000 reproducing watercolour sketches by Marko. To call them miniature sheets is misleading as they actually measure 200 x 160mm/8 x $6\frac{1}{4}$in, but they each contain a single stamp reproducing the same scene in miniature, measuring 50 x 40mm/2 x $1\frac{1}{2}$in, perforation to perforation.

11

12

13

14

15

16

17

18

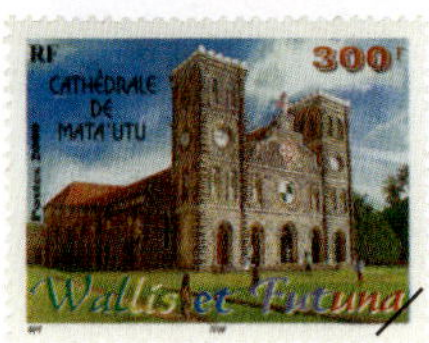

19

protectorate in 1888 and were then attached to New Caledonia for administrative purposes, but obtained their own stamps in 1920, the inaugural series being the stamps of New Caledonia suitably overprinted [17]. A series issued under Free French rule in 1942 featured an ivory head [18]. In 1961 the islands became a French overseas territory, and since then the stamps have become much more prolific, though still sticking fairly closely to subjects of specific island interest, with landmarks [19], scenery and wildlife well to the fore. Other issues highlight the interdependence of the French Pacific territories.

FRENCH SOUTHERN AND ANTARCTIC TERRITORIES

This name was applied in 1955 to a scattering of French islands and isolated territories across the southern Indian and Pacific Oceans, as well as bases on the Antarctic continent. Before that date these areas had used stamps of France or Madagascar and, in fact, the very first stamp issued by the combined territories was one of the latter suitably overprinted. The first distinctive series appeared in 1956 and it has since been followed by many stamps, issued either as singles or short sets, and generally released in December or January, which is the height of the polar scientific research season.

Subjects are largely concerned with the history of exploration and various scientific surveys, with immense scope for the ships of the explorers and scientists of the past two centuries, although the vegetation and wildlife of the region have not been overlooked. The vast majority of these stamps have been printed in intaglio with a restrained use of colour.

1

2

3

4

5

6

7

8

9

10

NEW ZEALAND DEPENDENCIES

A number of territories in the South Pacific came under New Zealand administration at one time and this included control of the postal services. Today, only the Tokelau Islands and Ross Dependency in the Antarctic are under the direct rule of New Zealand, but until the 1960s it was also responsible for the Cook Islands and Western Samoa. The Cook Islands were an independent kingdom that had been declared a British protectorate in 1888. Samoa had also been an independent kingdom, but was partitioned by Germany and the USA in 1900. In 1914 the German colony (Western Samoa) was occupied by New Zealand forces and was then mandated to New Zealand in 1920, becoming an independent state in 1962.

Left: The great hurricane that struck Samoa in 1889 destroyed the British, American and German warships anchored at Apia. The islanders, who resented foreign interference, regarded it as an act of God.

COOK ISLANDS

The Cook Islands, a federation of 15 islands, introduced postage stamps in 1892, and these portrayed Queen Makea Takau [1]. The islands were ceded to the British crown in 1900 and transferred to New Zealand in June 1901. New Zealand stamps were overprinted for use in Aitutaki, Penrhyn and Rarotonga [2–4], followed in 1920–31 by pictorial stamps that were separately inscribed for each island but otherwise had identical designs [5–6]. In 1932 a general series was introduced, followed by a more detailed scenic set in 1949 [7].

Following the Cook Islands' grant of self-government in 1965 stamps became more colourful and very prolific for a number of years, covering a wide range of subjects, from royalty [8] to the Apollo space missions. Separate postal services were resumed in Aitutaki [9] and Penrhyn [10] in 1972 and 1973 respectively, the latter covering all the northern islands.

NIUE

The island of Niue, formerly part of the Cook Islands, was annexed by Britain in 1900 and transferred to New Zealand with the other islands. However, in deference to the wishes of the inhabitants it was made a separate dependency in 1902. It used overprinted New Zealand stamps from time to time [11] as well as the Cook Islands pictorial designs of the 1920s, distinctively inscribed [12]. A distinctive pictorial set appeared in 1950 [13] and this was followed by a floral series in 1969 [14]. Self-government was granted in 1974 and since then Niue's stamps have become more liberal in subject and design, though they often reflect the island's strong ties with Britain [15].

SAMOA

As in Fiji, Samoa's first stamps, which were introduced in 1877, were produced for a service operated by a newspaper, the *Samoa Express*, mainly for distribution [16]. A general postal service was organized throughout the kingdom in 1886 and had stamps portraying King Malietoa [17].

Following the partition of the island in 1900 German colonial keytype stamps inscribed "Samoa" were used in the western area, whereas ordinary American stamps were in use in the eastern districts. The German stamps were overprinted "G.R.I." for Georgius Rex Imperator (George King Emperor) after the occupation in September 1914. These were followed by stamps inscribed "Samoa" and then, from 1935, more correctly inscribed "Western Samoa".

Several stamps from 1939 onwards alluded to Robert Louis Stevenson [18; 20], recalling both his literary fame and his ardent advocacy of the islanders' rights against the German administration. After Samoa gained independence in 1962 stamps were inscribed "Samoa I Sisifo" (Western Samoa) but since 1981 they have been inscribed simply "Samoa". Many recent issues highlight the country's tourist attractions [19].

TOKELAU ISLANDS

Formerly known as the Union Islands, this archipelago used the stamps of the Gilbert and Ellice Islands from 1911 until 1926, when they were transferred to Samoa and used its stamps until 1948. For several years the islands were quite content with three stamps, from 1/2d to 2d, but these were augmented by short sets and special issues from 1969 onwards. The issue policy remains relatively conservative, with only two or three a year, almost entirely devoted to indigenous topics even for the celebration of Christmas.

Below: One of the three stamps of the Tokelau Islands, which sufficed for many years (top), and Shackleton and Scott on one of the first stamps of Ross Dependency (bottom).

Splashdown

As the drop zone for many of the American space flights has been located in the South Pacific, it is hardly surprising that many of the stamps from the Cook Islands should illustrate this subject.

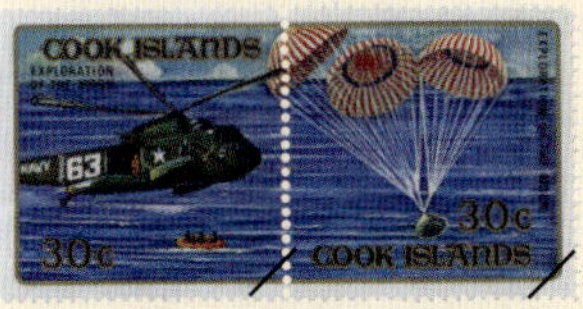

ANTARCTICA

Many of the British expeditions to the Antarctic started from New Zealand and on two occasions the postal service provided stamps for use on polar mail. Shackleton's expedition of 1908 was provided with a quantity of Penny Universal stamps vertically overprinted "King Edward VII Land", while Scott's expedition of 1911–12 had 1/2d and 1d stamps of the Edward VII series overprinted "Victoria Land".

In 1923 Britain laid claim to a sector of the Antarctic continent known as Ross Dependency and transferred it to New Zealand control soon afterwards, although it was not until 1957 that distinctive stamps were introduced, portraying the queen, showing a map and featuring HMS *Erebus* and the explorers Shackleton and Scott. Ten years later the stamps were re-issued with values in decimal currency. A set of six appeared in 1972 with new motifs featuring scenery and methods of communication, while a further set of five in 1982 extended these themes. Since 1995 a set of six has been issued each November, at the start of the scientific research season, featuring such subjects as polar explorers, landscapes and ice formations.

11

12

13

14

15

16

17

18

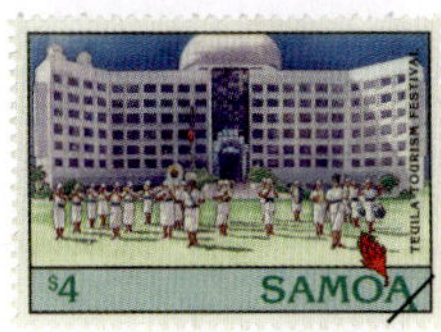

19

20

INSCRIPTIONS

Most stamps can be identified by their inscription, language and expressions of value, but there are others that baffle even the collector of long standing. Below is a list of key-words and abbreviations found in inscriptions and overprints, with their country, state or district of origin.

A & T Annam and Tonquin
Acores Azores
Afghanes Afghanistan
Africa Portuguese Africa
Akahi Keneta Hawaii
Amtlicher Verkehr Wurttemberg
AO (Afrika Ost) Ruanda-Urundi
Allemagne/Duitschland Belgian occupation of Germany
A Payer Te Betalen Belgium (postage due)
A Percevoir postage due Belgium (francs and centimes); Egypt (paras, milliemes)
Archipel des Comores Comoro Islands
Avisporto Denmark
Azad Hind Free India (unissued stamps prepared for use in India after Japanese "liberation")
B (on Straits Settlements) Bangkok
Bani (on Austrian stamps) Austrian occupation of Romania
BATYM Batum (now Batumi)
Bayer, Bayern Bavaria
BCA British Central Africa (now Malawi)
Belgique/Belgie/Belgien, also **Belge** Belgium
Böhmen und Mahren Bohemia and Moravia
Bollo delta Posta Napoletana Naples
Bosnien Bosnia
Braunschweig Brunswick
C CH Cochin China
Cechy a Morava Bohemia and Moravia
CEF (on India) Chinese Expeditionary Force
CEF (on German colonies) Cameroons under British occupation
Centesimi (on Austria) Austrian occupation of Italy
Centimes (on Austria) Austrian POs in Crete
Centrafricaine Central African Republic
Ceskoslovensko Czechoslovakia
Chiffre taxe France
Chine French POs in China
Comunicaciones Spain
Confed. Granadina Granadine Confederation (Colombia)
Cong Hoa Mien Nam National Liberation Front for South Vietnam
Congo Belge Belgian Congo
Continente Portuguese mainland
Coree Korea
Correio Brazil, Portugal
Correos Spain, Cuba, Porto Rico, Philippines
Côte d'Ivoire Ivory Coast
Côte Française des Somalis French Somali Coast
Danmark Denmark
Dansk Vestindien Danish West Indies
DDR German Democratic Republic
Deficit Peru
Deutsch Neu-Guinea German New Guinea
Deutsch Ostafrika German East Africa
Deutschösterreich Austria
Deutsch Siidwestafrika German South West Africa
Deutsche Flugpost/ Reichspost Germany
Deutsches Reich Germany
Dienstmarke Germany
Dienstsache Germany
Diligencia Uruguay

DJ Djibouti
Drzava, Drzavna Yugoslavia
EEF Palestine
Eesti Estonia
EE UU de C Colombia
EFO French Oceania
Eire Republic of Ireland
Elua Keneta Hawaii
Emp. Franc. French Empire
Emp. Ottoman Turkey
Equateur Ecuador
Escuelas Venezuela
España, Espanola Spain
Estados Unidos de Nueva Granada Colombia
Estensi Modena
Estero Italian POs in the Levant
Etablissements de l'Inde French Indian Settlements
Etablissements de l'Oceanie French Oceanic Settlements
Etat Ind. du Congo Congo Free State
Filipinas Spanish Philippines
Franco Switzerland
Francobollo Italy
Franco Marke Bremen
Franco Poste Bollo Neapolitan provinces and early Italy
Franqueo Peru
Franquicia Postal Spain
Freimarke Wurttemberg, Prussia
Frimerke Norway
Frimaerke Denmark
G (on Cape of Good Hope) Griqualand West
G & D Guadeloupe
GEA Tanganyika
Gen. Gouv. Warschau German occupation of Poland, World War 1
General Gouvernement German occupation of Poland, World War II
Georgie Georgia
Giuba Jubaland
GPE Guadeloupe
GRI British occupation of New Guinea and Samoa
Grossdeutsches Reich Nazi Germany
Guine Portuguese Guinea
Guinea Ecuatorial Equatorial Guinea
Guine French Guinea
Gultig 9 Armee German occupation of Romania
Guyane Française French Guiana
Haute Volta Upper Volta
Hellas Greece
Helvetia Switzerland
HH Nawab Shah Begam Bhopal
Hrvatska Croatia
HRZGL Holstein
IEF Indian Expeditionary Force
IEF 'D' Mosul
Imper. Reg. Austrian POs in Turkey
Impuesto de Guerra Spain (war tax)
Inde French Indian Settlements
India Port. Portuguese India
Irian Barat West Iran
Island Iceland
Jubile de l'Union Postale Switzerland
Kamerun Cameroons
Kaladlit Nunat, Kalaallit Nunaat Greenland
Karnten Carinthia
Karolinen Caroline Islands
KGCA Carinthia
Kgl. Post. Frim. Denmark, Danish West Indies
Khmere Cambodia
Kongeligt Post Frimaerke Denmark
KK Post Stempel Austria, Austrian Italy
KPHTH Crete
Kraljevina, Kraljevstvo Yugoslavia
Kreuzer Austria
KSA Saudi Arabia
K.u.K. Feldpost Austrian military stamps
K.u.K. Militärpost Bosnia and Herzegovina
K. Württ. Post Wurttemberg
La Canea Italian POs in Crete
La Georgie Georgia
Land-Post Baden
Lattaquie Latakia
Latvija Latvia
Lietuvos Lithuania
Litwa Srodkowa Central Lithuania
Ljubljanska Pokrajina Slovenia
L. McL. Trinidad (Lady McLeod stamp)
Lösen Sweden
Magyar Hungary
MAPKA Russia
Marianen Mariana Islands
Maroc French Morocco
Marruecos Spanish Morroco
Marschall-Inseln Marshall Islands
Mejico Mexico
Militär Post Bosnia and Herzegovina
Mocambique Mozambique
Modonesi Modena
Montevideo Uruguay
Moyen-Congo Middle Congo
MViR German occupation of Romania
Nachmarke Austria
Napoletana Naples
NCE New Caledonia
Nederland Netherlands
Ned. Antillen Netherlands Antilles
Ned./ Nederl. Indie Dutch East Indies
NF Nyasaland Field Force
Nippon Japan
Nieuwe Republiek New Republic (South Africa)
Nlle Caledonie New Caledonia
Norddeutscher Postbezirk North German Confederation
Norge, Noreg Norway
Nouvelle Caledonie New Caledonia
Nouvelles Hebrides New Hebrides
NSB Nossi-Be (Madagascar)
NSW New South Wales
NW Pacific Islands Nauru and New Guinea
NZ New Zealand
Oesterr., Oesterreich, Österreich Austria
Offentligt Sak Norway (official stamps)
Oltre Giuba Jubaland
Orts Post Switzerland
OS Norway (official stamps)
Ottoman, Ottomanes Turkey
P, PGS Perak (Government Service)

Pacchi Postale Italy (parcel stamps)
Pakke-Porto Greenland
Para Egypt, Serbia, Turkey, Crete
Parm[ensi] Parma
Pesa (on German) German POs in Turkey
Piaster German POs in Turkey
Pilipinas Philippines
Pingin Ireland
Poblact na hEireann Republic of Ireland
Poczta Polska Poland
Pohjois Inkeri North Ingermanland
Port Cantonal Switzerland (Geneva)
Porte de Conduccion Peru
Porte Franco Peru
Porte de Mar Mexico
Porteado Portugal and colonies
Porto Austria, Yugoslavia
Porto-pflichtige Wiirttemberg
Post & Receipt/Post Stamp Hyderabad
Postage and Revenue United Kingdom
Postas le n'ioc Republic of Ireland
Postat e Qeverries Albania
Poste Estensi Modena
Poste Locale Switzerland
Postes (alone) Alsace and Lorraine, Belgium, Luxembourg
Poste Shqiptare Albania
Postgebiet Ob. Ost German Eastern Army
Postzegel Netherlands
Preussen Prussia
Provincie Modonesi Modena
Provinz Laibach Slovenia
PSNC Pacific Steam Navigation Co., Peru
Qeverries Albania
R Jind
Rayon Switzerland
Recargo Spain
Regno d'Italia Venezia Giulia, Trieste
Reichspost German Empire
RF France and colonies
RH Haiti
Repoblika Malagasy Malagasy Republic
Republica Oriental Uruguay
Repub. Franc. France
Republique Libanaise Lebanon
Republique Rwandaise Rwanda
Rialtas Sealadac na hEireann Provisional Government of Ireland
RO Eastern Roumelia
RSA Republic of South Africa
Rumanien (on German) German occupation of Romania
Russisch-Polen German occupation of Poland
Sachsen Saxony
Scrisorei Moldavia and Wallachia
Segnatasse Italy
Serbien Austrian or German occupation of Serbia
SH Schleswig-Holstein
SHS Yugoslavia
Shqipenia, Shqipenie, Shqypnija, Shqiptare Albania
Sld., Soldi Austrian Italy,
Slesvig Schleswig
Slovensky Stat Slovakia
SO Eastern Silesia
SPM St Pierre and Miquelon
S. Thome e Principe St Thomas and Prince Islands
Suidwes Afrika South West Africa
Sul Bolletina, Sulla Ricevuta Italy
Sultunat d'Anjouan Anjouan
Suomi Finland
Sverige Sweden
SWA South West Africa
TAKCA Bulgaria
Tassa Gazzette Modena

Te Betalen Port Netherlands and colonies
TEO Cilicia. Syria
Terres Australes et Antarctiques Françaises French Southern and Antarctic Territories
Territoire Français des Afars et les Issas French Territory of the Afars and Issas
Tjanste Frimarke Sweden
Tjeneste Frimerke Norway
Tjeneste Frimaerke Denmark
Toga Tonga
Toscano Tuscany
UAE United Arab Emirates
UAR United Arab Republic (Egypt)
UG Uganda
UKTT United Kingdom Trust Territory (Southern Cameroons)
Uku Leta Hawaii
Ultramar Cuba. Porto Rico
UNEF Indian Forces in Gaza
UNTEA Western New Guinea
Vallees d'Andorre Andorra
Van Diemen's Land Tasmania
Venezia Giulia (on Italian stamps) Trieste
Venezia Tridentina Trentino
Viet Nam Dan Chu Cong Hoa North Vietnam
Vom Empfanger Einzuziehen Danzig (postage due)
YAR Yemen Arab Republic
YCCP Ukraine
YKP. H. P. Ukraine
Z Armenia
ZAR South African Republic (Transvaal)
Z. Afr. Republiek South African Republic (Transvaal)
Zeitungsmarke Austria, Germany (newspaper stamps)
Zil Eloine Sesel Seychelles Outer Islands
Zuid West Afrika South West Africa
Zulassungsmarke German military parcel stamp

GLOSSARY

Stamp collectors have a language all of their own, which can be puzzling to a newcomer. Some of the more commonly used terms are given below. References to glossed terms appear in bold.

Adhesive Stamp issued with **gum** on the reverse for sticking on mail, as opposed to one printed directly on the envelope, card or wrapper. *See also* Self-adhesive.

Aerogramme Specially printed air letter sheet on lightweight paper.

Airgraph World War II forces mail sent by micro-film, then enlarged for dispatch to the addressee.

Alphabets The different styles of lettering printed in the corners of British stamps 1840–87.

Backstamp Postmark on the back of an envelope, usually applied in transit or arrival.

Bantams South African stamps printed as a reduced format in World War II to save paper.

Bilingual pairs Stamps printed alternately in two different languages, as seen in issues from South Africa (1926–50) and Ceylon (1964).

Bisect Stamp cut in half for use at half the usual value, in times of shortage. Bisection may be made horizontally, vertically or diagonally.

Blind perforation Perforation in which the paper is merely dented, owing to blunt teeth in the perforating machine.

Block Four or more stamps joined together; also used in continental Europe as a synonym for a **miniature sheet**.

Bogus Label purporting to be a genuine stamp but without any validity or even a reason for issue other than to defraud collectors. Bogus overprints may be found on genuine stamps for the same reason.

Booklet One or more panes (small blocks) of stamps, usually held together with card covers.

Cachet Mark applied to cards and covers, other than the postmark, and often private or unofficial in nature.

Cancellation Postmark applied to stamps to prevent their re-use. Often hand- or machine-struck from steel or brass stamps, but may also be applied from a rubber, cork or wood stamp, or even by pen and ink.

Cancelled to order (CTO) Stamps postmarked in bulk, usually for sale to philatelists below face value; usually recognized by still having the gum on the backs.

Cantonals The earliest issues of Switzerland (e.g. Basle, Geneva and Zurich).

Carriers Stamps issued by private carriers, mainly in the United States, 1842–59.

Centred A stamp whose design is equidistant from the edges of the perforations is said to be well centred. Off-centre stamps have perforations (or scissor cuts if imperforate) cutting into the design on one or more sides.

Chalk-surfaced paper Security paper used for many British and colonial stamps to prevent re-use by cleaning off the cancellations. Can be detected by means of a silver pencil.

Chalky paper Special paper with a glossy surface used for many modern British definitive stamps, and also widely used for multicoloured stamps.

Chalon heads Name given to some early stamps of British colonies, e.g. Bahamas, Ceylon, New Zealand, Tasmania. reproducing a full-face portrait of Queen Victoria by Edward Chalon, RA.
Classics The earliest stamps of the world, 1840–1870.
Cliché Stereo or electro unit used in letterpress printing. These are assembled in a **forme** to form a printing plate.
Coils Stamps issued in reels or coils and often collected in **strips**. Can often be identified by being **imperforate** on two opposite sides.
Colour trials Impressions, or **proofs**, created in various colours prior to issue, for the purpose of determining the most suitable colours in actual production.
Combination cover Cover bearing stamps of two or more postal administrations, mainly from the early period when stamps had no franking validity beyond the frontiers of the country of issue.
Comb perforation **Perforation** on three sides of a stamp made at one stroke of the perforator, resulting in perfectly even corner teeth, compared with **line perforation**.
Commemorative A stamp sold in limited quantities for a period of time, often honouring a person, place, or event, but also used to promote certain current events.
Compulsory Stamp Charity stamps, issued at one time by countries such as Portugal and Yugoslavia, for compulsory use on mail.
Controls Letters and numerals found on British sheet margins, 1881–1947, for accounting purposes.
Cork cancellation Obliterators cut from corks, usually with fancy devices; widely used by 19th century American postmasters. Also used in Britain to obliterate incorrect datestamps.
Corner block Stamps taken from the corner of a **sheet**, adjacent to marginal paper showing **controls**, **cylinder numbers**, plate numbers or printer's imprint.
Corner letters Double alphabet sequence of letters found in the corners of British stamps, 1840–87, indicating the position of the stamp in the **sheet**.
CTO Widely used abbreviation for "**Cancelled to order**"
Cover Envelope or wrapper with stamps affixed or imprinted. Stamps are said to be "on cover" when the envelope is intact, as opposed to "on front" or "on piece".
Cut to shape Imperforate stamps of unusual shapes, with margins trimmed accordingly.
Cylinder number Tiny numeral printed in the sheet margin to denote the cylinder(s) used in production.
Dandy roll Wire gauze cylinder used in the manufacture of paper and impregnation of **watermarks**.
Definitives Stamps in general use over a period of years, as opposed to **commemoratives**, charity or semi-postal stamps and other special issues.
Demonetized Obsolete stamps declared invalid for postage.
Die The original piece of metal on which the stamp design is engraved.
Die proof Impression pulled from the **die** to check its accuracy.
Dominical labels Small labels attached below Belgian stamps, 1893–1914, instructing the postmen not to deliver the letter on Sunday. Where no objection was raised the labels were detached.
Dumb cancellation Postmarks with the town name erased for security reasons in wartime, and also special anonymous obliterations produced for the same purpose.
Engine-turning Intricate pattern of spiral lines forming the background to the earliest British and colonial stamps. This security device was copied from banknotes.
Entire Complete envelope, card or wrapper.
Entire letter Complete envelope or wrapper, with the original contents intact.
Embossed Stamps, or a portion of their design, die-struck in low relief, often colourless against a coloured background. Widely used for postal stationery.
Error Stamps deviating from the normal in some respect: missing or inverted colours, **surcharges** and **overprints** or mistakes in the design which may later be corrected. Usually worth more than normals, although in some cases (e.g. the Hammarskjold issue in the United States), the postal authority may take steps to minimize the rarity of the original.
Essay Preliminary design, not subsequently used.
Fake Genuine stamp that has been tampered with in some way to make it more valuable: e.g. fiscally used high-value stamps with the pen markings erased and a postmark substituted, or a stamp converted to a valuable rarity by the addition of an overprint.
First Day Cover or FDC Envelope bearing stamps used on the first day of issue.
First Flight Cover Cover carried on first airmail by a new route, or new aircraft.
Fiscal Stamp intended for fiscal or **revenue** purposes.
Flaw Defect in the printing **plate** or **cylinder**, resulting in a constant

blemish on the same stamp in every sheet; plate flaws are useful in sheet reconstruction.
Forme Printer's term for the frame clamped around stereos or **clichés** to make a printing **plate** in the letterpress process.
Frank Mark or label indicating that a letter or card can be transmitted free of postage. Widely used by government departments. Military franks have been issued by France, Vietnam etc for use by personnel.
Gum Mucilage on the back of unused stamps. British stamps changed from gum arabic (glossy) to polyvinyl alcohol gum (matt, colourless) and later PVA Dextrin gum (with a greenish tint).
Gutter Area between panes of a sheet. Stamps from adjoining panes with the gutter between are known as gutter or interpanneau pairs.
Half tone Black-and-white photographic image appearing on a stamp; often a feature of early 20th century **essays** where they were created by a simplified form of the photogravure process.
Healths Stamps issued by New Zealand since 1929 and Fiji (1951 and 1954), with a premium in aid of children's health camps.
Imperforate Stamps issued without any means of separating them, thus requiring them to be cut apart with scissors. Stamps with no perforations on one or more sides may come from **booklets** and those with no **perforations** on two opposite sides are from **coils**.
Imprint Inscription giving the name or trademark of the printer.
Imprint block Block of four or more stamps with marginal paper attached bearing the imprint.
Intaglio Printing process where the design is engraved in "recess", or below the surface of the printing plate.
Issue New stamp or stamps issued by a postal authority.
Jubilee line Line of printer's rule reinforcing the edges of the plate and first used on the British "Jubilee" series of 1887. Appears as bars of colour in the margin at the foot of the sheet.
Key plate Printing plate used to generate the design of the stamp.Used in conjunction with a duty plate, which prints the value.
Keytype Collectors' term for stamps of the British, French, German, Portuguese and Spanish colonies which used identical designs, differing only in the name of the colony and the denomination.
Kiloware Originally sealed kilogram bags of stamps on paper, but now applied to any mixtures sold by weight.
Line perforation Perforation where holes are punched out on one side of a stamp at a time, with the result that two sets of perforated lines do not register at the corners of the **sheet**.
Lithography Surface printing method where a design is photographically transferred to a zinc or aluminium **plate**. *See also* Offset lithography.
Locals Stamps whose validity is restricted to a single town or district and cannot be used for sending national or international mail.
Marginal markings Marks on the margins of sheets include **controls**, **cylinder numbers**, "traffic lights", printers' imprints, **jubilee lines**, sheet serial numbers, arrows showing the middle of the sheet,

values of rows or sheets, ornament and even commercial advertising (France, Germany).
Meter marks Marks applied by a postage meter used by firms and other organizations. They comprise the indicium (or imitation "stamp" with the value), the town die (with the date) and an advertising slogan, or may combine these elements in a single design. Invented in New Zealand (1904) and used internationally since 1922.
Miniature sheet Small sheet containing a single stamp or a small group of stamps, often with decorative margins.
Mint Unused stamp with full, original **gum** on the back.
Obsolete Stamp no longer on sale at the post office but still valid for postage.
Obliteration Post-marking of stamps to prevent re-use. *See also* cancellation.
Offset lithography Printing process whereby an image is transferred from an aluminum or zinc plate to a rubber blanket, and then from the rubber blanket to the paper.
Omnibus issue Commemoratives issued by several countries simultaneously, using similar designs.
Overprint Printing applied to a stamp some time after the original printing, to convert it to some other purpose (e.g. **commemorative**, charity, or for use overseas).
Pane Originally a portion of a **sheet** (half or quarter) divided by **gutters**, but also applied to the blocks of stamps issued in **booklets**.
Patriotics Covers and cards with patriotic motifs, fashionable during the American Civil War, the Boer War and both World Wars.
Perfins Stamps perforated with initials or other devices as a security measure to prevent pilfering or misuse by office staff.
Perforation Form of separation using machines which punch out tiny circles of paper. *See also* Comb perforation; Line perforation.
Phosphor band Almost invisible line on the face of a stamp, created by the application of a chemical, to facilitate the electronic sorting process.
Photogravure Printing process where the design is photographed onto the printing **plate** using a fine screen which breaks the copy up into very fine square dots. The tiny depressions that form around the squares retain the ink.
Plate Flat or curved piece of metal from which stamps are printed.
Plate proof Impression of a **sheet**, **block** or **strip** of new issues, pulled from the **die**, usually in black ink, or sometimes in various colours.
Plebiscites Stamps issued in towns and districts, mainly after World War I, pending the vote of the population to decide which country they should join, e.g. Memel, Marienwerder, Carinthia and Silesia.
Postage dues Labels denoting the amount of postage unpaid or underpaid (often including a fine).
Postage paid impressions (PPIs) Marks printed on envelopes, cards or wrappers, often used in bulk business mail.
Postal stationery Envelopes, cards and wrappers bearing **imprinted** or **embossed** stamps.
Pre-cancels Stamps used in bulk postings, with marks previously overprinted to prevent reuse. Widely used by Canada, Belgium, United States and France, but now largely superseded by **meter marks** and **postage paid impressions**.
Printer's waste Stamps with defective, double or misaligned printing, usually **imperforate**, and discarded during stamp production. Though usually strictly controlled, such material occasionally comes on to the market and is of interest to the specialist.
Proof Impression of a stamp design, pulled from the **die**. With perforated proofs, an overprint is often added to cancel the design and prevent it being used for postal purposes. *See also* Die proofs; Plate proofs
Provisionals Stamps **overprinted** or **surcharged** to meet a shortage of regular issues. Also used by emergent nations pending a supply of distinctive stamps, the stamps of the former mother country being overprinted.
Recess printing Term used in catalogues to signify **intaglio** printing.
Re-entry Portion of an **intaglio plate** which is re-engraved or re-entered by the transfer roller, usually detected by slight doubling of the lines.
Redrawn Stamps in which the basic design has been retained but various changes made in a subsequent edition.
Remainders Stocks of stamps on hand after an issue has been **demonetized** are sometimes sold off cheaply to the philatelic trade, with some form of cancellation to distinguish them from unused stamps sold at full value during the currency of the stamps.
Reprints Stamps printed from the original plates, sometimes long after the issue has ceased. They can be detected by differences in the paper, watermark and colour.

Retouch Repairs to letterpress plates and **photogravure** cylinders to touch out a flaw may result in stamps that can still be detected as slightly different from the normal. The corrected versions are known as retouches.
Revenue Stamp intended for **fiscal** or revenue purposes.
Rouletting Form of separation in which serrated instruments cut or pierce the paper without actually removing any, as in **perforation**.
Secret marks Tiny letters, numbers, dates and other devices introduced into the design of some stamps (notably the United States and Canada) for security reasons.
Self-adhesive A stamp in a **coil** or **booklet** with backing paper from which it is peeled and affixed to mail without the necessity to lick or moisten the back.
Selvedge Stamp edging or sheet marginal paper.
Se-tenant Two or more stamps of different designs, values or colours, printed side by side.
Sheet A complete set of stamps taken from a single printing **plate**. This may then be cut into individual **panes** for sale at a post office.
Sheetlet Small sheet of stamps, of varying quantities depending the on country of issue.
Specimen Stamp perforated or overprinted thus, or its equivalent in other languages, for record or publicity purposes and having no postal validity.
Straight edge Stamps with no **perforations** on one or more sides, mainly found in **coils** and **booklets** but including **sheets** of stamps from countries such as Canada and the United States.
Strip Three or more stamps that have not been separated.
Surcharge An **overprint** that alters the face value of a stamp.
Tablet Adjoining section of a stamp that bears an inscription, advertisement or other design.
Tabs Stamps with marginal inscriptions alluding to the subjects depicted, widely used by Israel and also by Switzerland and the United Nations.
Tied Postmarks that overlap the stamp and the envelope or card, a useful feature in establishing the genuineness of **bisects**.
Toughra (also tughra) Calligraphic markings indicating the signature of the former Sultan of Turkey, prevalent on Turkish issues predating the Ottoman Empire's demise in 1920.
Typography Collector's term for letterpress printing, abbreviated in catalogues to "typo".
Unused Stamp lacking a cancellation, but in less perfect condition than **mint**.
UPU Universal Postal Union.
Used Stamp bearing a cancellation.
Variety Any variation from the normal issue, relating to its shade, **perforation**, **watermark**, **gum** or phosphorescence, usually listed in the more specialized catalogues.
Vignette The main motif or central portion of a stamp design, as opposed to the frame, value **tablet** or inset portrait or effigy of the ruler.
Watermark Translucent impression used as a security device in the paper from which stamps are printed.
Zemstvos Russian local postal network which prepaid postage from the many smaller towns to the nearest imperial post office.

INDEX

PAKISTAN پاکستان পাকিস্তান
13
PAISA
POSTAGE
RAILWAY CENTENARY 1861-1961

TÜRKİYE CUMHURİYETİ
80.YILI
600.000 LİRA
POSTA

REPUBLIQUE FEDERALE DU CAMEROUN
45F
FEDERAL REPUBLIC OF CAMEROON

Notes

Notes

Notes

Notes

Notes

NOTES

NOTES

NOTES